THE PILLAR NEW TESTAMENT COMMENTARY

*General Editor*
D. A. CARSON

# *The Letters of*
# 2 PETER *and* JUDE

PETER H. DAVIDS

William B. Eerdmans Publishing Company
Grand Rapids, Michigan / Cambridge, U.K.

APOLLOS
NOTTINGHAM, ENGLAND

First published in the United States of America by
Wm. B. Eerdmans Publishing Co.
2140 Oak Industrial Drive N.E., Grand Rapids, Michigan 49505 /
P.O. Box 163, Cambridge CB3 9PU U.K.
www.eerdmans.com

and in the United Kingdom by
APOLLOS
Norton Street, Nottingham,
England NG7 3HR

Printed in the United States of America

29 28 27 26 25 24 23 14 13 12 11 10 9

**Library of Congress Cataloging-in-Publication Data**

Davids, Peter H.
The letters of 2 Peter and Jude / Peter H. Davids.
p. cm. (The Pillar New Testament commentary)
Includes bibliographical references and indexes.
ISBN 978-0-8028-3726-4 (cloth : alk. paper)
1. Bible. N.T. Peter, 2nd — Commentaries.
2. Bible. N.T. Jude — Commentaries. I. Title. II. Series.

BS2795.53.D38 2006
227'.93077 — dc22

2006012780

**British Library Cataloguing in Publication Data**

A catalogue record for this book is available from the British Library.

ISBN 978-1-84474-151-9

# *Contents*

## THE LETTER OF 2 PETER

## INDEXES

# *Series Preface*

Commentaries have specific aims, and this series is no exception. Designed for serious pastors and teachers of the Bible, the Pillar commentaries seek above all to make clear the text of Scripture as we have it. The scholars writing these volumes interact with the most important informed contemporary debate, but avoid getting mired in undue technical detail. Their ideal is a blend of rigorous exegesis and exposition, with an eye alert both to biblical theology and the contemporary relevance of the Bible, without confusing the commentary and the sermon.

The rationale for this approach is that the vision of "objective scholarship" (a vain chimera) may actually be profane. God stands over against us; we do not stand in judgment of him. When God speaks to us through his Word, those who profess to know him must respond in an appropriate way, and that is certainly different from a stance in which the scholar projects an image of autonomous distance. Yet this is no surreptitious appeal for uncontrolled subjectivity. The writers of this series aim for an evenhanded openness to the text that is the best kind of "objectivity" of all.

If the text is God's Word, it is appropriate that we respond with reverence, a certain fear, a holy joy, a questing obedience. These values should be reflected in the way Christians write. With these values in place, the Pillar commentaries will be warmly welcomed not only by pastors, teachers, and students, but by general readers as well.

* * *

The two epistles treated in this volume, 2 Peter and Jude, present peculiar challenges to the twenty-first-century commentator. Their strong denunciations seem out of tune with the times; their allusions to non-biblical Jewish sources raise some eyebrows; their transparent interdependence (one of them is borrowing from the other) raises the kinds of issues faced by those commenting on the Synoptic Gospels or on 1 and 2 Chronicles. Morever, historical criticism has sometimes left us with a legacy of suspicion about these two brief contributions to the NT. So I am grateful for the work of Peter Davids, whose lifelong interest in the General Epistles is well known and widely respected, and whose mix of service, in both academic and ecclesiastical settings, has doubtless contributed to his ability, on the one hand, to form sharp, independent judgments, and, on the other, to apply them to the contemporary church. In epistles so controverted, no commentary, including this one, will win universal agreement. But all of us will happily acknowledge how much we stand in debt to Dr. Davids.

D. A. Carson

# *Author's Preface*

When Don Carson presented me with the opportunity to write the present volume, I was both humbled and thankful. Humbled, because I realized that he was trusting me to complete the job of exegeting some difficult literature. Thankful, because, having written commentaries on James (NIGTC, 1982) and 1 Peter (NICNT, 1990), I had wanted to complete my work on the General Epistles. I had thought that having given away the 2 Peter–Jude NICNT volume (to Robert L. Webb), I might never get to finish my coverage of these letters.

What I did not realize at the time I accepted the invitation to write was that life would take me from Langley, British Columbia, where I could foresee having time to do significant writing, to Mittersill, Austria, where I had little time at all to write, to Innsbruck, Austria, where Jude and half of 2 Peter were finished, and finally to Meadows Place, Texas, where the work was completed. A project I had expected to complete in three to five years has taken more than ten. I appreciate the patience of the editors and the publishers for waiting all of that time.

While I was not actively writing all of that time, I was certainly learning. Parts of this volume could not have been written as well as they are without various experiences along the way, ranging from what I learned from Ralph P. Martin, Daniel Reid, and the many contributors during the editing of the *Dictionary of the Later New Testament and Its Developments* (Downers Grove, IL: InterVarsity Press, 1997) to what I learned from colleagues in seminars of the Studiorum Novi Testamentum Societas and Colloquium Biblicum Lovenienses and the four-year-long Bard College James project chaired by Bruce Chilton and Jacob Neusner and sponsored by Frank T. Crohn. I also must not forget the Facharbeitsgemeinschaft für Neuen Testament of Arbeitsgemeinschaft für evangelikale Theologie

(AfeT), the members of which encouraged me by their collegial friendship and example during my time in Austria.

The Pillar commentaries aim to combine good scholarship with application to church life. Here again our time in Austria was helpful. During much of this time Martin Bühlmann, the leader of the Vineyard movement in the German-speaking world, allowed me to advise and teach the leaders of the movement that he led. His friendship and support allowed us to remain in Europe, his interest in scholarship goaded me to continue to write, and his opening of the movement to me, a foreigner, kept me in contact with real churches with real problems, enriching my insights into the text. Among these churches one stands out, Vineyard Innsbruck, whose leader, Gernot Kahofer, was the reason for our move to Innsbruck. That church provided us with friendship, financial support, and a place to study — much of this material was written in my office under the stairs of that church. It is to Martin Bühlmann and Gernot Kahofer that I dedicate this book.

I am also thankful to my wife, Judith, who has continued to believe that I would eventually complete this book. Furthermore, for the past two years it has been her salary as a pastoral counselor that has enabled me to continue to write here in Meadows Place, Texas.

PETER H. DAVIDS

# *Abbreviations*

## I. JOURNALS, PERIODICALS, REFERENCE WORKS, AND SERIES

| | |
|---|---|
| AB | Anchor Bible |
| AnBib | Analecta biblica |
| ANTC | Abingdon New Testament Commentaries or Augsburg New Testament Commentary |
| *APOT* | *Apocrypha and Pseudepigrapha of the Old Testament*, by R. H. Charles |
| BAG | W. Bauer, W. F. Arndt, and F. W. Gingrich, *A Greek-English Lexicon of The New Testament and Other Early Christian Literature* |
| *BBR* | *Bulletin for Biblical Research* |
| BDF | F. Blass, A. Debrunner, and R. W. Funk, *A Greek Grammar of the New Testament and Other Early Christian Literature* |
| BETL | Bibliotheca ephemeridum theologicarum lovaniensium |
| BFCT | Beiträge zur Förderung christlicher Theologie |
| *Bib* | *Biblica* |
| BNTC | Black's New Testament Commentaries |
| *BSac* | *Bibliotheca sacra* |
| BTN | Biblica Theologica Norvegica |
| *BZ* | *Biblische Zeitschrift* |
| BZNW | Beihefte zur Zeitschrift für die neutestamentliche Wissenschaft |
| *CBQ* | *Catholic Biblical Quarterly* |

| | |
|---|---|
| CBSC | Cambridge Bible for Schools and Colleges |
| CEJL | Commentaries on Early Jewish Literature |
| CGTSC | Cambridge Greek Testament for Schools and Colleges |
| ConNT | Coniectanea biblica: New Testament Series |
| *CTJ* | *Calvin Theological Journal* |
| *DLNT* | *Dictionary of the Later New Testament and Its Developments* |
| *DPL* | *Dictionary of Paul and His Letters* |
| EB | Etudes bibliques |
| EKK | Evangelische-katholischer Kommentar |
| *EvQ* | *Evangelical Quarterly* |
| *ExpT* | *Expository Times* |
| HNT | Handbuch zum Neuen Testament |
| HTKNT | Herders theologischer Kommentar zum Neuen Testament |
| *HTR* | *Harvard Theological Review* |
| ICC | International Critical Commentary |
| *JBL* | *Journal of Biblical Literature* |
| *JETS* | *Journal of the Evangelical Theological Society* |
| *JNES* | *Journal of Near Eastern Studies* |
| *JSJ* | *Journal for the Study of Judaism* |
| *JSNT* | *Journal for the Study of the New Testament* |
| *JSOT* | *Journal for the Study of the Old Testament* |
| L&S | H. D. Liddell and R. Scott, *A Greek-English Lexicon* |
| MNTC | Moffatt New Testament Commentary |
| MSGVK | Mitteilungen der schlesischen Gesellschaft für Volkskunde |
| NAC | New American Commentary |
| NCB | New Century Bible |
| NIBC | New International Biblical Commentary |
| NICNT | New International Commentary on the New Testament |
| NIGTC | New International Greek Testament Commentary |
| NovTSup | Novum Testamentum Supplements |
| NTD | Das Neue Testament Deutsch |
| *NTS* | *New Testament Studies* |
| *OTP* | *Old Testament Pseudepigrapha*, edited by James H. Charlesworth |
| *RB* | *Revue biblique* |
| SB | Sources bibliques |
| SBLDS | Society of Biblical Literature Dissertation Series |

| | |
|---|---|
| SBLSCS | Society of Biblical Literature Septuagint and Cognate Studies |
| SBT | Studies in Biblical Theology |
| *Scr* | *Scripture* |
| SD | Studies and Documents |
| *ST* | *Studia Theologica* |
| SVTP | Studia in Veteris Testamenti pseudepigrapha |
| *TDNT* | *Theological Dictionary of the New Testament* |
| *TLZ* | *Theologische Literaturzeitung* |
| TNTC | Tyndale New Testament Commentaries |
| TU | Texte und Untersuchungen |
| *TynBul* | *Tyndale Bulletin* |
| *TZ* | *Theologische Zeitschrift* |
| WBC | Word Biblical Commentary |
| *WTJ* | *Westminster Theological Journal* |
| WUNT | Wissenschaftliche Untersuchungen zum Neuen Testament |
| *ZNW* | *Zeitschrift für die neutestamentliche Wissenschaft und die Kunde der älteren Kirche* |

## II. BIBLE TRANSLATIONS

| | |
|---|---|
| ASV | American Standard Version (1901) |
| ESV | English Standard Version |
| GNB | Good News Bible |
| JB | Jerusalem Bible |
| KJV | King James Version |
| LXX | Septuagint, i.e. the main Greek translation of the Hebrew Scriptures |
| NAB | New American Bible |
| NASV | New American Standard Version |
| NEB | New English Bible |
| NET Bible | New English Translation (©1996, Biblical Studies Press) |
| NKJV | New King James Version |
| NIV | New International Version |
| NLV | New Living Version |
| NRSV | New Revised Standard Version |
| RSV | Revised Standard Version |
| RV | English Revised Version |
| TEV | Today's English Version (1966) |

## III. APOCRYPHA

Because they are part of the Septuagint, and thus part of the Bible of the early Jesus movement, the Apocrypha are cited in the same manner as any other biblical book.

| | |
|---|---|
| 1 Esdr | First Esdras |
| 2 Esdr | Second Esdras |
| Jdt | Judith |
| 1 Macc | First Maccabees |
| 2 Macc | Second Maccabees |
| 3 Macc. | Third Maccabees |
| 4 Macc. | Fourth Maccabees |
| Sir | Sirach, or the Wisdom of Jesus ben Sira, or Ecclesiasticus |
| Tob | Tobit |
| Wisd | Wisdom of Solomon |

## IV. PSEUDEPIGRAPHA

| | |
|---|---|
| *Aḥikar* | *Aḥiqar (The Words of Aḥiqar) or Aḥikar* |
| *1 Enoch* | *First (Ethiopic) Enoch* |
| *2 Enoch* | *Second (Slavonic) Enoch* |
| *2 Apoc. Bar.* | *Second Apocalypse of Baruch* (also called 2 *Bar.*) |
| *3 Apoc. Bar.* | *Third Apocalypse of Baruch* |
| *Asc. Isa.* | *Ascension of Isaiah* |
| *4 Ezra* | *Fourth Ezra* (an expanded form of 2 Esdr) |
| *Jub.* | *Jubilees* |
| *Paral. Jer.* | *Paraleipomena Jeremiou* (*Things Omitted from Jeremiah*, also known as 4 *Bar.*) |
| *Pss. Sol.* | *Psalms of Solomon* |
| *Sib. Or.* | *Sibylline Oracles* |
| *Test. Abr.* | *Testament of Abraham* |
| *Test. Moses* | *Testament of Moses* |
| *T. Ash.* | *Testament of Asher* in the *Testaments of the Twelve Patriarchs* |
| *T. Benj.* | *Testament of Benjamin* in the *Testaments of the Twelve Patriarchs* |
| *T. Jud.* | *Testament of Judah* in the *Testaments of the Twelve Patriarchs* |

| | |
|---|---|
| *T. Levi* | *Testament of Levi* in the *Testaments of the Twelve Patriarchs* |
| *T. Naph.* | *Testament of Naphtali* in the *Testaments of the Twelve Patriarchs* |
| *T. Reub.* | *Testament of Reuben* in the *Testaments of the Twelve Patriarchs* |
| *T. Zeb.* | *Testament of Zebulun* in the *Testaments of the Twelve Patriarchs* |

## V. DEAD SEA SCROLLS

| | |
|---|---|
| 1QapGen | The *Genesis Apocryphon* from Cave 1 in Qumran |
| 1QH | The *Thanksgiving* scroll from Cave 1 in Qumran |
| 1QM | The *War* scroll from Cave 1 in Qumran |
| 1QpHab | *Commentary (Pesher) on Habakkuk* from Cave 1 in Qumran |
| 1QPs[a]Zion | *Psalms of Zion* scroll from Cave 1 in Qumran |
| 1QS | The *Rule of the Community* from Cave 1 in Qumran |
| 1QSa | The *Rule of the Congregation* or *Messianic Rule* from Cave 1 of Qumran |
| 4QAmram | The scroll about Amram from Cave 4 of Qumran |
| 4QEn[a] | 4QEnoch[a] |
| 4QEn[c] | 4QEnoch[c] |
| 4QEnGiants[a] | Aramaic Fragments of *1 Enoch* from the *Book of Giants* from Cave 4 of Qumran (4Q203) |
| 4QFlor | *Florilegium* from Cave 4 of Qumran |
| 4QpNah | *Commentary (Pesher) on Nahum* from Cave 4 in Qumran |
| 4QTest [4Q175] | *Testimonia* from Cave 4 of Qumran |
| CD | Cairo *Damascus Document* |

## VI. RABBINIC WRITINGS

| | |
|---|---|
| *m. Abot* | *Mishnah* tractate *Abot* |
| *m. Sanh.* | *Mishnah* tractate *Sanhedrin* |
| *m. Sot.* | *Mishnah* tractate *Sotah* |
| *b. B. Bat.* | *Babylonian Talmud,* tractate *Baba Bathra* |
| *b. Hag.* | *Babylonian Talmud,* tractate *Hagigah* |

| | |
|---|---|
| *b. Kidd.* | *Babylonian Talmud,* tractate *Kiddushin* |
| *b. Menah.* | *Babylonian Talmud,* tractate *Menahoth* |
| *b. Mes'ia* | *Babylonian Talmud,* tractate *Mes'ia* |
| *b. Sanh.* | *Babylonian Talmud,* tractate *Sanhedrin* |
| *b. Yoma* | *Babylonian Talmud,* tractate *Yoma* |
| *y. Ta'an.* | *Jerusalem Talmud,* tractate *Ta'anit* |
| *Gen. R.* | *Genesis Rabba* (the great midrash on Genesis) |
| *Lev. R.* | *Leviticus Rabba* (the great midrash on Leviticus) |
| *Num. R.* | *Numbers Rabba* (the great midrash on Numbers) |
| *Pirqe R. El.* | *Pirqe de Rabbi Eliezer* |
| *Sifré Num.* | *Sifré on Numbers* |
| *Tg. Neof.* | *Targum Neofiti* |
| *Tg. Ps.-J.* | *Targum Pseudo-Jonathan* |

## VII. JEWISH WRITERS

| | |
|---|---|
| Josephus | Flavius Josephus |
| *Ant.* | *Jewish Antiquities* |
| *C. Ap.* | *Contra Apion (Against Apion)* |
| *Life* | *Life of Flavius Josephus* |
| *War* | *The Jewish War* |
| Philo | Philo Judaeus of Alexandria, |
| *Abr.* | *De Abrahamo (Abraham)* |
| *Aet.* | *De aeternitate mundi (On the Eternity of the World)* |
| *Cher.* | *De cherubim (on the Cherubim)* |
| *Conf.* | *De confusione linguarum (On the Confusion of Tongues)* |
| *Cong.* | *De congressu quaerendae eruditionis gratia (On Mating with the Preliminary Studies)* |
| *Decal.* | *De decalogo (On the Decalogue)* |
| *Ebr.* | *De ebrietate (On Drunkenness)* |
| *Fug. et inv.* | *De fuga et inventione (On Flight and Finding)* |
| *Leg. alleg.* | *Legum allegoriae (Allegorical Interpretation)* |
| *Migr. Abr.* | *De migratione Abrahami (On the Migration of Abraham)* |
| *Mut.* | *De mutatione nominum (On the Change of Names)* |
| *Opif. mundi* | *De opificio mundi (On the Creation)* |
| *Plant.* | *De plantatione (Concerning Noah's Work as a Planter)* |
| *Post. Caini* | *De posteritati Caini (Descendants of Cain)* |

| | |
|---|---|
| *Quaest. Gen.* | *Questiones et solutiones in Genesin (Questions and Answers on Genesis)* |
| *Quis her.* | *Quis rerum divinarum heres (Who Is the Heir of Divine Things)* |
| *Sacr. Abel* | *De sacrificiis Abelis et Cain (On the Sacrifices of Abel and Cain)* |
| *Somn.* | *De somniis (On Dreams)* |
| *Spec. leg.* | *De specialibus legibus (The Special Laws)* |
| *Vit. Mos.* | *De vita Moses (Life of Moses)* |
| Pseudo-Philo *Bib. Ant.* | The *Biblical Antiquities* of Pseudo-Philo |

## VIII. EARLY CHRISTIAN WRITINGS

| | |
|---|---|
| *Acts Paul* | *Acts of Paul* |
| *Apoc. Paul* | *Apocalypse of Paul* |
| *Barn.* | *Epistle of Barnabas* |
| *1 Clem.* | *First Epistle of Clement to the Corinthians* |
| *2 Clem.* | *Second Epistle of Clement to the Corinthians* |
| Clement of Alexandria | Clement of Alexandria |
| *Clem. Hom.* | *Pseudo-Clementine Homilies* |
| *Did.* | *Didache (Teaching of the Twelve Apostles)* |
| *Diogn.* | *Letter of Diognetus* |
| *Ep. Apost.* | *Epistle of the Apostles (Epistula Apostolorum)* |
| Eusebius | Eusebius |
| *Eccl. Hist.* | *Ecclesiastical History.* In some works abbreviated as *H.E.* or cited as *Church History* |
| Gnostic writings | |
| *Corp. Herm.* | *Corpus Hermeticum* |
| *G. Thomas* | *Gospel of Thomas* |
| *Testim. Truth* | *The Testimony of Truth* |
| *Treat. Seth* | *The Second Treatise of the Great Seth* |
| Hermas | The Shepherd of Hermas |
| *Man.* | *Mandate* or *Command* |
| *Sim.* | *Similitude* or *Parable* |
| *Vis.* | *Vision* |
| Hippolytus | Hippolytus |
| *Apos. Trad.* | *The Apostolic Tradition* |

| | |
|---|---|
| Ignatius | Ignatius |
| *Eph.* | *The Letter of Ignatius to the Church in Ephesus* |
| *Philad.* | *The Letter of Ignatius to the Church in Philadelphia* |
| *Rom.* | *The Letter of Ignatius to the Church in Rome* |
| *Smyrn.* | *The Letter of Ignatius to the Church in Smyrna* |
| Irenaeus | Irenaeus |
| *Adv. haer.* | *Adversus haereses (Against Heresies)* |
| Justin | Justin Martyr |
| *1 Apol.* | *First Apology* |
| *2 Apol.* | *Second Apology* |
| *Dial.* | *Dialogue with Trypho the Jew* |
| *Mart. Pol.* | *Martyrdom of Polycarp* |
| Maximus Confessor | Maximus Confessor |
| Origen | Origen |
| *C. Cels.* | *Against Celsus* |
| Polycarp | Polycarp |
| *Phil.* | *The Letter of Polycarp to the Church in Philippi* |
| *Sent. Sextus* | *Sentences of Sextus* |
| Tatian | Tatian |
| *Or.* | *Oratio* (*Oration* or *Address*) |
| Tertullian | Tertullian |
| *Apol.* | *Apology* |
| Theophilus of Antioch | Theophilus of Antioch |
| *Autolycus* | *Letter to Autolycus* |

## IX. GREEK AND ROMAN LITERATURE

| | |
|---|---|
| Aristotle | Aristotle |
| *Rhet.* | *Rhetoric* |
| Cicero | Cicero (Marcus Tullius Cicero) |
| *De nat. deor.* | *De natura deorum (On the Nature of the Gods)* |
| Dionysius of Halicarnassus, | Dionysius of Halicarnassus |
| *Ant. Rom.* | *Antiquities of Rome* |
| Epictetus | Epictetus |
| *Disc.* | *Discourses* |
| Homer | Homer |

| | |
|---|---|
| *Il.* | *Iliad* |
| *Od.* | *Odyssey* |
| Juvenal | Juvenal (Decimus Iunius Iuvenalis) |
| Lactantius | Lactantius |
| *Div. Inst.* | *Divinarum institutionum (Divine Institutions)* |
| Lucian | Luciano of Samosata |
| *Peregr.* | *The Passing of Peregrinus* |
| Minucius Felix | Minucius Felix |
| *Oct.* | *Octavius* |
| Pausanias | Pausanias (Pausanius) |
| *Arcad.* | *Description of Greece,* bk. 8: *Arcadia* |
| Plato | Plato of Athens |
| *Phaed.* | *Phaedrus* |
| Pliny | Pliny the Elder |
| *Hist. Nat.* | *Natural History* |
| Plutarch | Plutarch |
| *Mor.* | *Moralia (Morals)* |
| *Sera numinis vindicta* | *De sera numinis vindicta (On the Delay of Divine Justice) = Moralia* 548-68 |
| Severus | Severus Iatrosophista Medicus |
| *Clyst.* | *De instrumentis infusoriis seu clysteribus ad Timotheum* |

# *Select Bibliography*

## I. COMMENTARIES ON 2 PETER AND JUDE


Bauckham, Richard J. *Jude, 2 Peter.* WBC 50; Waco, TX: Word Books, 1983.

Bigg, Charles. *A Critical and Exegetical Commentary on the Epistles of St. Peter and St. Jude.* ICC; Edinburgh: T&T Clark, 1901.

Calvin, John. *Commentaries on the Catholic Epistles.* Ed. and trans. J. Owen. Calvin's Commentaries 22; Grand Rapids: Baker (1551), 1979.

Cantinat, Jean. *Les Épitres de Saint Jacques et de Saint Jude.* SB; Paris: J. Gabalda et Cie, 1973.

Chaine, Joseph. *Les épîtres catholiques: La Seconde Épître de Saint Pierre, Les Épîtres de Saint Jean, L'épître de Saint Jude.* EB; Paris: J. Gabalda, 1939.

Charles, J. Daryl. *2 Peter, Jude.* In *1–2 Peter, Jude.* Believers Church Bible Commentary; Scottdale, PA: Herald, 1999.

Chase, Frederic Henry. "Jude, Epistle of." In James Hastings, ed. *Dictionary of the Bible.* 2:799-206.

Danker, Frederick W. "2 Peter." In Gerhard Krodel, ed. *The General Letters.* Proclamation Commentaries; Minneapolis: Fortress, 1995. 84-93.

Deichgräber, Reinhard. *Gotteshymnus und Christushymnus in der frühen Christenheit.* Göttingen: Vandenhoeck & Ruprecht, 1967.

Elliott, John H. *I-II Peter/Jude.* ACNT; Minneapolis: Augsburg, 1982.

Green, E. M. B. (Michael). *The Second Epistle of Peter and the Epistle of Jude.* TNTC; Grand Rapids: William B. Eerdmans, 1968.

Grundmann, Walter. *Der Brief des Judas und der zweite Brief des Petrus.* Berlin: Evangelische Verlagsanstalt, 1974.

Hillyer, Norman. *1 and 2 Peter, Jude.* NIBC; Peabody, MA: Hendrickson, 1992.

James, M. R. (Montague Rhodes). *The Second Epistle General of Peter and the Epistle of Jude.* CGTSC; Cambridge: Cambridge University Press, 1912.

Kelly, J. N. D. (John Norman Davidson). *The Epistles of Peter and of Jude.* BNTC; London: Adam and Charles Black, 1969.

Kraftchick, Steven J. *Jude, 2 Peter.* ANTC; Nashville: Abingdon, 2002.

Krodel, Gerhard. "Jude." In Gerhard Krodel, ed. *The General Letters.* Proclamation Commentaries; Minneapolis: Fortress, 1995. 94-109.

Lucas, Dick, and Christopher Green. *The Message of 2 Peter and Jude: The Promise of His Coming.* The Bible Speaks Today; Leicester, UK/Downers Grove, IL: Inter-Varsity Press, 1995.

Mayor, Joseph B. *The Epistles of Jude and II Peter.* Grand Rapids: Baker (1901), 1979.

Moffatt, James. *The General Epistles: James, Peter and Jude.* MNTC; London: Hodder and Stoughton, 1928.

Neyrey, Jerome H. *2 Peter, Jude.* AB 37C; New York: Doubleday, 1993.

Perkins, Pheme. *First and Second Peter, James, and Jude.* Interpretation; Louisville: John Knox, 1995.

Plumptre, Edward Hayes. *The General Epistles of St. Peter and St. Jude.* CBSC; Cambridge: Cambridge University Press, 1892.

Reicke, Bo Ivar. *The Epistles of James, Peter, and Jude.* AB 37; Garden City, NY: Doubleday, 1964.

Schelkle, Karl Hermann. *Die Petrusbriefe, der Judasbrief.* HTKNT XII.2; Freiburg: Herder, 1980[5].

Schrage, Wolfgang. "Der zweite Petrusbrief, der Judasbrief." In Horst R. Balz and Wolfgang Schrage. *Die "Katholische" Briefe: Die Briefe des Jakobus, Petrus, Johannes und Judas, übersetzt und erklärt.* NTD 10; Göttingen: Vandenhoeck & Ruprecht, 1973.

Schreiner, Thomas R. *1, 2, Peter, Jude.* NAC 37; Nashville: Broadman and Holman, 2003.

Sidebottom, E. M. *James, Jude and 2 Peter.* NCB; London: Thomas Nelson, 1967.

Skaggs, Rebecca. *The Pentecostal Commentary on 1 Peter, 2 Peter, Jude.* Cleveland, TN: Pilgrim, 2004.

Spicq, C. *Les Épitres de Saint Pierre.* SB; Paris: J. Gabalda et Cie, 1966.

Spitta, Friedrich. *Die zweite Brief des Petrus und der Brief des Judas.* Halle an der Saale: Verlag und Buchhandlung des Waisenhauses, 1885.

Vögtle, Anton. *Der Judasbrief, Der 2. Petrusbrief.* EKK 22; Solothurn and Düsseldorf/Neukirchen-Vluyn: Benzinger/Neukirchener, 1994.

Windisch, Hans. *Die katholischen Briefe.* HNT 15; Tübingen: J. C. B. Mohr (Paul Siebeck), 1930.

## II. ARTICLES AND MONOGRAPHS

Abrahams, Israel. *Hebrew Ethical Wills.* Philadelphia: Jewish Publication Society, 1926.

———. *Studies in Pharisaism and the Gospels,* second series. Cambridge: Cambridge University Press, 1924.

Adams, Edward. "Where Is the Promise of His Coming? The Complaint of the Scoffers in 2 Peter 3.4." *NTS* 51 (2005) 106-22.

Allison, Dale C., Jr. *Testament of Abraham.* CEJL; Berlin/New York: Walter de Gruyter, 2003.

Andersen, Francis I. "Yahweh, the Kind and Sensitive God." In Peter T. O'Brien and David G. Peterson, eds. *God Who Is Rich in Mercy: Essays Presented to Dr. D. B. Knox.* Homebush West, NSW, Australia/Grand Rapids: Lancer/Baker, 1986. 41-88.

Aune, David E. *Prophecy in Early Christianity and the Ancient Mediterranean World.* Grand Rapids: William B. Eerdmans, 1983.

Bailey, Robert Edson. "Is 'Sleep' the Proper Biblical Term for the Intermediate State?" *ZNW* 55:3-4 (1964) 161-67.

Baltzer, Klaus. *The Covenant Formulary.* Oxford: Basil Blackwell, 1971.

Banks, Robert J. *Going to Church in the First Century.* Hexagon, 1980.

Barnes, Thomas. "The Epistle of Jude: A Study in the Marcosian Heresy." *JTS* 6 (1905) 391-411.

Barrett, C. K. (Charles Kingsley). "Myth and the New Testament: The Greek Word *Mythos*," *ExpT* 68 (1957) 345-48.

———. "Things Sacrificed to Idols," *NTS* 11 (1964-65) 138-53.

Bauckham, Richard J. "The Delay of the Parousia." *TynBul* 31 (1980) 3-36.

———. "James, 1 and 2 Peter, Jude." In D. A. Carson and H. G. M. Williamson, eds. *It Is Written: Scripture Citing Scripture. Essays in Honour of Barnabas Lindars.* Cambridge: Cambridge University Press, 1988. 303-17.

———. *Jude and the Relatives of Jesus in the Early Church.* Edinburgh: T&T Clark, 1990.

———. "A Note on a Problem in the Greek Version of *1 Enoch* i.9." *JTS* 32 (1981) 136-38.

Belleville, Linda. "Ἰουνιᾶν . . . ἐπίσημοι ἐν τοῖς ἀποστόλοις: A Re-examination of Romans 16.7 in Light of Primary Source Materials." *NTS* 51:2 (2005) 231-49.

Berger, Klaus. "Der Streit des guten und des bösen Engels um die Seele: Beobachtungen zu 4QAmr[b] und Judas 9." *JSJ* 4 (1973) 1-18.

Bieder, Werner. "Judas 22f.: *"Hous de eleate en phobō̧,"* *TZ* 6 (1950) 75-77.

Birdsall, J. Neville. "The Text of Jude in P[72]." *JTS* 14 (1963) 394-99.

Black, Matthew. "Critical and Exegetical Notes on Three New Testament

Texts: Hebrews xi.11, Jude 5, James 1.27." In *Apophoreta: Festschrift für Ernst Haenchen.* BZNW 30; Berlin: Alfred Töpelmann, 1964. 39-45.

———. "The Doxology to the *Pater Noster* with a Note on Matthew 6:13b." In Philip Davies and Richard White, eds. *A Tribute to Geza Vermes.* Sheffield: JSOT Press, 1991. 327-32.

———. "The Maranatha Invocation and Jude 14, 15 (I Enoch 1:9)." In Barnabas Lindars and Stephen S. Smalley, eds. *Christ and Spirit in the New Testament: Studies in Honour of Charles Francis Digby Moule.* Cambridge: Cambridge University Press, 1973. 189-96.

Blass, F., and A. Debrunner. *A Greek Grammar of the New Testament and Other Early Christian Literature.* Trans. and rev. Robert W. Funk. Chicago: University of Chicago Press, 1961.

Bloomquist, Gregory. *"The Epicurean Tag in Plutarch: Implications for New Testament Study."* http://www.bloomquist.ca/publications/articles/Epicurean%20Tag%20in%20Plutarch.html.

Bonus, A. "2 Peter III.10." *ExpT* 32 (1920-21) 280-81.

Boobyer, G. H. "The Indebtedness of 2 Peter to 1 Peter." In A. J. B. Higgins, ed. *New Testament Essays: Studies in Memory of T. W. Manson.* Manchester: University of Manchester Press, 1959. 34-53.

———. "The Verbs in Jude 11." *NTS* 5 (1958) 45-47.

Borgen, Peder. *Bread from Heaven: An Exegetical Study of the Concept of Manna in the Gospel of John and the Writings of Philo.* NovTSup 10; Leiden: E. J. Brill, 1965.

Boyd, Gregory A. *Repenting of Religion: Turning from Judgment to the Love of God.* Grand Rapids: Baker, 2004.

Bowker, John. *The Targums and Rabbinic Literature.* Cambridge: Cambridge University Press, 1969.

Brown, Raymond E. "Does the New Testament Call Jesus God?" In Raymond E. Brown, *Jesus, God and Man.* Milwaukee: Bruce, 1967. 1-38.

Bruce, F. F. *The Canon of Scripture.* Downers Grove, IL: InterVarsity Press, 1988.

Buchanan, George W. "Eschatology and the 'End of Days.'" *JNES* 20 (1961) 188-93.

Bultmann, Rudolph. *Theology of the New Testament.* New York: Charles Scribner's, 1955.

Burer, Michael H., and Daniel B. Wallace. "Was Junia Really an Apostle? A Re-examination of Rom 16.7." *NTS* 47:1 (2001) 76-91.

Charles, J. Daryl. "Jude's Use of Pseudepigraphical Source-Material as Part of a Literary Strategy." *NTS* 37 (1991) 130-45.

———. "Literary Artifice in the Epistle of Jude." *ZNW* 82 (1991) 106-24.

———. "'Those' and 'These': The Use of the Old Testament in the Epistle of Jude." *JSNT* 38 (1990) 109-24.

———. "The Use of Tradition Material in the Epistle of Jude." Undated paper read at a SBL meeting.

———. *The Apocrypha and Pseudepigrapha of the Old Testament.* Oxford: Clarendon, 1913.

———. *The Assumption of Moses.* London: A & C Black, 1897.

Charlesworth, James H. *The Old Testament Pseudepigrapha.* Garden City, NY: Doubleday, 1983.

Chester, Andrew, and Ralph P. Martin. *The Theology of the Letters of James, Peter, and Jude: New Testament Theology.* Cambridge: Cambridge University Press, 1994.

Chilton, Bruce D. "The Transfiguration: Dominical Assurance and Apostolic Vision." *NTS* 27 (1980-81) 120-21.

Collins, John N. *Diakonia: Reinterpreting the Ancient Sources.* Oxford: Oxford University Press, 1990.

Conti, Martino. "La Sophia di 2 Petr. 3.15." *Rivista biblica* 17 (1969) 121-38.

Danby, Herbert. *The Mishnah.* Oxford: Clarendon, 1933.

Daniel, Constantin. "La mention des Esséniens dans le texte grec de l'épître de S. Jude." *Muséon* 81 (1968) 503-21.

Danker, Frederick W. "2 Peter: A Solemn Decree," *CBQ* 40 (1978) 64-82.

Davids, Peter H. *A Commentary on the Epistle of James.* NIGTC; Grand Rapids: William B. Eerdmans, 1982.

———. *The First Epistle of Peter.* NICNT; Grand Rapids: William B. Eerdmans, 1990.

———. "Themes in the Epistle of James That Are Judaistic in Character." Ph.D. dissertation. Manchester, U.K.: University of Manchester, 1974.

———. "The Use of Second Temple Traditions in 1 and 2 Peter and Jude." In Jacques Schlosser, ed. *The Catholic Epistles and the Tradition.* BETL 176; Leuven: Peeters, 2004. 409-31.

Deissmann, Gustav Adolf. *Bible Studies: Contributions Chiefly from Papyri and Inscriptions to the History of the Language, the Literature, and the Religion and Hellenistic Judaism and Primitive Christianity.* Trans. Alexander Grieve. Edinburgh: T&T Clark, 1901, 1903.

Delling, Gerhard. "ΜΟΝΟΣ ΘΕΟΣ." In *Studien zum Neuen Testament und hellenistischen Judentum: Gesammelte Aufsätze 1950–1968.* Göttingen: Vandenhoeck und Ruprecht, 1970. 396-400. Previously in *TLZ* 77 (1952) 469-76.

Donfried, Karl P. *The Setting of Second Clement in Early Christianity.* NovTSup 38; Leiden: Brill, 1974.

Dubarle, André M. "Le péché des anges dans l'épître de Jude." In *Memorial J. Chaine.* Lyons: Facultés Catholiques, 1950. 145-48.

Duke, Rodney K. "Priests, Priesthood." In T. Desmond Alexander and David W. Baker, eds. *Dictionary of the Old Testament: Pentateuch.* Downers Grove, IL: InterVarsity Press, 2003. 646-55.

Dunn, James D. G. *Jesus and the Spirit.* London: SCM, 1975.

du Plessis, O. J. "The Authorship of the Epistle of Jude." In *Biblical Essays 1966: Proceedings of the Ninth Meeting of "Die Ou-Testamentiese Werkgemeenskap in Suid-Afrika," and Proceedings of the Second Meeting of "Die Nuwe-Testamentiese Werkgemeenskap van Suid-Afrika."* Potchefstroom, South Africa: Potchefstroom Herlad (Edms.) Beperk, 1966. 191-99.

Dupont, Jacques. *Gnosis: La connaissance religieuse dans les épîtres de Saint Paul.* Louvain/Paris: Nauwelaerts/Gabalda, 1949.

Edgar, Thomas R. "Robert H. Gundry and Revelation 3:10." *Grace Theological Journal* 3 (1982) 19-49.

Ellis, E. Earle. *Paul and His Recent Interpreters.* Grand Rapids: William B. Eerdmans, 1961.

———. *Pauline Theology: Ministry and Society.* Grand Rapids: William B. Eerdmans, 1989.

———. "Prophecy and Hermeneutic in Jude." In E. E. Ellis, *Prophecy and Hermeneutic in Early Christianity.* Grand Rapids: William B. Eerdmans, 1978. 220-36.

Erickson, Millard J. *Christian Theology.* Grand Rapids: Baker, 1985.

Ferguson, Everett. *Backgrounds of Early Christianity.* Grand Rapids: William B. Eerdmans, 1993[2].

Finegan, Jack. "The Original Form of the Pauline Collection." *HTR* 49 (1956) 85-104.

Fitzmyer, Joseph A. "The Name Simon." In J. A. Fitzmyer, *Essays on the Semitic Background of the New Testament.* London: Geoffrey Chapman, 1971. 105-12.

Fossum, Jarl. "*Kurios* Jesus as the Angel of the Lord in Jude 5-7." *NTS* 33:2 (1987) 226-43.

Friedrich, Gerhard. "Lohmeyers These über das paulinische Briefpräscript kritisch beleuchtet." *TLZ* 81 (1956) 158-64.

Gamble, Harry. "The Redaction of the Pauline Letters and the Formation of the Pauline Corpus." *JBL* 94 (1971) 403-18.

García Martínez, Florentino. *The Dead Sea Scrolls Translated: The Qumran Texts in English.* Trans. Wilfred G. E. Watson. Leiden: E. J. Brill, 1994.

Gilmour, Michael J. *The Significance of Parallels between 2 Peter and Other Early Christian Literature.* Atlanta: Society of Biblical Literature, 2002.

Green, E. M. B. (Michael). *2 Peter Reconsidered.* London: Tyndale, 1960.

Gross, J. *La divinisation du chrétien d'après les pères grecs.* Paris: Gabalda, 1938.

Gunther, John J. "The Alexandrian Epistle of Jude." *NTS* 30:4 (1984) 549-62.

Haaker, Klaus, and P. Schäfer. "Nachbiblische Traditionen vom Tod des

Mose." In O. Betz, K. Haaker, and M. Hengel, eds. *Josephus-Studien: Untersuchungen zu Josephus, dem antiken Judentum und dem Neuen Testament: Otto Michel zum 70. Geburtstag gewidmet.* Göttingen: Vandenhoeck & Ruprecht, 1974. 147-74.

Hamilton, Edith. *Mythology.* New York: New American Library, 1942.

Harris, Murray J. *Slave of Christ: A New Testament Metaphor for Total Devotion to Christ.* New Studies in Biblical Theology 8; Downers Grove, IL/ Leicester, U.K.: InterVarsity Press/Apollos, 2001.

Harris, William V. *Restraining Rage: The Ideology of Anger Control in Classical Antiquity.* Cambridge: Harvard University Press, 2001.

Hartin, Patrick J. *James of Jerusalem: Heir to Jesus of Nazareth.* Interfaces; Collegeville, MN: Liturgical Press, 2004. 1-43.

Hennecke, Edgar. *New Testament Apocrypha.* Ed. Wilhelm Schneemelcher. Trans. R. McL. Wilson. London: Lutterworth/SCM, vol. 1, 1963; vol. 2, 1965.

Hiebert, D. Edmond. "Selected Studies from Jude, Part 2: An Exposition of Jude 12-16." *BSac* 142 (1985) 245-49.

———. "Selected Studies from Jude, Part 3: An Exposition of Jude 17-23." *BSac* 142 (1985) 355-66.

Holladay, Carl R. Theios Anēr *in Hellenistic Judaism.* SBLDS 40; Missoula, MT: Scholars, 1977.

Hornblower, Simon, and Antony Spawforth. *The Oxford Companion to Classical Civilization.* Oxford: Oxford University Press, 1998.

Hunter, Archibald M. *Paul and His Predecessors.* London: SCM, $1961^2$.

Hurtado, Larry W. *At the Origins of Christian Worship.* Grand Rapids: William B. Eerdmans, 1999.

Isenberg, Sheldon R. "Anti-Sadducee Polemic in the Palestinian Targum Tradition." *HTR* 63 (1970) 433-44.

Jackson, Howard M. "Ancient Self-Referential Conventions and Their Implications for the Authorship and Integrity of the Gospel of John." *JTS* n.s. 8:1 (1999) 1-34.

Jastrow, Marcus. *A Dictionary of the Targumim, the Talmud Babli and Yerushalmi, and the Midrashic Literature.* New York: Judaica, 1975.

Jeffers, James S. *The Greco-Roman World of the New Testament.* Downers Grove, IL: InterVarsity Press, 1999.

Jeremias, Joachim. "Isolated Sayings of the Lord." In Hennecke, *New Testament Apocrypha,* 1:85-90.

———. *Unknown Sayings of Jesus.* Trans. R. H. Fuller. London: S.P.C.K., 1957.

Jobes, Karen H. "The Syntax of 1 Peter: Just How Good Is the Greek?" *BBR* 13:2 (2003) 159-73.

Josephus, Flavius. *The Works of Josephus.* Oak Harbor, WA: Logos Research Systems, 1997.

Käsemann, Ernst. "An Apologia for Primitive Christian Eschatology." In *Essays on New Testament Themes.* Trans. W. J. Montague. SBT 41; London: SCM, 1964. 169-95. = "Apologie der urchristlichen Eschatologie," in *Exegetische Versuche und Besinnungen,* vol. 1. Göttingen: Vandenhoeck und Ruprecht, 1960, 1970. 135-57.

Kee, Howard Clark. "The Terminology of Mark's Exorcism Stories," *NTS* 14 (1968) 232-46.

———. "The Transfiguration in Mark: Epiphany or Apocalyptic Vision?" In John Reumann, ed. *Understanding the Sacred Text* (*Festschrift* for M. S. Enslin. Valley Forge, PA: Judson, 1972. 137-52.

Kellett, E. E. "Note on Jude 5." *ExpT* 15 (1903-04) 381.

Klijn, Albertus K. J. "Jude 5-7." In William C. Weinrich, ed. *The New Testament Age: Essays in Honor of Bo Reicke.* Macon, GA: Mercer University Press, 1984. 1:237-44.

Koester, Helmut. *Introduction to the New Testament,* vol. 2: *History and Literature of Early Christianity.* Philadelphia: Fortress, 1982.

Kraus, Thomas J. *Sprache, Stil und historischer Ort des zweiten Petrusbriefes.* WUNT 2. Reihe 136; Tübingen: Mohr-Siebeck, 2001.

Kubo, Sakae. "Jude 22-23: Two-division Form or Three?" In E. J. Epp and G. D. Fee, eds. *New Testament Text Criticism: Its Significance for Exegesis.* Oxford: Clarendon, 1981. 239-53.

Landon, Charles. *A Text-Critical Study of the Epistle of Jude.* JSNTSup 135; Sheffield: Sheffield Academic Press, 1996.

Lightfoot, Joseph B. *The Apostolic Fathers.* London: Macmillan, 1890.

Lövestam, Evald. *Son and Saviour: A Study of Acts 13,32-37.* ConNT 18; Lund: C. W. K. Gleerup/Copenhagen: E. Munksgaard, 1961.

Loewenstamm, Samuel E. "The Death of Moses." In G. W. E. Nickelsburg, ed., *Studies on the Testament of Abraham.* SBLSCS 6; Missoula, MT: Scholars, 1976. 185-217.

Lohmeyer, Ernst. "Probleme paulinischer Theologie, 1: Briefliche Grussüberschriften." *ZNW* 26 (1927) 158-64.

Louw, Johannes P., and Eugene A. Nida. *Greek-English Lexicon of the New Testament Based on Semantic Domains.* New York: United Bible Societies, 1988, 1989.

Magass, Walter. "Semiotik eine Ketzerpolemik am Beispiel von Judas 12f." *Linguistica biblica* 19 (1972) 36-47.

Maher, Michael, trans. and ed. *Targum Pseudo-Jonathan: Genesis.* In *The Aramaic Bible,* vol. 1B. Collegeville, MN: Liturgical Press, 1992.

Maier, Freidrich. "Zur Erklärung des Judasbriefes (Jud 5)." *BZ* 2 (1904) 391-97.

Malina, Bruce J. "Christ and Time: Swiss or Mediterranean?" *CBQ* 51:1 (1989) 1-31.

Marín, F. "Apostolícidad de los escritos neotestamentarios." *Estudios eclesiasticos* 50 (1975) 226.

Marshall, I. Howard. *Last Supper and Lord's Supper.* Exeter, U.K./Grand Rapids: Paternoster/William B. Eerdmans, 1980.

McNamara, Martin. *The New Testament and the Palestinian Targum to the Pentateuch.* AnBib 27; Rome: Pontifical Biblical Institute, 1966.

———., trans. and ed. *Targum Neofiti 1: Genesis.* In *The Aramaic Bible,* vol. 1A. Collegeville, MN: Liturgical Press, 1992.

———. "The Unity of Second Peter: A Reconsideration." *Scr* 12 (1960) 13-19.

McRae, G. W. "Why the Church Rejected Gnosticism." In E. P. Sanders, ed. *Jewish and Christian Self-Definition.* London: SCM, 1980. 1:128-30.

Mees, Michael. "Papyrus Bodmer VII ($p^{72}$) und die Zitate aus den Judasbrief bei Clemens von Alexandrien." *Ciudad de dios* 181 (1968) 551-59.

Meier, Sam. "2 Peter 3:3-7 — An Early Jewish and Christian Response to Eschatological Scepticism." *BZ* 32 (1988) 255-57.

Metzger, Bruce M. *A Textual Commentary on the Greek New Testament.* New York: United Bible Societies, 1971.

Michaels, J. Ramsey. "1 Peter," *DLNT* 914-23.

Millard, Alan Ralph. *Reading and Writing in the Time of Jesus.* Biblical Seminar 69; Sheffield: Sheffield Academic Press, 2000.

Milligan, G. "2 Peter III.10." *ExpT* 32 (1920-21) 331.

Molland, Einar. "La thèse 'La prophétie n'est jamais venue de la volonté de l'homme' (2 Pierre I, 21) et les Pseudo-Clémentines." In *Opuscula patristica.* BTN 2; Oslo: Universitetsforlaget, 1970. 64-77. = *ST* 9 (1955) 67-85.

Mowry, Mary Lucetta. "The Early Circulation of Paul's Letters." *JBL* 63 (1944) 73-86.

Neusner, Jacob. *The Mishnah: A New Translation.* New Haven and London: Yale University Press, 1988.

Neyrey, Jerome H. "The Apologetic Use of the Transfiguration in 2 Peter 1:16-21." *CBQ* 42:2 (1980) 504-19.

———. "The Form and Background of the Polemic in 2 Peter." *JBL* 99:3 (1980) 407-431.

———. "The Form and Background of the Polemic in 2 Peter." Unpublished Ph.D. dissertation. Yale University, 1977.

Oleson, John P. "An Echo of Hesiod's *Theogony* vv 190-92 in Jude 13." *NTS* 25 (1979) 492-503.

Osburn, Carroll D. "The Christological Use of *1 Enoch* 1.9 in Jude 14–15." *NTS* 23 (1977) 334-41.

———. "The Text of Jude 5." *Bib* 62 (1981) 107-15.

———. "The Text of Jude 22–23." *ZNW* 63 (1972) 139-44.

Pagels, Elaine H. *The Gnostic Paul: Gnostic Exegesis of the Pauline Letters.* Philadelphia: Fortress, 1975.

Pearson, B. A. *The* Pneumatikos-Psychikos *Terminology in 1 Corinthians.* SBLDS 12; Missoula, MT: Scholars Press, 1973.

Perkins, Pheme. *Peter: Apostle for the Whole Church.* Minneapolis: Fortress, 2000.

Pfitzner, Victor C. *Paul and the* Agon *Motif: Traditional Imagery in the Pauline Literature.* NovTSup 16; Leiden: E. J. Brill, 1967.

Philo Judaeus. *The Works of Philo.* Oak Harbor, WA: Logos Research Systems, 1997.

Picirelli, Robert E. "The Meaning of 'Epignosis.'" *EvQ* 47 (1975) 85-93.

Pilch, John J., and Bruce J. Malina, eds. *Biblical Social Values and Their Meaning.* Peabody, MA: Hendrickson, 1993.

Raphael, Lawrence W. "The Teaching of Writing an Ethical Will." *Judaism* 48 (1999) 174-80.

Reicke, Bo Ivar. "The Law and This World according to Paul." *JBL* 70 (1951) 259-76.

Reimer, Andy M. "'In the Beginning . . .': Lessons Learned in Teaching Genesis 1 to Evangelical College Students." *Canadian Evangelical Review* 29 (2005) 32-44.

Richards, E. Randolph. *Paul and First-Century Letter Writing: Secretaries, Composition and Collection.* Downers Grove, IL: InterVarsity Press, 2004.

———. "Silvanus Was Not Peter's Secretary: Theological Bias in Interpreting *dia Silvanou . . . egrapsa* in 1 Peter 5:12," *JETS* 43:3 (2000) 417-32.

Riemer, Jack, and Nathaniel Stampfer. *Ethical Wills: A Modern Jewish Treasury.* New York: Schocken, 1983.

Riesner, Rainer. "Der zweite Petrus-Brief und die Eschatologie." In Gerhard Maier, ed. *Zukunftserwartung in biblischer Sicht: Beiträge zur Eschatologie.* Wuppertal: R. Brockhaus, 1984. 124-43.

Roberts, J. W. "A Note on the Meaning of II Peter 3:10d." *ResQ* 6 (1962) 32-33.

Ross, John M. "Church Discipline in Jude 22–23." *ExpT* 100 (1989) 297-98.

Schaff, Philip. *The Ante-Nicene Fathers.* Electronic ed. Garland, TX: Galaxie Software, 2000.

Schlosser, Jacques. "Les jours de Noé et de Lot: A propos de Luc, XVII, 26-30." *RB* 80 (1973) 13-36.

Schmithals, Walter. "Zur Abfassung und ältesten Sammlung der paulinischen Hauptbriefe." [On the Composition and Earliest Collection of the Major Epistles of Paul.] *ZNW* 51 (1960) 225-45.

Schrage, Wolfgang, and Horst Balz. *Die "katholischen" Briefe: Die Briefe des Jakobus, Petrus, Johannes und Judas.* NTD 10; Göttingen: Vandenhoeck & Ruprecht, $1973^{11}$.

Sellin, Gerhard. "Die Häretiker des Judasbriefes," *ZNW* 77:3-4 (1986) 206-25.

Sibinga, J. Smit. "Une citation du Cantique dans la Secunda Petri." *RB* 73 (1966) 107-18.

Sickenberger, Joseph. "Engels- oder Teufelslästerer im Judasbrief (8-10) und im 2. Petrusbriefe (2,10-12)?" In T. Siebs, ed. *Festschrift zu Jahrhundertfeier der Universität zu Breslau.* MSGVK 13-14; 1911-12. 621-39.

Smith, Terence V. *Petrine Controversies in Early Christianity: Attitudes towards Peter in Christian Writings of the First Two Centuries.* WUNT 2:15; Tübingen: J. C. B. Mohr, 1985.

Snyder, Graydon F. "The *Tobspruch* in the New Testament." *NTS* 23:1 (1976-77) 117-20.

Snyder, John I. *The Promise of His Coming — The Eschatology of 2 Peter.* San Mateo, CA: n.p., 1986.

Strobel, August. *Untersuchungen zum eschatologischen Verzögerungsproblem auf Grund der spätjudisch-urchristlichen Geschichte von Habakuk 2,2ff.* NovT-Sup 2; Leiden: E. J. Brill, 1961.

Taylor, Vincent. "Does the New Testament Call Jesus 'God'?" In Vincent Taylor, *New Testament Essays.* London: Epworth, 1970. 83-89.

Thiede, Carson Peter. "A Pagan Reader of 2 Peter: Cosmic Conflagration in 2 Peter 3 and the *Octavius* of Minucius Felix." *JSNT* 26 (1986) 79-96.

Thurén, Lauri. "The Relationship between 2 Peter and Jude — A Classical Problem Resolved?" In Jacques Schlosser, ed. *The Catholic Epistles and the Tradition.* BETL 176; Leuven: Peeters, 2004. 451-60.

Towner, Philip H. *The Goal of Our Instruction: The Structure of Theology and Ethics in the Pastoral Epistles.* JSNTSup 34; Sheffield: Sheffield Academic Press, 1989.

Townsend, Michael J. "Exit the Agape?" *ExpT* 90 (1978-79) 356-71.

van der Horst, Pieter W. *The Sentences of Pseudo-Phocylides.* SVTP 4; Leiden: E. J. Brill, 1978.

Vermes, Geza. "The Targumic Versions of Gen 4:3-16." In Geza Vermes, *Post-Biblical Jewish Studies.* Leiden: Brill, 1975. 96-100.

Vögtle, Anton. *Das neue Testament und die Zukunft des Kosmos.* Düsseldorf: Patmos, 1970.

von Allmen, Daniel. "L'apocalyptique juive et le retard de la parousie en II Pierre 3:1-13." *Revue de Théologie et Philosophie* 16 (1966) 255-74.

Wallace, Daniel B. *Greek Grammar beyond the Basics: An Exegetical Syntax of the Greek New Testament.* Electronic ed. Garland, TX: Galaxie Software, 1999, ca. 1996.

Waltke, Bruce K., with Cathi J. Fredricks. *Genesis: A Commentary.* Grand Rapids: Zondervan, 2001.

Ward, Roy Bowen. "Partiality in the Assembly: James 2-2-4," *HTR* 62 (1969) 87-97.

Watson, Duane Frederick. *Invention, Arrangement, and Style: Rhetorical Criticism of Jude and 2 Peter.* SBLDS 104; Atlanta: Scholars Press, 1988.
Wenham, David. "Being 'Found' on the Last Day: New Light on 2 Peter 3.10 and 2 Corinthians 5.3." *NTS* 33 (1989) 477-79.
Werdermann, Hermann. *Das Irrlehrer des Judas- und 2. Petrusbriefes.* BFCT 17/6; Gütersloh: C. Bertelsmann, 1913.
Whallon, William. "Should We Keep, Omit, or Alter the *hoi* in Jude 12?" *NTS* 34 (1988) 56-59.
Whitaker, G. H. "Faith's Function in St Jude's Epistle," *ExpT* 29 (1917-18) 425.
White, John L. *The Form and Function of the Body of the Greek Letter.* Missoula, MT: Scholars Press, 1972[2].
Wikgren, Allen P. "Some Problems in Jude 5." In B. L. Daniels and M. Jack Suggs, eds. *Studies in the History and Text of the New Testament in Honor of Kenneth Willis Clark.* SD 29; Salt Lake City: University of Utah Press, 1967. 147-52.
Wilson, W. E. "*Heurethēsetai* in 2 Pet. iii.10." *ExpT* 32 (1920-21) 44-45.
Wolters, Al. "'Partners of the Deity': A Covenantal Reading of 2 Peter 1:4." *CTJ* 25 (1990) 28-44.
———. "Postscript to 'Partners of the Deity.'" *Calvin Theological Journal* 26 (1991) 418-20.
———. "Worldview and Textual Criticism in 2 Peter 3:10." *WTJ* 49 (1987) 405-13.
Wright, Nicholas Thomas. *The Challenge of Jesus.* Downers Grove, IL: InterVarsity Press, 1999.
———. *Jesus and the Victory of God.* Minneapolis: Fortress, 1996.
———. *The New Testament and the People of God.* Minneapolis: Fortress, 1992.
Zahn, Theodor. *Introduction to the New Testament.* New York: Scribner's, 1909.

# *General Introduction*

A person could think of a number of reasons for writing a commentary on 2 Peter and Jude. One reason might be, to put it crassly, that they are there. That is, they are in the canon of the NT, for better or worse, so one must write on them if one is to have a commentary series on the NT. Surely there are some who would embrace this reason for writing. It is simply a job that needs to be done. Some of these writers would consider it a mistake that these works were included in the canon (and, as we shall see, many people in the church of the first centuries would have agreed with them, especially when it comes to 2 Peter), but since the books are there, one must write on them.

A second reason might be to counterbalance Paul. The overwhelming focus in NT studies has clearly been on the four Gospels and Paul's letters. For many since the Reformation Paul's letters have been more central than the Gospels. They have been a canon within the canon. By focusing on 2 Peter and Jude (and along with them on James and perhaps 1 Peter) one shows that Paul was not the only voice in the earliest phases of the Jesus movement. There were other voices and other theologies, even if their output was not so prolific (or, perhaps, not so well preserved). Certainly there are scholars who embrace this view. Both of these views would get the job done, but neither of them does justice to these letters.

Thus a third reason for writing on these letters would be that they are so fascinating and make a significant contribution to the NT. In them we see communities of the Jesus movement coming to terms with Greco-Roman culture. The author of 2 Peter, does this in some daring ways as he appropriates the language and thought forms of that culture. This appropriation of culture can be instructive for us as we come to terms with our postmodern culture. In these works we see communities using the Jewish traditions we know from the OT. But they do not simply quote their Greek OT (the LXX). Instead they cite the traditions as they were being retold in their first-century world. This methodology needs to be taken into account as we explore how to apply the OT to a community that lives after Jesus. In these works we see communities coming to terms with teachers who were rejecting the ethical teachings of Jesus but who still claimed to be followers of Jesus. In Jude we do not learn how these teachers justified their position. Jude is not about to set out their arguments as the teachers would have done. But judging from his vehemence, they must have been at least somewhat effective in their presentation. In 2 Peter we discover that one of the justifications used by the teachers he confronts (not necessarily the same group that we meet in Jude) was that there would be no final judgment. Did they think that this had already happened in Jesus? Did they justify this as the only position worthy of a perfect God (who should therefore not have to meddle with his creation)? We do not learn the answer to those questions, but we do learn how 2 Peter confronts them. Perhaps these writers are particularly important today when there is a tendency in the Western church to ignore the teaching of Jesus as a practical way of life — and sometimes to emphasize grace so much that it seems as if the final judgment does not matter.

Along the way there are some surprises for us. We will see the compassion that Jude has for those involved in the error that he is attacking. Jude, compassionate? See if this is not the case. We will learn how these authors define belief in Jesus. We will discover that "Savior" is not so much attached to Jesus' cross as to his return in power. We will marvel again at how our Father has shared himself with us, giving us abilities that we may not believe that we have (or perhaps do not want to use). Perhaps we will recognize that we in the West have become entrapped in the very things from which our Father's plan was to free us. And we will certainly receive a new appreciation for coming judgment, which perhaps stands out most clearly here since it is separated from a presentation of the nature of the resurrection and the details of the coming new age (which are subjects for Paul and Revelation). Yet, more than the final judgment, we will see that the coming new age of the earth is the hope of the believer in Jesus and that that vision should determine how he or she lives in the present.

There is a final pair of fascinating things we can learn from this literature. In it we meet a Peter who is different from 1 Peter and even more different from the Peter most people find in Galatians. He is not Jesus' delegate to the Jews (Galatians), nor even a believer steeped in the OT who is writing to the Gentiles (1 Peter), but a follower of Jesus who is fully acculturated to the Gentile world. Are we seeing the development of a man who starts out as a Galilean fisherman attracted to the revolution announced by John the Baptist that he later came to believe had come in Jesus? Certainly if Peter bar Jonah wrote 2 Peter (an issue that we will discuss at some length), that is just what we are seeing. Could that say something about our own adaptation as we go through life?

The second of these fascinating things is that 2 Peter uses Jude, which is why we will discuss Jude first. This usage (the evidence for which belongs in the introduction to 2 Peter) should not raise the old smokescreen, "Why would an apostle use the work of another church leader?" The answer to that would be, "And why would he not use the work of another church leader?" The first question surely tells more about us and our conception of an apostle than it does about 2 Peter. If one found a gold mine of material, why would one not use it, just as Matthew uses Mark (or, for some, Mark uses Matthew)? What is fascinating is to discover how 2 Peter uses Jude. He does not slavishly copy it as if he knew it would become holy writ, but instead he adapts it to his own perspective and his own argument. This is why we need separate sections of commentary on each of these books, that 2 Peter is not Jude expanded but Jude adapted. We need to look at Jude on its own to understand Jude's own argument and perspective, and then we need to look at 2 Peter on its own to find out his somewhat different perspective. Great minds in the first century were no more cookie-cutter images of some ideal type than they are now. The differing situations and the originality in thinking of the two writers are instructive in an age when many are tempted to parrot party lines or adopt slogans from great leaders without thoroughly digesting them and making them their own.

Thus these works are well worth our time. They are well worth a commentary of this size and even larger. So it is with anticipation that we dive in and examine the two books in order, first Jude and then 2 Peter.

One further issue is worth mentioning. The danger in reading the NT is that we will read our present culture and history back into the text. In order to help us avoid this pitfall, this commentary will reserve the terms "church" and "Christian" for the post-first-century period, when there was a clear break between the Christian movement and Judaism. During the first century the Jesus movement viewed itself and was often viewed as another movement under the larger Jewish umbrella. This does not mean that the followers of Jesus saw themselves as just one Jewish movement or party among other equally valid Jewish movements or parties, but that they saw themselves as *the* true remnant of Israel or *the* true renewed Judaism. Thus "from the inside" they viewed themselves as the only true expression of the faith of Israel (e.g., Acts 4:12); they were, as Paul states, the "Israel of God," whether ethnically Jewish or Gentile in origin (Gal 6:16). Whether for reasons of legitimacy (Judaism had limited legal recognition by the Roman Empire) or of theology (and for Paul the theological continuity with Abraham and Israel certainly dominated), the Jesus movement firmly insisted that they were the sole true expression of Judaism and thus heirs of its promises and protections.

On the other hand, "from the outside" they were just another sect or party within Judaism, a sect that other Jewish sects often claimed was outside the Jewish umbrella (especially the Pauline version with its inclusion of Gentiles) and that Gentiles mockingly named "Christians" because of their claim to follow a Messiah who translated into Greek as "Christ" (which would sound strange as a title). Yet, although they were called "Christians" by others, they seem to have referred to themselves as believers or followers of Jesus or of the Way or simply as brothers and sisters. So we shall adopt this language of referring to them as the Jesus movement to continually remind ourselves that we are in a different world, before the many developments of church history, when Judaism reorganized with a far more unified theology and practice than it had in most of the first century and when the church both rejected Judaism (as we see, e.g., in *Barnabas*) and adopted Roman structure and organization. Similarly, when we come across other language that was not religious in the first century but became religious later, we will often use a modern nonreligious synonym to keep us from importing our contemporary conceptions into the text. It is not the goal of this commentary to change modern Christian language, but to help us as much as possible to climb into the world of the first century and then apply it to the twenty-first.

# The Letter of JUDE

# *Introduction to Jude*

## I. INTRODUCTION

Jude is a book that has often been treated with "benign neglect."[1] Rarely the text for a sermon, even in the university or seminary classroom it is often given only brief treatment at the end of a course on the General Epistles, perhaps as part of the last lecture on the final day of the course. Apparently it was more valued in the period right after it was written, for it is the only letter in the NT to be extensively incorporated into another (i.e., into 2 Peter). Indeed, 2 Peter is the earliest evidence for the existence of Jude. Jude was circulated as a separate book in Egypt and Italy by the end of the second century, for both Clement of Alexandria and Origen cite it (both lived in Egypt), and it was included in the Muratorian Canon (which was Italian). However, subsequent to this doubts arose (so Eusebius, *Eccl. Hist.* 2.23.25; 3.25.3) since Jude cites works such as *1 Enoch* that by then were considered noncanonical. Of course, this was the age of the consolidation of authority and of the delimitation of the canon (meaning the list of what was to be read in church as reflecting the rule of faith).[2] Thus a work that did not fit the developing patterns was doubted

1. Elliott, *I-II Peter/Jude*, 161.

2. A "canon" means a rule or a list, in this case the list of which works should be read publicly in church as reflecting the rule of faith (i.e., canon meaning "list" took on the sense of canon meaning "rule" because the term was applied to the rule of faith before it was applied to a list of books). In an oral-mnemonic society most people received their only scriptural knowledge through this public reading. The concern was that works would be read that misled the congregation in the house church and later the larger church. This concern was stimulated by Marcion's truncated canon (and his truncating of Luke to fit his position), but became even more significant as Gnostic works became

despite its relatively good pedigree.[3] These doubts appear to have been short lived everywhere but in Syria (where it was accepted only in the sixth century).[4] Jude appears in the major fourth-century canon lists (which are from the southern and northern Mediterranean areas, not the eastern end where Syria is located). This acceptance, of course, did not make the letter popular. Its shortness, its apparent absorption into 2 Peter (although we will see that in reality each work has its own perspective), and its apparent lack of theological discussion all worked against it. In modern times its seemingly harsh tone has also contributed to its neglect. We will discover, however, that many of these issues are the result of reading an ancient work through later lenses, or the imposition of Reformation or modern concern or standards on a first-century work. Thus the neglect is more the result of our problems than of Jude's problems.

## II. AUTHORSHIP

Problems with Jude start with the first verse, where the author is named. Jude claims to be written by "Jude, a servant of Jesus Christ and a brother of James." While the name Judah (the Hebrew form) or Judas (the Greek form) was extremely frequent in Jewish groups (Jesus, according to Luke,

---

available, some of which were written under the names of apostles (the *Apocryphon of John, Apocryphon of James, Gospel of Thomas, Gospel of Philip, Apocalypse of Paul,* etc.). This defensive stance produced a tendency to "play it safe," so works that were valued tended to be attributed to apostles whether or not the apostle took an active part in their production (Mark was associated with Peter and Luke-Acts with Paul; Matthew was attributed to Matthew) and works that were nonapostolic stopped being read, even if they were orthodox and helpful (e.g., the *Didache*). Jude did not reflect this "canon consciousness" (since it came from before the period when the canon was actively discussed) and had some ideas to which certain later church leaders objected. Besides, Jude was not known to be either an apostle or a major leader in the early Jesus movement. On canon see F. F. Bruce, *The Canon of Scripture* (Downers Grove, IL: InterVarsity Press, 1988), especially 17-18 on the definition of the term.

3. Jude was never cited frequently, but contrast Jude's early use by Clement of Alexandria and Tertullian with that of James, which is *never* explicitly cited until Origen (although a word that James may have invented does appear more than once in the *Shepherd of Hermas,* which *could* indicate that James was known in Rome by the end of the first century). One would not expect a short work like Jude to be cited often.

4. Bigg, *The Epistles of St. Peter and St. Jude,* 305-10, lists the evidence, as do Mayor, *The Epistles of Jude and II Peter,* cxv-cxxiii, and Cantinat, *Les Épitres de Saint Jacques et de Saint Jude,* 276-82. The main issue was apparently Jude's citation of *1 Enoch* by name (and for Didymus the Blind the content of his citation of the *Testament of Moses*). While Tertullian believed that this made *1 Enoch* canonical (*De cultu feminarum* 1.3), other church leaders thought that this disqualified Jude.

had two men named Judas among the Twelve, Judas son of James and Judas Iscariot; Luke 6:16, NIV), this Jude/Judas expected his identity to be recognized by members of the Jesus movement, at least by those members to whom the letter was written. Who could this person be? The issue is important, for it will tell us where this letter fits into the story of the Jesus movement.

We know for sure who it could not be, namely Judas son of Simon Iscariot (to use John's designation, John 6:71), since every tradition about him indicates that he felt so much shame as a result of his betrayal of Jesus that he committed suicide about the time of Jesus' crucifixion. A more realistic possibility would be the prophetic Judas Barsabbas, who, according to Luke (Acts 15:22, 27, 32), accompanied Silas in carrying the letter from the Apostolic Council. However, while this person was surely capable of giving a prophetic denunciation such as that found in this letter, he is never identified with a James (Jacob in its Hebrew form).[5] Another possibility would be that other Judas who was part of the Twelve (mentioned in Luke 6:16; John 14:22; Acts 1:13). John identifies him simply as "not Iscariot," but both Lucan references identify him as "Judas son of James" (NIV; Greek translation, "Judas of James"). (He is apparently the same person whom Mark 3:18 [followed by Matt 10:3] identifies as Thaddaeus [glossed as Lebbaeus in some later manuscripts of both Mark and Matthew]). On the one hand, this person could not have been very well known if the tradition contains some confusion about his name (although it is possible that Mark was trying to avoid identifying him with Judas Iscariot, and that Matthew follows him in this). On the other hand, while he is associated with a "James," the "of James" probably indicates "son of James" rather than "brother of James" (unless one argues that "brother" has dropped out of the text, for which there is no evidence). Thus our apparently well-known "Judas brother of James," the designated author of Jude, most likely does not intend to indicate that he is the otherwise obscure Judas of the Twelve.

Therefore, the most likely Judas being designated as the author of

5. E. Earle Ellis, *Prophecy and Hermeneutic in the Early Church* (Tübingen: J. C. B. Mohr [Paul Siebeck], 1978; repr. Grand Rapids: William B. Eerdmans, 1978), 226-30, argues that "brother" means "co-worker"; thus our Jude is indeed Judas Barsabbas, who had been a co-worker of James. However, (1) the argument that Jude would have called himself "brother of the Lord" had he been a brother of Jesus would have to mean that the James who wrote the letter of James also could not have been a brother of the Lord since he does not call himself by that title (Jas 1:1), and (2) while "brother" can mean "co-worker," it means this only when someone is referring to another person as "my brother" or "our brother," not when a person calls himself "brother of." In each of its occurrences in biblical literature, "brother of" indicates that the individual is a relative of the person in question.

this letter is Judas the younger brother of Jesus (Matt 13:55; Mark 6:3).[6] Even here there is some uncertainty in the tradition, for while the two Synoptic Gospels agree on the order of the first two brothers (although not on the form of the name of the second), they disagree on the order of the last two.[7] Despite this uncertainty, however, we clearly have a Judas who had a brother James who was well known in the early Jesus movement, for James the brother of Jesus was the main leader of the Jesus movement in Jerusalem (and probably in all Palestine) from at least A.D. 44 (the latest date when Peter had to flee Jerusalem, although James was probably the leader long before this) to his martyrdom in A.D. 61.

This Judas brother of Jesus and James has in some parts of the church been identified with Thomas the Twin, one of the Twelve. The fact that the name "Thomas" is a transliteration of the Aramaic term for "twin" and thus was not a personal name lends credence to the idea that his personal name could have been Judas, dropped to avoid confusion with the two other members of the Twelve.[8] However, the further identification of this Judas Thomas with the brother of Jesus is unlikely, for it does not appear to be the position of the earlier sources, and those sources that do make the identification (e.g., the some manuscripts of the Syriac translation of John 14:22; *Gospel of Thomas*) have a theological reason for doing so.[9] Furthermore, while Judas Thomas may well have been the name of this member of the Twelve, he is never said to have a brother James (this is not even brought out in passages calling him the twin brother of Jesus) and thus does not qualify as a candidate for our author, whose brother James appears to be better known than he is.

We remain, then, with Judah bar Joseph, that is, Judas son of Joseph, a younger brother of Jesus. We have very little information about this

6. If one takes one of the views about the family of Jesus in which his "brothers" were either stepbrothers (sons of Joseph from before he married Mary) or cousins (sons of Clopas, John 19:25 with Matt 27:56), this Judas could be the same as Judas of James, but, while that was once a popular position in the Roman Catholic Church, few Catholics take that position today. On the other hand, many would argue that Jesus' "brothers" were all either older (if Joseph had sons before he married Mary) or contemporaneous with him (if they were cousins). For a modern presentation of the view that Jesus' brothers were cousins, see Patrick J. Hartin, *James of Jerusalem: Heir to Jesus of Nazareth* (Interfaces; Collegeville, MN: Liturgical Press, 2004), 1-43.

7. Richard J. Bauckham, *Jude and the Relatives of Jesus in the Early Church* (Edinburgh: T&T Clark, 1990), 6-9. This probably indicates an uncertainty about which brother was older.

8. Gary M. Burge, "Thomas, the Apostle," in Walter A. Elwell, ed., *Baker Encyclopedia of the Bible* (Grand Rapids: Baker, 1988), 2:2057.

9. Bauckham, *Jude, 2 Peter,* 32-36. The theological reason was to make Judas Thomas the twin of Jesus, at least in a spiritual sense.

brother, who could have been younger than twenty when Jesus died.[10] We are told that Jesus' brothers were not his followers at one point during his ministry (John 7:5); while Johannine references are difficult to evaluate in the light of the data in the Synoptics, the reference to Judas in Mark 6:3 points to his still living in Nazareth and leading a "normal" life at a time in Jesus' ministry when Jesus had already moved to Capernaum. Yet whatever the situation before Jesus' last trip to Jerusalem, Acts 1:14 identifies Jesus' mother Mary and his brothers as being among those in the upstairs room right after Jesus' ascension. One suspects that the author of Luke-Acts also assumes that they were in that same room for Passover forty days earlier, but he does not say that. Only the Johannine tradition (John 19:25) places Mary with Jesus at that time. At the least the tradition indicates an awareness that Jesus' brothers were part of the Jesus movement from its earliest days in Jerusalem. But after this single reference all of Jesus' brothers except James disappear from the text of the NT.

There is a series of later traditions about this Judas. The *Acts of Paul* apparently identifies our Judas with the one mentioned in Acts 9:1, which is an understandable confusion.[11] Eusebius cites a tradition from Julius Africanus to the effect that Jesus' relatives spread the good news throughout Palestine (*Eccl. Hist.* 1.7.14). This tradition is hardly improbable, given that we know that they were committed members of the Jesus movement, although it may or may not exaggerate their influence and/or range of travel. Eusebius also reports Hegesippus claiming that the grandsons of Jude were brought before the Roman emperor Domitian as being politically dangerous, but that they persuaded him that they were simply poor farmers (*Eccl. Hist.* 3.19–3.20.8). Despite the fact that one fragment of Hegesippus actually identifies these men as Zoker (Zecha-

10. Judas was the youngest or the next to the youngest of Jesus' brothers and thus at least the third child born after Jesus, since we are not told where the sisters came among the siblings (he would be third as all of the sisters were born after Jesus' three oldest brothers and of these brothers Judas was born third; if Judas was the youngest sibling, he could be the sixth or seventh child, assuming that at least two (sisters is plural) and possibly three or more sisters were older than he (and that no children died in infancy). Given this latter assumption, if Jesus was born in 4 B.C., it would hardly be surprising if he were fourteen years or so older than Judas (that would mean a child every two years, which would not be surprising for a woman who nursed her children for two or three years, as was normal in that day). Since the crucifixion is usually dated A.D. 29 or 30, that would mean that Judas may well have been younger than twenty. However, we must remember that in that culture he certainly carried adult responsibilities and may well have been married and had a family by that age.

11. E. Hennecke, *New Testament Apocrypha* (London: Lutterworth, 1965), 2:388. "[In Damascus] I entered into a great church with the blessed Judas, the brother of the Lord, who from the beginning gave me the exalted love of faith," says Paul.

riah) and James,[12] there are enough historically dubious parts to this tradition that it is highly suspect. We are far wiser to say that we know nothing about the later life of Jude/Judas other than that it is probable that for the rest of his life he remained part of and (at some level) a leader in the Jesus movement in Palestine.

Whether this Judas son of Joseph was the actual writer of Jude is a matter of dispute. Many scholars believe that the son of a carpenter would not have been equipped to write such a letter. Others argue that the evidence points in that direction. In order to examine this question, we need to take other information into account, namely, the place and date of composition, the addressees, and the language and structure.

## III. PLACE AND DATE OF COMPOSITION

If this Jude wrote this letter, if he is, then, the main character in the implied story contained in the document, where and when did he write it? The issue of the "when" is easier to answer than the "where." That is, if 2 Peter did indeed use Jude, then Jude must have been written first. But that answer begs the question since the date of 2 Peter is disputed. That is, if Simon Peter bar Jonah wrote 2 Peter, then it was probably written before A.D. 68, the death of the Roman emperor Nero, assuming the accuracy of the tradition that Peter was martyred under Nero. (As we will discuss in the Introduction to 2 Peter [p. 125], it probably is accurate, although, given its late date, one cannot be certain that it is.) That would put Jude around A.D. 60 at the latest, given that Peter would have to get it and read it before he could use it. However, if 2 Peter is, as Richard Bauckham claims,[13] a posthumous *testament*, then the dates of 2 Peter and of Jude could easily be a couple of decades later. Even this *could* have been within Jude's lifetime, for while we have no information as to how long he lived, it is conceivable that in that age a man might have written a letter like this in his late 70s or 80s, although not many actually did. Those who place 2 Peter in the early to middle of the second century tend to date Jude toward the end of the first century, and for them neither of these books was actually written by its implied author.[14] As we continue our discussion, we shall be looking for information that proves or disproves these various hypotheses.

12. This fragment is found in Carl de Boor, *Neue Fragmente des Papias, Hegesippus und Pierius* (TU 5/2; Leipzig: J. C. Hinrichs, 1888), 169.

13. Bauckham, *Jude, 2 Peter,* 158-62.

14. See Vögtle, *Der Judasbrief, der zweite Petrusbrief,* 128-29.

A story involves place as well as date, so the question of date is connected to the question of where the letter was written. Given that the letter was accepted early in Egypt, some scholars have argued for an Alexandrian place of composition.[15] While the reception of the letter there might point in this direction (as well as the fact that it was not well accepted in Syria until the sixth century), the strongest argument in this direction is the quality of the Greek. But here we must be careful. It is not so much the style of Jude that is so excellent as his rhetorical skill and use of relatively rare vocabulary. The author is well educated and knows at least the basics of classical rhetoric, but one could learn that in Jerusalem or Antioch as well as in Alexandria. Furthermore, the finding of manuscripts of *1 Enoch* in Qumran shows that that source of Jude was in circulation in Palestine and so would not make the Egyptian provenance more likely due to our having found Ethiopic manuscripts.

The other likely location for the beginning of our implied story is somewhere in Palestine or Syria. Helmut Koester argues for Syria on the grounds that Judas Thomas Didymus was revered in Gnostic circles there and that opposing him to Judas brother of James would make sense.[16] The argument, however, depends on Jude's having been written against Gnostics, and that identification of his opponents is not persuasive since he does not describe any specifically Gnostic teaching. There is also no tradition placing any of the relatives of Jesus that far north. Thus it is more likely that Jude was written toward the southern end of this range, which would be Palestine. A number of commentators opt for this location.[17] What the decision turns on is the degree to which one believes that Jude reflects Palestinian sources. That is, we have learned long ago that there was plenty of Hellenistic culture in first-century Palestine (e.g., there was a gymnasium, among other Hellenistic institutions, in Jerusalem), so one can easily conceive of a writer obtaining a good Hellenistic education there (if he had not obtained the education elsewhere before arriving in Jerusalem) and writing in proper Hellenistic style (if he or she were writing to recipients in the wider Greco-Roman world), but it is harder to imagine an author who lived outside of Palestine consulting sources in Hebrew or Aramaic or an author born outside of Palestine allowing Semitisms or Semitic enhancements to creep into his Greek (unless, like Paul, they had done significant study in Palestine). As we will see, there is some evidence that our author did have contact with Hebrew or Aramaic source material.

15. John J. Gunther, "The Alexandrian Epistle of Jude," *NTS* 30:4 (1984) 549-62.

16. Helmut Koester, *Introduction to the New Testament*, vol 2: *History and Literature of Early Christianity* (Philadelphia: Fortress, 1982), 246-48.

17. E.g., Bauckham, *Jude, 2 Peter*, 15-16; Kelly, *The Epistles of Peter and of Jude*, 234.

A further argument for a Palestinian place of writing is that Jude and especially James were well known in Palestine. Neither they nor the other relatives of Jesus appear to have been revered outside the eastern Mediterranean. The simple attribution implies that this work was written where Jude was known and where James was better known.

Thus our decision is for a Palestinian provenance. This does not have a definitive effect upon authorship. We simply do not know enough about the life of Jude to argue that, if he wrote it, it must have been written in Palestine. For all we know, Jude could have traveled extensively. On the other hand, all we know about Jude and even all of the traditions that we have about him and his descendants are connected to Palestine, so a Palestinian provenance might make his authorship somewhat more likely. Still, surely plenty of people in the Palestinian Jesus movement were well educated in Greek even after the scattering of the Hellenists (Acts 8:1). Thus someone other than Jude could have written the letter even if it was written in Palestine.

The story implied in a letter is that it was written at a given time from someone in a given place to someone in another place. Date is thus also dependent upon the decisions that one makes about the addressees and their circumstances. A number of authors have viewed the following statements as indicating circumstances that fit the late first century.[18]

| | *Content* | *Comment* |
|---|---|---|
| v. 3 | The faith that was once for all entrusted to the saints | The faith entrusted in the past |
| v. 17 | Remember what the apostles of our Lord Jesus Christ foretold | Apostles are remembered, not present. |
| v. 18 | In the last times | This is an issue only if it separates the addressees from former times. |
| v. 20 | Build yourselves up in your most holy faith | The faith |

These authors argue that references to "the faith" indicate a later date, particularly because "the faith" is a body of faith and practice that was entrusted to the church in the past. Furthermore, the apostles are spoken of as a group, and that group does not appear to be present. Many scholars think that this indicates that they are now dead. What are we to

18. E.g., Vögtle, *Der Judasbrief, der zweite Petrusbrief,* 8; Kelly, *The Epistles of Peter and of Jude,* 234.

make of these indications of time? First, frequent references to "the faith" do appear to come late in the NT period.[19] Such references appear in Acts 13:8 and 14:2, but also in 1 Cor 13:16, 2 Cor 13:5, and Gal 1:23. In the Prison Epistles the expression is rare (Phil 1:27 and Col 2:7 are the only possible instances). The term occurs in Heb 4:14 (and perhaps in 1 Pet 5:9) and then some thirteen times in the Pastoral Epistles. In other words, while it does occur on occasion by the 50s of the first century (Galatians and Corinthians), it is clearly far more common in works that are dated in the 60s or later.[20] It does tend to appear in conflict situations ("fight for the faith" contexts), and while this is especially true in the Pastoral Epistles, it is also true for Hebrews and other references to "the faith." We conclude that the reference to "the faith" is not a sure indicator of a post-60 date, but that it would tend toward grouping this work with the Pastoral Epistles.

Interpreters also point out that Jude refers to the apostles as a group involved with the past history of his addressees. This is clearly the case, but the accompanying assumption that the apostles are dead and therefore Jude comes from the late first century assumes a position on a number of issues. First, who are these "apostles of our Lord Jesus Christ"? If this is a second-century book, then we are talking about the Twelve and Paul, or some such fixed group as that. In that case it is a little surprising that "holy" or some such adjective has not been added. But in the first century many missionaries were referred to as "apostles." Paul refers to a couple (or perhaps to a group of missionaries) by this designation in Rom 16:7,[21] and even in the early second century a Chris-

19. In the listing that follows some data will be assumed that do not show up in English. The issue will be where the definite article indicates "the faith" and where it is only a (Greek) case indicator, meaning "with respect to faith" or something like that. Since this commentary is for English readers, we will not go into detail about these data.

20. We will not discuss the date of the Pastoral Epistles in this commentary. If they are by Paul and if the tradition of his martyrdom under Nero is correct, then they were written before 68. But of course many scholars believe that they come from a later period of the church. Thus they do not help us until we have settled the question of their dating.

21. Michael H. Burer and Daniel B. Wallace, "Was Junia Really an Apostle? A Re-examination of Rom 16.7," *NTS* 47:1 (2001) 76-91, argue that "outstanding among the apostles" is a construction that most likely means "well known by the apostles" or "whose fame is known to the apostles." However, (1) if they are correct, then it is likely that "apostles" means the wider group of missionaries rather than the Twelve since Paul is writing to Rome, not to people resident in Palestine, which is the only place where the Twelve were as a group, (2) the authors admit that the NIV translation is possible, even if they do not think that it is probable, and (3), upon reading their evidence, we found that at least some of what they felt supported the "exclusive" position ("well known by the apostles") could as naturally be read as supporting the "inclusive" position ("outstanding among the apostles"). Yet it is unlikely that they are correct, for Linda Belleville again

tian writer can refer to traveling apostles (*Did.* 11:3-6), so to assume that this refers to a deceased group that is identical with the Twelve may say more about our reading than about Jude's writing. All we know is that these were individuals commissioned at some time (before or after Easter) by Jesus Christ.

Second, the assumption that the expression means that this group of apostles has died is unfounded. Clearly they are no longer present (for if they were present, one would not need to remember what they said), but missionaries often moved on. We need think only about Paul, whose longest stay in a church he founded was about three years. During the founding of the church the missionaries (or the Twelve, if this church were founded by a pair or more of them) made predictions of dangers in the future. Acts records Paul as sometimes doing this when he left a church (e.g., Acts 14:22; 20:29-30). This means that at least by the time of Luke's writing such prophetic warnings were deemed appropriate for traveling missionaries; if Luke is referring to an accurate tradition, then such prophetic warning goes back to the 40s and 50s. Thus the expression in Jude does not necessarily mean that the apostles are dead.

Finally, even if Jude is talking about apostles who are dead, not apostles who have left, there is no reason why this fact should put the date of Jude past A.D. 70. If our traditions are correct, by then Peter and Paul and James were all dead, and likely many of the rest of the Twelve as well.[22] Before the execution of James, Peter, or Paul many Christians had died (2 Corinthians and 1 Thessalonians both deal with that issue, and both were written before A.D. 60) and certainly missionaries would be among the most likely to die, given the rigors of travel, not to mention the dangers of persecution (Paul survived his travels, but it was not because people did not try to kill him; Stephen did not even leave Jerusalem before he was killed). Thus well within the lifetime of a reasonably long-lived brother of Jesus this language makes sense.

But, we might ask, did such false teachers as those mentioned in Jude live before the end of the first century? For that we will have to consider a wider set of issues, which we will handle below, but let us say at this point that unless the addressees turn out not to have existed during the first century, there are no other date indicators in the work that would

---

lays out the evidence in "'Ιουνιᾶν . . . ἐπίσημοι ἐν τοῖς ἀποστόλοις: A Re-examination of Romans 16.7 in Light of Primary Source Materials," *NTS* 51:2 (2005) 231-49, showing that "outstanding among the apostles" is indeed the better translation.

22. If the tradition about the writing of Mark is correct, then it was the silencing or the threat of silencing the apostolic voice that led to the writing of that Gospel, which is the earliest of the Gospels.

not be at home in pre-70 Palestine, although we freely admit that a date later in the first century is also possible.[23]

## IV. ADDRESSEES

Our implied story requires a group of addressees for whom the instruction is needed. We could diagram this as follows:[24]

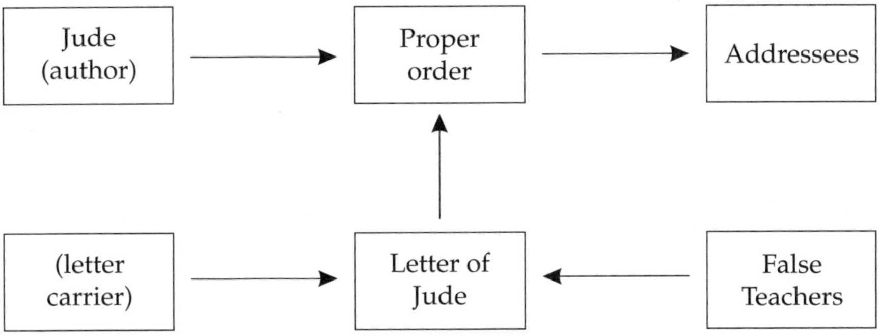


What this diagram shows is that Jude is trying to bring proper order to his addressees or, perhaps more accurately, to their community. His "agent" is the letter we are reading. The opponent is the false teachers. The presumed letter carrier (without a public postal system there had to be one) functions as the helper. (In those days he would indeed have been a helper, for he may well have read the letter to the addressees and then explained its contents.) Thus, having talked about the author, we now turn to the addressees and then to the false teachers. We take up the letter itself in the commentary text.

Turning to the issue of addressees, then, we discover that Jude does not address a specific group. "Those who have been called, who are loved by God the Father and kept by Jesus Christ" could designate any group of people committed to Jesus as Lord, whether they were Jewish or Gentile, whether they were Palestinian, Egyptian, or northern Mediterranean. There is neither a geographic descriptor nor even the use of a gen-

23. Jude does not refer to the type of argument found in 2 Peter 3. So we must be careful not to read into Jude a doubting of the Parousia. Jude was useful to 2 Peter, but some of the issues in 2 Peter are unknown to Jude.

24. For a discussion of this type of diagramming of an implied narrative, see N. T. Wright, *The New Testament and the People of God* (Minneapolis: Fortress, 1992), 69-77. Its origin is in the literary analysis of A. J. Greimas.

eral term like "Diaspora" (as in Jas 1:1) that would at least indicate that the addressees were external to Palestine. The only thing that we can discern from this address is that Jude is not an evangelistic tract.

Thus we must examine the internal data of the letter to see if we can discover more about this community, however large and scattered it may be. (Any larger believing community in that period, such as the church in Corinth, was a network of house churches, but some letters, e.g., 1 Peter, were not addressed to a single network but to a large, scattered group of networks.) The internal data about the community itself are limited. That is, as noted above, the people are described as believers (Jude 1) whose community is threatened by "intruders" of some type (i.e., "certain men have secretly slipped in among you"; Jude 4). Whether these "intruders" are traveling teachers, who appear to have been common in the first century, or whether by referring to them as intruders Jude is indicating that their teaching means that they are not really part of the Jesus movement or that their teaching is foreign to the movement, we cannot tell. By calling them "intruders" Jude separates them from the community and thus implies that the community itself has not succumbed, which may or may not be a polite or charitable assumption.[25]

These believers apparently respect James, since Jude identifies himself with respect to James rather than with respect to his own location or parentage.[26] We know that the letter of James circulated in the eastern Mediterranean (and possibly Rome) before being widely accepted, and that James was the leader of the Jesus movement in Palestine, so that would be one possible location, although James was also respected in other parts of the church where he was not personally known and his letter was not read. The community Jude addresses is expected to be familiar with the narratives of the Hebrew scriptures, but while many groups in the Jesus movement probably could not afford their own copies of either the Hebrew texts or the Septuagint (the choice of version depending on where they lived and which languages they read), all valued those texts. More telling is the fact that they are expected to be familiar with both *1 Enoch* and the *Testament of Moses.* The former was probably composed in Palestine (fragments were found among the Dead Sea Scrolls),

25. Neyrey, *2 Peter, Jude,* 51-53.

26. Jude does include his relationship to Jesus: servant. In other words, he is representing the king, as a servant of Caesar represented Caesar. Paul also likes to use this designation. Both Paul and Peter often add "apostle." This latter is also a relationship to Jesus in that he had commissioned them to travel with the message of the kingdom, making it appropriate for them to relate to far-flung communities of believers. The titles are not so much offices as "bishop" would become as they are functional relationships vis-à-vis Jesus. They are saying, "I represent Jesus in what I am doing."

although it later circulated more widely in both Greek and Ethiopic translations.[27] The latter was probably written in a Semitic language by members of the Hasidic movement in Palestine in the early first century.[28] It was later translated into Greek and then into Latin. As we look at these data, we conclude that either the author or the addressees probably lived in Palestine since that is where the lines converge (James, *1 Enoch*, *Testament of Moses*), and that if the author lived in Palestine, then the addressees were a group in the Jesus movement who lived in a Greek-speaking area not too far away. Anywhere in the eastern Mediterranean, including Syria and Egypt, would fit that description. We cannot tell what the racial makeup of the group was. We might suspect that they were predominantly Jewish given the biblical-prophetic tone of the work and the expectation that they will revere the name of James, but then many readers know people who grew up without any significant contact with the church who, after conversion, became fluently bilingual in King James biblical vocabulary, and, as we noted above, Jewish believers were not the only ones to revere the name of James. Still, the evidence does point in a Jewish direction, even if it is far from decisive.

Can the identification of the false teachers tell us anything about the addressees? This is a far more difficult issue. First, we possess little information about the false teachers. Not only do we lack their own presentation of their doctrines, but also Jude does not try to give us a systematic presentation of those doctrines. He gives enough information so that his readers would presumably recognize whom he was referring to, but we are not in their privileged position. Second, it is risky to mirror-read the doctrines of a group from its critics. The language of the critic may be stereotyped rather than a literal description of the people he or she is criticizing, for an important part of rhetoric was to describe the opponent as dishonorable. Thus we have to be careful to read the descriptions through eyes attuned to the first-century culture in which it was written.[29] With these caveats in mind, however, we must still attempt to describe those whom he considers false teachers.

27. E. Isaac, "1 Enoch," in Charlesworth, *OTP* 1:6-8.

28. J. Priest, "Testament of Moses," in Charlesworth, *OTP* 1:920-22.

29. Robert J. Karris pointed this issue out for the Pastoral Epistles ("The Background and Significance of the Polemic of the Pastoral Epistles," *JBL* 92 [1973] 549-64). See also Frederik Wisse, "The Epistle of Jude in the History of Heresiology," in Martin Krause, ed., *Essays on the Nag Hammadi Texts in Honor of Alexander Boehlig* (Leiden: E. J. Brill, 1972), 133-43. While we are not as sceptical as either Karris or Wisse, the point we need to take from these studies is that ancient authors did use stereotyped terms to attack their opponents, and thus we should be cautious about reading detailed descriptions out of their accusations.

| | *Charge* | *Comment* |
|---|---|---|
| v. 4 | They are godless. | General statement of impiety |
| v. 4 | They change the grace of our God into a license for immorality. | Immoral |
| v. 4 | They deny Jesus Christ, our only Sovereign and Lord. | We are not told in what sense they deny Jesus, but the titles indicate that it has to do with his authority. |
| v. 8 | These dreamers pollute their own bodies, reject authority, and slander celestial beings. | Immoral and rebellious |
| v. 10 | These men speak abusively against whatever they do not understand. | Rebellious |
| v. 11 | They have taken the way of Cain; they have rushed for profit into Balaam's error; they have been destroyed in Korah's rebellion. | Immoral and rebellious |
| v. 12 | Shepherds who feed only themselves | Greedy |
| vv. 12-13 | They are clouds without rain, blown along by the wind; autumn trees, without fruit and uprooted — twice dead. [13]They are wild waves of the sea, foaming up their shame; wandering stars. . . . | Images that will take their meaning from other texts, although "waves of the sea" appears to indicate immorality |
| v. 16 | These men are grumblers and faultfinders; they follow their own evil desires; they boast about themselves and flatter others for their own advantage. | Immoral, greedy, rebellious |
| v. 18 | Scoffers who will follow their own ungodly desires | Immoral |
| v. 19 | These are the men who divide you, who follow mere natural instincts and do not have the Spirit. | Immoral, cause divisions |

When we look at this list, a consistent picture begins to appear. First, we do not see any doctrinal issues appearing. Contrary to what is true of most second-century splinter groups, there is hardly any mention of a christological issue. Some have seen the denial of "Jesus Christ, our only Sovereign and Lord" (Jude 4) as a proto-Gnostic denial that the human Jesus was the exalted Christ. While this verse is found in the commentary literature, it is not the position of modern commentators because Jude never discusses the nature of Christ. If some form of Docetism was the belief of his opponents, then Jude totally misses the point. Unlike 2 Peter, Jude does not discuss the delay of the Parousia. Vögtle and Neyrey believe that a denial of the Parousia (or a claim that the Parousia had already taken place) on the part of the false teachers may be implied in (1) the denial of "our Lord Jesus Christ" and the following emphasis on judgment, and (2) the slandering of the angels, whom the NT often pictures as coming with Christ at the time of the judgment.[30] This is certainly far more defensible than the proto-Gnostic arguments of a previous age, but it still raises the question as to whether it accurately reflects Jude. It is 2 Peter that defends the Parousia, not Jude. Jude's false teachers are threatened with judgment, but we never learn on what basis they apparently did not fear it. Did they argue that they were free from the law? Did they argue that deeds done in the body did not matter? (Both of these arguments appear among Paul's opponents.) Or did they argue that the final judgment would not come,[31] or, if it did come, that it would not involve them, perhaps like modern church members who do not believe that they will face judgment for their bad behavior because they have "accepted Christ as [their] Savior"? We do not know, for the doctrinal issue is not one that concerns Jude.

So, second, what we do see is a pattern of two basic charges: (1) immorality[32] and (2) rebellion. The rebellion is against the angels, Je-

30. Vögtle, *Der Judasbrief, der zweite Petrusbrief,* 7-8; Neyrey, *2 Peter, Jude,* 31-32.

31. While the delay of the Parousia is not mentioned in Jude, even if it were, it would not necessarily indicate a date later than A.D. 60. Given Jesus' language about everything being fulfilled in "this generation" and the repeated language in the NT about the climactic events happening "soon," and given that the average life span in that day was about thirty-five to forty years, within thirty years of Jesus' resurrection some people must have wondered what the delay was about and by forty years most of the first generation was dead. That reality would lead to the question of whether Jesus was wrong about "this generation" and whether "soon" could be stretched that long. The idea that it had somehow already happened (seen in 2 Thessalonians 2) was only one solution; another was surely that the Christian leaders had interpreted Jesus wrongly and there was no Parousia, at least none in the way it had been presented.

32. Since immorality in Jude generally points to sexual misconduct, and since it certainly does in the minds of modern readers, we should note that there is also the less

sus (in that they are not following his lifestyle), and probably the leadership of the Jesus movement (this would explain the reference to Korah, those in vv. 10 and 16 to evil speech, and that in v. 19 to their causing divisions). The immorality is at root a giving way to their "desires." What we have, then, is some form of antinomianism in which the teachers whom Jude opposes are following a lifestyle that he believes is characterized by unbridled desire and whose position is an honor challenge to the leadership of the Jesus movement and the holy angels (whom Paul believes have something to do with the holiness of the community — 1 Cor 11:10). While these descriptions are general and stereotyped, they are the only information that he gives us and thus must have been enough to let his readers know which group or groups he was warning against. We do not think that this is merely an honor challenge and that the immorality accusations are simply a way of labeling the opponents impure,[33] for if that were the case, too much space is devoted to the issues of immorality and not enough to the issue of rebellion. Also, somewhere one would expect Jude to indicate what the challenge was about.

When and where did such teaching arise? If it arose in Palestine, it certainly was not in circles of the Jesus movement influenced by Pharisaism. Most likely we are talking about communities in areas whose surrounding community was Gentile and where there was less support for Jewish moral standards. Syria (Antioch) and Egypt (Alexandria) would both fit this description, for in both places there are highly Hellenized cities where we know that there were communities of the Jesus movement. Furthermore, both had concentrations of Jews and thus of Jewish followers of Jesus, which would ensure contact with the core of Jewish followers of Jesus in Palestine and ensure that Gentiles joining the community would be well versed in the Jewish scriptures and traditions. Given that there is no language that we can specifically identify with Alexandrian thought and that the sphere of influence of James appears to have extended north of Judea more than south, Galilee (with its Gentile cities such as Sepphoris and Tiberias) and Syria might be the more likely areas (one should include in this area the largely Gentile coastal cities of Palestine such as Joppa and Caesarea), but given that Jude is as much a tract as a letter, there is no real reason not to include the whole sweep of the eastern Mediterranean where the Jerusalem leaders were revered.

As for date, we should think of a time after Paul's law-free teaching had become accepted. Our letter often cites stories of judgment from the

---

frequent charge of their being greedy. But we include greed under immorality, since a person is controlled by desire whether he or she is greedy for money, sex, or food.

33. So Neyrey, *2 Peter, Jude,* 51-52.

OT, but it never cites the decalogue as law. Apparently a "you shall not" from the Torah would not have been a convincing argument or was not an argument that our author was inclined to use. Yet the stories carry weight. It is difficult to tell whether or not the temple in Jerusalem is still standing. One would think that the destruction of Jerusalem and its temple would be a fine example of divine judgment on sinners. But given that the sins of Jerusalem were not of the same type as the apparent sins of the false teachers, the destruction of Jerusalem might not have been thought relevant. Virtually any date after 50 or 55 could be defended.[34] It does not take too long for libertinism to infiltrate a church, at least in a Gentile context, as Paul would attest from his experience in Corinth. Furthermore, the later one goes after the death of James (A.D. 61 or 62), the more likely that James would have received some title (e.g., "holy," "blessed," "martyr"). Whatever the case with the titles for James, the latest date possible is the date of 2 Peter, since we will argue in the Introduction to 2 Peter that 2 Peter uses Jude (pp. 136-43). But, as we noted above (pp. 14-17), that allows a wide range of dates, given that the date of 2 Peter is disputed. With this vagueness we have to be content, for Jude did not see fit to give us more specific information.

## V. LANGUAGE AND STRUCTURE

Jude is an actual letter. That is, unlike 2 Peter where the letter salutation appears to be tacked onto something that is more like a tract (there is no letter closing), Jude follows the conventions of Hellenistic letter writing, producing an outline like this:

- Letter Opening: Salutation (vv. 1-2)
- Letter Body
    - Body Opening (vv. 3-4)
    - Body Proper (Sometimes Called "Body Middle") (vv. 5-16)
    - Body Closing (17-23)
- Letter Closing: Benediction (vv. 24-25)

34. Even if Paul's teaching was officially accepted by A.D. 50 (i.e., the Jerusalem Council came after Gal 2:11-14) — and this is not at all sure, for many scholars believe that Gal 2:1-10 indicates Paul's version of the Jerusalem Council rather than its coming after Galatians, and in this case Peter had not gotten the point fully sometime later (Gal 2:11-14) — it would take some time for the teaching to become widespread and teachers to start taking it to extremes that Paul would not have countenanced.

Having noted that this structure is clearly visible, we should also note that Jude's use of it differs somewhat from the standard forms that we have in the NT. First, while the letter opening is normal enough (although the recipients are described only as believers with no location being given or implied), there is no thanksgiving. This is not unprecedented in the NT letters (e.g., Galatians also has none), but it is a bit different. Second, the letter closing has only a benediction. There are no greetings, summary, health wish, or purpose statement such as we find in many NT letters. Given the general nature of the addressees, one would not expect personal greetings, and it is possible that the purpose statement is implied in the benediction, which also serves as a type of health wish, but even if we accept those as the reasons for the truncation, Jude has a rather sudden and brief letter closing.

Rhetorically the letter is deliberative rhetoric, which is to say that it is asking its readers to make decisions on a course of action with reference to the future.[35] Watson's rhetorical analysis looks like this:[36]

*Epistolary Prescript* (vv. 1-2)
*Exordium* (v. 3) (Purpose)
*Narratio* (v. 4) (Shared Assumptions)
*Probatio* (vv. 5-16) (Arguments)
  First Proof (vv. 5-10)
  Second Proof (vv. 11-13)
  Third Proof (vv. 14-16)
*Peroratio* (vv. 17-23) (Concluding Exhortation)
Doxology (vv. 24-25)

The only problem with this neat structure is that, while an educated Greco-Roman would in all likelihood consciously structure his argument following more or fewer such steps, in Jude the letter form has an over-riding literary structure, and within the letter structure rhetorical form is secondary and often modified.[37] This is why Jude's rhetorical pattern does not fit the Greco-Roman ideal. What we can say is that Jude has had some rhetorical education, but it is unclear whether he has had

35. Duane Frederick Watson, *Invention, Arrangement, and Style: Rhetorical Criticism of Jude and 2 Peter* (SBLDS 104; Atlanta: Scholars Press, 1988), 32-33.

36. Watson, *Invention, Arrangement, and Style,* 77-78.

37. Neyrey, *2 Peter, Jude,* 26-27. This is also true for the Pauline letters, which is one reason why Galatians, e.g., starts out looking very much like forensic rhetoric in a letter format and then becomes more deliberative in style, the rhetorical structures blurring after the start of ch. 3. The rhetorical handbooks were studied during one's education, but in the practice of letter writing they were often not followed too closely.

more than the rhetorical education that would come with a basic Hellenistic education.

It is also clear that Jude uses repetitive patterns for emphasis. The most obvious are the triplets that he cites from Jewish tradition:

> People who left Egypt — Angels who did not keep position — Sodom/Gomorrah (vv. 5-7)
> Cain — Balaam — Korah (v. 11)

However, notice these other repetitive patterns, some triplets and some longer:

> Called — loved — kept (v. 1)
> Grace — mercy — love (v. 2)
> Pollute — reject — slander (v. 8)
> Clouds — trees — waves — stars (vv. 12-13)
> Ungodly — ungodly — ungodly (v. 15)
> Divide — follow — without the Spirit (v. 19)
> Be merciful — save — show mercy (vv. 22-23)

Various authors have detected far more patterns in Jude than this, some of which are convincing and some less convincing.[38] The point is that Jude loves to pile up terms for rhetorical effect, a phenomenon that appears elsewhere in the OT and NT. This means that the individual terms need to be taken as less important than the total picture generated, which fact is often forgotten given the atomistic nature of modern exegesis.

Clearly Jude has a good command of Greek vocabulary. He introduces eighteen words into the vocabulary of the NT (four may be borrowed from one or another Greek translation of the OT), only three of which were picked up by 2 Peter. He also uses another twenty-two words that are rare in the NT. Now, as Bauckham notes, these data require careful evaluation. Jude uses some unusual images, so his use of unusual vocabulary is not surprising. Furthermore, some of the terms he uses are quite common in nonbiblical Greek, just not in the NT. At the end of the day only a few of his words turn out to be truly rare.[39] Still, we certainly have an author who is skillful in Greek, although not without the occasional Semitism, which may come from his familiarity with biblical literature.

38. See the list in Neyrey, *2 Peter, Jude,* 28. He is following J. Daryl Charles, "Literary Artifice in the Epistle of Jude," *ZNW* 82 (1991) 106-24.

39. Bauckham, *Jude, 2 Peter,* 6.

It is surprising that Jude does not show great familiarity with the Septuagint (LXX). The fact is that, while he has picked up some expressions from the LXX (expressions that were probably common in the community in which he lived), there is no place in the work where he actually quotes it and there are some places where what he does say is significantly different from it, assuming that he is indeed alluding to the OT and not using a phrase that has passed into Christian usage (see Jude 11 and Num 26:9; Jude 12 and Ezek 34:2; Jude 23 and Amos 4:11 or Zech 3:3). Richard Bauckham argues that in two places (Jude 12 alluding to Ezek 34:2 and likely to Prov 25:14, and Jude 13 alluding to Isa 57:20) Jude must be referring to the *Hebrew* text since the LXX text does not make the point that Jude is making.[40] Bauckham's point is that the phrase "clouds without rain," "feed only themselves," and "foaming up their shame" (with respect to waves) allude to these Old Testament passages and the phrases that they allude to are not found in the LXX, but only in the Hebrew text of the respective passages. In order to establish this, he has to argue two things: (1) Jude is consciously referring to these passages, and (2) the language is not found in the LXX but is in the Hebrew. He certainly does establish (2), for in two of the three cases the LXX diverges enough from the Hebrew that Jude cannot be directly referring to the LXX (in the case of "clouds without rain" and Prov 25:14 Jude is rather unlike either the LXX or the Hebrew). What is not as well established is (1) in that "clouds without rain" could have become proverbial (as noted above, the Hebrew text has "clouds and wind without rain," so it is not identical) even if it did come from the Hebrew text. The same is true for "shepherds who feed only themselves" (Jude shares only the grammatical form and the meaning with the Hebrew). "Foaming up" in Jude is also not identical to the Hebrew "waves [of the sea] cast[ing] up mire and mud," although, since the Isaiah reference is to "the wicked," it does fit Jude's context. Our conclusion is that Bauckham could be right, but the evidence is not conclusive. If he is correct, then Jude clearly knows Hebrew as well as Greek. If he is not, all we know about Jude is that he is educated in Greek and knows at least some phrases that came from the Hebrew OT. We believe that, while the evidence is not conclusive, it is at least likely that Jude lived in a community that was in contact with the Hebrew text, whether or not his reference to that text is totally conscious.

This discussion of language and structure also has something to say about the cultural background of the work. What it indicates is that our author was a person who had roots in a community where the Hebrew

40. Bauckham, *Jude, 2 Peter,* 7. He further argues that in Jude 6 and 14 Jude is using the Aramaic text of *1 Enoch,* although in Jude 15 he shows knowledge of the Greek text.

scriptures were used and who quite possibly read Hebrew and Aramaic himself. In addition, he had a good Hellenistic education. We should not think of him as being among the intellectually elite, but neither was he an uneducated peasant. It is not that he simply knows the Bible, but that he knows the Bible and has a decent education. Whether or not this describes Jude the brother of Jesus we cannot know. The level of education our author has was available in Palestine, but for him (whether he is Jude or someone else) to receive it someone had to value it enough to finance it. While Jude appears to be "normal" enough in the eyes of his surrounding culture when he appears in the Gospels, we do not know his profession and thus do not know if he had somehow received an education. When it comes to how much education Jude the brother of Jesus had, we are going by guesswork.

In our discussion of authorship above, we put off any decision until we had examined the addressees and the literary style of Jude. Without samples of writing known to be from Jude and without knowledge of his education and history, we cannot establish that Jude is the author of this work. But without significant speculation about what Jude *could have* written and what education he *could have* received, we cannot know that he could not have written this work. Could a carpenter working on Sepphoris (a major building project within walking distance of Nazareth that was under construction during the years of Jesus' youth) have developed contacts that enabled one of his sons to gain a good Hellenistic education? Would the son of a Jewish carpenter have wanted that education if he had had the opportunity?[41] We are told that his brother Jesus could read Hebrew and possibly Greek (he could certainly converse in Greek); had that stimulated Jude to seek an education?[42] Might a carpenter's son who joined the Jesus movement in his late teens or early twenties have pursued a Hellenistic education in support of his ministry? We do not know the answers to any of these questions. What this means is that we do not have the capacity to evaluate the quality of Greek that Jude could or could not write.[43] "Carpen-

41. See A. R. Millard, *Reading and Writing in the Time of Jesus* (Biblical Seminar 69; Sheffield: Sheffield Academic Press, 2000), for an examination of the issue of the extent of reading and writing in Palestine in the first century.

42. In Luke 4:16 Jesus is reported to have read the Scriptures (which would have been in Hebrew unless it were a Greek-speaking synagogue, and there is little reason to suppose that it was). If Mark 12:16 (and parallels) indicates that Jesus knew the content of the inscription on the coin (e.g., the claims of divinity for Augustus and the claim to be high priest), then he may well have been able to read Greek. But it is possible that he guessed the inscription from the picture and did not intend to make any other point than the identity of the image on the coin.

43. One can, of course, assert that a secretary or amanuensis was responsible for

ter" may sound lower class enough that one may think that the quality of Greek is problematic for his son.

On the other hand, none of the explanations why someone would use Jude as a pseudonym is convincing. There were too many better-known leaders in the Jesus movement. The name does fit the likely provenance of the author and his obvious saturation with stories from the OT, but his brother James was far better known, and Peter would have been an even better pseudonym if one wanted a wide circulation. Jude was not so well known to his target audience that he did not have to identify himself by James. Thus, unless we posit a person with a particular personal interest in Jude, there is no good explanation for the choice of the name unless Jude were indeed the author. Perhaps we should let the language of the letter define for us Jude's education rather than to posit a possible education for the relative unknown Jude, and then argue that he could not have written the letter because he did not have the required education. Was Jude the author of Jude? God alone knows, but the arguments against his authorship do not have the type of historical data needed to establish them.

## VI. THEOLOGY

Theology in its broadest sense is reflection upon a worldview (worldview including especially the nature of God and his relationship to the world)[44] and its implications; thus for our purposes it is shorthand for the

---

the Greek, but given that the Greek style is intricate, that makes the amanuensis in some sense the co-author of the letter (assuming that the named author had a chance to read the work and agreed to what had been written). This also introduces a complicating hypothesis. It is not that anyone doubts that an amanuensis was used. Most people in the first century A.D. used an amanuensis for any actual writing that they did, since such people were skilled not only in writing but also in preparing and keeping ink and papyrus in the proper condition for writing. (See E. Randolph Richards, *Paul and First-Century Letter Writing: Secretaries, Composition and Collection* [Downers Grove, IL: InterVarsity Press, 2004].) However, to posit that such a scribe (whose name, skills, and relationship to our author we know nothing about) was a co-author (or the dominant author if the named author gave him only a general impulse for writing the letter and/or did not have a chance to review and correct it) of the letter is a step into the hypothetical. Is it possible? It certainly is. Do we have any reason to assume that it is what happened? The only reasons would be that (1) we are convinced that the attribution to Jude is historically accurate, and (2) we are convinced that this Jude that we know so little about could not have written the letter that we have before us.

44. Strictly speaking, theology is "the study or science of God" (so Millard J. Erickson, *Christian Theology* [Grand Rapids: Baker, 1985], 21), but, as Erickson himself

worldview that informs the letter. To put it a different way, theology arises from the story or set of stories that underlies the worldview of the author.

Jude is an extremely short letter, so the first thing one must say about its theology is that since it comes from the Jesus movement we must assume that most of his theology is held in common with that movement, that is, the expectation of the kingdom of God, come in Jesus of Nazareth and coming to fruition in the future. This is the interpretation of the phase of the story of Israel that the early Jesus movement held. However, even such a short letter as this reveals the particular shape of the story that is the focus of Jude's attention, the implied story that he is applying.

Returning to our narrative diagram, the general story looks like this:

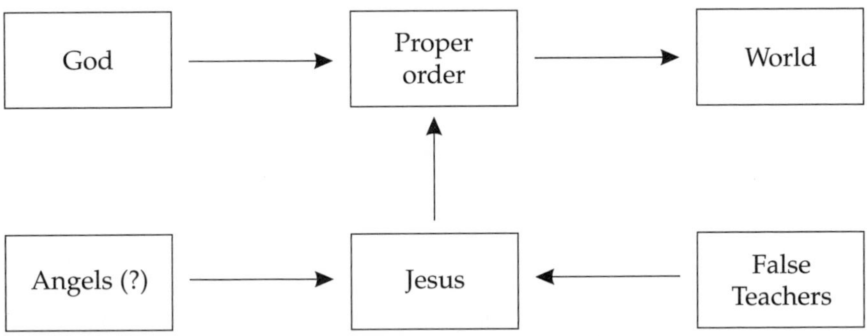


Jude reveals the most about four of the narrative functions: (1) the sender, namely, God, (2) the agent, namely, Jesus, (3) the opponents, namely, the false teachers (who show the nature of evil in general), and then (4) what good order looks like, namely, judgment. This judgment recalls a number of earlier phases of the larger story, phrases found in the Pentateuch and literature that expanded on the Pentateuch. We will look at these narrative functions in order.

First, the letter is framed by references to God. In v. 2 it is "God the

goes on to state, this includes reflection upon creation as a work of God and issues of general culture and learning (e.g., natural science, psychology, and philosophy, all of which are named by Erickson, whom we chose because he does carefully define theology). In other words, it reflects upon the elements of a worldview. Properly speaking, it should be a theistic worldview, but given that nontheistic worldviews often have elements that function as God does in theistic worldviews, broadly speaking we could say that to the extent that they are reflective they also have a theology, even if it is a theology without an acknowledged *theos* (god).

Father" or "Father God" who loves his people (or in whom they are loved, depending on how one reads the Greek *en,* although the passive could be a circumlocution for the active), and in v. 25 it is "God our Savior" who is keeping them from falling and preparing to present them in his royal court. In both cases this being is distinguished from "Jesus Christ"/"Jesus Christ our Lord." Unlike 2 Peter, Jude does not allow for the possibility that the title "God" is being applied to Jesus. But this means that God the Father is the "sender," the active agent in loving, probably in selecting, protecting, and saving his readers. This is not an austere or absent God, but a God very much involved in their lives. He has been present in their selection, he is present in his love, and he will be present in their salvation, since the title "Savior" here as everywhere in the NT is connected to eschatological deliverance rather than to the event of the cross (see the discussion of the title in the Introduction to 2 Peter, pp. 152-54). With a "Father" (or family head) like this, his readers are in a privileged position.

If God is presented as the family head, as the framework, so to speak, of all the good his people have received, Jesus is presented as his agent, as the leader of the people of God, as the sovereign of God's kingdom. Jude is Jesus' servant, probably thought of in relationship to a king. They are kept "by" (NIV) or "for" (NRSV) Jesus Christ (depending on how the Greek dative is read), the one reading viewing him as the king protecting his people and the other viewing him as the king who will receive his people. Jesus is "our only Sovereign and Lord," a politically explosive title, given that Caesar was known by those terms[45] (it would be similar to calling Jesus "our only Commander in Chief and President" in the United States).[46] This Sovereign has delegates whom he sends out with his message (Jude 17, remembering that "delegate" or "one who is sent" is the meaning of "apostle"). He is expected to come with mercy for those who keep themselves "in God's love"; that is, he will bring them eternal life (v. 21). Finally, this Sovereign is the one through whom honor is given to God (v. 25), which means that he is viewed as a subking under God as high king.

Quite possibly Jude is not only viewing Jesus as the Sovereign

45. Josephus (*War* 7.418-19) reports of a group of Jewish rebels that, despite severe torture, none of them would "confess or seem to confess that Caesar was their lord [Sovereign — same word as in Jude]." See further Karl Heinrich Rengstorf, *"doxa," TDNT* 2:45.

46. We pick the United States because its President is simultaneously head of state and head of government and thus in a sense more sovereign (and viewed as more sovereign) than is the case in such English-speaking countries as the United Kingdom and Canada where those roles are separated between the Queen (or Governor General in Canada as the Queen's representative) and the Prime Minister (although, as those who know these countries realize, the theory may not match the reality).

within the contemporary period but also seeing him as God's agent in the Hebrew scriptures and other Jewish literature. Having mentioned Jesus as Lord in v. 4, he goes on in v. 5 to refer to "the Lord" who delivered "his people out of Egypt." Some of the oldest manuscripts have "Jesus" or "Christ" instead of "Lord," showing at least a very old interpretation of the text and possibly the original text itself. At the least the juxtaposition of the term "Lord" in Jude 4 and 5 suggests that the same person is in view (especially since Jude never clearly uses "Lord" for God) and that Jude is reading the Exodus account in terms of Jesus. In that case Jude may be viewing Jesus as the one who imprisoned the fallen angels (Jude 6) and to whom Michael appeals in Jude 9. Whether that is the case or not, it is likely that Jude views *1 Enoch's* "Lord" as Jesus, who is coming with his angels to execute judgment. This is what we would expect from God's sovereign executive. It also fits the eschatological picture of 1 Thess 4:16; 2 Thess 1:7; and Rev 19:11-21. In other words, it is the common NT eschatological picture. Jesus, then, in Jude is the Sovereign who is coming at the end of the age to establish God's good order, but whose involvement with the world stretches back to the great events of Israel's history, as Jude, in common with other NT writers, retells Israel's history in terms of Jesus. He is God's executive agent indeed, a Sovereign who is to be respected.

In contrast to Jesus, the Holy Spirit is barely mentioned, a viewpoint that Jude shares with 2 Peter (which differs from 1 Peter, which mentions the Spirit relatively frequently). Jude's two references to the Spirit come in Jude 19 and 20. The false teachers do not have the Spirit, which is another way of saying that their inspiration is from another source than God. The positive use of the Holy Spirit is related to prayer, for true believers are to "pray in the Holy Spirit" (a similar usage occurs in 1 Cor 14:15, where Paul speaks of praying "in the Spirit," i.e., under divine inspiration or in tongues, versus praying "in my mind"). Thus the Spirit is the one who inspires the true believer and is absent from the pseudo-believer. This function of the Spirit is also similar to that referred to by 2 Peter, although in 2 Peter it is the ancient prophets who were inspired by the Spirit, while in Jude it is contemporary believers. At any rate, the Spirit's activity in this literature is limited to inspiration. We do not find the same connection of the Spirit to sanctification or evangelization that we find elsewhere in the NT.

When it comes to the human condition and its solution, the main problems mentioned are (1) the rejection of the authority of the Sovereign, whether in the past (as in the case of the angels who abandoned their honorable position) or in the present (as in the case of the false teachers who reject the authority of the Sovereign by their rebellious lifestyle), and (2) the giving in to desire (implied in v. 4 and stated explicitly in vv. 16 and 19). The charges of greed and slander are probably subspecies of these two basic charges. Salvation, or eternal life, is obtained by submitting to the authority of the Sovereign, which means holding "the faith," a faith or commitment that was given to the "holy ones," that is, those who are separate from impurity. Thus we have the contrast impurity (desire)–holiness paralleled by rebellion against–submission to the Sovereign. God grants grace or mercy so that one can shift from the dishonorable group into the holy/honorable group. This is the same mercy that the true believers received and thus should show toward the false teachers and their followers: they are not (yet) beyond hope. However, despite being capable of receiving mercy (and thus the believers are not to cut them off totally), the false teachers are polluting (apparently it is their sexual misbehavior that he views as especially polluting). It is polluting to the true believers to have these teachers in their celebrations of the Lord's Supper (at that time a full meal); thus, when these followers of the false teachers respond to mercy and submit to the Sovereign (including his ethical standards), one must be careful not to allow their pollution to come with them. Here we have a first-century version of "love the sinner and hate the sin," in which the focus is on rescue. While purity issues are not to be ignored, the main point is not "Kick these folk out and keep yourselves pure" but "Rescue as many as you can (but do take care, for they have a contagious disease)."

Although people who have been "delivered" can be destroyed (Jude 5), true believers are not to live in fear (other than fear of the pollution that the false teachers might bring with them), for God is able to keep them from falling. They will not be overcome by evil against their will. In this part of Jude the community becomes the agent and Jesus fades back to the position of overlord.

The ultimate hope of the believing community (i.e., the description of the ultimate proper order) is for "the mercy of our Lord Jesus Christ to bring you to eternal life." That is, eternal life is in the future and not a present possession. This phrase apparently refers to the coming of Christ to usher his true followers into the full experience of his reign. What will happen to those who do not receive this mercy is never stated explicitly except in the words of *1 Enoch,* which speaks about "these men." Still, even without this more explicit statement, all of the examples given are of men or angels who experienced judgment and destruction as a result of their way of life and specifically as a result of their rebellion or living lives controlled by desire. Indeed, one wonders whether an explicit description of the fate awaiting them could be as dark as the implications from the repeated references to these well-known stories. Jude leaves it to the imagination of the readers to fill in the unexpressed blanks, and shudder.

# *Commentary on Jude*

## I. LETTER OPENING: SALUTATION (vv. 1-2)

> [1]*Jude, a servant of Jesus Christ and a brother of James,*
> *To those who have been called, who are loved by God the Father and kept by Jesus Christ:* [2]*Mercy, peace and love be yours in abundance.*

A Greek letter normally begins with a salutation in the form x to y. Jude 1-2 forms that salutation in our letter. Compared to some of the Pauline letters it is quite brief (perhaps because, unlike Paul's, Jude's position and influence were not in dispute), yet it covers the basic parts of a salutation: identification of the author, identification of the addressees, and a greeting formula.

**1** The author identifies himself as Jude. Obviously, Jude or Judas (the Greek form of the Hebrew name Judah) was a common name among Jewish Christians since it was a common name among Jews. For example, Jesus chose only twelve apostles, and two of them were named Judas. Therefore, to which of the many Judases in the early church does Jude 1 refer?

First, we need to look at the other elements in the author's self-description to see if they give us any more information. In the next element he identifies himself as "a servant of Jesus Christ." This type of formula is common in the NT, especially in the greetings in letters. For example, look at the following:

Rom 1:1 Paul, a servant of Christ Jesus, called to be an apostle and set apart for the gospel of God —

| | |
|---|---|
| Gal 1:10 | If I were still trying to please men, I would not be a servant of Christ. |
| Col 4:12 | Epaphras, who is one of you and a servant of Christ Jesus, sends greetings. |
| Titus 1:1 | Paul, a servant of God and an apostle of Jesus Christ for the faith of God's elect and the knowledge of the truth that leads to godliness — |
| Jas 1:1 | James, a servant of God and of the Lord Jesus Christ, |
| 2 Pet 1:1 | Simon Peter, a servant and apostle of Jesus Christ, |
| Jude 1 | Jude, a servant of Jesus Christ and a brother of James. |

We quickly see that this was not a fixed formula, but a common way of referring to oneself and esteemed colleagues. It could be varied by including God with Christ or by simply saying "servant of God" rather than "servant of Christ." Yet even with this variation, it was clearly meaningful to the writers of NT epistles. The Greek term for "servant" used in this formula is *doulos,* meaning "slave," which was not a high-status position in society. Therefore, it is not immediately obvious why free men (which is the status of these NT writers) would use such a title. Is it because of their humility? If so, why would they couple the term with "delegate" (i.e., "apostle"), as is done in several of the examples in our table? This combination of terms indicates that in the minds of the users of "servant," it is not a term of humility per se ("I am just a nobody"), but an indication that in their eyes their status comes, not from themselves but from the one to whom they belong and whose delegate they are. In the Greek OT Moses, among others, is called the "servant of the Lord" (e.g., Exod 14:31; Deut 34:5; Josh 1:1-2 plus fifteen more times in that book).[1] Thus "servant" or "slave" is clearly an honorific term if it is connected with "of Jesus" or "of the Lord," not because of the personal honor status of the slave but because of the honor status of the owner. This fits with what we know of the culture of the Roman Empire, in which highly placed imperial slaves had tremendous authority, for they represented their master, Caesar. While technically they held only the social rank of slave (i.e., a social zero), because of whose slaves they were they were to be treated with respect, for to disregard Caesar's slave doing Caesar's business was to disregard Caesar.

So Jude is, in a quiet way, using a stereotyped phrase that indicates

1. Jesus is also referred to as the servant of the Lord (Acts 3:13; 4:27, 30), although in these references Acts uses a different Greek term than the one Jude does. The term in Acts can mean either "child" or "slave."

that his authority is the authority of one who represents Jesus. That is, he is recalling the implied narrative that Jesus rules and will return as world ruler and identifying his relationship to that ruler as one of "servant." It is not that Jude himself has any authority (that he is in some way "God's anointed") or that Jude himself has personal social status, but that he participates in a larger story in which there is a Sovereign, whose authority Jude (and others in the NT period) represents. This is humility — or, even better, honesty as to his status — but it is a humility that also recognizes his delegated authority.[2]

He further identifies himself as "a brother of James." John Calvin thought that this indicated that Jude was the member of the Twelve referred to as "Judas of James" (Luke 6:16; John 14:22; Acts 1:13).[3] However, Jude clearly identifies himself as the brother *(adelphos)* of James, and the phrase "Judas of James" would normally be understood as "Judas son of James." Furthermore, Jude nowhere refers to himself as a delegate (i.e., "apostle")[4] or one of the Twelve. Finally, Calvin complicates his theory further by arguing that this apostle Jude was also a brother of Jesus, which is unlikely because Jesus' brothers are never said to be among his followers until after his resurrection (Mark 3:20-21; John 7:5; Acts 1:14). However, Calvin is correct in recognizing that there was only one James in the early church who was well enough known to be referred to simply

2. On the use of this phrase and slavery in the Greco-Roman world, see Simon Hornblower and Antony Spawforth, *The Oxford Companion to Classical Civilization* (Oxford: Oxford University Press, 1998), 670-73; James S. Jeffers, *The Greco-Roman World of the New Testament* (Downers Grove, IL: InterVarsity Press, 1999), 189-91; and Murray J. Harris, *Slave of Christ: A New Testament Metaphor for Total Devotion to Christ* (New Studies in Biblical Theology 8; Downers Grove, IL/Leicester, U.K.: InterVarsity Press/Apollos, 2001).

3. Calvin, *The Catholic Epistles*, 428.

4. Because the term "apostle" has developed a religious connotation, we will generally use the term "delegate." For the NT writers the term itself was used in many contexts. Although in secular Greek it was limited to military expeditions and seafaring ventures, Jews used an Aramaic/Hebrew term that our term translates to indicate a variety of people who were sent to conduct business in the name of the sender. (See the proverbial use of the Greek term in John 13:16: "delegate" and "the one sending.") It is only by adding "of Jesus Christ" either explicitly or in the context that the NT authors are able to indicate whose delegate they are. See K. H. Rengstorf, *"apostolos," TDNT* 1:407-46. Interestingly enough, the Twelve are normally called "trainees" or "apprentices" (i.e., "disciples") or just "the Twelve" except in contexts referring to Jesus' sending them on a mission (where "delegate"/"apostle" is used) until we enter the post-resurrection period in Luke–Acts. After that normally the Twelve are meant until Acts 14, with 14:14 making it clear that Barnabas and Paul are also authorized delegates (i.e., "apostles"). Paul, of course, is very conscious of his direct commission from Christ, as well as of the fact that being an authorized delegate of Jesus is a gift that others may receive (1 Cor 12:28-29 in the context of the discussion on spiritual gifts).

as "James" and who is known to have a brother named Jude. This person was not a member of the Twelve, James son of Alphaeus (the "of Alphaeus" tips us off to the fact that it was how he was distinguished from other Jameses) or James son of Zebedee (who was in the background in the early church even before his execution between A.D. 41 and 44), but James the brother of Jesus (Matt 13:55; Mark 6:3).

Therefore, it is also unlikely that Jude should be identified with the prophetically gifted "Judas called Barsabbas" (Acts 15:22, 27, 32), for he is not known to have had a brother called James. It is true that some scholars[5] have argued that "brother" is a designation for a member of those gathered around James and thus his spiritual brothers (Acts 11:1; 15:22); however, the term is never elsewhere specifically connected with James. Instead it is used collectively so that a believer might be designated "one of the brothers" or even as "a brother" but never as "a brother of x" unless he was actually related. Besides, in Acts the author felt it necessary to identify Judas with his nickname Barsabbas, so it is unlikely that the plain "Jude" of our passage would be enough to identify him.

We conclude, then, that in Jude 1 the author intends to identify himself as that Jude who is listed as the third or fourth of the brothers of Jesus, James always being listed first. It has, of course, been objected that Jude does not call himself the brother of Jesus, but then neither does James (Jas 1:1). It appears that while others would refer to these men as brothers of Jesus (Mark 3:31 = *Gospel of Thomas* 99; Acts 1:14; 1 Cor 9:5; Gal 1:19; Eusebius, *Hist. Eccl.* 2.23.4), they themselves chose a simpler self-designation, which any Christian leader could use. According to Eusebius, Jude was married and had children, for his grandsons were reportedly small farmers in Galilee during the time of Domitian (*Hist. Eccl.* 3.19.1–3.20.1), although there is good reason to doubt the reliability of the tradition about his grandchildren. (See further the discussion in the Introduction, pp. 9-12).

The addressees are identified, not by name or location, but by three descriptors. The main descriptor is "called." This descriptor appears ten times in the NT, primarily in Romans (1:1, 6, 7; 8:28) and 1 Corinthians (1:1, 2, 24). It is found only once in the Gospels (Matt 22:14, "For many are called, but few are chosen" [NRSV]). Otherwise it appears here and in Rev 7:14. Interestingly, in three of these passages it is part of an epistolary salutation. Paul twice speaks of himself as called to be an apostle, but more frequently he speaks of Christians as called to be holy people (i.e.,

5. O. J. du Plessis, "The Authorship of the Epistle of Jude," in *Biblical Essays 1966* (Potchefstroom, South Africa: Potchefstroom Herlad [Edms.] Beperk, 1966), 191-99; E. Earle Ellis, "Prophecy and Hermeneutic in Jude," in E. E. Ellis, *Prophecy and Hermeneutic in Early Christianity* (Grand Rapids: William B. Eerdmans, 1978), 220-36.

"saints"; he does this twice) or called to belong to Jesus Christ. In fact, in three of our passages Christians are referred to simply as those who are "called." The point is that God has selected people for a destiny. While in the case of Paul it included becoming a delegate of Jesus, in the case of all Christians it includes holiness and belonging to Christ. Here our author does not immediately describe the destiny (this will come out in the rest of the letter), although the following descriptors indicate that it is good, but simply leaves us with the implication that believers are caught up in the plan of God.

This calling is further defined by two participles, each connected to a member of the Trinity. The first speaks of Christians as those who are loved by or in God the Father.[6] Paul says the same in Rom 1:7 (although he uses a different grammatical form). The point Paul makes and that Jude would make if we accept the translation "by" is that God called us out of sheer love. It is not that Jesus delivered us and the Father had to accept us, but that the Father loved us and in that love called us. Yet what would the other translational possibility mean, being loved "*in* God the Father" (NRSV; the NIV has "by")? Certainly the NIV translation "by" is possible (i.e., it translates the Greek word *en* instrumentally), but that would be an unusual way of expressing the subject of a passive verb (normally *hypo* is used). That leads us to suspect that the NRSV is correct with its "in God the Father." Could this phrase be expressing something similar to the Johannine references to Christians being "in God" (John 17:21 ["in us"]; 1 John 2:24 ["abide . . . in the Father"]; 3:24 ["abide in him"]; 4:13, 15, 16)? This is probably the case in that Jude 21 commands believers, "keep yourselves in the love of God" (NRSV), and 1 John 4:16 connects abiding in the Father to the Father's love for us and our abiding in love. Thus Jude is indicating that we are loved by God (God is the implied subject of the verbal noun "called" as well as of the participles) as we are "in God." Perhaps this could be depicted by a child picked up into a father's arms and experiencing the father's love while he or she remains there. The intent of the perfect tense of the participle is probably to stress the present reality of the love.[7] Every Christian can say, "I am loved

6. Some translations, e.g., NKJV, read "sanctified." The manuscripts reading "sanctified" date from the ninth century and later, while those reading "loved" date from the fourth century. Furthermore, "loved" is widespread among the geographical regions of the church. It appears that the frequent use of "sanctified" (fifteen times in the epistles and twice in Acts), and particularly its use in the salutation in 1 Cor 1:2, influenced some copyist to make an accidental change (the first two and last six letters of each term are identical; only the middle three letters are different).

7. There are two sides or aspects to the perfect, i.e., "The *action* is portrayed *externally* (summary), while the *resultant state* proceeding from the action is portrayed *inter-*

by my Father."[8] One aspect of pastoral care is to make this objective reality an experiential reality.

The second participle speaks of Christians as those who are guarded by or for Christ Jesus. Christians view this age as hostile to faith. The teachers Jude opposes have clearly succumbed to these forces, and even believers need to be rescued, as we shall see toward the end of the letter. How can one hope to make it through? Has the promised future with Christ been held out like a carrot only to be whipped away when we struggle forward and perhaps stumble? The answer is, "No, God not only began my Christian life, but he is also protecting me." He himself guards us and keep us safe in a hostile age. The Greek dative could be translated either as instrumental ("by Jesus Christ," NIV) or as a dative of advantage ("for Jesus Christ," NRSV). Probably the latter is the more natural way of reading the Greek, in which case the idea is that the Father is guarding us so that we will belong to Jesus, that is, remain loyal to him as our ruler, at the end of the age. If 1 Pet 1:4 can speak of an inheritance guarded for us, then here Jude can speak of a people guarded for Jesus. This underlines the eschatological focus of the idea of guarding. The present is not our goal; the future is. Furthermore, Jesus is the future. Again, as was the case in being loved, the Greek used the perfect tense, for while the guarding is a divine action (one could say a past act in that temporality is not entirely absent from the participle, even if it is not the emphasis), it is experienced as a state or condition. (Thus the NIV correctly translates, "are loved . . . and kept.") Those who are called and loved are also those who are protected.

Where did Jude get these ideas? Certainly Jesus is part of the answer, yet we must remember that the early church also mined the OT. Bauckham[9] suggests that we look at the Servant Songs of Isaiah, where Israel is said to be called (Isa 41:9; 42:6; 48:12, 15; 49:1; 54:6), loved (Isa 42:1; 43:4; cf. Deut 7:7-8; Jer 31:3; Hos 11:1; 14:4), and guarded (Isa 42:6;

---

*nally* (continuous state)" (Daniel B. Wallace, *Greek Grammar beyond the Basics: An Exegetical Syntax of the Greek New Testament,* [electronic ed.; Garland, TX: Galaxie Software, 1999, ca. 1996]). While both aspects are normally present in the perfect, any given use can stress one or the other. In our judgment the stress in this passage is on the experience of the resultant state of being loved in God (without forgetting the action that created this state). That is, we think that this is an intensive perfect.

8. We recognize that Jude uses "loved" and "guarded" collectively for the group, which is the primary reference. However, in moving this into our individualistic culture, there is surely an individual application, even though we would not wish to imply that the absoluteness of the collective (i.e., the followers of Jesus as a group were loved and guarded, and Jude is confident that they will not fall away as a group) can be applied to the individual.

9. Bauckham, *Jude, 2 Peter,* 26.

49:8) by God. In fact, in the Greek translation of the OT "loved one" (the term used in our text) appears as a name for Israel (e.g., Deut 32:15; Ps 28:6; Isa 44:2) or a tribe of Israel (Deut 33:12) many times, so that the Jews in 3 Macc 6:11 can refer to themselves in prayer as "your loved ones." What has happened, then, is that what was true of Israel is seen by Jude (and by Paul and other early Christians) as also true of the renewed Israel, that is, the Jesus movement that we call the church. If the Israel of the past were God's chosen, loved, and guarded ones, so much more must we, the Israel of the present, be. Yet now this benefit is seen to come through Jesus Christ. In this way the Jesus movement appropriated the titles and benefits of ancient Israel as its own, for it saw itself in continuity with and as the fulfillment of Israel, not as a separate entity. Its story is a continuation of the retelling of Israel's story.

**2** The greeting formula is a blessing or short prayer. Such a prayer or blessing in the name of an appropriate deity was typical in the salutation of a Greek letter. As for the most part in the previous verse, in Jude the deity remains unnamed, for in the monotheistic environment of Jude that was not necessary. Furthermore, Jews preferred not to use the name of God unless it was necessary. Instead Jude expresses the wish that God will "multiply" to these called individuals "mercy, peace and love."

The term "mercy" *(eleos)* brackets Jude (here and in v. 21). Paul uses it along with peace in a letter closing (Gal 6:16). When it comes to salutations, "grace, mercy and peace" is found in three letters (1 Tim 1:2; 2 Tim 1:2; 2 John 3), but normally mercy stands by itself and is related to redemption (Titus 3:5), prayer (Heb 4:16), or final judgment (2 Tim 1:18; Jas 2:13). In the Greek OT it most frequently stands for the Hebrew *hesed*, which, while often found in covenantal contexts, means (at least when God is involved) going beyond the obligations to duty and showing exceptional faithfulness or mercy.[10]

"Peace" is a typical part of the Pauline word pair "grace and peace" (Rom 1:7; 1 Cor 1:3; 2 Cor 1:2; Gal 1:3; Eph 1:2; Phil 1:2; Col 1:2; 1 Thess 1:2; 2 Thess 1:2; Titus 1:4; Phlm 3) and thus appears to have been the nor-

10. Francis I. Andersen, "Yahweh, the Kind and Sensitive God," in Peter T. O'Brien and David G. Peterson, eds., *God Who Is Rich in Mercy: Essays Presented to Dr. D. B. Knox* (Homebush West, NSW, Australia/Grand Rapids: Lancer/Baker, 1986), 41-88, points out that the data do not sustain the thesis of N. Glueck that *hesed* is simply covenant faithfulness. The term indicates action beyond covenant obligation, especially in divine-human relationships (in human-human relationships it can be reciprocal and so involve some obligation). It is paired with "compassion" and with "justice" (the latter especially in the prophets). Thus while only context can determine its meaning in any given case, Andersen concludes that the LXX translation is not a bad one, although we might read it as a mere feeling statement and not as a term that indicates action beyond obligation in a situation that often, but not always, involves a covenantal relationship.

mal Christian greeting (1 Pet 1:2; 2 Pet 1:2; Rev 1:4). The idea of grace *(charis)* is a Christianized form of the Greek greeting *chairein* (Jas 1:1), whereas peace picks up the Hebrew greeting *shalom* (which is a wish for well-being, since *shalom* includes ones health and the health of one's farm and family as well as peace). Given the frequency of the "grace and peace" pair, one wonders whether Jude is substituting mercy for grace in the typical greeting pair or is showing a more Jewish form of it. "Mercy and peace" do appear in the salutation of a Jewish letter in *2 Apoc. Bar.* 78:2-3, "Thus speaks Baruch, the son of Neriah, to the brothers who were carried away in captivity: Mercy and peace be with you."[11]

The third item in the prayer is "love" *(agapē).* Again we have a bracketing of the letter with a term (here and in v. 21). This term does not appear in any other NT letter salutation, although it is common enough elsewhere in the NT. Interestingly enough, the *2 Baruch* passage cited above continues, "I remember, my brothers, the love of him who created me, who loved us from the beginning and who never hated us, but, on the contrary, chastised us." In other words, reflection on the love of God quite naturally follows a call for his mercy and peace. Given that Jude has already said that Christians are loved "in God the Father," this interpretation is more likely than that he is praying that their love for others may increase (which is a good NT sentiment but is not found in letter salutations; Eph 1:4; Phil 1:9; Col 1:4; 1 Thess 1:3; 2 Thess 1:3).

Whatever the source of the greeting, it was still used by the church in the second century. The preface to the *Martyrdom of Polycarp* (ca. A.D. 155) reads, "The Church of God which sojourns in Smyrna, to the Church of God which sojourns in Philomelium, and to all the sojournings of the Holy Catholic Church in every place. Mercy, peace and love of God the Father, and our Lord Jesus Christ be multiplied." Given the verbal similarity, it may be that the writer knew Jude, although it could be the coincidence of the use of a greeting brought from the East.[12]

In this salutation Jude has set a tone. His readers are in a secure position. They are not only receiving God's love and protection, but Jude is praying that this mercy, peace, and love that they have received will be

11. There is an issue here in that Charlesworth, *OTP,* has "grace and peace" while Charles, *APOT,* has "mercy and peace." There is no textual note, so either the Syriac is multivalent or Charlesworth has been unconsciously influenced by the NT.

12. Jude and the *Martyrdom of Polycarp* are verbally close only in their salutations, which both refer to God the Father and Jesus Christ (Polycarp adds Lord) and both have "mercy, peace and love" and "be multiplied." However, their subject matter is so different that we neither expect nor find common vocabulary after this point. Thus we are left with a possibility and wish that we had more information about the beliefs of those in the church in Smyrna.

multiplied (paralleled in the salutations of both 1 Pet 1:2 and 2 Pet 1:2). This secure position of the faithful will soon be contrasted with the insecurity of the interlopers whom he will denounce later in the letter. Furthermore, the salutation makes a positive connection with his readers, who will have to act against those who are condemned. Thus its rhetorical function includes both joining with the church and setting the stage for contrasting them with the interlopers.

## II. LETTER BODY (vv. 3-23)

### A. Body Opening: Thematic Statement *(exordium/narratio)* (vv. 3-4)

> 3*Dear friends, although I was very eager to write to you about the salvation we share, I felt I had to write and urge you to contend for the faith that was once for all entrusted to the saints.*

3 The thematic statement sets out the major issue of the letter, which is the need of the church receiving the letter to defend the true faith in the face of certain people who have "slipped in" among them.

Jude begins by addressing his readers as "dear friends" or "beloved." Of the twenty-nine times this term appears in the NT, eighteen are in the General Epistles. More important, while Paul almost always uses the term in the conclusion of an argument (1 Cor 10:14; 15:58; 2 Cor 7:1; Phil 2:12; 4:1; 2 Thess 2:8), in the General Epistles, and especially in 1 and 2 Peter and Jude, it introduces a new section addressed to the readers. It also picks up on the "loved" of v. 1 and the "love" of v. 2, implying that Jude views these Christians as God does.[1] Furthermore, like those terms, it appears in both the opening and closing (vv. 17, 20) of the letter. Thus it is not that these believers are specially loved by Jude, but that he using the warm greeting of a leader of the Jesus movement to address them, placing himself on their side and taking God's perspective as he does it.

Our author points out that he was "eager" to write to them about "the salvation we share." Eagerness (which also occurs in 2 Pet 1:5, 10) is a good classical Greek idiom found in Isocrates and Plato and meaning "to want very much to" or "to make every effort to" do something (cf. *Barn.* 4:9 for a similar expression of writing out of friendship). It could

1. The terms are related in Greek, "loved" *(agapēmenois),* "love" *(agapē),* and "dear friends" *(agapētoi)* all coming from the same root.

mean either that while he was planning to write to them this particular occasion of writing came up, or that critical news reached him as he was in the act of writing them. Since there is no evidence of a previous topic in the letter, the NRSV captures the probable sense best, "While eagerly preparing to write to you." The general topic he was planning to write on was "the salvation we share," which contrasts with the condemnation of the false teachers. God is portrayed in this letter as the readers' Savior (cf. v. 24)[2] and as the one before whom the false teachers stand condemned. Thus again Jude has joined with his readers and drawn a line between them as sharers of salvation and the false teachers.

Whatever he was previously going to address about the topic of their common salvation, this letter now has a new agenda: the need to exhort his readers to "contend for the faith." Unlike the previous topic, this one is a necessity, something about which he does not think he has a choice (1 Cor 7:37; Phlm 14). As he will indicate in the next verse, his "friends" are apparently unaware of the nature of the interlopers in their midst, so Jude has to exhort or urge them to take appropriate action. This clearly indicates that the purpose of this letter is to motivate. It is a letter of exhortation, like Hebrews (Heb 13:22).

The action required is "to contend for the faith that was once for all entrusted to the saints." The idea of contending is that of carrying on "a conflict, contest, debate, or legal suit"; although not prevalent in the NT or the LXX, it was common in Greek in relationship to the contests in the stadium.[3] In other words, this is a serious struggle. While the opponents have yet to be introduced, the prize to be kept is clear: the faith.[4] In v. 20 this is described as "the most holy faith" (perhaps in contrast to the unholiness of the false teachers), but here it is "the faith once for all entrusted to the saints," indicating that (1) no new revelation can change the essence of this faith, and (2) it is the faith that they have received (the word for "entrusted" indicates the passing on of a tradition) from their teachers, possibly including Jude.

> [4]*For certain men whose condemnation was written about long ago have secretly slipped in among you. They are godless men, who change the grace*

2. On "Savior" as a title see the discussion in the Introduction to 2 Peter, pp. 152-54. This is not a reference to the atonement, but to God's deliverance of believers from evil powers or to his general beneficence, given that no specific danger is in sight.

3. E. Stauffer, *"agōn, ktl." TDNT* 1:134-40. Cf. V. C. Pfitzner, *Paul and the* Agon *Motif* (NovTSup 16; Leiden: E. J. Brill, 1967).

4. On faith in Jude see Grundmann, "Zum Glaubensverständnis des Judasbriefes," in *Der Brief des Judas und der zweite Brief des Petrus,* 26-27; and G. H. Whitaker, "Faith's Function in St Jude's Epistle," *ExpT* 29 (1917-18) 425.

*of our God into a license for immorality and deny Jesus Christ our only Sovereign and Lord.*

4 While one might contend for the faith against those who are not part of the believing community, such language is never used in that context in the NT. The debate in this situation is far more problematic, for the "in"–"out" demarcation lines are not clear. That is, the problem is the presence in their midst of people who teach by word and deed an alternative version of Christian belief. These individuals (NIV's "men" translates *anthrōpoi,* which means "human beings" and so designates either sex) have "secretly slipped in among you." By this Jude indicates that the false teachers were not originally part of that church, but have come from outside, probably presenting themselves as traveling Christian teachers or prophets (who were a feature of the first-century church, with both salutary [Acts 11:27-30; 21:10-11] and negative [2 John 10] effects; cf. *Didache* 11–12; Ignatius, *Eph.* 9:1). Their entrance was not secret in the sense that no one knew they were there. In fact, the designation "certain" is frequently used in the NT for an unnamed group whom the readers know well (1 Cor 4:1; 2 Cor 3:1; 10:12; Gal 1:7; 1 Tim 1:3, 19; 2 Pet 3:9). Their entrance was secret in that the way they presented themselves and (perhaps) their original behavior did not alert the church to the reality that these teachers had an unacceptable alternative view of the faith. Jude is attempting to unmask them.

Jude makes a series of four charges about these people: (1) the Scriptures condemn them, (2) they are godless or impious, (3) they change God's grace into "a license for immorality," and (4) they deny "Jesus Christ our only Sovereign and Lord."

The first charge, "whose condemnation was written about long ago," could mean one of three things. First, it could mean that their condemnation had been written in the heavenly books, perhaps even before the world was created (Clement of Alexandria, Windisch, Kelly). While in Jewish and Christian circles it was common to speak about everyone's sins having been written in the heavenly books (Rev 20:12; *2 Apoc. Bar.* 24:1; *1 Enoch* 89:61-71; 104:7), some literature also indicated that the names and punishment of sinners were written down before they sinned (*1 Enoch* 108:7). However, since the passage in *1 Enoch* is a later addition to *1 Enoch* that Jude most likely did not know, since Jude does not indicate that he has received any divine revelation about such heavenly writing, and since he does indicates that at least some of these people can repent (Jude 22-23), it is unlikely that this is what he intended by this phrase.

Second, it could mean that Jude or some other Christian writer had written about their condemnation a long time before (e.g., Acts 20:29-30;

1 Tim 4:1-3; 2 Tim 3:13), some suggesting that this writing was 2 Pet 2:1–3:4.[5] However, we do not have any such Christian writing prophesying interlopers like those Jude is writing about, except possibly in 2 Peter, which we argued in the Introduction (p. 23; see also pp. 136-43) is later than Jude. Therefore, this identification is also unlikely.

Third, the phrase could mean that the condemnation was written in some form of Jewish prophecy (Grundmann, Mayor, Chaine, Cantinat). In the light of Jude's use of scriptural and extracanonical literature, including the prophecy of Enoch from *1 Enoch,* in the rest of the book, this identification is surely the most likely. Thus this charge that their condemnation was written about in Jewish prophecy will clarify itself as we continue to read the letter.

The second charge is that they are godless, or, better, impious (*asebēs,* also occurring in Jude 15). The term denotes moral outrage against a deity (or deities, in the case of the Greek city-state) rather than disbelief in the deity. Thus in the Greek OT (especially in poetic literature) it is the opposite of the fear of God and parallel to being unrighteous or sinful, which is also true of its few uses in the NT (outside our literature only in Rom 4:5; 5:6; 1 Tim 1:9; 1 Pet 4:18; in the last two of these it is paired with "sinners"). In other words, Jude is not accusing these people of disbelief in God, but of moral rebellion against God. Morality rather than theology is the issue, even if sometimes bad theology leads to bad morality (and vice versa).

The third charge confirms the second charge in that it states that the interlopers change God's grace into a "license for immorality" (NIV) or, better, "into licentiousness" (NRSV). The term *aselgeia* appears in vice catalogues in Mark 7:22, Rom 13:13, Gal 5:19, and 1 Pet 4:3, and in shorter descriptions of vice in 2 Cor 12:21 and Eph 4:19. This term designates "sensual indulgence, especially sexual immorality" (Bauckham). It is contrasted with the grace of God, a phrase appearing twenty-seven times in the NT. This "grace" or "favor" is in contrast with judgment or condemnation, which is what humanity deserves from God. Yet such grace was easily understood as indulgence, which made moral behavior unnecessary. In fact, in some cases living immorally was thought of as glorifying God by making his grace more magnificent (Rom 6:1; 1 Cor 5:1-2; 6:12-20). A similar ignoring of morality may be behind Jas 2:14-26. The fact is that as soon as one says that God forgives sins rather than demands full payment for every sin, the temptation is to presume upon such grace. What this attitude ignores is that it is upon repentance and

5. Theodor Zahn, *Introduction to the New Testament* (New York: Scribner's, 1909), 249-52.

commitment to God (i.e., faith, which means commitment rather than belief when followed by a personal object) that forgiveness takes place. The basic Christian confession was not a statement about Jesus forgiving sin, but about Jesus as Lord (Rom 10:9-10). In fact, Paul himself several times underlined the fact that those who show no repentance but continue in sin are not citizens of the kingdom (e.g., 1 Cor 6:9-11; Gal 5:19-21). Jude encounters the teaching of "cheap grace," that is, grace without repentance or even grace that grants license to sin more than before, in the interlopers, and it becomes one of the charges against them.

Finally, these people deny "Jesus Christ our only Sovereign and Lord." It is not that these men and women actually denied any particular doctrine about Jesus. In terms of the creed that they could sign they may well have been as orthodox as Jude himself. But their behavior is a denial of Christ. Jude uses two terms in making his point, both of which could be translated "master." The second, "Lord," is so common in the NT that we often fail to realize that in that world there were "lords" of various types, from husbands to masters to rulers, whom one had better obey and who had the right to inflict punishment if one did not obey. In that world Caesar was the supreme Lord. To confess that Jesus was one's *only* Lord was to make a statement of independence from Caesar as well as a statement of submission to Jesus. The first term, *despotēs* (the root of the English term "despot"), is rarer, occurring only ten times in the NT. While it is used in Luke-Acts and Revelation for God as master (Luke 2:29; Acts 4:24; Rev. 6:10), its common use is for the master that a slave must obey (1 Tim 6:1, 2; Titus 2:9; 1 Pet 2:18). The point is that if people fail to obey someone, whether or not they call him "lord" or "master," they are in fact denying that he *is* their lord or master. Thus their behavior with respect to the commands of Jesus (perhaps those found in the Sermon on the Mount or perhaps those given to the Jesus movement later through various prophets) reveals the true state of their hearts. However orthodox their words may be, their behavior denies that Jesus is really their only Sovereign and Lord.

Some scholars read this description of the interlopers and argue that it is not to be taken as an actual description of known behavior of the teachers Jude opposes. Idolatry and immorality are often paired in the OT, so if someone departed from right doctrine it would be assumed that he or she was also immoral. These charges are not actual, but are part of vilifying and demonizing opponents with whom the author does not agree.

While the pairing does take place in the OT, and Jude will call upon the OT repeatedly to support his case, this argument overlooks one cardinal fact: these opponents are never charged with theological error or with opposing the leadership of the Jesus movement, much less the leadership of Jude. In fact, the *only* thing that they are charged with is ignoring Christian morality. Doctrinal error has not led to the accusation of moral error since doctrinal error is never attributed to these teachers. Thus, while Jude does use stock phrases and descriptions (more to demonstrate the judgment of these teachers than that their behavior is evil), it appears that he is describing real behavior that, at least in his opinion, in one way or another fits those stock descriptions. We have already seen above that such behavior was not unknown in the early church, so there is no reason to suppose that Jude would not be confronting it.

## B. Body Proper: Proof for the Thematic Statement (vv. 5-16)

### *1. First Proof (vv. 5-7 and 8-10)*

*[5]Though you already know all this, I want to remind you that the Lord delivered his people out of Egypt, but later destroyed those who did not believe. [6]And the angels who did not keep their positions of authority but abandoned their own home — these he has kept in darkness, bound with everlasting chains for judgment on the great Day. [7]In a similar way, Sodom and Gomorrah and the surrounding towns gave themselves up to sexual immorality and perversion. They serve as an example of those who suffer the punishment of eternal fire.*

**5** The evidence adduced for the seriousness of the thematic statement consists of three examples from the OT. Jude begins with "I want to remind you," to which is attached "although you already know all this." The phrase is a disclosure formula that may begin a letter body or show a transition within it.[1] Here it forms the transition between the thematic statement and the arguments supporting that statement. The transition is made with this formula in that it softens the instruction, preserving the honor of the readers rather than shaming them. It functions similarly to Paul's statement, "I do not want you to be ignorant," but it is an even gentler introduction, making the charitable assumption that the readers already know all of this and that Jude is only reminding them. This style contrasts with Paul's shaming language in Gal 3:1, "O ignorant Galatians!" Apparently, while Jude perceives a danger to the community, either because the community has not yet sided with the interlopers

1. John L. White, *The Form and Function of the Body of the Greek Letter* (Missoula, MT: Scholars Press, 1972[2]), 3, 11-15, 38.

against him or because the politics of the situation dictate a gentle approach, he proceeds in a manner that preserves the honor of his readers.

The examples he gives are all biblical examples of judgment cited several times in Jewish literature in various orders (Sir 16:7-10; 3 Macc 2:4-7; *T. Naph.* 3:4-5; CD 2:17–3:12; *m. Sanh.* 10:3). Since they all deal with people within the community who morally or otherwise defected from the community and received God's judgment, they show that the pre-Jesus Jewish community also saw the need to deal with such defectors from their community.

Each of these examples is a reference to a story that is part of the larger story of Israel, which the followers of Jesus retold with their being the climax of that story. Each of these stories is told, not with direct reference to the OT, but in the form in which it was told in various Jewish circles during the Second Temple period.

The first example is drawn from the story of Israel in the wilderness, the original version being in either Numbers 14 or Exodus 32 (cf. 1 Cor 10:6-13, which combines this incident with two others, as Jude may also be doing). The decision as to the exact passage for the origin of the story revolves around whether the lack of faith that is referred to ("those who did not believe") has to do with turning to idolatry as in Exodus 32 or with the failure to trust God as in Numbers 14. In both of these events (and the others mentioned by Paul in 1 Corinthians 10) the "back to Egypt" cry demonstrated a failure to trust God (lack of faith), although the Israelites worked it out in different ways.

The passage itself presents two major textual issues. The first concerns the placement of the "once," which some manuscripts place with the act of salvation ("once for all saved a people out of the land of Egypt," NRSV) and others with their previous knowledge ("though ye once knew this" [KJV], or "you have been informed of all things once and for all" [Bauckham]; the NIV drops any explicit reference to the "once" but appears to side with the NRSV). The manuscript evidence slightly favors the KJV reading,[2] but (1) the protection of honor in the rest of the disclosure statement, (2) the placement of the "once" before the verb it modifies in the previous verse, and (3) the need to insert a "but later" *(to deuteron)* for a corresponding "first" incline us to think that the texts used by the NRSV are more likely the original reading.[3]

2. While א and C, along with many miniscules and versions, support the NRSV reading, A, B, and 𝔓72 support the KJV reading.

3. So also Matthew Black, "Critical and Exegetical Notes on Three New Testament Texts, Hebrews xi.11, Jude 5, James i.27," in Walter Eltester, ed., *Apophoreta: Festschrift für Ernst Haenchen* (BZNW 30; Berlin: Alfred Töpelmann, 1964), 39-45; Allen Wikgren, "Some Problems in Jude 5," in B. L. Daniels and M. Jack Suggs, eds., *Studies in the History and*

The second concerns whether it is "the Lord" who delivered his people or "Jesus" or "God Christ." The manuscript evidence is similar to that for "once" in that those manuscripts reading "once" where the KJV has it also usually read "Jesus" or "God Christ" and those that the NRSV follows read "Lord." While it is tempting to accept "Jesus," which reading does clearly show how many early Christians interpreted the reference, because of our arguments above for the placement of "once" and because "Jesus" would be so unusual as to be not just the more difficult reading but a highly unlikely one (even Paul uses "God" and "the Lord" for the judgments described in 1 Corinthians 10), we believe that the original reading was "Lord." Jude may well understand this term as referring to Jesus; at the least he intends it to be an analogy to Jesus as "Sovereign and Lord" in the previous verse.

What, then, is Jude saying? After politely introducing this section of argumentation, he points out to his readers as his first piece of evidence that while the Lord on the one hand delivered the whole nation out of Egypt, he also destroyed in the wilderness those who did not believe, that is, were not committed to him/did not trust him (the issue is not intellectual belief but trust/commitment). This situation parallels that of the interlopers who are showing "unfaith" in that they are denying "Jesus Christ our only Sovereign and Lord." Thus the implication is that although they are among the people of God whom "the Lord" has saved out of (spiritual) "Egypt," they will be destroyed in the end because of their lack of commitment to (faith in) the Lord.

**6** The second example comes from Gen 6:1-4 as interpreted through Jewish tradition. In Genesis the story of the "sons of God" occurs without reference to their fate:[4]

> [1]When men began to increase in number on the earth and daughters were born to them, [2]the sons of God saw that the daughters of men

---

*Text of the New Testament in Honor of Kenneth Willis Clark* (Salt Lake City: University of Utah Press, 1967), 147-52. But see also B. M. Metzger, *A Textual Commentary on the Greek New Testament* (New York: United Bible Societies, 1971), 725-26; and C. D. Osburn, "The Text of Jude 5," *Bib* 62 (1981) 107-15.

4. For a discussion of the meaning of the "sons of God" in the Genesis context, see Bruce K. Waltke, *Genesis: A Commentary* (Grand Rapids: Zondervan, 2001), 115-17. He argues that the idea that Genesis 6 refers to intermarriage between human groups (i.e., the "sons of God" are a race or group of human beings) "must be rejected for philological reasons" in favor of divine beings. With this conclusion we agree. Then, after discussing a number of other theories, he argues that rulers who claimed divine status might fit the Genesis account, despite the difficulties, if they were viewed as demon possessed. This compromise has yet to convince us. But we are, of course, dealing with Jude and not with Genesis, so we cannot go into the interpretation of Genesis itself in detail.

> were beautiful, and they married any of them they chose. [3]Then the LORD said, "My Spirit will not contend with man forever, for he is mortal; his days will be a hundred and twenty years."
>
> [4]The Nephilim were on the earth in those days — and also afterward — when the sons of God went to the daughters of men and had children by them. They were the heroes of old, men of renown.

However, Jewish tradition filled in the story by (1) refocusing the effect on humanity (i.e., making the angelic beings the origin of sin in humanity rather than just the origin of the limited life span) and (2) making the nature and rebellion of the "sons of God" explicit. While the tradition is found in various forms in the Jewish literature of the centuries surrounding Jude (2 *Apoc. Bar.* 56:10-14; *1 Enoch* 6–19; 21; 86–88; 106:13-17; *Jub.* 4:15, 22; 5:1; *T. Reub.* 5:6-7; *T. Naph.* 3:5; CD 2:17-19; 1QapGen 2:1; *Tg. Ps.-J.* Gen 6:1-4), Jude is clearly dependent upon the form found in *1 Enoch,* not least because he explicitly cites this work in vv. 14-15, but also because of the close parallels between Jude 6 and the account in *1 Enoch* 6–19.

We should note at this point that Judaism abandoned this interpretation of Genesis 6 as referring to angelic beings only after the time of R. Simeon b. Yohai (in the third-generation Tannaim, i.e., A.D. 130-60), insisting thereafter that the "sons of God" were human beings rather than angels. In Christian circles this interpretation of Genesis 6 as referring to angelic beings remained unanimous until the third century and continued until the fifth century (Bauckham). Thus the strangeness of the tradition to our ears does not mean that it was strange to Jude's readers. After all, there is no example of any other Jewish interpretation of Genesis 6 from two or more centuries before Christ (the formation of the early part of *1 Enoch*) to two centuries afterward (R. Simeon b. Yohai).[5]

Jude, then, refers to angels (also called "Watchers" by *1 Enoch* and some other literature), that is, "the angels, the children of heaven" (*1 Enoch* 6:2; adding in v. 6 that there were 200 of these angels). These angels had their own proper spheres of authority *(archē),* which was also a commonplace of Jewish literature and Christian teaching, going back at least to the interpretation of Deut 32:8 in the Greek translation of the OT (which has "according to the number of the sons of God" rather than "according to the number of the sons of Israel" as in the Masoretic text). This interpretation is found in the intertestamental literature (*Jub.* 2:2; 5:6), the Dead Sea Scrolls (1QH 1:11; 1QM 10:12), early Christian writings (Justin,

5. R. Simeon was a disciple of R. Akiba and is mentioned over 325 times in the Mishnah, normally cited simply as "R. Simeon."

*2 Apol.* 5:2, although he also refers to them as "spirits," "gods," and "demons"), and of course in *1 Enoch* (e.g., 82:10-20).

However, these angels did not "keep their positions of authority." There is a bit of irony here, for "keep" *(tērēsantos)* is the same verb as that used for God's keeping them in darkness *(tetērēken),* in each case meaning to "protect," "keep," or "guard." That is, those who would not guard their own positions of authority end up guarded in a place of darkness. The point Jude makes is that these angels "abandoned their own home" (*1 Enoch* 12:4 ["who have abandoned the high heaven, the holy eternal place"]; 15:3, 7) in descending to earth and taking human wives. Thus their apostasy (not in a doctrinal sense, but in the sense of transgressing their proper boundaries) is noted both negatively ("did not keep") and positively ("abandoned"). This, of course, is parallel to the apostasy of the interlopers in the congregation, who abandoned their place in the community by their own immorality.

The result of this apostasy was disastrous for these angels. They are presently "bound with everlasting chains" and "kept in darkness." The phrase "kept in darkness" refers to their imprisonment in the underworld, a use of "darkness" *(zophos)* found from Homer on in Greek literature (meaning "the gloom of the world below," "nether darkness," in Aeschylus; Homer, *Od.* 11.57; 20.356; *Il.* 15.191; 21.56; see further L & S; cf. Jude 13; the term appears twice in Jude, twice in the parallels in 2 Peter, and once in Heb 12:18, where it refers to the darkness surrounding Sinai). The reference to "everlasting chains" is also found in *1 Enoch* (13:1; 14:5; 54:3-5; 56:1-4; 88:1; 4QEnGiants[a] 8:14) and other Jewish literature referring to the Watchers (*2 Apoc. Bar.* 56:13; Jub. 5:6; cf. Origen, *C. Cel.* 5.52). As *1 Enoch* 10:4-6 puts it,

> [4]And secondly the Lord said to Raphael [an archangel], "Bind Azaz'el [the fallen angel who had taught war and oppression to human beings] hand and foot (and) throw him into the darkness!" And he made a hole in the desert which was in Duda'el and cast him there; [5]he threw on top of him rugged and sharp rocks. And he covered his face in order that he may not see light; [6]and in order that he may be sent into the fire on the great day of judgment.

In *1 Enoch* the other fallen angels suffer a similar fate ("bind them for seventy generations underneath the rocks of the ground until the day of their judgment and of their consummation, until the eternal judgment is concluded," *1 Enoch* 10:12).

Yet the imprisonment of these beings is not the worst result of their apostasy, for they are being kept in prison "for judgment on the great

Day." While the exact phrase "the great day of judgment" is relatively rare in Jewish and early Christian writings (but see *1 Enoch* 22:11; 84:4; *Tg. Neof.* Deut 32:34), "the great day of the Lord" or similar phrases are used in both the OT and the NT for the final judgment (Joel 2:11, 31; Zeph 1:14; Mal 4:5; Acts 2:20; Rev 6:17; 16:8; cf. *1 Enoch* 54:6; *2 Enoch* 18:6). Thus, bad as it is, imprisonment in the underworld is only a prelude to the still worse ultimate fate of these beings. Jude does not explain what this is, but *1 Enoch* 10:13-14 says,

> [13]In those days they will lead them into the bottom of the fire — and in torment — in the prison (where) they will be locked up forever. [14]And at the time when they will burn and die, those who collaborated with them will be bound together with them from henceforth unto the end of (all) generations.

While it may not be clear whether *1 Enoch* is talking about eternal fire or the final destruction of the Watchers, his image is consistent with that in Rev 20:11-15.

Where is the temporary prison where the fallen angels are imprisoned? Jewish writers located it either under the earth (the original meaning of the Greek phrases used in Jude) or in the second heaven (*2 Enoch* 7:2; 18:4). While this location is immaterial in terms of the nature of the place, it is probably the second heaven location that is reflected in 1 Pet 3:19-20. There the text refers to the same fallen angels as imprisoned in a location where Christ preaches something to them. Very likely this refers to Christ's proclamation of triumph to the fallen angels upon his ascension through the various heavens to the throne of God.[6] This locates 1 Peter and Jude in the same thought-world (even if they may locate the prison in different places), which is also that of Revelation and other NT writings.

7 If the fates of the Israelites in the wilderness and the fallen angels of the time of Noah, both of which once experienced God's favor and then abandoned it, were not warning enough, Jude now turns to his third example, Sodom and Gomorrah. While Sodom and Gomorrah are frequently cited in Scripture as examples of judgment (some of the references to the word pair are in Genesis's Sodom stories, and the rest refer to the judgment of the cities: Deut 29:23; Isa 1:9; 13:19; Jer 49:18; 50:40; Lam 4:6; Amos 4:11; Zeph 2:9; Matt 10:15; Luke 17:29; 2 Pet 2:6; Jude 7; cf.; 2 Esdr 2:8; 3 Macc 2:5) or as an example of evil (Isa 1:10; 3:9; Jer 23:14; Ezek 16:46-50; Rev 11:8), Jude cites them and "the surrounding towns"

6. Peter H. Davids, *The First Epistle of Peter* (NICNT; Grand Rapids: William B. Eerdmans, 1990), 138-43.

(Gen 19:25, 29, the other three cities being Admah, Zeboiim, and Bela or Zoar [Gen 14:8], the latter being saved as a concession to Lot) as examples of the results of "sexual immorality and perversion," of which the interlopers Jude is confronting are also accused.

Jude connects his charge to the previous discussion of the angels with the phrase "in a similar way" *(ton homoion tropon toutois),* indicating that the sin of the angels and the sin of these cities are similar. What Sodom and Gomorrah are charged with is giving themselves up to sexual immorality and perversion. The term for sexual immorality *(ekporneuō)* is a general term indicating any type of sexual intercourse outside of marriage. This is made specific by the following phrase that, more literally translated, reads, "departed after a different type of flesh." Virtually all commentators agree that this refers to the incident in Gen 19:4-11, and most believe that this means the attempt at homosexual relations, that is, as Neyrey puts it, a violation of the laws of purity, which prohibited the mixing of things, even between the sexes (Deut 22:5, 9-11). Thus seeking sexual intercourse with a person of the same sex would be seeking a different type of flesh than that which one was supposed to seek. See also Kelly. Bauckham, however, argues that the issue is that of seeking intercourse with angels, which would indeed be a different type of flesh. Thus the two incidents cited are the reverse of one another (the fallen angels seeking intercourse with human women, and the men of Sodom seeking intercourse with angels), but each clearly a crossing of a "species" boundary. As support he cites *T. Naph.* 3:4-5,

> But you, my children, shall not be like that [the Gentiles who worship idols and follow wandering spirits]: In the firmament, in the earth, and in the sea, in all the products of his workmanship, discern the Lord who made all things, so that you do not become like Sodom, which departed from the order of nature. Likewise the Watchers departed from nature's order; the Lord pronounced a curse on them at the flood. On their account he ordered that the earth be without dweller or produce.

The OT itself is not a lot of help in deciding between these interpretations. In the Sodom story itself it appears that the violation of hospitality is the main issue, particularly since the permitted rape[7] of two women was seen as a solution to the problem (cf. Judges 19). Later reflection focused on the violation of hospitality (Wisd. 19:14-15, "Others had refused

7. Since their father who had authority over them would "bring them out" (Gen 19:8), their rape would be "permitted" within the mores of that culture, although the father would suffer loss since they would no longer be virgins and thus not bring the expected bride price (or not be marriageable at all).

to receive strangers when they came to them"; Josephus, *Ant.* 1.194, "they hated strangers") and their selfish pride (Ezek 16:49-50 ["abominable deeds" is never defined]; 3 Macc 2:5 [although the author leaves their notorious "crimes" undefined]; Josephus, *Ant.* 1.194, "grew proud on account of their riches and great wealth"; Philo, *De Abrahamo* 134; *Tg. Ps.-J.* Gen 13:13; 18:20). However, some works accuse Sodom of at least general sexual immorality (*Jub.* 16:5-6; 20:5, "they were polluting themselves and they were fornicating in their flesh and they were causing pollution upon the earth."; *T. Levi* 14:6; *T. Benj.* 9:1, "You will be sexually promiscuous like the promiscuity of the Sodomites" [both *Testaments* cite an otherwise unknown prophecy of Enoch]), and Philo, in line with what may well be implied in some of the previously cited works, accuses them of homosexuality in particular (*De Abrahamo* 135–36, "those were men who lusted after one another, doing unseemly things, and not regarding or respecting their common nature . . . and so, by degrees, the men became accustomed to be treated like women"; cf. *Vit. Mos.* 2.58; Josephus, *Ant.* 1.194, "abused themselves with Sodomitical practices").

We conclude that Bauckham is right in arguing that the comparison with the fallen angels has to do with crossing a "species" boundary. However, even the evidence of *T. Naphtali* would be consistent with what Philo makes clear, that sexual intercourse with other males was viewed as crossing just such a boundary. In that none of the other references is at all concerned that the "strangers" involved were angels, it is more likely that Jude too is thinking of homosexual activity as the "different type of flesh" (different, not from themselves, but from the women they were supposed to desire). This would be in line with the general Jewish rejection of homosexual relations.

Like the fallen angels, the people of Sodom and Gomorrah "serve as an example of those who suffer the punishment of eternal fire." While the fallen angels were said to be destined for fire, Sodom and Gomorrah were destroyed by fire. Their fire is eternal in that that their destruction was complete, and, unlike most burned cities in Palestine, they were never rebuilt. (If, in fact, the cities discovered on the hills overlooking the south end of the Dead Sea are these cities, there is archaeological evidence that they were suddenly destroyed and burned at about the same time, although the cause of the fire cannot be determined.) This is an example (3 Macc 2:5 uses a similar term for "example"), for it was a theoretically visible (Wisd 10:7; Josephus, *War* 4.483; Philo, *Vit. Mos.* 2.56)[8] reminder of

8. Since the cities were long buried, they were not visible during most of the biblical period. However, in that their destruction lived in memory and in that their absence could be observed, they were still "visible" in the tradition.

the fire of coming judgment (fire and brimstone are associated with "eternal" temporal judgment in Deut 29:23; Isa 34:9-10; Jer 49:17-18; cf. Ezek 38:22; and with eschatological judgment in Rev 14:10-11; 19:3; 20:10; "eternal fire" also indicates judgment in Matt 18:8; 25:41; cf. 4 Macc 12:12; *3 Apoc. Bar.* 14:6; *T. Zeb.* 10:3; 1QS 2:8) that was coming upon the interlopers in Jude's community, who were also practicing immorality. God's past record of judgment serves to remind us that it is never safe to ignore his instructions; he tells us how the world was designed to operate, and any attempt to create our own version of reality is certain to be dysfunctional, sometimes in the short term and sometimes in the long term, with or without obvious divine intervention.[9]

> [8]*In the very same way, these dreamers pollute their own bodies, reject authority and slander celestial beings.* [9]*But even the archangel Michael, when he was disputing with the devil about the body of Moses, did not dare to bring a slanderous accusation against him, but said, "The Lord rebuke you!"* [10]*Yet these men speak abusively against whatever they do not understand; and what things they do understand by instinct, like unreasoning animals — these are the very things that destroy them.*

**8** Having laid out his first set of historical evidence for the fate of the interlopers, Jude now applies it using the transitional v. 8 and moves on to the second set of evidence. "In the very same way" refers back to the previous verses (Jude 5-7) and indicates that what these folk do is of the same order as what Israel, the fallen angels, and Sodom and Gomorrah did. There is a connective *(mentoi)* that is not translated but indicates that the activities of these interlopers took place despite the previous examples of what happens to such behavior.

Jude refers to the false teachers as "these dreamers." The Greek term for "dreamers" occurs in only one place elsewhere in the NT, Acts 2:17 (quoting Joel 2:28). There it is used positively for dreams sent by God, which was a well-known OT (and NT — e.g., Matt 1:20 plus five

9. God is always involved in the world, so there is nothing that happens in which he is not involved. Thus the idea of miracles, whether of healing or of judgment, that involves a normally distant God breaking into the world is not part of the biblical worldview. However, the actions of God are sometimes more obvious than at others. Yet this can leave us with questions. How does one evaluate the war of A.D. 66-70? From one point of view it was the boiling over of Jewish resentment of Roman occupation and the resultant destruction of much of Palestine and Jerusalem in particular that was an expected consequence of defying Rome. From another point of view, that of Mark 13, it was the judgment of God on that part of the Jewish people who had chosen the path of violence rather than the path of Jesus. God was present, but only for those with eyes to see.

more times in Matthew; Acts 2:17; 16:9; 18:9) form of revelation (e.g., Num 12:6; 1 Sam 28:6; 1 Kings 3:5). Here it is used negatively of false prophecy, just as the same Greek term is used in the Greek OT, especially in Jeremiah (Deut 13:1, 3, 5; Jer 23:25, 28; 29:8; cf. a related term in Jer 23:32; Zech 10:2). The same idea is found in *1 Enoch* 99:8. Because of its solid rooting in both the OT and early Christian experience of prophetic dreams and visions, this meaning is more likely than (1) that Jude is referring to their imagination (which is not the normal meaning of this word group), (2) that Jude is referring to the sleep of sin (Calvin), (3) that Jude is referring to their self-hypnotism (Reicke), or (4) that the term means "seers" and is thus a self-designation for Essenes.[10] What the reference to these people as "dreamers" means is that these individuals were claiming divine revelation as the basis of their practices, either because their visions gave them a superior status in general (Neyrey)[11] or because the content of their visions was a rival revelation (Bauckham). Jude is referring to them as false prophets in that they claim a prophetic basis for their practices. As noted above, dreams were and are, according to the NT, a legitimate form of divine revelation, but all prophetic revelation needs testing on the basis of the whole teaching of Scripture so that the true may be separated from the false. This prevents the two equally dangerous extremes: (1) accepting all dreams and prophetic words uncritically, and (2) rejecting all dreams and prophetic words out of fear of deception.[12]

Jude accuses these people of acting on the basis of their personal revelation and engaging in three sinful activities: (1) polluting their own bodies, (2) rejecting authority, and (3) slandering celestial beings. Two of these have already appeared in the examples previously cited. Both Israel in the wilderness and the fallen angels had rejected authority; both the fallen angels and the men of Sodom and Gomorrah had polluted their own bodies. It is the third charge that leads the discussion forward to the following verse. However, all three expressions are worthy of closer examination.

The first charge ("pollute their own bodies") could be translated more literally "defile the flesh." While the exact phrase is found only in later works (Hermas, *Man.* 4:1:9 [for adultery]; *Sim.* 5:7:2; *Sib. Or.* 2:279

10. C. Daniel, "La mention des Esséniens dans le texte grec de l'épître de S. Jude," *Museon* 81 (1968) 503-21. The fact is that the Greek term "dreamer" used in Jude is not how the Greek OT translates the Hebrew term for "seer." Furthermore, the Essenes did not refer to themselves as "seers."

11. Neyrey draws upon G. Sellin, "Die Häretiker des Judasbriefes," *ZNW* 77 (1986) 216.

12. In *Didache* 11 and 13 and in Hermas, *Mandate* 11, we find the early church wrestling with just such problems of discernment, trying to keep the good without accepting the evil.

[for licentiousness]; cf. the related "defile the body" in *T. Ash.* 4:4), the idea of defilement is frequently used for the sexual actions of the fallen angels (*1 Enoch* 7:1; 9:8; 10:11; 12:4; 15:3-4) and of the Sodomites (*Jub.* 16:5). Thus Jude is clearly accusing them of unspecified defiling sexual practices, that is, the same things that the fallen angels and the Sodomites of Jewish tradition had done.

The second charge ("reject authority") could be translated "disregard lordship." Three interpretations have been proposed for this phrase. Calvin and Luther believed that "lordship" means civil or ecclesiastical authority. These people rejected certain human authority. On the other hand, Moffatt and others argued that it means that a certain class of angels was being disregarded. Those angels are referred to in Eph 1:21; Col 1:16; *Asc. Isa.* 2:22; and Clement of Alexandria, *Strom.* 5.11.77, quoting the *Apocalypse of Zephaniah.* Finally, Bauckham and others believe that it refers to the lordship of God (*Did.* 4:1) or Christ (Hermas, *Sim.* 5:6:1). Of the three interpretations, the first is the least likely because nowhere else in this work does Jude refer to either civil or ecclesiastical authorities, nor were ecclesiastical authorities referred to at this time as "lords" (as was the case in the time of Luther and Calvin). The second is possible because of the appearance of the critical term in Pauline literature, but there it is plural and here it is singular. Thus either it was some specific angelic "lord" whose authority was being rejected (and none is named), or else this interpretation is problematic. The final interpretation is somewhat more likely than the second in that we already know that these people deny the authority of Jesus (Jude 4), although we have argued above that this was a practical denial rather than a theological denial. If this is indeed the meaning of "reject authority," then the first two charges are resumptive of the previous examples and charges.

The third charge ("slander celestial beings") states literally that they "slander the glorious ones." Who are these "glorious ones"? While in the OT the Hebrew equivalent of this Greek term can refer to famous people (Ps 149:8; Isa 3:5; 23:8; Nah 3:10; cf. the Dead Sea Scrolls 1QM 14:11; 1QpHab 4:2; 4QpNah 2:9; 3:9; 4:9), the Greek OT never translates that Hebrew terminology with the Greek term used here (*doxas*). Thus it is unlikely that famous people (either OT worthies or the apostles) are meant. The other possibility for this term is that it means angels (who unfortunately are rarely referred to in the OT, although the Greek translation of Exod 15:11 probably refers to them with this term), a usage found in the Dead Sea Scrolls (1QH 10:8; 1QPs$^{a}$Zion 22:13) and apocalyptic literature (*Asc. of Isa.* 9:32; *2 Enoch* 22:7, 10). This is the most likely meaning, especially since angels will be referred to in the next verse; it is also how Clement of Alexandria interpreted this passage.

Yet, if they were slandering angels, why would they do so? Several explanations have commended themselves to commentators. (1) Some argue that these angels were evil angels, and they were slandered either to show these teachers' superiority to them or to declare their freedom from them.[13] There are two further varieties of this position, one of which sees these teachers as denying any real existence to idols (i.e., denying that there was a spiritual entity behind the image), much as the Corinthians did,[14] and the other of which views them as speaking contemptuously of evil powers (the same evil powers of which they are accused of falling prey due to their immorality).[15] (2) Others agree that these teachers saw these angels as evil, but believe that Jude views them as good. Such writers usually attribute Gnostic beliefs to the group in which evil archons or angels, rather than the good God, created the world.[16] Thus Jude would view slander of the creator-angels or God as blasphemous, and they would view it as cursing evil beings. (3) A final group of commentators argues that the angels were good angels and that these people are either expressing their superiority as enlightened spiritual humans to such beings or that these teachers slander the angels as the givers of the law of Moses (so Bauckham, Chaine, drawing on the Jewish traditions found in *Jub.* 1:27-29; Josephus, *Ant.* 15.136; Acts 7:38, 53; Heb 2:2; Hermas, *Sim.* 8:3:3, the latter reference indicating the role of the angel Michael as the guardian of the law/gospel, an angelic role 1 Cor 11:10 may also refer to).

In evaluating these proposals, we notice first of all that *doxa* is never used elsewhere in Jewish or Christian writings to refer to an evil angel. Nor is it clear that Jude would object to dishonoring such beings, although he might not go as far as Qumran in cursing them (4Q280-82, 286-87, which are liturgies for cursing evil angels). The fact is that "slander" *(blasphēmeō)* does not mean "to deny the existence of" but rather "to shame" or "to speak insultingly about." It was thus a form of shaming or dishonoring, and in a society like Jude's that was based on honor and shame, this was appropriate for evil beings; indeed, to honor such beings would be wrong. Thus there is nothing in the verse itself that would make one think that the reference is to evil angels (on the following verse, see below).

13. H. Werdermann, *Das Irrlehrer des Judas- und 2. Petrusbriefes* (BFCT 17/6; Gütersloh: C. Bertelsmann, 1913), 33.

14. C. K. Barrett, "Things Sacrificed to Idols," *NTS* 11 (1964-65) 138-53.

15. Werdermann, *Das Irrlehrer des Judas- und 2. Petrusbriefes,* 33.

16. Among commentators, Sidebottom, *James, Jude and 2 Peter,* takes this position. R. Bultmann also champions it in his *Theology of the New Testament* (New York: Charles Scribner's, 1955), 1:170.

Second, we do not see any evidence of ontological dualism in Jude, which makes it unlikely that a Gnostic belief lay behind the practice. In other words, there is no evidence that the people he opposes were denying the creation, or attributing it to an evil deity. Some Gnostics were indeed accused of immorality, yet it is clear that one can become involved in immoral behavior without Gnostic theology. Furthermore, there is no evidence for developed Gnostic thought as early as the period of Jude.[17]

Third, we can understand why Jude would be concerned about the slander of God's angelic messengers. While this was not the usual problem in the church (Col 2:18; Rev 19:10; 22:8 all witness to the problem of worshiping angels, quite the opposite to what is going on here), if one were, as Jude claims, flouting the moral authority of Christ/God, then it would not be surprising to find them flouting the authority of angels, who were often pictured as enforcing the moral rule of Christ/God, including that expressed in the law.

Bauckham suggests that Paul may indeed be the background of this slandering of angels. Given that Paul spoke of the law's association with angels as being part of its lesser status (Gal 3:19), that he associated both angels and the law with "the basic principles of the world" (NIV; "elemental spirits of the world," NRSV) to which his readers had once been enslaved (Rom 8:33-39; Gal 4:3, 9; Col 2:8-23), one could easily see how some of Paul's readers might have overlooked his positive statements about the law (e.g., Rom 7:12) and associated both the law and its angelic mediators entirely with the slavery from which they had been freed.[18] Thus a distorted form of Paulinism may lie behind the actions of these interlopers.

There is no doubt that Paul did suffer from misinterpretation and that some of it took a libertine form (e.g., 1 Corinthians 5–6, 8–10). And there is no doubt that the rationale of freedom from the law and its mediating and enforcing angels would have formed a convenient basis for the actions of which these people are accused. However, Jude does not have a single reference to the law, nor, unlike James, does he reflect Pauline language that would tip us off to some use of Paul by his opponents. Thus,

17. Bauckham points out that later libertine forms of Gnosticism did flout the law and its associated angels, viewing the OT expressions as evil rather than good (Irenaeus, *Adv. haer.* 1:23:4; 1:24:5; *Treat. Seth* 64:1-10; *Testim. Truth* 29:11–30:17; G. W. McRae, "Why the Church Rejected Gnosticism," in E. P. Sanders, ed., *Jewish and Christian Self-Definition* [London: SCM, 1980], 1:128-30). However, this Gnosticism has a dualistic ontology that is totally absent from Jude, so it could hardly have formed a reason for slandering angels at this period of history.

18. Bauckham cites B. Reicke, "The Law and This World according to Paul," *JBL* 70 (1951) 259-76.

while this is an attractive and plausible hypothesis, it is too specific to be established by our text. All that we can say for sure is that the teachers Jude opposes were accused of slandering or dishonoring God's angels. (This is a theme that will also be taken up in 2 Pet 2:10b-11.)

This interpretation receives further support when we look at the structure of this verse with its three accusations. They parallel the accusations in Jude 5–7. Understood in their wider context, in Jude 5 we have a reference to the evil behavior of the Israelites, in Jude 6 a reference to the evil angels rejecting the authority of God, and in Jude 7 a reference to human beings dishonoring angels. Furthermore, the two charges in Jude 4, licentiousness and denying the authority of Christ, are also reflected in these three charges. Thus it appears that Jude is getting specific about items he has previously described in general.

Finally, we need to ask whether Jude is describing the actual behavior of those he accuses or simply using stock phrases to attack his opponents. The very fact that these phrases are so difficult to interpret indicates that they were not stock phrases. Instead, he appears to have specific behavior in view, which he will expand upon in the next verse.

**9** The example Jude gives is not that of an OT story, but of an intertestamental expansion upon such a story. The biblical story of the death and burial of Moses in Deut 34:1-12 is known, if not exactly familiar. The essential information is in the first six verses of the chapter, specifically in vv. 1 and 4-6:

> Then Moses went up from the plains of Moab to Mount Nebo, to the top of Pisgah, which is opposite Jericho, and the LORD showed him the whole land: Gilead as far as Dan, . . . [4]The LORD said to him, "This is the land of which I swore to Abraham, to Isaác, and to Jacob, saying, 'I will give it to your descendants'; I have let you see it with your eyes, but you shall not cross over there." [5]Then Moses, the servant of the LORD, died there in the land of Moab, at the LORD's command. [6]He was buried in a valley in the land of Moab, opposite Beth-peor, but no one knows his burial place to this day.

Clearly that story mentions neither "the archangel Michael" (found in the OT only in Dan 10:13, 21; 12:1) nor the devil (which is a Greek term appearing twenty-two times in the Greek OT, but only in translating postexilic books, i.e., Esther, Job, Zechariah, and once each in 1 Chronicles, Psalms [108:6], 1 Maccabees, and Wisdom of Solomon; when it translates a specific Hebrew term it is usually translating "Satan"). According to the church fathers, starting with Clement of Alexandria *(Fragments on the Epistle of Jude)*, the reason for this is that Jude is citing, not the OT, but the *Assumption of Moses.*[19] (Clement wrote, "'When Michael, the archangel, disputing with the devil, debated about the body of Moses.'" Here he confirms the *Assumption of Moses.* He is here called Michael, who through an angel near to us debated with the devil."[20] ) Thus there is universal agreement that Jude is citing an apocryphal work.

The problem arises in finding the work and thus the context to which Jude is referring. While no extant writing contains the story to which Jude refers, the so-called Milan manuscript contains the bulk of a first-century work called *The Testament of Moses,* and it is the lost ending to this book that Bauckham argues forms the basis for Jude's story.[21] From other references to this work the lost ending can be reconstructed: After the death of Moses Michael came to bury his body. The devil (Samma'el, one of a variety of Jewish names for the devil) came and argued that the body should be given to him, for Moses had been a murderer (i.e., he had murdered the Egyptian, Exod 2:12-14) and thus did not deserve an honorable burial. When Michael appealed to the judgment of God with "The Lord rebuke you!" the devil withdrew, knowing that God would decide in favor of Moses' honor and against his slander.

Given this background, we can now explore what Jude is trying to communicate. First, starting in the OT Michael is cited as an angelic being (called a "prince" in Daniel) who is the protector of Israel (Rev 12:7; 1 QM 17; cf. *b. Hagigah* 12b; *b. Menahot* 110a for rabbinic references to Michael). He is identified as one of the four or seven chief angels (e.g., *1 Enoch* 20:5; 40:9), and often as the head of the group. The term "archangel" appears in the NT only here and in 1 Thess 4:16; the term appears otherwise only in pseudepigraphical works (thirty-eight times), such as the Greek text of *1 Enoch* 20:7; *Jub.* 10:7; *Life of Adam and Eve* 1; 22:1; 37:4; *Test. Abr.* 1:4, 6; 10:1. It also appears in later Christian writings. "Archangel" indicates a chief angel, and thus is the equivalent of Daniel's "chief prince" or the

19. Further discussion of this work can be found in R. H. Charles, *The Assumption of Moses* (London: A. & C. Black, 1897) and *APOT,* 2:407-34, which abbreviates the earlier work.

20. Philip Schaff, *The Ante-Nicene Fathers* (electronic ed.; Garland, TX: Galaxie Software, 2000).

21. Richard Bauckham, *Jude and the Relatives of Jesus in the Early Church* (Edinburgh: T&T Clark, 1990), 235-80. Bauckham presents evidence for the existence of both the anti-Gnostic *Assumption of Moses* and the earlier *Testament of Moses,* arguing that Jude reflects the latter rather than the former. The Milan manuscript itself is translated by J. Priest in Charlesworth, *OTP,* 919-34. Bauckham also discusses the claim that 4QAmram lies behind the *Assumption* or *Testament of Moses.* However, since this document mentions Amram rather than Moses, does not use the phrase "the Lord rebuke you," and may or may not mention Michael, it clearly witnesses to a general Jewish tradition of disputes between the devil and an angel rather than to a specific source for our citation in Jude.

rabbinic "angels of the presence." Thus Michael is presented as a figure known to Jude's readers who is one of the chief angels of God.

Second, in our story Michael is involved in a dispute with the devil. There is a long tradition of disputes between the devil and angels, starting with the "angel of the LORD" in Zech 3:2 and stretching on through the Dead Sea Scrolls (CD 5:17-18; 1QS 3:18-25), pseudepigrapha (*T. Ash.* 6:4-6), and early Christian works (Hermas, *Man.* 6:2:1). This particular dispute involves the body of Moses. Thus Moses is already dead, and at issue is the disposition of his body. While Deut. 34:6 says that God buried him, by the time of the Greek translation of this text it was interpreted as "they buried him," probably indicating angels acting on God's command. Thus it would not surprise a reader of the Greek OT to discover the presence of Michael in this scene. What might surprise them a little would be the presence of the devil. The exact issue between Michael and the devil is not stated; we may presume that Jude expected his readers to be familiar with the story. Furthermore, the issue itself does not play a role in Jude, so it does not need to be mentioned explicitly.

Third, the point of the citation is the response of Michael. There are two parts to this response. The first is what he did not do, while the second is what, in contrast, he did do. What he did not do is "dare to bring a slanderous accusation against him." This is an extremely difficult phrase, which needs to be unpacked. The verb "to dare" appears sixteen times in the NT. It indicates taking a risk, and in particular a risk in terms of honor or shame. Thus in Matt 22:46 (par. Mark 12:34; Luke 20:40) people no longer dared to asked Jesus questions (which challenged his honor), for they saw what had happened in the previous instance. In Mark 15:43 Joseph risks his honor by going in and requesting Jesus' body from Pilate, as do the Philippians in preaching the gospel in Phil 1:14. In each of these cases people risked shame by stepping beyond the bounds of social propriety, but received honor from the writers of the respective books. In Acts 7:32 Moses does not dare, which indicates that he kept his proper place in relationship to God. Likewise Paul keeps his proper place in Rom 15:18; cf. 2 Cor 10:2, 12; 11:21. Thus Michael is pictured here as keeping his proper place, which contrasts with the angels of v. 6, who failed to remain in their proper place.

The phrase "to bring a judgment of slander" (to translate it literally) occurs in the NT only in here and in 2 Pet 2:11, which we believe is dependent upon this passage. The closest that the LXX comes is in Isa 42:3, but that passage does not include the critical term "slander" *(blasphēmia).* Thus it is unlikely that Jude is depending upon a text that we know. Two interpretations of our passage in Jude are currently argued. The first, argued by Kelly, is that of the NIV, "he did not dare to bring a slanderous accusation" against the devil. This fits into the context in that it would contrast with the actions of the false teachers who "slander *(blasphēmousin)* celestial beings." The problem with this is that (1) it is difficult to see how one *could* slander the devil, and especially in a situation in which he was opposing the command of God, and (2) it is not characteristic of Scripture to be considerate of the devil's reputation (cf. John 8:44; Acts 13:10; 1 John 3:8; Rev 12:9, all of which speak negatively of the devil).

The other interpretation, argued by Bauckham and Neyrey, is that of the NRSV, "to bring a condemnation of slander against him." This would be parallel to Acts 19:40, where the charge of rioting is mentioned.[22] While this interpretation does not fit the charges against the interlopers in the previous verses as well, which would mean that the verses are linked by a catchword connection, it does fit the flow of the argument. The false teachers slander angels, probably accusing them of foisting the law with its moral requirements upon Moses. By way of contrast, Michael, whose position was indisputable, when disputing with the devil in a narrative in which the devil was slandering the character of Moses, would not accuse this fallen angel, whom all agree is evil, of slander. In doing this Michael refused to overstep his proper boundaries and take the place of God in judging evil.

It is this latter position that appears to have the most evidence to commend it. First, it avoids the problem of having to figure out how one could slander the devil. Second, it provides a cogent reason for Jude's citing the particular incident that he does, namely, an incident in which the devil is slandering Moses. Third, it provides a counterexample to the false teachers in that Michael does not overstep his bounds on a topic on which his accusation would be justified, while they do overstep theirs in an area in which their accusations are not justified.

Jude's negative statement leads to a description of what Michael did do; he said, "The Lord rebuke you!" This phrase is itself a quotation of Zech 3:2. There in another judgment scene the Satan (the article indicates that in Zechariah Satan is the name of an office and not yet a personal name) stands ready to fulfill his function of accusing Joshua, who is present there in filthy clothing, indicating at least cultic impurity and possibly moral guilt. "The angel of the LORD" is also present, and he utters the phrase "the LORD rebuke you" and then informs Joshua that his

22. In both cases the substance of the charge is in the genitive, and thus the genitive does not describe the act of making the charge (slanderously, riotously) but the charge itself (judgment of slander, charge of riot). See BDF #178 on the genitive with verbs of accusing. (A genitive with a term of judgment can also indicate the punishment to which a person is condemned, as in Matt 23:33, or the object judged, as in John 12:31, or the one judging, as in 2 Thess 1:5.)

guilt has been removed. This phrase, then, is an appeal to the judgment of God. Rather than assert his own authority over Satan, Michael calls upon God to render the appropriate judgment. One cannot be further from the arrogance of the false teachers in their taking the place of God in their slanderous accusations against his angels.[23] Clearly, Jude, like James (4:11-12; 5:9), believes that judging others is totally inappropriate behavior for a follower of Jesus. They are to be like Michael, who refrains from such behavior.

**10** In contrast to Michael, who would not bring a justified judgment of slander against Satan, these (the emphatic "these" picks up from Jude 8 and is repeated in 12, 16, and 19 as Jude catalogues his accusations against the false teachers) teachers slander "whatever they do not understand," meaning the angels. Most likely they justified their behavior on the basis of some type of "higher" knowledge of the structure of the spiritual world (this reference to not understanding is probably not specific enough to refer back to the Sodomite ignorance of the angels who visited Sodom, as in *T. Ash.* 7:1). Far from displaying higher knowledge, Jude argues, they slander angels in their ignorance.

What they do understand is what they know by "instinct," like "unreasoning animals." Instinct (only here in the NT, although a cognate term appears in Rom 1:26-27 and 2 Pet 2:12) is often contrasted with rationality. That animals were "unreasoning" was considered a truth that pointed to their lower natures when compared with human rationality (4 Macc 14:14, 18 [even unreasoning animals love their young]; Wisd 11:15 [where plagues of irrational animals are the punishment for human beings' worship of irrational creatures]; Josephus, *Ant.* 10.262 [the lions in the story of Daniel]; *C. Ap.* 2.213); because sin was seen as unreasonable, it was at times compared with animal behavior (*4 Ezra* 8:29-30: "Let it be your will to destroy those who have the ways of cattle; but regard those who have gloriously taught your Law"). Thus these teachers, who probably claimed a higher spirituality, a higher knowledge, actually are ignorant of the true spiritual world; all that they really know about is their instinctual desires, probably referring to their sexual desires.

This situation is, of course, disastrous. Whether their source was

23. While H. C. Kee, "The Terminology of Mark's Exorcism Stories," *NTS* 14 (1968) 232-46, argues that rebuke (*epitimaō*) indicates a word of power that controls demonic forces and hence is used in God's eschatological subjugation of demons (*2 Bar.* 21:23; *Asc. Isa.* 4:18), this passage in Jude refers neither to the eschatological judgment of the devil nor to the use of a word of power. Rather, it recognizes that God is judge and that even an archangel should not usurp that judgment. In this sense Jude is more in line with later Jewish thought expressed in *The Life of Adam and Eve* 39:1 (12:1) (Then Seth said to the beast, "May the Lord God rebuke you. . . .") and *b. Kiddushin* 81a-b.

Jewish or Christian teaching, those in the early Jesus movement knew that the instinctual desires needed to be curbed. For the Jew they were influenced by the *yetser hara'*, or evil impulse, which needed control through the Torah. Paul was aware of the problem when he wrote Rom 7:7-12, calling it the "sin" that was in our "members" (which is where the Jews thought of *yetser* as dwelling; Jas 1:14 refers to it as "desire," as does 1 Pet 2:11 and 1 John 2:16-17), but Paul had discovered that the law, or Torah, far from solving the problem, only compounded the problem, revealing how out of control the human being really is. His solution is found in Rom 8:1-8, where the solution is the Spirit (James's solution is to ask for "wisdom from above"), who alone can control the human impulses.[24] These teachers, however, are justifying their instinctual desires, which desires are "the very things that destroy them," not meaning that they lead to some relatively immediate negative result (e.g., death from sexually transmitted diseases), but divine judgment (1 Cor 3:17, the one other place where this refers to divine judgment in the NT).

### 2. *Second Proof (vv. 11-13)*

*11 Woe to them! They have taken the way of Cain; they have rushed for profit into Balaam's error; they have been destroyed in Korah's rebellion.*

*12 These men are blemishes at your love feasts, eating with you without the slightest qualm — shepherds who feed only themselves. They are clouds without rain, blown along by the wind; autumn trees, without fruit and uprooted — twice dead. 13 They are wild waves of the sea, foaming up their shame; wandering stars, for whom blackest darkness has been reserved forever.*

**11** The reference to the destruction (through divine judgment) of the teachers he opposes leads Jude to break out into a woe oracle. While the term "woe" can be used in other contexts (Ps 120:9; Prov 23:29), its most frequent use is in prophetic oracles (including that in Num 21:29), especially in Isaiah and Jeremiah, where it expresses the sad situation of

24. See further P. H. Davids, *The Epistle of James* (Grand Rapids: William B. Eerdmans, 1982), 36 and the literature cited there. Jews did not think that instinctual desires (*yetser*) were in themselves evil, for they recognized that they belonged to physical life and thus were created by God. However, they were out of control, and thus, unless they were controlled, they would cause the person to step over God's boundaries and bring disaster. Likewise those in the early Jesus movement saw nothing negative in the body and its desires, and they could enjoy physical pleasure, but they recognized that when these were in control they did transgress God's boundaries, as they witnessed in the pagan world around them.

those under divine judgment (e.g., Isa 3:9, 11; 45:9-10; Jer 4:13, 31; 10:19, but note the ironic use in Jer 6:4). This form of speech was also used by intertestamental writers (Jdt 16:17; Sir 41:8-9; *1 Enoch* 92–105), Jesus (e.g., Matt 23:13-36; Luke 6:24-26; 11:42-52), and later Christian writers (*Barn.* 6:2). The form of the oracle here is unusual in that it says "Woe to them!" (as in Hos 7:13 in the LXX) rather than "Woe to you!" or "Woe to those who . . . !" but this form comes from Jude's addressing the church rather than the false teachers themselves. The oracle itself shows that Jude is at least copying a prophetic form, and probably that Jude is himself speaking prophetically.

Typically in such oracles the following clauses (introduced by the Greek word *hoti*) give (1) sins because of which the judgment is pronounced, and/or (2) the judgment that is coming upon the sinners. Such judgment is not necessarily eschatological; indeed, in the OT it was normally temporal. But the very form "woe" implies that there is some negative consequence coming upon those to whom it is applied (or who apply it to themselves); indeed, "woe" can be almost another word for judgment (Rev 8:13; 9:12; 11:14). If vv. 11-13 are taken as a unit, then Jude lists both the sins and the judgment.

The first charge is that "they have taken the way of Cain." The expression "have taken the way of" (or, more literally, "walked in the way of") is common in the Greek translation of the OT for following the moral example of someone, usually an ancestor (1 Kings 15:26, 34; 16:2, 19, 26; 2 Kings 8:18, 27; 16:3; 2 Chron 11:17; 21:6; Ezek 23:31). Thus these teachers follow the example of Cain. But what is the example that they are following? Is our author attributing murder to them? The answer is, Probably not. However, Cain's murder was viewed metaphorically as an example of hatred of one's brothers and sisters (1 John 3:11; *T. Benj.* 7:5; *1 Clem.* 4:7, "You see, brothers and sisters, jealousy and envy produced fratricide"). Other ancient authors go beyond this to see Cain not only as guilty of a variety of sins but also as one who taught them to others (Josephus, *Ant.* 1.52-62: "He excited his acquaintances to procure pleasures and spoils by robbery, and became a great leader of people into wicked courses . . ."; Philo, *De posteritati Caini* 38–39). In other words, not only were a variety of sins, including lust, attributed to him, but he was presented as one who taught such sins to others. Thus Cain as understood in Jewish tradition became a good picture of the activities of the false teachers.[25]

25. Bauckham, *Jude, 2 Peter,* 80, points out that in the targumic tradition Cain was also known as the archetypal heretic, in particular one who denied final judgment along with rewards for the righteous and punishments for the wicked. While at least some of this is clearly an anti-Sadducean polemic (so S. Isenberg, "Anti-Sadducee Polemic in the Palestinian Targum Tradition," *HTR* 63 [1970] 433-44), it might still pre-date Jude, for it is

The second charge is that "they have rushed for profit into Balaam's error." The OT presents a dual picture of Balaam. On the one hand, in Num 22:18; 24:13 he refuses to curse Israel for money. On the other hand, Deut 23:4 and Neh 13:2 present Balaam as being hired to curse and the Lord turning the curse into a blessing. Later Judaism certainly attributed greed to Balaam (e.g., *m. Abot* 5:22). More importantly, picking up on Num 31:16 (and perhaps the references in Num 31:8 and Josh 13:22, which place Balaam in Moab after his first encounter with Balak), Balaam was portrayed as the one who advised Moab to entice Israel to sin through fornication, that is, who was behind the incident of Baal Peor (Num 25:1-3). This concept is found throughout later Jewish tradition (e.g., Josephus, *Ant.* 4.126-30; Philo, *Vit. Mos.* 1.292-99; *b. Sanhedrin* 106a). Josephus puts it this way:

> (126) But Balak, being very angry that the Israelites were not cursed, sent away Balaam without thinking him worthy of any honor. Whereupon, when he was just upon his journey, in order to pass the Euphrates, he sent for Balak, and for the princes of the Midianites, (127) and spake thus to them: — "O Balak, and you Midianites that are here present (for I am obliged even without the will of God to gratify you), it is true no entire destruction can seize upon the nation of the Hebrews, neither by war, nor by plague, nor by scarcity of the fruits of the earth, nor can any other unexpected accident be their entire ruin; (128) for the providence of God is concerned to preserve them from such a misfortune; nor will it permit any such calamity to come upon them whereby they may all perish; but some small misfortunes, and those for a short time, whereby they may appear to be brought low, may still befall them; but after that they will flourish again, to the terror of those that brought those mischiefs upon them. (129) So that if you have a mind to gain a victory over them for a short space of time you will obtain it by following my directions: — Do you therefore set out the handsomest of such of your daughters as are most eminent for beauty, and proper to force and conquer the modesty of those that behold them, and these decked and trimmed to the highest degree you are able. Then do you send them to be near the Israelites' camp and give them in charge, that when the young men of the Hebrews desire their company, they allow it them; (130) and when they see that they are enamored of them, let them take their leaves; and if they entreat them to stay, let them not give

---

widespread in the targumic tradition. Yet this argument would at most show that the reasoning that Jude implies is that of the false teachers, namely, that they, like the Sadducees, did not believe in a final judgment and thus did not believe that there would be any punishment for doing evil. The texts cited do not present Cain as one who *taught* this and thus was a false teacher, only as one who believed this.

> their consent till they have persuaded them to leave off their obedience to their own laws and the worship of that God who established them, and to worship the gods of the Midianites and Moabites; for by this means God will be angry at them." Accordingly, when Balaam had suggested this counsel to them, he went his way.[26]

The error of Balaam, then, is the error of proposing moral entrapment for profit. Both motives (i.e., moral entrapment and the desire for profit) appear to be involved in Jude's condemnation of these teachers. The desire for financial gain, of course, is warned against elsewhere in the NT (e.g., 1 Tim 6:5-10), and its corrupting influence is not limited to the first century.

The third charge is that "they have been destroyed in Korah's rebellion." The name "Korah" appears in three different contexts in the OT. First, it appears in a positive context in the titles of eleven psalms, and so is associated with the temple officials mentioned in 1 Chronicles (1 Chron 1:35; 2:43; 6:22, 37; 9:19; 26:19), Levites who were responsible for music as well as other temple affairs. Second, it appears in a more ominous context as the name of several descendants of Esau (Gen 36:5, 14, 16, 18). However, even if its use in Esau's genealogy may be a foreshadowing, this reference in Jude is clearly to the Levite leader mentioned first in Exod 6:21, 24, who led a rebellion in Numbers 16 and so earns a final reference in Num 26:10-11. The rebellion itself associated Korah, who is from a different branch of the same Kohathite clan as Moses and Aaron, with the leaders of the tribe of Reuben. Their attack on Moses and Aaron is based on the charge that since the whole people of God is holy and had God in their midst, Moses and Aaron have usurped authority in setting themselves up as political and priestly leaders (Num 16:3). The text later makes clear that the issue for Korah was the exclusive reservation of the priesthood to Aaron's family (Num 16:10-11), while the issue for the Reubenite leaders was Moses' leadership (Num 16:13-14). The result of the challenge was that the leaders and their households were swallowed in an earthquake, while their followers were destroyed by divine fire (Num 16:31-35). Korah therefore became proverbial for a rebellious or schismatic person, not just in the Jewish tradition (Josephus, *Ant.* 4.14-21; Pseudo-Philo, *Biblical Antiquities* 16) but also in Christian tradition (*1 Clem.* 4:12; 51:1-4, although Clement mentions only Korah's associates Dathan and Abiram by name, not Korah himself).

The reference to Korah makes two points. First, the issue for Jude is that Korah *disputed* the authority of Moses. That is why Jude uses

26. Flavius Josephus, *The Works of Josephus* (Oak Harbor, WA: Logos Research Systems, 1997).

*antilogia* (dispute, contradiction) rather than *stasis* or *episystasis,* which the LXX, Josephus, and *1 Clement* use and which does mean "rebellion" or "sedition." Korah's failure in Jude's eyes was a verbal challenge to the authority and status of Moses and Aaron. As the Mishnah states, "And what is [a dispute] which is not for the sake of Heaven? It is the dispute of Korach and all his party."[27] This means that Jude is accusing the teachers he opposes of challenging the authority of at least the teaching of the Jesus movement (understood to be the teaching of Jesus), and likely of its leaders as well. Second, Korah was destroyed, and this is prophetically applied to the false teachers by asserting that they "have been destroyed" (Greek aorist tense, indicating an action looked on externally as a whole) in Korah's dispute. In order to emphasize this, Korah is moved from his chronological position in the list of three (chronologically he should come before Balaam) to last in the series, and the Greek word for "have been destroyed" is placed at the end of the verse. Cain was exiled and Balaam died in the context of a battle, but Korah's fate was public and dramatic. He went down into the ground, and so these teachers will go down, for Jude is implying that they will end up in hell.

**12** Having made his series of three charges characterizing the teachers by comparing them to notorious sinners in the past (all of whom were people who in one way or another apostatized from the truth), Jude now turns to their effect on the local community of the Jesus movement. As teachers they promise benefit to the community, but in fact they have no benefit to offer.

When the community gathers, they are "blemishes at your love feasts." Virtually the only type of meeting of the early Jesus movement that is described in Scripture and the literature of the second century is that involving a common meal. Here the meal is called "love" (the translation "love feasts" (pl.) is simply an attempt to get at the meaning of the plural of *agapē,* the Greek term for love; the idea that these are meals or feasts is understood from the context).

While some writers view these meals as something separate from the Lord's Supper or Eucharist,[28] we are not convinced that the evidence

27. *Abot* 5:17. Jacob Neusner, *The Mishnah: A New Translation* (New Haven and London: Yale University Press, 1988).

28. E.g., I. Howard Marshall, *Last Supper and Lord's Supper* (Grand Rapids: William B. Eerdmans, 1980), 127, argues that the meal and the "breaking of bread" were separate parts of the service in Acts 2, although on 144-45 he argues that by 1 Corinthians 11 the meal and the "breaking of bread" were integrated (cf. 130-31, where he cites a variety of theories held by various scholars). Larry W. Hurtado, *At the Origins of Christian Worship* (Grand Rapids: William B. Eerdmans, 1999), 84-85, views the whole meal as being cultic from the beginning.

supports that position. Instead, it appears to us that at least until A.D. 250, when the concepts of priest, sacrifice, and altar begin to appear with respect to the Eucharist,[29] the Lord's Supper was a reenactment of the Last Supper or the fellowship meals of Jesus and his disciples. That is, it was a common potluck meal with bread broken at the beginning and a cup of wine shared at the end (cf. Ignatius, *Smyrn.* 8:2; Hippolytus, *Apostolic Tradition* 26; *Epistle of the Apostles* 15).[30] We see this custom reflected in 1 Cor 11:20-22, where an abuse of the meal allowed social distinctions in the church to be underlined as the upper-class Christians ate and drank their rich food, leaving either only poorer food or scraps for the slaves and other lower-class folk in the church; this practice followed the normal social customs for a *collegia* (club).[31] However accepted the social custom might be in the Greco-Roman world around them, Paul is upset that rather than celebrating the unity of Christians (i.e., that they were one family), it reinforced social distinctions that belonged to the surrounding pre-Jesus humanity.

Here in Jude the problem at the meals is different: these teachers whom Jude opposes are a danger to the community. They are "reefs" or "rocks" (the term is used for rocks on the seashore that can wreck ships), and so not people with whom one wants to be in close proximity. In choosing *spilas* ("reef" or "rock") Jude may intend a wordplay with *spilos* ("blemish," the word that some commentators and translations, including the NIV and NRSV, believe our author intended) and so indicate that they are also a danger to the purity of the community. And since the meal was at least in part a reenactment of the Last Supper, where the participants were to be ritually pure and the animal "without blemish," it would be quite improper that such "blemishes" be present. However, this remains at the wordplay level. There is no textual evidence that Jude wrote anything other than "reef" (thus the NIV is misleading). The focus

29. As early as *Didache* 13, that is, the early second century, we discover that prophets who settle within a community are "high priests" for the community and so deserve the tithe. There is also one reference to the Eucharist as a sacrifice in *Did.* 14:1, although the concern there is that one not defile the communal meal through a lack of reconciliation with a fellow community member.

30. Cf. M. J. Townsend, "Exit the Agape?" *ExpT* 90 (1978-79) 356-71; Marshall, *Last Supper and Lord's Supper,* 110-11. See also R. J. Banks, *Going to Church in the First Century* (n.p.: Hexagon, 1980), which reconstructs such a meeting in narrative form. By Justin Martyr's time (A.D. 130-65, probably toward the end of this period) there is some evidence that the meal and the Eucharist, which had by now become a ritual, were separating, at least in some locations.

31. See E. Earle Ellis, *Pauline Theology: Ministry and Society* (Grand Rapids: William B. Eerdmans, 1989), 123-47, for an extensive discussion of the place of the Jesus movement in the social setting of the Greco-Roman world.

remains on the danger these teachers posed to the community. At the meal they "feast with" the community. The idea of feasting (*syneuōcheomai,* not the normal word for eating, *esthiō*) is not an issue. That is what the meal was for, since for many in the church it was likely the best meal of the week. In that sense it parallels the feast that would take place in the tabernacle or temple after a fellowship offering was offered. Feasting in the presence of the deity was the climax of both Hebrew and Christian worship. The problem is that these teachers are dangerous to have around, especially since the meal was the time when prophetic words and teaching were shared.

Many interpreters take the next term "fearlessly" ("without a qualm" in the NIV) with the feasting, indicating that they do it without appropriate fear of God, either in their attitude toward (and perhaps behavior at) the meal or in their failing to recognize the presence of God at the meal[32] (cf. 1 Cor 11:20-22, 33-34; for the use of *aphobos* [the term used here in Jude] as "irreverent," see Prov 15:15, LXX). While this interpretation does make sense, Jude appears to include the "feasting together" with the previous terms (in Greek *hoi . . . syneuōchomenos*" brackets "blemishes" and "your love feasts"); he also has a tendency to put adverbs before the participles they modify (Jude 3, 4, 8). Thus it appears more likely that he intends to communicate "fearlessly shepherding themselves." The meals of the church were intended as times of unity when Christians cared for one another. Jude has already stated that these people are leaders or teachers, and thus "shepherd" is an appropriate designation of their function (cf. John 21:16; Acts 20:28; Eph 4:11; 1 Pet 5:2; so also Ignatius, *Phil.* 2:1 and *Rom.* 9:1). Here Jude uses the image of "shepherd" taken from Ezek 34:2-3,

> "Son of man, prophesy against the shepherds of Israel; prophesy and say to them: 'This is what the Sovereign LORD says: Woe to the shepherds of Israel who only take care of themselves! Should not shepherds take care of the flock? You eat the curds, clothe yourselves with the wool and slaughter the choice animals, but you do not take care of the flock.'"

These teachers are out for their own profit (like Balaam), not that of the "flock"; their interest is in feeding themselves, which they do without fear of the consequences (i.e., without fear of God).

It is not that these people fail to contribute anything. They are teachers, so they certainly speak. However, Jude sees their teaching as promis-

32. Bauckham, *Jude, 2 Peter,* 86.

ing a lot and delivering nothing: "clouds without rain, blown along by the wind." This may allude to Prov 25:14, "Like clouds and wind without rain is a man who boasts of gifts he does not give."[33] In Jude's eyes the wind that blows them along is certainly not the Holy Spirit, as in John 3:8. Rather, it is either part of the imagery (that of a farmer who sees the wind bringing clouds which then blow right past without giving the hoped-for rain) or perhaps alludes to their being moved along by their desires, as in Jas 1:6.

This image and two of the following ones may well be influenced by *1 Enoch* 80 (especially since Jude will quote *1 Enoch* 1 immediately following this section). For instance, *1 Enoch* 80:2-6 reads,

> In respect to their days, the sinners and the winter [rainy season] are cut short. The seed(s) shall lag behind in their lands and in their fertile fields, and in all their activities upon the earth. He will turn and appear in their time, and withhold rain, and the sky shall stand still at that time. The vegetation shall slacken and not grow in its season, and the fruit shall not be born in its (proper) season. The moon shall alter its order, and will not be seen according to its (normal) cycles. . . . Many of the chiefs of the stars shall make errors with respect to the orders given

33. Bauckham argues that in his references both to Prov 25:14 and to Ezek 34:2 Jude is probably dependent on the Hebrew text, for the LXX of these passages expresses a different sense. Prov 25:14 LXX reads, "Like winds and clouds and apparent showers, thus is the one who boasts about a false gift," while a wooden translation of the Hebrew would be, "Mists (clouds) and wind and there is not rain, a person boasting in (of) a gift emptily." The sense of the two is not significantly different; Jude is, at any rate, only making an allusion to the passage. Turning to Ezek 34:2, one can read the Hebrew as "Son of man, prophesy against the shepherds of Israel, prophesy and say to them, to those shepherding, 'Thus says the Lord YHWH, "Woe, shepherds of Israel, <u>who are shepherding themselves</u>. Should not those shepherding shepherd the sheep?"'" The LXX reads, "Son of man, prophesy to the shepherds of Israel, prophesy and say to the shepherds, 'Thus says the Lord Lord [*kyrios* is repeated], "O shepherds of Israel, shepherds don't feed themselves, do they? Don't the shepherds feed the sheep?"'" In this case the Hebrew does continually play on the same root (shepherds/shepherding), including its participial form ("who are shepherding themselves"), while the LXX drops the wordplay and so uses a different root for shepherds than it does for feeding/tending/grazing. It could have kept the wordplay, for there is a verb for feeding or tending sheep that is cognate with the term for shepherd, but either for stylistic reasons (to avoid repeating the same root too many times) or perhaps differences in register or meaning in the dialect of the translators, it chose not to do so. In this case Jude does appear to know the Hebrew construction (underlined above), although such a conclusion is based on only two words that parallel the grammatical structure in the Hebrew text, those words being translations of the Hebrew, not direct citations of the Hebrew. In both cases it could well be that the phrases are proverbial rather than direct allusions to the Hebrew text. See the discussion in the Introduction of this commentary (p. 26).

> them; they shall change their courses and functions and not appear during the seasons which have been prescribed for them. . . .

The reference to lack of rain, trees not bearing fruit, and the stars changing course all fit with the description of these teachers, and the fit is especially good if we translate the beginning of the quotation with Bauckham, "in the days of the sinners," rather than the way E. Isaac has translated it in Charlesworth's *OTP.* However, knowledge of this background simply underlines rather than changes the point Jude is making: the "sinners" do not yield what they promise.

In Jude the disappointment in these teachers is further driven home with the image "autumn trees, without fruit." While some commentators view these as trees in late autumn past the time of fruit-bearing (Bigg, Kelly), the reference is more likely to the fact that one expects to find fruit on trees in the autumn (cf. Luke 13:6). However, these "trees" are fruitless. If a prophet is recognized by his or her fruit (Matt 7:15-20), these teachers are recognizable as false by their lack of fruit. Again using the prophetic present, Jude describes them as "uprooted" (equivalent to Jesus' "cut down" in Matt 7:19) and "twice dead." Mayor argues that this latter term refers to their being dead because they bear no fruit and then doubly so because they are uprooted in response, while Bauckham believes that the term refers to the "second death" (Rev 2:11; 20:6, 14; 21:8), which is an idea also found in the Targums.[34] However, while this is attractive, the reference is not to a "second death" but to "dying twice" (the Greek is a participle), which would lead one to lean toward Mayor's view. The "uprooted" is in the final emphatic position in the sentence, indicating the judgment awaiting those who now show by their fruit that they are really "dead." So certain is their "uprooting" that Jude can use an aorist participle, that is, a Greek tense that shows that he is viewing the event of their judgment as an accomplished act.

**13** Continuing his series of metaphors drawn from four spheres of nature — land (trees), air (clouds), sea, and heaven (stars) (paralleled in *1 Enoch* 80, quoted above, as well as possibly paralleled in *1 Enoch* 2:1–5:4)[35] — Jude now comes to the sea. Drawing an image from Isaiah, he

34. I. Abrahams, *Studies in Pharisaism and the Gospels* (second series; Cambridge: Cambridge University Press, 1924), 41-49; M. McNamara *The New Testament and the Palestinian Targum to the Pentateuch* (AnBib 27; Rome: Pontifical Biblical Institute, 1966), 117-25.

35. While Jude may well be conscious of the material in *1 Enoch,* especially since he quotes the verse right before *1 Enoch* 2:1, *1 Enoch* gives positive examples from the four spheres in 2:1–5:4. It is only in 80:2-8 that one finds the negative examples that are similar to those in Jude. Thus what *1 Enoch* appears to contribute most is the idea of taking examples from the four spheres.

calls the teachers "wild waves of the sea, foaming up their shame." In Isa 57:20 we read, "But the wicked are like the tossing sea, which cannot rest, whose waves cast up mire and mud." (Note that this last phrase, "whose waves cast up mire and mud," is extant only in the Hebrew, not in the LXX, a possible indication of Jude's knowledge of the Hebrew text, although Jude has "their own shame" instead of "mire and mud.") While not a people given to using lots of images from the sea, other Jewish writers also used this image. For example, in the Dead Sea Scrolls 1 QH 2:12-13 (10:12-13) contains the complaint, "The assembly of the wicked is roused against me, they roar like the turbulence of the seas when their waves beat and spew out ash and mud."[36] Here in Jude the teachers are the wicked; they are wild waves of the sea, restlessness being a characteristic of the wicked and the demonic (Jas 3:8, 16).[37] Like a stormy sea they spew out foam and debris, but at this point Jude drops the metaphor. What they are "foaming up" is "their shame." While the literature debates whether the "shame" is their deeds or their words, both could be in Jude's mind, for with these teachers there is no charge of inconsistency of word and deed. The important thing to note, however, is that they certainly did not name their deeds "shame." They surely considered them honorable, even enlightened, much as the person Paul cites in 1 Cor 5:1 surely did (and the church agreed with him, 1 Cor 5:2). Jude, however, is giving a prophetic denunciation, speaking of them from what he feels is God's perspective, and from that perspective what they call "honor" is "shame" indeed.

Moving on to his final image, Jude calls these teachers "wandering stars." While the image fits the "restlessness" of the previous image, it also picks up two other concepts. First, as a rule stars (which were thought to be guided by angels) remain in their courses and do not wander. Jude's phrase *(asteres planētai)* is the normal term for planets, which were originally thought to be stars that were wandering from their courses, although by Jude's time it was a case of a name sticking even after astronomers realized that the planets were regular in their movements.[38] A king wandering from the right way could be viewed as a

36. Cf. 1QH 8:15-16 (16:15-16), "But I have become the mockery of the raging torrents, which throw their mire over me."

37. For further discussion of the relationship between restlessness and the demonic, see the comment on the James verses in Davids, *A Commentary on the Epistle of James.*

38. See H. Braun, *"planaō," TDNT* 6:229. Cf. Cicero, *De nat. deor.* 2.51 ("Most remarkable, too, are the movements of the five planets, mistakenly labelled 'those which stray'; mistakenly, because nothing can be said to 'go astray' which through all eternity maintains in a steady, predetermined pattern its various movements forward, backward, and in other directions").

wandering or fallen star (Isa 14:12-15). More significantly, fallen angels could be viewed as fallen stars (Rev 9:1), and the Watchers of *1 Enoch* (the "sons of God" of Gen 6:1) are described in this way several times. "And the stars which roll over upon the fire, they are the ones which have transgressed the commandments of God from the beginning of their rising because they did not arrive punctually" (*1 Enoch* 18:15). Later we read, "These [seven stars bound in a chaotic place] are among the stars of heaven which have transgressed the commandments of the Lord and are bound in this place until the completion of ten million years . . ." (21:6). Similar images are repeated in other sections of the book (86:1, 3; 88:1, 3), with the added information that these "stars" are eventually thrown into "an abyss, full of fire and flame"(90:24). By using this image, then, Jude is comparing these teachers to the Watchers or fallen angels of *1 Enoch.* While these teachers were never angels, like them they had the "commandments of the Lord" and have departed from them.

Second, the accusation that they are "wandering stars" uses the term *planētai,* which reminds us again of Balaam (Jude 11, "Balaam's error"), since the Greek word for "error" is *planē,* a root frequently used to describe false teachers or false prophets (Matt 24:5, 11, 24; 1 Tim 4:1; 2 Tim 3:13; 2 Pet 3:17; 1 John 4:6; Rev 2:20; 13:14; cf. Matt 22:29; 27:64; Mark 12:24; John 7:12; Rom 1:27). Movement is good, but not when it is into error. They have rushed, not to obey God, but into Balaam's error; they are stars, but not shining where God has commanded them, but wandering or erring stars. The catchword connection ties together the two types of images, the nature images and the OT images.

Unlike those who remain true to God and will "shine like the stars in heaven" (Dan 12:3), for these teachers (like the fallen angels of *1 Enoch*) "the blackest darkness has been reserved forever." Truly, the end judgment of the fallen angels in *1 Enoch* is fire and their proximate judgment is darkness and chaos (*1 Enoch* 88:1), while in Jude the darkness appears to be eternal. However, the images of both fire and blackest or outer darkness are used by Jesus in Matthew as metaphors for final judgment (darkness: Matt 8:12; 22:13; 25:30; fire: Matt 25:41), and the darkness image was popular in Jewish literature (Tob 14:10; *Pss. Sol.* 14:9; 15:10). Sometimes they occurred together ("darkness, nets, and burning flame" [*1 Enoch* 103:7; *1 Enoch* 108:4]; "to the gloom of everlasting fire" [1QS 2:8]; "without end with the humiliation of destruction by the fire of the dark regions" [1QS 4:13]; "cruel darkness and lightless gloom . . . a black fire blazes up perpetually" [*2 Enoch* 10:2]; "[God] will also send the impious down into the gloom in fire" [*Sib. Or.* 4:43]).

Because his primary image is that of stars, Jude apparently finds eternal darkness the fitting contrast, as did Jesus in some contexts. In other contexts Jude, like Jesus, might well have chosen fire. The points these authors are making is not literal: they are describing the place of judgment as a place of utter isolation (darkness) and/or destruction or torment (fire). Whatever metaphors a writer uses for it, it is not a pleasant situation even to think about. Yet for such people the place of judgment is "reserved" or, more literally, "kept forever." If Jude knew the teaching of Jesus in Matt 25:41, this thought may have been triggered by his reference to these teachers as "wandering stars." That is, according to Jesus "the eternal fire" was created "for the devil and his angels"; it was never designed for human beings (even if the passage makes it clear that human beings will receive this fate although it was not *designed* for them). These teachers, by copying the behavior of the fallen angels, will receive the "reserved" *(tetērētai)* punishment designed for those fallen angels. Meanwhile there is also a "reserving" in Jude for faithful believers: they are kept *(tetērēmenois)* by Christ (Jude 1) and are at the same time to keep *(tērēsate)* themselves in God's love (Jude 21). Jude uses the same verb three times, twice for God's/Christ's action and once for human action. What a difference it makes as to which usage of reserving/guarding applies to any one of us!

### 3. *Third Proof (vv. 14-16)*

*14Enoch, the seventh from Adam, prophesied about these men: "See, the Lord is coming with thousands upon thousands of his holy ones 15to judge everyone, and to convict all the ungodly of all the ungodly acts they have done in the ungodly way, and of all the harsh words ungodly sinners have spoken against him." 16These men are grumblers and faultfinders; they follow their own evil desires; they boast about themselves and flatter others for their own advantage.*

**14** Having described his analysis of the behavior of the teachers he opposes, Jude seeks an ancient authority to back up his argument. We would have expected him to cite the Hebrew Scriptures, but instead he cites the work of *1 Enoch,* making the only explicit quotation in his book. Jude obviously believes that *1 Enoch* is authoritative in that he cites it as a prophecy ("prophesied"). Given the frequency of prophecy in the OT and, for that matter, in the NT Jesus movement, such language indicates that Jude believes that this is divinely inspired speech. Furthermore, he introduces it with a quotation formula (*legōn* in Greek, sometimes translated as "saying," but properly indicated in the NIV by means of the colon and quotation marks, which in English indicate that a direct quotation is beginning). That is how written sources, especially scripture, are cited in the NT. Did Jude, then, consider this scripture to be like Genesis or Isaiah? Certainly he did consider it authoritative, a true word from God. We cannot tell whether he ranked it alongside other prophetic books such as Isaiah and Jeremiah.

What we do know is, first, that other Jewish groups, most notably those living in Qumran near the Dead Sea, also used and valued *1 Enoch,* but we do not find it grouped with the scriptural scrolls. They at least thought of the first two divisions of the Hebrew Scriptures, the *Torah* (Pentateuch) and *Nevi'im* (Prophets, including Joshua–2 Kings as well as Isaiah, Jeremiah, Ezekiel, and the "Book of the Twelve") as in a different category of writing. Whether they would have included *1 Enoch* in the third division, *Kethubim* (Writings, including Psalms, Proverbs, Ecclesiastes, Ruth, Daniel, and 1 and 2 Chronicles) we do not know.

Second, for the most part canonical consciousness came later than the time of Jude. That is, while there had been discussions since the persecution of 169 B.C. as to which scrolls one could surrender to the authorities and which one should die for, there was no developed canon consciousness in the Second Temple Judaisms we know.[39] We know that the Sadducees viewed only the Torah as fully authoritative (so Jesus is reported to have used only the Torah [Pentateuch] in arguing with them in Mark 12:18-27). If there was a lectionary cycle in any of the synagogues during this period (a thesis that is possible but also debated), then the Torah reading was certainly the main reading with a reading from the *Nevi'im* being a secondary one — the *Kethubim* were probably read only at certain festivals. While the Jews did discuss the Hebrew Scriptures in Jamnia in A.D. 90, it was not a discussion of the canon but rather a discussion of *why* certain books were assumed to be holy ("defiling the hands").

It was Christians who started asking two questions in the second century: (1) which works should be bound together in a codex (book)? And (2) which works should be read in church (since most people could not read and so were dependent upon what was read in church) as reflecting the rule of faith? These were the questions that led to modern canon consciousness. Thus without visiting Jude's church or watching how he treated his various scrolls (assuming he personally owned any), we cannot tell whether he would have rated *1 Enoch* as one of the

39. By a "developed canon consciousness" I mean: (1) consensus on which books were authoritative or inspired, (2) in the case of the Hebrew Scriptures that they clearly indicate that all three groups (Law, Prophets, and Writings) were "closed," and (3) that they make a significant distinction between the closed grouping of Scripture and other writings. As I will argue below, at least one major group did not view two of the groups that would make up the Hebrew Scriptures as fully authoritative and other groups seem to have considered what we would now call noncanonical writings as authoritative.

Prophets or as one of the Writings. All we can tell is that he treats *1 Enoch* as authoritative and does not distinguish it in any way from the Hebrew Scriptures other than that he quotes *1 Enoch* and does not quote any of the scriptures that we have in our Bibles (whether our Bibles include only the thirty-nine books of the OT or also include the so-called Apocrypha, as the Greek version that was the Bible of the NT authors did[40]).

Setting aside the issue of the fact that Jude does cite *1 Enoch,* we notice that in citing the work Jude names Enoch and calls him "the seventh from Adam." That is, in Gen 5:3-20 we have the list: Adam — Seth — Enosh — Kenan — Mahalalel — Jared — Enoch. Counting both the first and last person in the list in typical Semitic style, one gets seven. This number was applied to Enoch in more than one Jewish text (e.g., *1 Enoch* 60:8; 93:3; *Jub.* 7:39, "When he was alive in his seventh generation"; and later *Lev. R.* 29.11, "Among generations, the seventh is preferred: Adam, Seth, Enosh, Kenan, Mehallel, Jered, and Enoch: 'And Enoch walked with God'"). Since seven was a significant number (while much later than our text, the meditation on seven in *Lev. R.* 29:11 illustrates this point), the number of perfection, Jude mentions it specifically to note the importance of Enoch and thus of what he prophesies, although he does not go into any other details about the history of Enoch.

The passage quoted in Jude 14-15 is from *1 Enoch* 1:9, at the end of the first chapter as we know the book today. The work in its totality is found only in Ethiopic, but it was composed in either Hebrew or Aramaic (there are debates over which was the language of composition or whether both were used) and our passage is also found in a Greek translation (Codex Panopolitanus), a Latin translation (Pseudo-Cyprian, *Ad Novatianum* 16), and an Aramaic fragment from Qumran (4QEn$^c$ ar = 4Q202). Unfortunately, the Aramaic text is rather fragmentary, for it begins the damaged scroll, the previous eight verses having completely disappeared. In its context in *1 Enoch* this passage comes right after a description of God's coming to reward the righteous. Jude and two versions appear at the top of page 78.

Which text Jude knew is debated. That is, he clearly had not read the Ethiopic, since it is a later translation, but had he seen something like the Greek version or only something like the Aramaic version, or did he know both? The evidence is unclear since we do not know when he is purposefully altering the text and when he is quoting it exactly. Yet, as

40. The NT authors make allusions to the material in such works as 1 and 2 Maccabees and Sirach, which is an indication that such works were part of their reading. It is also clear that, with some exceptions, they normally quote from the Greek version of the Scriptures. Thus it is not unreasonable to believe that their Scriptures included at least some of what we know as the Apocrypha.

| *Ethiopic/Greek*[41] | *Jude (NRSV)* | *Aramaic*[42] |
|---|---|---|
| Behold, he [= God] will arrive with ten million of the holy ones in order to execute judgment upon all. He will destroy the wicked ones and censure [or rebuke] all flesh on account of everything that they have done, that which sinners and the wicked ones committed against him. | See, the Lord is coming with ten thousands of his holy ones, [15]to execute judgment on all, and to convict everyone[43] of all the deeds of ungodliness that they have committed in such an ungodly way, and of all the harsh things that ungodly sinners have spoken against him. | [16][when he comes with] the myriads of his holy ones [to carry out the sentence against everyone; and he will destroy all the wicked] [17][and he will accuse all] flesh for all their [wicked deeds which they have committed by word and deed] [18][and for all their] arrogant and wicked [words which wicked sinners have directed against him] |

the comparison shows, there is good evidence that he knew something like the Aramaic version that we have, for there are places where his translation appears to show a better understanding of the Aramaic than the Greek version does, and yet he is close enough to the Greek version, especially in v. 15, that he most likely knew at least something close to it.[44] If Jude does cite the Aramaic of *1 Enoch,* it makes the argument that he knows the Hebrew text of the traditional Hebrew Scriptures stronger.

41. Translation from E. Isaac in *APOT* 1:13-14.

42. Translation from Florentino García Martínez, *Dead Sea Scrolls Translated: The Qumran Texts in English,* trans. W. G. E. Watson (Leiden: E. J. Brill, 1994), 250. The parts in square brackets [ ] are missing or unclear in the manuscript and have been interpolated by the editors. This shows the condition of the text. The numbers are the line numbers in the column on the manuscript, not "verse" numbers. The text cited is 4QEnoch$^{c}$ (4Q204 [4QEn$^{c}$ ar]), although 4QEnoch$^{a}$ (4Q201 [4QEn$^{a}$ ar]), lines 5-6, are similar but also lack the key verb.

43. The standard Greek text reads *pasan psychēn,* or "every soul," more idiomatically "every person" (backed by $\mathfrak{P}^{72}$ and א). However, significant fourth- and fifth-century manuscripts read *pantas tous asebeis,* or "all the ungodly," which would fit better in Jude. While on the principle of the more difficult reading one would prefer the text, the textual evidence is well enough balanced that the alternative reading is correct. It would be helpful if we knew whether any of the scribes knew *1 Enoch* and might have changed the reading in Jude to fit *1 Enoch,* for if we accept the alternative reading, Jude has edited the quotation in *1 Enoch* to fit his purposes.

44. See further Bauckham, *Jude, 2 Peter,* 94-96 and Vögtle, *Der Judasbriefe, der zweite Petrusbrief,* 71-77.

More important is the fact that he has altered the text. First, instead of "he" (which in context clearly means God) Jude has inserted "the Lord" (probably meaning Jesus) in line with a common early Christian practice of taking OT texts and interpreting them in terms of Jesus or his Parousia (Isa 63:1-6 in Rev 19:13, 15; Isa 66:15 in 2 Thess 1:7; Zech 14:5 in 1 Thess 3:13) or the interpretation of Psalms using "Lord" for the divine name to shift the image to Jesus. Second, instead of having "all flesh" stress universal judgment, he has focused the quotation on "all" (the "ungodly" of the NIV is not explicit in Greek, which means "every person"), allowing the focus to remain on the teachers whom he opposes. Third, he leaves out any reference to their destruction, which is a bit surprising since he mentions it elsewhere. Finally, he focuses on their words rather than on both their words and their deeds, for the sins he is most concerned with have to do with their teaching.

Looking at the text in greater detail, we see that the picture of God coming with his angelic hosts is drawn from Deut 33:2, "The LORD came from Sinai and dawned over them from Seir; he shone forth from Mount Paran. He came with myriads of holy ones from the south, from his mountain slopes." This is a poetic description of the Sinai theophany that begins the Mosaic blessing at the end of Deuteronomy. At Sinai the Lord was coming to bless his holy people (indeed, in the Hebrew text it is unclear whether the "myriads of holy ones" are angels at all, for in the next verse the "holy ones" appear to be his people, whom the Lord loves), but the verse is being used both in *1 Enoch* and (via *1 Enoch)* here as descriptive of the divine court coming for the final judgment. In his reading of *1 Enoch* Jude does not use the present tense used in the Greek version we have of *1 Enoch* and in the LXX of Deut 33:2, which would look at the event from within, as if it were unfolding before one, but the aorist,[45] which looks at the event as a whole, as something that is happening external to one's experience. This could place him closer to the Hebrew OT text, since there is a tendency to translate the Hebrew perfect with the aorist (if the word were extant in the Aramaic text of *1 Enoch,* it might also be a perfect), or it could indicate the certainty with which he views the event, that is, he sees it as a complete event.[46] Since English lacks a way to

45. Due to its fragmentary nature, we do not know what tense the Aramaic used, nor do we know whether the Aramaic is the version of *1 Enoch* that Jude knew. However, one suspects that he is reflecting that text, although he could be reflecting the OT text upon which it was predicated.

46. Since it speaks of a future event, it is likely a proleptic aorist. As Wallace, *Greek Grammar beyond the Basics,* 563, says, "The aorist *indicative* can be used to describe an event that is not yet past as though it were already completed." He goes on to comment on the next page, "An author sometimes uses the aorist for the future to stress the cer-

code this nuance of complete/externally observed or ongoing/internally observed action into the verb tense, a nuance found in both Hebrew and Greek, the NIV rightly focused on the fact that Jude views the passage as predictive and translates it accordingly ("is coming").

In *1 Enoch* God (understood christologically by Jude as "the Lord") comes with a host of angels. This picture of Jesus appears several times in the Son of Man sayings in the Synoptics: Matt 16:27 = Mark 8:38 = Luke 9:26; Matt 24:30-31 = Mark 13:26-27; Matt 25:31; Luke 12:8-9(?); cf. John 1:51(?). Bauckham argues that this picture is drawn from Zech 14:5, "Then the LORD [i.e., YHWH] my God will come, and all the holy ones with him." This is a judgment passage, and the shifting of "the LORD my God" to Jesus would not be unlike the NT, which expected Jesus as Messiah to do the judging in the final judgment. However, another passage may also have influenced this development. The Son of Man sayings themselves are probably using imagery from Dan 7:13 (Mark 14:62 and parallels certain intend this reference). Just a few verses earlier in Dan 7:10 we read, "A river of fire was flowing, coming out from before him. Thousands upon thousands attended him; ten thousand times ten thousand stood before him. The court was seated, and the books were opened." This is another judgment scene, this time describing the court of the "Ancient of Days." Given that three verses later the Son of Man appears to receive dominion in this context of judgment, it is quite possible that the images of the heavenly court in Daniel 7 were transferred to Jesus by the NT writers (e.g., 2 Thess 1:7; perhaps 1 Thess 3:13). Certainly, then, Jude had ample precedent in the sayings of Jesus and the context of the Jesus movement to apply this picture of the coming of God to Jesus.

**15** The purpose of this coming is judgment. While the term *krisis* itself (translated "judgment") does not necessarily indicate judgment (e.g., John 7:24 could be using the term to indicate discernment), in the idiom used here, "to make *krisis,*" it does. Thus the meaning is "to decide a question of legal right or wrong, and thus determine the innocence or guilt of the accused and assign appropriate punishment or retribution — 'to decide a legal question, to act as a judge, making a legal decision, to arrive at a verdict, to try a case.'"[47] Jude quotes *1 Enoch* because he is convinced that the verdict will be negative for these people. While the Gospel tradition points out that Jesus did not come to judge (e.g., John 3:17), it also states that he will judge at the final judgment (e.g., John 5:22, 27,

tainty of the event. It involves a 'rhetorical transfer' of a future event as though it were past."

47. Johannes P. Louw and Eugene A. Nida, *Greek-English Lexicon of the New Testament Based on Semantic Domains* (New York: United Bible Societies, 1988, 1989).

30). Thus the church now lives in the time of mercy and forgiveness (although sometimes Christians wrongly live as though they were the judges of the world and judgment had already started), but the church is also mindful that this time is limited and that dire consequences await those who persist in disobedience in the face of divine mercy.[48]

The Lord's specific concern in this judgment, according to Jude, is to convict ungodly people (in context meaning the teachers Jude opposes) of (1) ungodly acts and (2) harsh words spoken against him. The passage calls us back to Jude 4, where the teachers are labeled "ungodly" *(asebeis),* a root that appear three times in the quotation from *1 Enoch* and was perhaps the reason for using the passage (the other common word is "all," which appears four times, almost punctuating the passage). That is, these teachers are not only people whom he has already labeled and continues to label as "ungodly," meaning that they "live in a manner contrary to proper religious beliefs and practice,"[49] but people who are accused of both ungodly acts (Jude 4, 8) and harsh words (Jude 4[?], 8, 10).[50] *1 Enoch* accuses the fallen angelic beings repeatedly of "harsh words," which are always words spoken against God: *1 Enoch* 5:4 ("you have spoken slanderously grave and harsh words with your impure mouths against his greatness"); 27:2 ("those who speak . . . against the Lord and utter hard words concerning his glory"); 101:3 ("you utter bold and hard words against his righteousness"). This speaking harshly against God is Jude's major concern in selecting this verse to apply to the teachers he opposes, for it will be on their teaching that Jude chooses to focus in the next verse, perhaps because that was the most dangerous to the congregations to which he was writing. Behavior alone may simply be ungodly, but when it is taught as justified and even advocated and the authorities teaching otherwise are slandered, then it can be most dangerous to the health of others.

**16** Jude finishes this section by making three charges against the teachers he opposes. First, expanding upon the idea that these people speak harshly against God, he calls them "grumblers and faultfinders"

48. There are, of course, relatively immediate, present consequences for disobedience to God — such "judgment" God has not put off — but we are referring to the consequences that flow from the final judgment.

49. Louw and Nida, *Greek-English Lexicon of the New Testament Based on Semantic Domains,* §53.10.

50. The term means "harsh," "violent," or "strong" when connected to "winds" or "words" (John 6:60; Jas 3:4; cf. Matt 25:24), or "stubborn" when connected to "heart" (Rom 2:5; cf. Mark 10:5; 16:14; Acts 7:15; Heb 3:8, 13, 15; 4:7). Cf. Louw-Nida, *Greek-English Lexicon,* §§20.3 and 26.4. In terms of precedents for our text, Joseph speaks harshly in Gen 42:7, 30, LXX; in 1 Kgdms 20:10 (1 Sam 20:10, LXX) David wonders whether Saul will speak harshly to Jonathan; in 3 Kgdms 12:13 (1 Kings 12:13, LXX) Rehoboam answers the people harshly.

or, better, "people who grumble about their fate." The first term *(gongystai)* in what is actually a word pair (i.e., it is a pair with the second term) takes one back to Jude 5 and Israel in the wilderness (and perhaps Korah in Jude 11). When Israel had a hard time, the people murmured or grumbled (Exod 15:24; 16:2; 17:3; Num 14:2, 36; 16:41; 17:5), and while this grumbling was often verbally directed against Moses, God takes it as directed at him (Num 14:27; 16:11; 17:10; Deut 1:27; Ps 106:25). Our term in Jude is a form of the root used to translate this grumbling in the Septuagint, which root Paul also uses when referring back to Israel in the wilderness, "Do not grumble, as some of them did — and were killed by the destroying angel" (1 Cor 10:10).

The second term *(mempsimoiroi)*, which is not found anywhere else in either the LXX or the NT, refers to complaining about fate. While in its original context it is a pagan idea (the Fates being the gods that determined the lots of people), by the time of Jude it had already been used as something of a synonym for our first term. Philo, for example, uses it to refer to Israel in the wilderness (*Vit. Mos.* 1.181), "But when water failed them, so that for three days they had nothing to drink, they were again reduced to despondency by thirst, and again began to *blame their fate* as if they had not enjoyed any good fortune previously; for it always happens that the presence of an existing and present evil takes away the recollection of the pleasure which was caused by former good."[51] This term in Jude is an adjective modifying the main term, "grumbling."

What Jude is saying is that these people "grumble about their fate." Are they grumbling against their church leaders (like Jude), against their fate as created beings,[52] or against their fate in terms of God's (and especially Christ's) moral demands? While both the first and the last could be in view in terms of the parallels with Israel in the wilderness, the focus of the charge in the Enoch prophecy and in Jude 4 is that they speak against Christ ("the Lord" in Jude's version of the Enoch prophecy). They complain that the moral demands of the teaching of Jesus are inhuman or unfair or too hard, probably backing up their charges with reasons, perhaps even citations of the Hebrew Scriptures. Jude sees them as Israel in the wilderness, and he also sees the same fate in store for them, which should serve as a warning to those today who find the teaching of Jesus (when properly understood within the context of the first century) unfair or too hard, something to be modified or even ignored.

51. Philo Judaeus, *The Works of Philo* (Oak Harbor, WA: Logos Research Systems, 1997).

52. See Vögtle, *Der Judasbrief, der zweite Petrusbrief*, 79-80, who discusses the arguments of some who hold these to be Gnostic teachers and thus their negative fate of being embodied. Vögtle rightly dismisses this position as not finding support in context.

Jude's second charge is that "they follow their own evil desires" (while the text has simply "desires," the NIV interprets the term as implying "evil"). While "desire" can be good (Luke 22:15; 1 Thess 2:17) or bad in Scripture, to be controlled by or to follow one's desires is always bad. Jewish thought realized that desire (they called it *yetser*) was without boundaries, so one needed the law to control it. Jas 1:14-15 points out that desire without control leads to sin. Thus to follow one's desires is to end up sinning, often with the implication that sexual sin is involved (see also Rom 1:24; 6:12; 13:14; Col 3:5; 1 Thess 4:5; Titus 2:12; 3:3; 1 Pet 1:14; 2:11; 4:2-3). In making this reference to desire, Jude is repeating the claim that he made earlier about their ungodly deeds (Jude 4, 7-8, 15).

Finally, in chiastic fashion Jude returns to a version of his first charge, "They boast about themselves and flatter others for their own advantage." The first part of the clause is more woodenly translated, "They speak huge [words]" (the last term appears elsewhere in the NT only in 2 Pet 2:18, which is dependent upon our passage). In Theodotion's translation of Daniel this idiom is used in Dan 11:36 for arrogant speech against God. In other words, this charge appears to be a repetition of the type of charge we find in *1 Enoch* 5:4, 27:2, and 101:3 (all quoted above), which pairs two types of speaking against God (variously expressed). One immediately thinks of the Antichrist in Rev 13:5, but of course many others have dared to rise up against God and speak huge claims in his face (with or without recognizing that he existed and was listening). Thus the issue in this charge is not that these teachers are proud of themselves, but that they are making claims against God.

The last part of this charge is that they "show partiality for the sake of gain/favor." The first term ("flatter others" in the NIV) is common in the OT as a translation of the Hebrew for showing partiality (Gen 19:21; Deut 10:17; 28:50; 2 Chron 19:7; Job 13:10; 22:8; Prov 18:5), sometimes in a positive sense, but more often in a negative sense connected with taking bribes. In what way are they doing this? Could it be that like those in Jas 2:1-4 they are showing partiality toward the wealthier members of their church to gain their favor (and financial support)? Or are they currying the favor of the wealthier members of their community to gain acceptance of their teaching (i.e., acceptance is the "gain" or "favor" that they seek)? Or are they as teachers giving judgments from the law that favor wealthier members of their community in order to gain their favor or support?[53] In this case they are like those in *Test. Moses* 5:5, "For those who are their leaders, their teachers, in those times will become admirers of avaricious persons, accepting (polluted) offerings, and they will sell

53. Bauckham, *Jude, 2 Peter,* 99-100, argues for this last position.

justice by accepting bribes." Now if the *Testament of Moses* is the work alluded to by Jude in Jude 9, there would be a clear basis for this claim. Unfortunately, as mentioned above, the end of this work is missing, so we cannot tell whether Jude's information comes from this work or from another lost work (referred to as the *Assumption of Moses*). However, Jas 2:1-4 (noted above) may clarify this situation more than was obvious at first, for if R. B. Ward is correct,[54] then what James is referring to is a Christian court (cf. 1 Cor 6:1-6) and thus partiality in matters of judgment among church members. Furthermore, given that the idea of partiality itself is so often connected in the OT with taking bribes for giving judgments in someone's favor, the term itself adds some strength to the last position. That is, these teachers are so expressing their teaching as to gain the support of wealthier members of their community (picking up on the Balaam charge in Jude 11). Whether they had the authority to actually give judgments in their favor, we do not know. What it does look like is that Jude is accusing them of distorting the teaching of God (i.e., Christian ethics) to gain the financial support of members of the community who are listening to them. Thus what this final charge underlines is that in Jude's eyes one of the reasons for some of their teaching is financial gain, an affliction that is not uncommon in the church today.

## C. Body Closing (vv. 17-23)

### 1. *Final Prophecy (vv. 17-19)*

> [17]*But, dear friends, remember what the apostles of our Lord Jesus Christ foretold.* [18]*They said to you, "In the last times there will be scoffers who will follow their own ungodly desires."* [19]*These are the men who divide you, who follow mere natural instincts and do not have the Spirit.*

Jude has come to the closing of the body of his letter. At this point he turns from his description of the teachers and begins to address his readers. In doing this he forms an *inclusio* with vv. 3-5:[1]

54. Roy Bowen Ward, "Partiality in the Assembly: James 2-2-4," *HTR* 62 (1969) 87-97. This is a section from his Ph.D. dissertation, "The Communal Concern of the Epistle of James" (Harvard University, 1966).

1. As one sees, there is a common noun of address, a common title for Christ (which appears thirty-eight times in the NT, but in terms of appearances per length of a book Jude has the greatest number, 2 Peter being the next), and a common idea of remembering. The content of the remembering differs, although the faith once delivered to the saints surely included the prophetic messages of the apostles.

| Jude 3–5 | Jude 17 |
|---|---|
| *Dear friends* | *Dear friends* |
| *I want to remind you* | *Remember* |
| *The faith that was once for all entrusted to the saints* | *The apostles of our Lord Jesus Christ foretold* |
| *Deny our Lord Jesus Christ* | *Apostles of our Lord Jesus Christ* |

Thus Jude appears to be doing two things in this section. First, he is adding apostolic prophecy to the prophecy of Enoch predicting the coming of these teachers. In that sense this is a continuation of the previous section and not unlike the strategy used in 2 Pet 1:16-21 (where the apostolic testimony is added to prophecy that is presumably from the OT). Second, he is beginning his *peroratio* in that he is starting to exhort the believers and instruct them on how to behave. In the following verses several more key terms will be picked up from the beginning of the letter and applied to the conduct of his readers.

**17** Jude begins by addressing his readers ("you" is the first word in Greek) in contrast to ("but" contrasts two statements) his description of the false teachers. Now his readers, again addressed as "dear friends" (or "loved ones"; see Jude 3), are called back to active involvement. The letter has never lost sight of them, but they have been passive since v. 5 (while they are mentioned in v. 12, they are simply the people the teachers feast with). Now they are again in focus, and what these readers are to do is "remember." The function of the remembering is to give a final proof that the presence of the teachers he opposes is not something unexpected but part of the apostolic teaching, and thus forms an eschatological sign.

The readers are to remember "what the apostles of our Lord Jesus Christ foretold." That is, they are to remember prophetic ("foretold") sayings ("what" translates *rhēmatōn* or "sayings") of the apostles, one of which he is about to cite. The verb "foretold" is imperfect, suggesting the possibility that this type of teaching was something that the apostles said repeatedly. In this they are like Paul in 1 Thess 3:4; 2 Thess 2:5; 3:10. In each of these cases Paul uses the imperfect of a verb of saying to refer to predictions that he made while in Thessalonica. This warns us that (1) such a prediction may come true shortly after it is made, and that (2) the imperfect indicates a habitual theme rather than a long period of instruction (since Paul was in Thessalonica at most three months and perhaps as little as three weeks). Unlike Paul, Jude is not the one who gave the prophecy, but "the apostles." This is often taken as an indication that the author of Jude lives in the postapostolic generation in that (1) the apostles appear as a group, (2) Jude does not group himself with them, and (3) the apostles are mentioned as active only in the past. That, however, is only partially true. We need to examine the points one by one.

Point (2) may be true in that it does not appear that Jude groups himself with the apostles. However, the text is not conclusive on this point. That is, if certain apostles were the founders of the communities to which Jude writes and he was not among them, he would not group himself with those apostles. But it does not necessarily follow that he did not consider himself an apostle, just that he did not consider himself one of those responsible for that community. Yet, while Paul does refer to James as an apostle (Gal 1:19; cf. Gal 2:9), none of the other brothers of Jesus is referred to as an apostle. One could be a significant leader in the church without being an apostle. While this reference makes it look as if Jude does not group himself with the apostles, we cannot be certain given that we do not know the full historical context.

That the apostles appear as a group (point [1]) indicates only that the communities receiving this letter were not all founded by a single apostle or that Jude is referring to teachings or prophecies that were considered apostolic without being traceable to this or that apostle. Thus such teachings or prophecies might be referred to the apostles as a group. For example, no single apostle was the source of the teaching that Jesus had risen from the dead and ascended into heaven. Nor is a single apostle credited with the prophetic claim that Jesus would return.

Point (2) is true in that the activity of the apostles is indeed in the past, but we cannot tell how distant that past is. Paul could write in similar terms relatively soon after leaving Thessalonica. What Jude does indicate is that the apostles are no longer parts of the communities to which he writes. Their speaking is in the past, although it was a speaking to members of the community ("they said to you" in v. 18) rather than a tradition that the community had received through intermediaries.

What Jude is referring to is a common phenomenon in the early church, that of prophecy. In this case the speakers of the prophecy were apostles of "our Lord Jesus Christ" (the same Lord Jesus Christ that the teachers denied, Jude 4), who spoke this (and other) prophecies as part of the foundational teaching of the communities of which these believers are part. Thus the prophecy is also part of "the faith once delivered to the saints."

**18** The prophecy itself consists of three elements: (1) time ("in the last times"), (2) character ("scoffers"), and (3) lifestyle ("follow their own ungodly desires"). In terms of the time element, the prophecy is about "the last times," which means the times in which his readers were living since the prophecy describes people they were encountering. The expression itself is quite unusual in Greek, for normally we find the expression "the last days" (Acts 2:17; 2 Tim 3:1; Heb 1:2; Jas 5:3; 2 Pet 3:3 — note especially the first two and the last of these references) or "last day" (John 6:39-40, 44, 54; 11:24; 12:48), although we do find "last hour" (1 John 2:18), "last time" *(kairos)* in 1 Pet 1:5, and the "latter times" in 1 Tim 4:1 (also with *kairos;* cf. *Did.* 16:2; Ignatius, *Eph.* 11:1). Here we find "the last of time" (*chronos,* sing.; cf. 1 Pet 1:20, "last of times," pl.). In the Hebrew Scriptures we often find the phrase "the latter days" (Deut 4:30; 31:29; Isa 2:2; Jer 23:20; 30:24; 48:47; 49:39; Ezek 38:16; Hos 3:5), and this is frequently translated relatively literally in the LXX (Deut 4:30; 31:29; Isa 2:2; Jer 23:20; 25:19; 37:24; Ezek 38:16; Dan 2:28-29; 10:14; Hos 3:5; Mic 4:1). The NT often uses the LXX's translation, but also feels free to create parallel expressions at times, perhaps finding its own way of expressing the Hebrew.[2] The phrase itself was a flexible one for the future and thus not eschatological in itself,[3] but it certainly was used eschatologically by some first-century Jewish communities (CD 4:4; 6:11; 1QSa 1:1; 2 *Apoc. Bar.* 6:8; 41:5; 78:5) and by the early Jesus movement for both the coming of Christ inaugurating the last days (Heb 1:2; 1 Pet 1:20) and the future time of judgment and salvation (Jas 5:3; 1 Pet 1:5).

Here the prophecy is that in the end times certain events would take place, and in particular certain types of people would show up. In 1QpHab 2:5-6[4] we read (on Hab 1:15), "The interpretation of the word [concerns the trai]tors in the last days. They shall be violators of [the coven]ant who will not believe. . . ." We also find this type of eschatological denunciation in 1 Tim 4:1 ("in later times some will abandon the faith") and 2 Tim 3:1 ("There will be terrible times in the last days"). All of these have to do with circumstances that the writers and readers of this literature were experiencing at the time of the writing, identifying those experiences with the last days/latter times. Jude's prophecy is similar, and the presence of the false teachers is thus an indication that the community is living in "the last time." In this he again picks up on Jude 4, also echoing the frequent threats of judgment found throughout the book (5, 6, 7, 10,

2. Bauckham, *Jude, 2 Peter,* 104, argues that this is more evidence that Jude is reading the Hebrew Scriptures and not the LXX. But while Jude is clearly not dependent upon the LXX, given similar expressions in works that do not show signs of knowing the Hebrew text, it is more likely that this was simply a common expression in the early church.

3. G. W. Buchanan, "Eschatology and the 'End of Days,'" *JNES* 20 (1961) 188-93. See especially the uses in Deuteronomy, which are noneschatological.

4. The parts of the quotation in square brackets [ ] represent tears or holes in the scroll. The text in those places is reconstructed from context, other copies of the document or remaining bits of letters on the edges of the tear or hole.

15). How near did Jude view this day of judgment as being? We do not know. He certainly expected it to overtake these teachers whom he opposes, but the text is not clear about how quickly he expected the event to happen. Still, he views himself as living at the climactic point of eschatological tension.

Rather than characterizing those who are coming as false teachers or false prophets (a type of denunciation that is common enough in the NT; see, e.g., Matt 7:15; 24:11; Mark 13:22; Acts 20:29-30; 1 Tim 4:1-3; 1 John 2:8; 4:1-3), this prophecy designates them as "scoffers." The root itself appears only in biblical Greek, with the same term appearing in Isa 3:4 LXX, 2 Pet 3:3 (probably because of this passage), and here. The scoffer in the Hebrew Scriptures is the person who despises religion and the morality based on it. Where the idea appears we find actual mocking (Pss 42:3, 10; 79:10; Jer 17:15), usually in terms of "Where is . . . ?" and we find a term for such a person, that is, "scoffer." The scoffer is not an atheist (an abstract position that is more modern than ancient), yet the scoffer does not believe that God will judge, or at least that God will judge him or her for what they are doing, and so feels free to indulge in behavior that others see as immoral. In 2 Pet 3:3-4 the scoffers explicitly reject the Parousia of Christ and the concomitant judgment ("Where is this 'coming' he promised?"). In our passage we do not know why they feel justified in rejecting traditional moral teaching (which included teaching on a final judgment), but the issue for Jude is their behavior rather than its justification.

Jude has already described their lifestyle in v. 16, namely, they follow their own desires. Here he adds a descriptor to "desires" not found in the previous passage (which has no descriptor in Greek), which is "ungodly." This term *(asebeiōn)* picks up the *1 Enoch* passage, which uses the root repeatedly. Is this term what made Jude select this prophecy, or has he chosen this term to translate the prophecy into Greek? Either way it is clear that he wishes to identify those *1 Enoch* condemns with those whom the apostles predicted would come. The expression is awkward, but it is paralleled in Hermas, *Vis.* 3:7:3, where a similar construction refers to "evil desires." The prophecy allows Jude to keep his focus on the antinomian lifestyle of these teachers. They betray themselves, not so much by what they say and certainly not by what they think, but by what they do. We in our age would do well to remember that those who claim commitment to Jesus must live as he lived. Claiming to "be saved" without following the way of the King is, according to Jude, simply ungodliness — or he might be happy to call it demonic nonsense.

**19** The apostolic prophecy ends with v. 18, but Jude goes on to comment upon it. He addresses first the effect of the teachers he opposes on the church, and then their nature.

As to their effect on the church, "these are the men who divide you." The Greek term for "divide" is found only here in all of biblical literature and is rare in Greek as a whole. Some scholars note that it was used by Aristotle in his *Politics* (4.4: "as, if we wished to make a classification of animals, we should have to begin *by setting aside* that which all animals have in common") in the sense of "defining" or "making a distinction" in order to classify, a usage that is found in some post-NT literature as well (Maximus Confessor 2.103d, 131c; Severus, *Clyst.* 32.25).[5] However, another use of this term meaning "to separate" is found in *Corp. Herm.* 3:2a, where it indicates "the separation of the upper from the lower elements in the creation of the cosmos."[6] If the former meaning were chosen, then Jude would be talking about Gnostic or proto-Gnostic teachers classifying Christians according to whether they were spiritual or simply "soulish." If the latter were chosen, then Jude would be indicating that these teachers are dividing the church. This cannot be a division that has led to outright separation since the teachers are still taking part in the Eucharist along with those whom Jude considers faithful (Jude 12). Yet one can build a recognizable clique without outright separation (as has happened, e.g., in 1 John 2:19). 1 Corinthians 1 refers to cliques formed within the church, and Jas 3:14, 16 cites "party spirit" as one of the key vices he is combating. In neither case is there outright separation.

It is difficult to decide between the two meanings, and indeed they shade into each other (for if one says, "We are this and they are that," it usually either leads to or results from the fact that the person making the statement is meeting with the "we" group and in one way or another is drawing a boundary between it and the "they" group). However, it is clear that the early Jesus movement did struggle with schism. While the Jesus movement itself was either a group within or a split from the synagogue (e.g., Acts 19:9), there were times when the Jesus movement tended to split internally (Gal 2:12; both this text and Acts 19:9 use *aphorizō,* which is related to the term Jude uses). There may have been a prophetic expectation of such schism. Joachim Jeremias, for example, cites an agraphon or non-Gospel saying attributed to Jesus (contained in Justin, *Dial.* 35.3) that predicts such events: "There will be dissensions *(schismata)* and squabbles *(haireseis).*"[7] Paul certainly would have agreed with this, for in 1 Cor 11:18 he notes that "there are divisions *(schismata)*

5. Mayor, *The Epistle of St. Jude and the Second Epistle of St. Peter,* 47-48.

6. Bauckham, *Jude, 2 Peter,* 105.

7. Joachim Jeremias, "Isolated Sayings of the Lord," in in E. Hennecke, ed., *New Testament Apocrypha* (London: SCM, 1963), 1:88. We have no idea whether Jude knew about this saying, but if he did, then it may be in his mind when he refers to the teachers separating people.

among you," and then he goes on in the next verse to say, "there have to be differences *(haireseis)* among you." It seems that for Paul the divisions are God's eschatological sign as to who is approved by God or not. Here in Jude it looks as if the divisions in the church are functioning in that way as well, but there the leaders are disputing which group has God's approval. The teachers Jude opposes certainly did not say, "We are denying the Lord and going to destruction. Follow us!" Rather, they must have said, "We have true insight, and Jude and his group do not. Follow us!" Jude, of course, is arguing a contrary opinion.

Jude's argument against the teachers he opposes comes down to its nub when he discusses their nature. Jude states that they "follow merely natural instincts (*psychikoi,* or "soulish") and do not have the Spirit *(pneuma mē echontes).*" There is a consensus among commentators that Jude's language comes from his opponents. That is, they claimed to have the Spirit, and because of that were free to behave as they did. However, what they or Jude means by these terms is open to discussion. Naturally, if one believes that those Jude opposes are Gnostics, then this is evidence that they made the pneumatic-psychic distinction known in some later Gnostic literature.[8] This distinction, however, appears to be a second-century derivative from Paul (1 Cor 2:14-15),[9] and so even if one argued that this is the distinction that Jude is arguing for, one still does not know where along the continuum that starts with Paul and extends to the second century Gnostics he or she should locate Jude. While Paul himself does use this terminology, scholars are not sure where he gets it. Certainly something like this language was known in Hellenistic Judaism. For instance, Philo, *Leg. alleg.* 3.247 uses it. The problem is that in Hellenistic Jewish literature it is far more common that mind *(nous)* is contrasted with soul *(psychē)* as the higher element in a person than that spirit is contrasted with soul. There is not even a clear distinction between soul and spirit in Hellenistic Jewish literature. Thus it appears that Christians introduced this form of the distinction because they were aware of the presence of the Holy Spirit within them.[10]

8. The problem is, as Vögtle, *Der Judasbrief, der zweite Petrusbrief,* 90-91, points out, that there is no evidence that these people believed that they had received some form of higher spiritual revelation, for language for revelatory experiences is lacking in Jude, nor is the full Gnostic schema of the Valentinians (*pneumatikos — psychikos — choikos,* the latter term meaning "earthly" or "out of earth" and thus totally unable to obtain salvation) present. In other words, it is highly unlikely that this language comes from Gnostic opponents.

9. B. A. Pearson, *The Pneumatikos-Psychikos Terminology in 1 Corinthians* (SBLDS 12; Missoula, MT: Scholars Press, 1973), ch. 6.

10. So Bauckham, *Jude, 2 Peter,* 106.

Furthermore, Jude does not use Paul's term "spiritual" *(pneumatikos)*, but only the term for "soulish," and that term is found elsewhere in the NT only in Jas 3:15, "Such 'wisdom' [in contrast to God's wisdom 'from above'] does not come down from heaven but is earthly *(epigeios)*, unspiritual *(psychikē)*, of the devil *(daimoniōdēs)*." In this passage in James we see the reason for Jude's use of his terminology. The teachers he opposes claim to have the Spirit and probably claimed that their licentious behavior was justified by the presence of the Spirit in them. Jude disputes that. He does not go as far as James and call them "demonic" (although he certainly might have had the question been put to him), but he does say that they are "unspiritual" or "follow mere natural instincts" rather than the Spirit. And to underline this he expands and says that they "do not have the Spirit." He appears to disqualify them from using their own terminology of being "spiritual." This, then, is not the Gnostic terminology of the second century or an indication of a tripartite anthropology held by Jude, but a rejection of the claims of his opponents to have the Spirit.

How the teachers he opposes used their claim to possess the Spirit we do not know. Did they think that their possessing the Spirit brought them superior insight that allowed them to rise beyond the "petty moral distinctions" that Jude's followers were convinced were right? Or did they believe that they received revelations from the Spirit (although, as noted above, revelatory language is not used, other than the single reference to "dreamers" in Jude 8) that pointed to a different, divinely revealed ethic? Or did they think that their ability to teach was a spiritual gift? We do not know. What we do know is that Jude looks at their behavior and says, "They do not even have the Spirit; everything they say and do comes from the human level, not from anything beyond it." Furthermore, it was also clear to the early Jesus movement that if one did not have the Spirit, he or she was no true follower of Jesus Christ (Rom 8:9; 1 Cor 12:13; cf. the importance of the presence of the Spirit in Acts and the importance of divine wisdom in James). Thus at this point Jude has totally disqualified these teachers, not just from teaching but also from being considered followers of Jesus. He knows that not everyone who calls Jesus Lord, or has had a conversion experience, or has prayed the "sinner's prayer," or has had spiritual experiences is in fact a true follower of Jesus. One recognizes the true followers by their obedience to their Lord.

## 2. *Closing Exhortation (vv. 20-23)*

*20But you, dear friends, build yourselves up in your most holy faith and pray in the Holy Spirit. 21Keep yourselves in God's love as you wait for the mercy of our Lord Jesus Christ to bring you to eternal life. 22Be merciful to those who doubt; [23]snatch others from the fire and save them; to others show mercy, mixed with fear — hating even the clothing stained by corrupted flesh.*

Jude has finished his condemnation of the teachers he opposes. With the apostolic prophecy he rests his case. Having delivered his warning and proved his thesis (the thesis of Jude 3-4), he closes his letter with an exhortation to his readers.

**20** Jude repeats verbatim the address to his readers we found in v. 17 ("But *you,* beloved," would be another translation). There he exhorted them to remember an apostolic prophecy about the teachers, a prophecy of which he believed the readers were aware. Now he wants to talk to his readers, not about the teachers. Interestingly enough, he does not instruct his readers to do anything about the teachers (e.g., "Kick the heretics out!"), but rather focuses on what they should do about themselves. Only secondarily does he instruct them what to do about those the teachers have led astray. This is indeed instructive for those facing errant teaching in a modern context.

Grammatically his only imperative is to "Keep yourselves in God's love."[11] There are three participial clauses that modify this command, telling them how to live it out: (1) "build[ing] yourselves up in the most holy faith," (2) "pray[ing] in the Spirit," and (3) "wait[ing] for the mercy of our Lord Jesus Christ to bring you to eternal life." Possibly all four are to be read as commands, that is, the so-called imperatival use of the participle, but, if so, we must still keep in mind that the one true imperative is the core of the sentence and thus the central command.

In structural terms there are several interesting features to these verses (see the table at the top of p. 93). First, we notice that they resume topics mentioned in the opening verses of the letter. What becomes clear is the deliberateness with which Jude picks up themes from the opening of the letter as he comes to close the letter. Yet this is not mere repetition; there is also a shift. While in the opening Jude was in the indicative mood — they are kept and they are loved — now he is in an imperative mood: keep yourselves in God's love. That is, divine action and human respon-

11. Vv. 20 and 21 are one sentence in Greek. They are retained as one sentence in the NASV (following the ASV), NKJV (following the KJV), and the NET Bible, resulting in some rather awkward English. The ESV (following the RSV) also keeps the two verses in one sentence, but at the cost of changing the participles into imperatives, so one loses the sense of what is the main thought and what are the modifications. Most modern translations (such as the NIV) break the sentence into two (or even three) sentences, usually at the verse division, which makes for far more readable English. German translations do not have this problem given the structure of German.

| | Term | Term in vv. 20-21 | Comment |
|---|---|---|---|
| v. 1 | Kept (by Jesus) | Keep (yourselves). | Shift to their responsibility |
| vv. 1, 2 | Loved (by God) | (God's) love | Keep yourselves. |
| v. 2 | Mercy (= beloved) | Mercy (of Jesus) (= beloved) | This mercy received becomes the mercy they show in vv. 22-23. |
| v. 3 | Dear friends | Dear friends (= beloved) | This address clearly signals a major transition in the letter. |
| v. 3 | Faith (once for all entrusted) | (Most holy) faith | |
| v. 3 | Saints (holy ones) | Holy (faith) | Shift from people to the faith |

sibility are both clearly stated by this single author within one short letter. (We should note now that he will move back to divine action in the closing doxology, where the focus is again on God.)

Second, there is a double trilogy here: faith — love — waiting (a paraphrase of hope)[12] and Holy Spirit — God — Lord Jesus Christ. Now it is true, as we have seen, that Jude loves sets of three, but one strongly suspects that these groups were influenced by the traditional groupings in the tradition of the Jesus movement.

The exhortations themselves are quite traditional, shared by Jude with many others in the church. "Build yourselves up" comes from the picture of the church as a temple. Paul uses the same verb in 1 Cor 3:10, 12, 14; Eph 2:20; and Col 2:7, although the image of the temple or house that must be built goes far beyond the use of this particular verb (e.g., Matt 16:18; Acts 9:31; 15:16; 20:32; 1 Pet 2:5; *Barn.* 16:8-10; Ignatius, *Eph.* 9:1; Polycarp, *Phil.* 3:12; 12:2).[13] So traditional is the usage that one won-

12. A. M. Hunter, *Paul and His Predecessors* (London: SCM, 1961²), 33-35, argues that this trio is a pre-Pauline formula. This is surely correct, as Bauckham, *Jude, 2 Peter,* 112, also argues.

13. Such references are, of course, part of a theme in the Jesus movement that goes back to Jesus himself, his critique of the Jerusalem temple and his prediction of its destruction. Just as he replaced the temple for his movement during his life, so his followers viewed their community as replacing it afterward (since Jesus was in the community by the Spirit), and especially after its destruction. The eschatological vision of Revelation is of a renewed earth without a temple, but rather with God in the middle of the commu-

ders whether the building metaphor has been forgotten, as it has when in English we use the term "edify" and do not realize that it originally had to do with building an "edifice." What is clear is that the building is collective. It is not that the individual follower of Jesus is to build himself or herself up, but that the follower(s) of Jesus (individually or together) is (are) to build the community of Jesus up. This building up contrasts with the activities of the teachers Jude opposes, who divide or split the community (Jude 19).

Christians are to build the church "in your most holy faith" or "with respect to your most holy faith." This "most holy faith" may be thought of as a foundation, as Bauckham argues,[14] but it may also be thought of as the building material. Again our author implies a contrast with the teachers he is opposing. The most holy faith belongs to his readers (it is *your* faith); they are the ones who need to fight for "the faith once for all entrusted to the saints" (Jude 3). This contrasts with the work of the teachers who have not kept the faith, but have departed. Furthermore, the faith is holy (as are the people to whom it is entrusted), but the teachers are anything but holy, as Jude's description of their lifestyle has indicated. The holiness of the faith, since it comes from God (the only source of holiness in the NT), contrasts with the ungodliness of the teachers who have denied Jesus Christ. Naturally, as in most NT contexts, "faith" means primarily a commitment, not a body of data believed, and it is precisely their commitment to Jesus as "our only Sovereign and Lord" (or, if a hendiadys, "our only Sovereign Lord") that Jude wants his readers to pursue and that the teachers have abandoned, since such a commitment requires obedience.

The next exhortation is that they should "pray in the Holy Spirit." This concept appears in the Gospels (John 4:23-24) and the Pauline writings (1 Cor 14:15-16; Eph 6:18). The last reference is especially close to our passage, "Pray in the Spirit on all occasions with all kinds of prayers and requests." Yet the first reference in Paul is also important, for in it Paul contrasts praying in the Spirit (i.e., in tongues) with praying with one's mind, arguing for the value of both in appropriate contexts. What this shows is that praying in the Spirit is in line with the usual sense of doing

---

nity of his people. See further N. T. Wright, *Jesus and the Victory of God* (Minneapolis: Fortress, 1996), 405-38.

14. Bauckham, *Jude, 2 Peter,* 113. He contrasts building on the foundation of the faith with building on the foundation of Jesus Christ (1 Cor 3:11). But Paul's metaphor is much more flexible than that, for in Eph 2:20 it is on the foundation of the apostles and prophets that the church is built. This image is close to that of Matt 16:18, where Peter is the rock upon which Jesus will build his church. A living metaphor is used by each writer in a way appropriate for his situation; it is not technical language.

something in the Spirit (Mark 12:36, prophecy produced by the Spirit; Acts 19:21, travel directed by the Spirit; Rom 14:17, joy produced by the Spirit; 1 Cor 12:3, speech controlled by the Spirit; Eph 5:18, controlled by alcohol versus controlled by the Spirit), which means that it refers to prayer *controlled* or *guided* by the Spirit. That the Spirit inspires true prayer is a much larger theme in the NT (cf., e.g., Rom 8:26-27, which follows from Rom 8:9, where the Spirit controls the Christian's life in general). That this prayer can be both rational and transrational (i.e., glossolalic) is also clear in the NT. We have no other information about the practices of Jude's community, but, given that the one place where Paul explains the phrase he does so in terms of glossolalic prayer (praying in tongues) and the widespread experience of glossolalia in the NT period according to both Paul and Acts, J. D. G. Dunn is probably correct when he writes, "A reference to charismatic prayer, including glossolalic prayer, may therefore be presumed for Jude 20."[15] Again the contrast with the false teachers is clear. While Jude's readers are empowered by the Holy Spirit, since they can pray in the Spirit (as opposed to praying in a merely human manner) as indicated by glossolalic prayer,[16] the teachers Jude opposes are devoid of the Spirit (Jude 19). They cannot do what Jude's readers can do, for, despite probable claims to the contrary, they are not properly equipped.[17]

**21** The central exhortation in this series (or in this sentence, if we think in terms of the Greek text) is that they should "keep [themselves] in

15. J. D. G. Dunn, *Jesus and the Spirit* (London: SCM, 1975), 245-46. Paul seems to assume the gift of tongues in 1 Corinthians 12–14; that is, its presence is not unusual. The problem in 1 Corinthians is that it got out of hand. So in 1 Cor 14:15-16 he defines praying in the Spirit by contrasting it with praying with the mind. Acts points to the experience of glossolalic prayer in Jerusalem (Acts 2), Caesarea (Acts 10), and Ephesus (Acts 19). Thus one would be hard put to argue that Jude's community would not at least include prayer in tongues under this phrase.

16. While the only other occurrence of the expression "praying in the Spirit" is to glossolalic prayer (as we indicated), and as an outward manifestation of the activity of the Spirit this would be a visible sign of praying in the Spirit, we do not want to limit praying in the Spirit to this one phenomenon, significant as it is. Surely from the viewpoint of spiritual theology various forms of contemplative prayer, including the prayer of silence, singing in worship (when inspired by the Spirit — many worship songs and hymns are sung prayers), and other forms of prayer can be and are Spirit-inspired, although perhaps in a less outward and visible way.

17. Given that some non-Christian religions also experience glossalalia, one cannot say that glossalalia per se divided those Jude addresses from the teachers he opposes (although it may have). But one can say that if those he opposed exhibited glossolalia or engaged in glossolalic prayer, Jude would not have attributed the phenomenon to the Spirit since on the basis of their lifestyle he believed that these teachers were devoid of the Spirit.

God's love." As we have seen, Jude 1 has already stated that God loves Jude's readers. Jude has also said in the same place that Jesus Christ keeps or guards them. Now he commands them to be actively involved in remaining in God's love. Is this love to be taken as a subjective genitive (God's love for us) or an objective genitive (our love for God)? While some commentators (e.g., Cantinat) opt for the latter as more in line with the idea of "keeping," that is, we can control our own behavior but not that of God, most commentators rightly opt for the former. This is partly on the basis of Jude 1 (where the construction is different, indicating that Christians are the object of the love) and partly on the basis of parallel ideas in the NT. God's love for us is often a topic of NT rhetoric (e.g., Rom 5:5; 8:39). However, a number of passages indicate a need for active involvement in maintaining that love relationship. For instance, in John 15:9-10 we read, "As the Father has loved me, so have I loved you. Now remain in my love. If you obey my commands, you will remain in my love, just as I have obeyed my Father's commands and remain in his love." Here in John as in Jude we have a situation in which the believers are already loved but still need to remain in that love. The way to do so is then explained. In 1 John 4:16 we read that God is love and loves believers, but they also need to "remain" in love. Thus here Jude is indeed balancing v. 1; they have experienced God's love, but it is possible to depart from that love, as one sees in the case of the teachers he opposes. They too were bought by the Lord, but now they deny him (Jude 4). Thus it is important that these Christian readers watch out so that they remain in their place and do not leave it, as the fallen angels in Jude 6 left theirs.

The final exhortation in our series, one which gives the context of the previous one, is to "wait for the mercy of our Lord Jesus Christ to bring you to eternal life." Waiting involves eschatological hope, for, as we will see, mercy is something experienced in the future rather than in the present. In the OT we find the command to wait in Hab 2:3, "For the revelation awaits an appointed time; it speaks of the end and will not prove false. Though it linger, wait for it *(hypomeinon auton);* it will certainly come and will not delay."[18] Many other texts in the OT also encourage waiting: Isa 30:18 ("Blessed are all who wait for him"); 49:23 ("Then you will know that I am the Lord; those who hope in me will not be disappointed"); 51:5 ("The islands will look to me and wait in hope for my arm"); 64:4 ("who acts on behalf of those who wait for him"; LXX Isa 64:3,

18. See A. Strobel, *Untersuchungen zum eschatologischen Verzögerungsproblem auf Grund der spätjudisch-urchristlichen Geschichte von Habakuk 2,2ff.* (NovTSup 2; Leiden: E. J. Brill, 1961), part 1, for the use of this text in Christian and Jewish eschatological expectation.

*ha poiēseis tois hypomenousin eleon* ["which you do to those waiting/enduring for mercy"]); Dan 12;12; Mic 7:7 ("I wait for God my Savior; my God will hear me"); Zeph 3:8 ("'Therefore wait for me,' declares the LORD"). While some of these passages were not eschatological in their OT context, others (e.g., Dan 12:12; Zeph 3:8) definitely are, and still others were interpreted eschatologically by the Jesus movement and parts of later Judaism. In the NT as a whole the idea of eschatological waiting is clearly expressed: there are those pious Jews waiting for God to act on behalf of Israel (Mark 15:43; Luke 2:25, 38; 23:51), and there are those waiting for a specifically Jesus-centered hope (Acts 24:15 ["I have the same hope in God as these men, that there will be a resurrection of both the righteous and the wicked"];[19] Titus 2:13 ["while we wait for the blessed hope — the glorious appearing of our great God and Savior, Jesus Christ]").[20] Each of these references uses the term found here in Jude (there is also a noneschatological use found in Acts 23:21 and Phil 2:29). While Christians are not often commanded to wait, waiting, using the term found here in Jude or any of several others, is the context of their existence "between the times" in this age.[21]

While various passages refer to different aspects of the coming of Christ that they are waiting for, in our passage the Christians are waiting for "mercy" that will "bring you to eternal life." Mercy is a term that is found in salutations (1 Tim 1:2; 2 Tim 1:2; 2 John 3), but also refers to the motive for God's saving action (Titus 3:5; 1 Pet 1:3), present assistance from God (Heb 4:16), and mercy in the Day of Judgment (Matt 5:7; 2 Tim 1:18). Usually it refers to mercy from God, but, given that the Jesus movement viewed judgment as being Christ's action at the end of the age (cf. John 5), in some passages as here the "Lord" who grants mercy is Christ. Our passage is clearly eschatological in that one is *waiting* for this mercy. Furthermore, this mercy is "unto eternal life" (a more formal equivalent translation than the NIV). That is, this is the type of mercy at the return of Jesus out of which he will grant eternal life (the life of the age to come) to his followers. Having said that, we realize that the translation "mercy" may itself be misleading. In English it may imply that one is crying out for favor (often undeserved favor) and does not know whether he or she will receive it, such as a prisoner asking a judge for mercy. However,

19. The statement quoted in Acts 24:15 could have been said by members of many Jewish sects, not just that sect that was committed to Jesus (and that appears to be its apologetic intention), but (1) the hope of the resurrection is not something that every Jewish sect believed in, and (2) given its wider context in Paul's teaching in Acts, in this case hope for the resurrection is connected to the resurrection of Jesus.

20. See also 2 Pet 3:12, which may well be dependent upon this passage.

21. For some of the other terms see Bauckham, *Jude, 2 Peter,* 114.

mercy's use in our passage is closer to the Hebrew *hesed,* which it often translates in the Greek OT (see the LXX of Gen 24:12; 40:14; Exod 20:6), or *hen* (Gen 19:19). The first term often carries the idea of covenant faithfulness, and the second the idea of (often deserved) favor, such as a king showing appropriate favor to a faithful citizen. Thus in Heb 4:16 it is not that one hopes that God will go beyond the line of duty and show mercy, but that one comes to God confident that one is in good standing because of Jesus and thus expects to experience his favor (translated "mercy"). Likewise in our passage with respect to the Day of Judgment; one is waiting for this day since one expects to receive the Lord's favor and enter into eternal life. Mercy is not something that we have already received, for the final judgment has not yet happened. But the image is that of coming before the lord one has faithfully served, confident that one will receive the reward that he has promised.

There is a stark contrast here with what has been said about the teachers Jude opposes. They too will come to judgment, but there is no hope of mercy for them. They will be judged and convicted (v. 15); the blackest darkness is reserved for them (v. 13), they have been destroyed (v. 11), and, it is implied, they will receive the punishment of eternal fire (v. 7). When it comes to his readers, Jude does not even use the term "judgment," but simply implies it in the term "mercy" (for in that culture in a time of judgment a king both punished his enemies and rewarded his followers). They have something worth waiting for (in fact, in other contexts the Greek term used here for "waiting" can mean "welcome"). There is every reason to keep themselves in the love of God, for by so doing they assure a bright future for themselves in contrast to that of the teachers who live for today and, despite what they may say, have no hope for the future.

**22** Having exhorted his readers how to behave in general and encouraged them as to their hope, Jude finally turns back to the issue of the teachers he opposes and their followers. How should his readers treat these people? Are they to be hated, fought, feared, or simply shunned? Jude implicitly rejects all of these approaches (so common in contemporary attitudes toward teaching considered to be false and misleading) and argues for a much more positive response. However, before we can discuss the response, we need to be aware that the text of these two verses is very uncertain.

It takes only a glance at the English translations to make this textual uncertainty clear (see p. 99). Each of these translations is based on a different reading of the NT textual evidence. The first and the last have the strongest textual evidence. While not adopted by any major translation, the last reading (i.e., two short lines) is supported by more than one mod-

| *Version* | *Translation* |
| --- | --- |
| NIV (also NLV, GNB, RV, NRSV) | Be merciful to those who doubt; [23]snatch others from the fire and save them; to others show mercy, mixed with fear — hating even the clothing stained by corrupted flesh. |
| RSV (also ASV, JB, NEB margin) | And convince some, who doubt; [23]save some, by snatching them out of the fire; on some have mercy with fear, hating even the garment spotted by the flesh. |
| KJV | And of some have compassion, making a difference: [23]And others save with fear, pulling *them* out of the fire; hating even the garment spotted by the flesh. |
| NEB (also TEV [1966], JB margin) | There are some doubting souls who need your pity; snatch them from the flames and save them. There are others for whom your pity must be mixed with fear. |
| Bauckham (also Moffatt) | Snatch some from the fire, but on those who dispute have mercy with fear, hating even the clothing that has been soiled by the flesh. |

ern commentator as well as by ancient manuscripts.[22] The first reading (i.e., three short lines) is the choice of most translators and commentators.[23] The fact is that one has ancient and widespread evidence on both sides of the argument, and both sides can explain how the other text forms arose if their chosen text was the original. This is one of the places in the NT in which scholars simply cannot state with any assurance what the original text was. We, however, are opting for the text translated by the NIV, for it makes the most sense in the context of Jude (and fits his predilection for threes) and most easily explains the origin of the other textual forms.[24]

22. Besides Bauckham, *Jude, 2 Peter,* 108-11, Neyrey, *2 Peter, Jude,* 85-86, follows this reading, supported by 𝔓[72] (which is the most ancient witness); Clement of Alexandria, *Strom.* 6.8.65; and some of the Latin, Syriac, and Sahidic versions.

23. Besides being the choice of many older commentators, it is also the choice of Vögtle, *Der Judasbrief, der zweite Petrusbrief,* 102-5. It is supported by א and comes close to the text in A and B (B is missing the relative and conjunction that would make it read the same as א), both of which latter readings probably arose from it. The Byzantine textual tradition and the Vg follow it, as do the latest editions of the United Bible Societies and Nestle-Aland texts.

24. In our view the *elenchete* of A is a corruption of the *eleate* of א, for having spoken of convicting in the sense of condemning in v. 15, it is unlikely that he would use that

Jude, then, is instructing his readers to do what they can to rescue those who have erred or are attracted by the doctrines of the teachers he opposes. While the teachers have been roundly condemned, their followers are to be rescued rather than ostracized. The three groups mentioned are probably not, strictly speaking, separate groups, but rather three ways of describing people in need of rescue.

The first descriptive approach to such people is "Be merciful to those who doubt." Mercy is what Christians are wished (Jude 2) and what they are expecting to receive (Jude 21). Thus it is appropriate that they show mercy rather than judgment to others. Judgment is left to Jesus (or in some epistles God) at the end of the age; Jesus' followers are called to demonstrate mercy and forgiveness in the present. Those to whom they show mercy are those who "doubt." This term can mean "arguing" or "disputing" as in Jude 9,[25] but in that case the text should mention with whom they are arguing. It can also mean "discerning" or "discriminating," as in Matt 16:3; 1 Cor 6:5; 11:29; and 14:29, but in such a case the text expresses an object that one is to discern. When used without the disputant with whom to argue or the object to judge or discern, the term means that the argument is going on inside the person, and he or she is in inner conflict or doubt, as in Acts 10:20; 11:13; Rom 14:23; Jas 1:6. That appears to be the use here. It is to people in such inner turmoil that one is to show mercy.

Mercy is indeed a core Christian virtue; Jesus taught it (Matt 5:7; Luke 6:36; 10:37), and later writers emphasize it (Jas 2:13, which appears in a context of showing mercy instead of judgment). The church has often preferred judgment to mercy, but that is not what the Scriptures teach, for there followers of Jesus are told to show to others the mercy that God has

---

strong term for those who merely doubt (which is the normal meaning of *diakrinō* when used without an object). The version in 𝔓72 probably arose by haplography, the triple use of *hous* and the double use of *eleate* causing a scribe in essence to leave out a line and then skip back and combine the end of the first line with the final line. Of course, damage to an early manuscript — perhaps even the original — could have contributed to such a problem.

25. While Bauckham, *Jude, 2 Peter,* 115, follows the reading of 𝔓72, which would read more smoothly without, it does have the participle we are translating "those who doubt." Bauckham understands it as meaning "those who dispute" or "argue," that is, "those who continue to argue in support of their antinomian behavior." It is not clear why Bauckham believes this interpretation fits the context better than "those who doubt," and he gives no clear reasons. J. N. Birdsall, "The Text of Jude in 𝔓72," *JTS* 14 (1963) 398, argues for the meaning "those who are under judgment," that is, excommunicated, as in 1 Cor 5:3-5. However, in no other passage in the NT is this term used with this meaning. Nor is there any indication in the text that the teachers have been excommunicated. Far from it, one of the problems is their shameless presence at the common meals (Jude 12).

already shown to them. So in Jude some are doubting, not sure who is right. Rather than condemning them for their uncertainty about the truth or their entertaining the possibility that the teachers whom Jude opposes could be right, Jude calls for mercy, being gracious toward them and showing the same type of acceptance and love that God shows.

**23** While the doubters may not have been sure who was right and thus may have held back from committing to either set of practices, some were already getting involved with the practices of the teachers Jude is opposing. Jude's counsel is to "snatch" them "from the fire" and "save them." While some see Amos 4:11 as background ("'I overthrew some of you, as I overthrew Sodom and Gomorrah. You were like a burning stick snatched from the fire, yet you did not return to me,' declares the LORD"), the picture in this case is probably drawn from Zech 3:2, for in the Amos passage judgment is still coming (Amos 4:12). In Zechariah we read,

> [1]Then he showed me Joshua the high priest standing before the angel of the LORD, and Satan standing at his right side to accuse him. [2]The LORD said to Satan, "The LORD rebuke you, Satan! The LORD, who has chosen Jerusalem, rebuke you! Is not this man a burning stick snatched from the fire?"
>
> [3]Now Joshua was dressed in filthy clothes as he stood before the angel. [4]The angel said to those who were standing before him, "Take off his filthy clothes."
>
> Then he said to Joshua, "See, I have taken away your sin, and I will put rich garments on you."
>
> [5]Then I said, "Put a clean turban on his head." So they put a clean turban on his head and clothed him, while the angel of the LORD stood by.

There are three elements here that appear to influence our passage: (1) "snatched from the fire," (2) "filthy clothes," and (3) deliverance instead of judgment (the whole passage being a judgment scene and the LORD refusing to condemn but rather choosing to remove the impurity of the priest). In the NT context in which Jude was living the fire of judgment (Jude 7) had become a fairly consistent image. John the Baptist speaks of the judgment of fire in Matt 3:10 (= Luke 3:17), and Jesus refers to the fire of Gehenna in Matt 5:22; 13:40-42; 18:8-9; 25:41; Mark 9:47-48 (cf. Matt 7:19; Luke 17:29). Paul and other writers employed the image more rarely (1 Cor 3:13; Heb 10:27; Rev 20:14-15; cf. 2 Pet 3:7), but they do indeed use it. Thus the "fire" to which Jude is referring is that of final judgment or, perhaps, the destruction that follows judgment. It is not that they are already in hell (so Windisch), but that they are, so to speak, teetering on its edge. The first-century Jesus movement expected the return of Jesus, and thus the final judgment, at any moment. It was seen as a near rather than a distant event. As a result, those who are erring are in great danger that that judgment will catch them unprepared. In Jude's picture the flames of judgment already lap around their feet; one must snatch them away before they are fully in flame and lost forever.

This, of course, is precisely the attitude of the NT in general toward those who stray. Matt 18:15-17 is not talking about how to judge fellow Christians, but how to restore them. It is only when all attempts to appeal to them have been rejected that the church reluctantly recognizes that they are on the outside, not the inside, of the community of Jesus. Luke 17:3-4; Gal 6:1-2; 2 Thess 3:14-15; 1 Tim 5:20; Titus 3:10 all show the church more ready to restore the erring than to exclude them, although boundaries must be drawn for those who insist on their error. Jas 5:19-20 sums this attitude up as well as any, when it indicates that turning a sinner (i.e., one of the followers of Jesus who has "wander[ed] from the truth") from his or her error will "save him [or her] from death" (i.e., the result of God's judgment) and cover many sins. There is in James no goal of publicly exposing or shaming people (although they might feel personal shame once they realized that they had sinned), no interest in making them examples so that others will learn, simply the desire to turn them from their error. That brings salvation from death. That desire to bring salvation is probably the purpose of James as a whole.[26] In our text we find the same attitude in Jude.[27]

Jude then introduces a third group to which one should "show mercy, mixed with fear." Whether those in this group are to be sharply

26. Jas 5:19-20 is the purpose statement of James. See further Davids, *The Epistle of James*, 26, 198-201.

27. Neither Jude nor James refers to what to do with "those who persist in sin" (1 Tim 5:20, NRSV — the present participle is translated as a customary present), whom the community tries to rescue but who refuse rescue. At some point the community must "rebuke [them] before all" (cf. 1 Corinthians 5) to put the lie to the idea that their behavior is compatible with commitment to Jesus. But the key term here is "at some point." Matt 18:15-20 describes a process of trying to rescue an individual, first privately, then with a small group, and finally through the appeal of the whole community. As in Jude, the point of Matt 18:15-20 in context is rescue, bringing a wandering sheep back, gaining a brother or sister. But it recognizes that we are not always successful and eventually, out of love for the willful wanderer as well as to protect the rest of the flock, we must declare to the person where he or she is, that is, outside the kingdom. This process, however, should not be hurried. One hopes as long as possible that one is still dealing with miscommunication and misunderstanding. Public rebuke and exclusion are the last resort, the point at which only one who lived in denial of human willfulness could still affirm that the person was not knowingly and deliberately choosing to act in rebellion against Jesus.

differentiated from the second group is not at all clear. In rhetoric of this type one may pile images together, the one showing the goal (rescue) and the next showing the attitude (mercy mixed with fear). What is clear is that this third group is clearly involved in the sins of the teachers since the image "clothing stained by corrupted flesh" may well refer back to Jude 8. One would think that such people were beyond hope, yet again Jude says, "Show mercy."[28]

This mercy is to be "mixed with fear." What are they to fear? Three suggestions have been made: (1) God's holiness, (2) God's/Christ's coming judgment, and (3) the polluting nature of sin. Kelly suggests that the fear is the awe of God that appears frequently in the OT and in such NT texts as 1 Pet 1:17 ("Since you call on a Father who judges each man's work impartially, live your lives as strangers here in reverent fear").[29] Certainly that is a relevant attitude, but it does not explain why showing mercy in particular should be "in fear." It is too general an attitude to explain this passage. Bauckham, on the other hand, argues that it is "fear of judgment," noting the contrast to the fearlessness of the teachers (Jude 12).[30] Certainly fear of judgment is an attitude that is referred to in the NT. Heb 12:21 is picked up in Heb 12:28-29, where God is depicted as a "consuming fire." It was fear of judgment that motivated Noah in Heb 11:7. And the expectation of judgment is fearful (Heb 10:27; cf. 4:1). Clearly, fear of judgment lies behind Jude 23. Yet even if fear of judgment is in the background, it does not seem to be in the foreground. Again we must ask why fear (of whatever type) is connected to showing mercy. The key appears to be in the final phrase, which states that one is to hate "even the clothing stained" by the flesh. That is, in showing mercy to those who are sinning it is quite possible to get drawn into their sin. Thus Jude advises showing mercy in fear. One is working on the edge of the fire, so to speak. Not only are those being rescued at risk, but the rescuers are also endangering themselves. Sin is deceitful enough that those trying to help others could themselves get

28. This statement has bothered some commentators, who have in turn conjectured that some other term (*ekbalate,* "throw them out," or *elasate,* "drive them out") must have been in the original than "show mercy" *(eleate).* The state of preservation of these verses in particular makes such a suggestion possible. Yet there is almost no evidence in the manuscripts that we have to justify such a change in wording. It is at the first "have mercy" (Jude 22) that some manuscripts (although not the earliest) read "rebuke" *(elenchete)* — the very few manuscripts that read "rebuke" for the second "have mercy" (Jude 23) have probably displaced it from the earlier position because they too thought that Jude was being too soft on these people. See further Vögtle, *Der Judasbrief, der zweite Petrusbrief,* 107.

29. Kelly, *The Epistles of Peter and of Jude,* 289.

30. Bauckham, *Jude, 2 Peter,* 116.

trapped. That is no reason not to "show mercy," but every reason to have fear.

This mercy-with-fear is to be characterized by "hating even the clothing stained by the flesh" (we are deliberately leaving out the NIV's interpretive addition of "corrupted"). This is a difficult statement precisely because it is probably metaphorical. Does it indicate the lack of bodily care of the wandering teachers Jude opposes?[31] Or is he talking about the libertine practices of his opponents? Could he be using the Gnostic language of his opponents?[32] Or is it a reference to a folk belief that the nature of a person impregnated his or her clothing with either healing (Mark 5:27-29; Acts 19:11-12) or damaging consequences, and thus that contact with one living in a "fleshly" way was dangerous?[33] Certainly the Gnostic theory seems untenable, for "flesh" is not contrasted with something else, such as "spirit," nor is the "clothing stained by flesh" contrasted with other clothing (as in *Acts of Thomas* 111 [line 62 of the poem; cf. line 72 and the wider context]; 125 [where "dirty garments" means sexual relations]). The idea that clothing in some way receives the nature of the person appears to take a metaphor literally (i.e., Rev 3:4 uses our expression as a metaphor, not as a literal description), as does the assertion that this refers to the lack of cleanliness of the wandering preachers. Bauckham is certainly right in arguing that the picture is taken from Zech 3:3-4, although his reference to the person's inner garment being stained by excrement strains the idea of a wordplay with Hebrew.[34]

What appears to be the case is that the image of dirty clothing = sin in Zechariah has been combined with Jude's own reference to these teachers polluting their own "flesh" (Jude 8) to produce the image here. Zechariah indeed says nothing about "flesh," yet the image of bodily de-

31. Gerhard Sellin, "Die Häretiker des Judasbriefes," *ZNW* 77:3-4 (1986) 223-24. There were certainly wandering philosophers such as some Cynics for which this was true.

32. Schrage, *Der zweite Petrusbrief, der Judasbrief*, 239.

33. Vögtle, *Der Judasbrief, der zweite Petrusbrief*, 106-7. He suggests that the implication is that of excommunication, that is, that one have no contact with such a person. He also cites Rev 3:4 ("a few people . . . who have not soiled their clothes"); *Mart. Pol.* 13:2 ("because each of the faithful was always zealous, which of them might the more quickly touch his flesh"). The latter mentions touching a holy person's body, not his clothing, and thus is not relevant, while the former has our expression as an idiom for sin to be contrasted with white festival clothing.

34. Bauckham, *Jude, 2 Peter*, 116. He is following F. H. Chase, "Jude, Epistle of," in J. Hastings, ed., *Dictionary of the Bible*, rev. ed. by F. C. Grant and H. H. Rowley (New York: Scribner's, 1963), 2:799-806. The argument is that the word for "filthy" in Zechariah is related to the terms for excrement or vomit found in Deut 23:14; 2 Kings 18:27; Prov 30:12; Isa 28:20; 36:12; Ezek 4:12. Thus the "stained clothing" in Jude is an interpretation of the "filthy clothes" of Zechariah as clothing stained by the body (i.e., "the flesh").

sires as those of the flesh was common enough in the NT. It is a Pauline image, but far more than simply a Pauline image (John 1:13; Gal 5:16-19, 24; 6:8; Eph 2:3; Col 2:23; 1 Pet 2:11; 1 John 2:16). Sometimes the phrase "desires of the flesh" is used, and sometimes simply "flesh." The metaphor indicates human drives that lack control and therefore physical and especially sexual sin. The "clothing" referred to by Jude is a specific article of clothing, the *chitōn*, the inner of the two articles of clothing in everyday use. Since it was worn constantly and next to the skin, it was quite likely to be stained by the body, as is a T-shirt today. The image in Jude, like that in Rev 3:4, arises quite naturally as a live metaphor. The metaphor itself was suggested by Zechariah, either directly or indirectly (if Rev 3:4 is enough to indicate that the metaphor was common in the first-century Jesus movement). The concept of "sin of the flesh" imposed itself on the garment image to create a garment stained by the flesh. In Zechariah the high priest is delivered from judgment with the order to change his clothing. Here people are also to be rescued, and their "clothing," meaning their sins, are to be "hated" and left behind. Such an image combines well with that of showing mercy "mixed with fear."

Does this "mixed with fear" indicate a distancing oneself from people? Does it mean that one should pray for them but have no personal contact with them (Vögtle)? Does the image of "hating the clothing" add to this impression? It is true that when people were excommunicated there was to be only limited contact with them, as we see in Matt 18:17 ("treat him as you would a pagan or a tax collector"); 1 Cor 5:11 ("you must not associate with anyone who calls himself a brother but is sexually immoral or greedy, an idolater or a slanderer, a drunkard or a swindler. With such a man do not even eat"); Titus 3:10 ("Warn a divisive person once, and then warn him a second time. After that, have nothing to do with him").[35] Yet all of these passages apply to people who are excommunicated. In Jude even the false teachers themselves still partake in the communal meal that was the Lord's Supper (Jude 12). Thus even if these people who wear "clothing stained by the flesh" are the teachers themselves, Jude cannot be suggesting no contact other than prayer (which interpretation is perhaps an attempt to read the second century into this passage). If we are correct that Jude has little hope for the teachers, but can conceive of the rescue of their followers, then these followers would

35. The often cited passage in 2 John 10-11 is not as relevant, for that passage concerns welcoming teachers into a house church (assuming that the "elect lady" is in fact a church) and thus giving them a platform to spread their teaching rather than welcoming people into a private home. The references often given to Ignatius, *Eph.* 7:1; *Smyrn.* 4:1 [which suggests absolutely no contact other than prayer]; 7:2; and Polycarp, *Phil.* 6:3, are relevant but appear to be a later strengthening of the NT instructions.

be even less likely to be excommunicated than the teachers. Thus it appears that Jude is saying that one should not simply condemn these people but is to "show mercy," meaning that one should attempt to persuade such people to reject the teaching of the false teachers and return to the orthodox standard of behavior. Yet at the same time one should have nothing to do with their sins and must in fact, as part of the rescue process, separate the people from their sins. Such advice is wise indeed. One cannot rescue people without personal contact, but one must also be cautious that what seduced them does not seduce you. It is quite possible to remain in positive contact and accept a person without at the same time condoning or accepting the person's sin. This appears to be Jude's position, a merciful one indeed.

## III. LETTER CLOSING: DOXOLOGY (vv. 24-25)

> [24]*To him who is able to keep you from falling and to present you before his glorious presence without fault and with great joy —* [25]*to the only God our Savior be glory, majesty, power and authority, through Jesus Christ our Lord, before all ages, now and forevermore! Amen.*

Jude has finished his letter. It is time to close, and Jude does so with a doxology, which is also a form of praise or prayer (often a prayer to the gods was included in the closing of a Greco-Roman letter). While closing prayers are common in NT letters, only four of them end with a doxology. Most NT letters end with greetings and then blessings for their readers, and this lack makes Jude look as much like a sermon as a letter. Doxologies, however, often punctuate Pauline letters, usually marking the closing of sections (Rom 11:36; Gal 1:5; Eph 3:20-21; Phil 4:20 [before the final greeting]; 1 Tim 1:17; 6:16 [before the final charge]; 2 Tim 4:18 [before final greeting]). Jude's doxology is relatively long and ends our letter on a positive note rather than the negative one of the condemnation of the teachers he opposes. Like the typical doxology, it consists of an addressee (i.e., God, indicated by "to"), ascribed honor (often using a variety of terms), the extent of the honor (usually "forever"), and an invitation for the hearers to affirm this honor (usually "Amen").[1] The table shows how this works out for letters ending in a doxology, three in the NT and two in the apostolic fathers.

1. Reinhard Deichgräber, *Gotteshymnus und Christushymnus in der frühen Christenheit* (Göttingen: Vandenhoeck & Ruprecht, 1967), 25-32.

| | *Addressee* | *Honor* | *Duration* | *Response* |
|---|---|---|---|---|
| Jude 24-25 | To him who is able to keep you from falling and to present you before his glorious presence without fault and with great joy — to the only God our Savior, | be glory, majesty, power and authority, through Jesus Christ our Lord | before all ages, now and forevermore! | Amen |
| 2 Pet 3:18 | To him [Jesus] | be glory | both now and forever! | Amen |
| Rom 16:25-27 | Now to him who is able to establish you by my gospel and the proclamation of Jesus Christ, . . . to the only wise God | be glory | forever through Jesus Christ! | Amen |
| *Mart. Pol.* 22:3 | To whom [Jesus] . . . with the Father and the Holy Spirit, | be glory | forever and ever, | Amen |
| *1 Clem.* 65:2 | The grace of our Lord Jesus Christ be with you and with all, in every place, who have been called by God through him, through whom be to him | glory, honor, power and greatness and eternal dominion, | from eternity to eternity. | Amen |

Despite the different practice in most Pauline letters, we are not surprised that such an exclamation of praise would end these letters.[2] Doxologies are found in OT literature and NT hymns, either in the form starting with "blessed" (1 Chron 29:10 and many psalms; Luke 1:68; 2 Cor 1:3;

2. The *Martyrdom of Polycarp* is in structure a letter from the church in Smyrna to the church in Philomelium. The *Epistle of Diognetus* also ends with a doxology, "to whom [the Father] be glory forever. Amen."

Eph 1:3; 1 Pet 1:3 — note that in the NT the doxology tends to open letters) or in a form starting with "to" (Ps 103:31; 1 Pet 4:11, and in the Pauline examples listed above the table).[3]

Deichgräber regards Jude's doxology as an indication of its late date due to (1) length, including the number of attributes recounted for God, (2) its use of the "through Jesus Christ" formula, and (3) its fuller form of the reference to eternity (indeed, he argues that references to eternity are found only in Hellenistic Jewish doxologies, not Palestinian ones).

However, with respect to (3), not only is the eternity formula found in *Pss. Sol.* 17:3 ("the kingdom of our God is forever over the nations in judgment") and in *Tg. Neof.* Exod 15:18, both of Palestinian origin, but there are also precedents in the OT (1 Chron 29:10; Ps 41:13 [40:14 LXX; "Praise be to the LORD, the God of Israel, from everlasting to everlasting. Amen and Amen"]; 72:19; 89:52; 106:48 ["Praise be to the LORD, the God of Israel, from everlasting to everlasting. Let all the people say, 'Amen!'"]; Dan 2:20). Even Jude's threefold time designation is found in Jewish and Christian literature, although not in doxologies (2 *Apoc. Bar.* 21:9 ["those who exist, those who have gone and those who will come"]; 23:3; Heb 13:8 ["Jesus Christ is the same yesterday and today and forever"]; Rev 1:4; 4:8).

When we turn to (2), the "through Jesus Christ" formula, there are some textual problems with Rom 16:27 (however, if it was indeed part of the original letter, it would date the formula to Paul's life). Yet 2 Cor 1:20 shows Paul using a "through Christ" formula in a prayer context similar to a doxology, as he does in other prayer contexts (e.g., Rom 1:8 ["I thank my God through Jesus Christ for all of you"]).

Finally, with respect to (1), the idea that length determines age is a problematic assumption. It is true that liturgical formulas often develop over time, but in the case of doxologies the OT is the base for all Christian formulas, and the prayer in 1 Chron 29:10-13 is certainly as extensive as the doxology in Jude:

> Praise be to you, O LORD, God of our father Israel, from everlasting to everlasting. Yours, O LORD, is the greatness and the power and the glory and the majesty and the splendor, for everything in heaven and earth is yours. Yours, O LORD, is the kingdom; you are exalted as head over all. Wealth and honor come from you; you are the ruler of all things. In your hands are strength and power to exalt and give strength to all. Now, our God, we give you thanks, and praise your glorious name.

3. Matthew Black, "The Doxology to the *Pater Noster* with a Note on Matthew 6:13b," in Philip Davies and Richard White, eds., *A Tribute to Geza Vermes* (Sheffield: JSOT, 1991), 327-32.

There is also a problem with Deichgräber's argument for lateness based on the assertion that the doxologies in Prayer of Manasseh 15 ("yours is the glory forever. Amen"); 4 Macc 18:24 ("to whom be glory forever and ever. Amen"); and 1 Esdr 4:40 are Hellenistic. First, it is not necessarily true that the Prayer of Manasseh is Hellenistic. Second, even if they all are Hellenistic, there is good evidence for the use of Hellenistic-Jewish literature in Jerusalem in the first century. The Aramaic- and Greek-speaking communities of the Jesus movement were mixed from the beginning, just as other Jewish communities of the time were mixed. Furthermore, one must not forget the doxologies in Revelation (e.g., 1:5-6; 5:13; 7:10; 19:1), which are found in a book full of Palestinian influence.

Thus there is no reason to think that this form of closing doxology must be later than the period when Jude flourished. Our author has taken a form often used by followers of Jesus (doxologies are more common in the literature of the Jesus movement, while blessing God is more common in Jewish literature coming from other Jewish groups, although no group is exclusive in its use of one form or the other) and made it into the ending of his letter. In this way he ends on a high note with the focus on God rather than on the teachers who are shaming God.

**24** God is described by Jude as the one "who is able to keep you from falling." God's ability to keep or guard (*phylassō,* a term close in meaning to *tēreō,* "to keep or watch out for") has already been celebrated in Jude. In v. 1 he has said that Christians are "kept [*tēreō*] by Jesus Christ." That God is able to guard or protect his people appears many times in NT literature: John 17:11 ("protect [*tēreō*] them by the power of your name"), 15; 2 Thess 3:3 ("he will strengthen and protect [*phylassō*] you from the evil one"); 1 Pet 1:5 ("who through faith are shielded by God's power"); Rev 3:10 ("I will also keep you [*tēreō*] from the hour of trial that is going to come upon the whole world"). There is another type of keeping that goes on in Jude in addition to that in Revelation and the other literature cited. In v. 6 the angels that did not keep their proper place are now being kept by God in darkness for judgment. Furthermore, the blackest darkness is being kept *(tēreō)* for the teachers Jude opposes (Jude 13). On a more positive note, Christians are to keep *(tēreō)* themselves in God's love (Jude 21). In our verse Jude flips to the other side of the coin and points to God as the one doing the keeping, using the alternative verb for variety.

God keeps them from "falling," a unique word in the NT. In fact, the only other place where it appears in biblical literature is in 3 Macc 6:39, where God is celebrated as the Lord who "most gloriously revealed his mercy and rescued them all together and unharmed" (NRSV). "Unharmed" is the same word as here. In our text God guards them "unfallen" or "unharmed," and in 3 Maccabees he rescues them "unharmed." The ideas are very similar. Yet the idea of stumbling or falling (usually meaning moral failure) is not unique to Jude. Rom 11:11 ("Did they [Israel] stumble so as to fall beyond recovery?"); Jas 2:10 ("whoever keeps *[tēreō]* the whole law and yet stumbles at just one point"); 3:2 ("We all stumble in many ways"); 2 Pet 1:10 ("if you do these things, you will never fall") all contain the idea, expressed in relation to the various topics of discussion in the respective books. The background of the idea is the image of falling or slipping in the Psalms (e.g., 38:16; 56:13; 66:9) and God's keeping the psalmist from falling (e.g., 121:3-8; 140:4; 141:9).

The second part of the description of God is that he is able to "present you before (*katenōpion*) his glorious presence without fault (*amōmous*) and with great joy." God "presents" us or, literally, "stands" us before his presence. While "present" is the better translation, the Greek reader would not miss the contrast of standing and falling. They are different aspects of the same thing: if one does not fall in the world, then one stands before God, and both standing and being without fault are products of God's action.

The background of being without fault is the OT, where that which was presented to God, whether a person coming to worship or an animal being brought for sacrifice, must be unblemished (e.g., Exod 29:1, 38; Lev 1:3; Num 6:14; Ps 15:2; Ezek 43:22; cf. the application to Christ in Heb 9:14; 1 Pet 1:19). Our passage in Jude is itself similar to several others in the NT. Eph 1:4 ("he [God] chose us in him [Christ] before the creation of the world to be holy and blameless [*amōmous*] in his sight [*katenōpion*]"); 5:27 ("to present her to himself as a radiant church, without stain or wrinkle or any other blemish, but holy and blameless [*amōmos*]"); Col 1:22 ("to present you holy in his sight [*katenōpion*], without blemish [*amōmous*] and free from accusation"); 1 Thess 3:13 ("May he strengthen your hearts so that you will be blameless and holy in the presence of our God and Father"). What we note in these passages is the repetition of similar vocabulary, leading some to suggest that this language may have been liturgical.[4] The language is certainly traditional. Yet it is difficult to tell whether or not it is actually liturgical, for the language flows so naturally from the OT that one would not be surprised at independent usage without the mediation of a liturgical form. At the same time, this flow from the OT could well have been mediated through the prayer and liturgical language of the community of the followers of Jesus. So we must not completely rule out liturgical derivation. There is just not enough information to answer the question of whether there was a liturgical source. What is

4. Bauckham, *Jude, 2 Peter*, 122.

clear is that one of these terms appears only in these passages and then later in the apostolic fathers (Polycarp, *Phil.* 5:2, "likewise must the deacons be blameless before [*katenōpion*] his righteousness, as servants of God").

Not only are the readers presented blameless or without fault, but also "with great joy." This joy is not a private joy ("I am so happy"), although certainly that is what would be felt, but a public joy ("We rejoice before him"). The great joy refers to an eschatological celebration, the appropriate festivity when God delivers his people (Isa 12:6; 25:9; 60:5; 61:10; Jer 31:7; 1 Pet 4:13; Rev 19:7). The term used for "great joy" is found only in Jewish and Christian Greek, with the exact phrase appearing in *1 Enoch* 5:10 ("their happiness shall be multiplied forever in gladness and peace all the days of their life"); Luke 1:44 ("the baby in my womb leaped for joy"); Acts 2:46 ("They broke bread in their homes and ate together with glad and sincere hearts"); *Mart. Pol.* 18:3 ("There [at the grave of Polycarp] the Lord will permit us to come together in gladness and joy"). In each of the passages cited there is public celebration.

The place where one is presented is before "his glory" (again, giving a more formal equivalent translation to aid our discussion). God's glory is due to his presence, of course, so this is a periphrasis for God, a typically Jewish way of referring to the deity. Examples of this usage in Jewish literature are found in Tob 12:12 ("it was I [an angel] who brought and read the record of your prayer before the glory of the Lord"); *1 Enoch* 27:2 ("those who speak . . . unbecoming words against the Lord and utter hard words concerning his glory"); 63:5 ("we should glorify, praise and have faith before his glory"); 102:2 ("will seek to hide themselves from the presence of the Great Glory"). Naturally, the hope of standing before God is the eschatological hope of the followers of Jesus. Moses could not see God's glory and live (Exod 33:18-23), but followers of Jesus are destined to stand in his very presence. They will stand there unblemished because they have kept themselves and God has kept them. And they will stand there in public celebration. The picture is that of a festival in the presence of God, a sea of people singing, praising, and dancing in joyous celebration in the very presence of the God they had served on earth.

**25** Jude now picks up the shout of praise that perhaps echoes the future praise of the believers. It begins, "to the only God," echoing the distinctive Jewish confession passed down through the centuries. That basic confession started, "Hear, O Israel: The Lord our God, the Lord is one." Since their god was considered the one God, the idols of the nations were not thought of as gods at all (e.g., Isa 41:21-24). Thus we are not surprised when Greek texts, both biblical and extrabiblical, refer to God as the "only" God: Neh 9:6 ("only Lord"); Ps 83:18 (= Ps 82:19 LXX; "you alone are the Most High"); Ps 86:10 (= LXX Ps 85:10; "you alone are God"); 2 Macc 1:24-25; 7:37; 4 Macc 5:24; and so on. This usage was naturally taken over in the NT (John 5:24; 17:3; Rev 15:4, "only Holy One"), and that was especially true in doxologies (Rom 16:27, "only wise God"; 1 Tim 1:17, "only God"; 2 *Clem.* 20:5, "the only invisible God"; cf. the prefaces to doxologies in 1 Tim 6:15-16, "blessed and only ruler . . . who alone is immortal"; *1 Clem.* 43:6, "the true and only God").[5] This usage is not something to be seen over against Gnostic speculation about the Demiurge, "an inferior creator-God,"[6] but in continuity with standard Jewish theology. Naturally there is an implied contrast with the false teachers, for here Jude is confessing the only God (presumably in deed as well as in word), while the teachers he opposed denied the "only Sovereign and Lord" (Jude 4).

The second epithet for God, "our Savior," is likewise traditional. Christians are familiar with the call to God "Hosanna" or "Save now." In the OT God was not only asked to save, but referred to as "God our Savior," with the LXX using the same Greek expression as in our passage (Ps 65:6 = LXX Ps 64:6; Ps 79:9 = LXX Ps 78:9; LXX Ps 94:1 [the Hebrew has "Rock of our Salvation"]; cf. Pss 27:9; 38:22; 42:5; Isa 17:10; 43:3; etc.). This usage carried on into the intertestamental period, for example, in *Pss. Sol.* 8:33 ("Lord, our Savior"); 17:3 ("God, our Savior"). In the NT it is more common to connect "Savior" to Jesus (Luke 2:1; John 4:42; Acts 5:31; 13:23; Eph 5:23; Phil 3:20; 2 Tim 1:10; Titus 1:4; 2:13; 3:6; 2 Pet 1:1, 11; 2:20; 3:2, 18; 1 John 4:14), although the term is sometimes connected to God, especially in 1 Timothy and Titus (Luke 1:47; 1 Tim 1:1; 2:3; 4:10; Titus 1:3; 2:10; 3:4). It is interesting to note (1) that Titus neatly balances references to God as Savior with those to Jesus as Savior, never mentioning one without the other, and (2) that 2 Peter never refers to God as Savior despite his having used Jude.[7] The application of the title "Savior" to God was apparently a Jewish usage that some sections of the Jesus movement used, but others did not find helpful.[8]

5. See further Gerhard Delling, "ΜΟΝΟΣ ΘΕΟΣ," in *Studien zum neuen Testament und hellenistischen Judentum: Gesammelte Aufsätze 1950-1968* (Göttingen: Vandenhoeck & Ruprecht, 1970), 396-400 or *TLZ* 77 (1952) 469-76.

6. So Kelly, *The Epistles of Peter and of Jude*, 291-92.

7. See the discussion of "Savior" in the Introduction to 2 Peter (pp. 152-54).

8. Vögtle, *Der Judasbrief, der Petrusbrief*, 110, argues that the concept of salvation is connected to Jesus and that this expression in our passage is like the theology of the Pastorals. First, we will argue in the next paragraph that "through Jesus Christ" is probably connected to the praise rather than to the term "Savior." Second, if indeed salvation *is* connected to Jesus, that is not particularly characteristic of the Pastorals. The Pastorals characteristically have more of an interest in *God* as Savior. Yet even when we admit that, with such good Jewish antecedents one realizes that a Jew would not need the the-

The phrase "though Jesus Christ our Lord" comes next in Greek. The NIV and many commentators connect it to the presentation of glory to God. Christians give glory to God through Jesus Christ. This fits with the words of 1 Pet 4:11, "that . . . God may be praised through Jesus Christ." It is certainly the way this phrase functions in many doxologies (Rom 16:27 as well as the postbiblical ones in *1 Clem.* 58:2; 61:3; 64:1; 65:2; *Did.* 9:4; *Mart. Pol.* 14:3). However, some scholars would argue that Jude is saying that God is our Savior "through Jesus Christ." Grammatically this is possible, but the parallels cited are not convincing. It is true that *2 Clem.* 20:5 connects a "through" clause to "the Savior and prince of immortality," but in this passage God is not called "Savior" nor is the structure entirely parallel to that in Jude, for the whole description of Jesus is in a relative clause giving a reason to praise God. *Mart. Pol.* 20:2 is close to Jude in structure, but here we run into a long clause describing God (somewhat parallel to what we find in *2 Clem.* 20:5) and a similar ambiguity to that found in Jude, so it does not form a clear case of the "through" phrase modifying "Savior." The fact is that the weight of evidence points toward the traditional understanding: followers of Jesus praise God through Jesus Christ.

The praise to be given to God starts with "glory." This attribution is found in most doxologies, and in many it is the only element of praise. Two exceptions are 1 Tim 6:16, where "honor and might" are ascribed to God, "honor" taking the place of "glory" as a more Greco-Roman synonym, and 1 Pet 5:11, where only "might" is ascribed, fitting the context, which requires God to use his might to help his people (God's glory was mentioned in the previous verse). The ascription of glory is found frequently in the OT, for example, in the hymn of Exod 15:11, "Who among the gods is like you, O Lord? Who is like you — majestic in holiness, awesome in glory, working wonders?" While the Hebrew lacks the common term for "glory" *(kabod),* the LXX uses our term. The reason for the importance of glory is that while God can be said to have a certain amount of "glory" objectively (when Moses asks to see his glory in Exod 33:18 God can respond that his glory will pass by [Exod 33:22], so "glory" is something that characterizes him; cf. Rev 21:23), glory is also something that human beings (and other beings) can give to him. That is, one meaning of glory is "reputation" or "honor." Honor was a very important theme in ancient Mediterranean societies. One could act honorably and in that sense have great honor, but other human beings might not recog-

---

ology of the Pastorals to refer to God as Savior. A more detailed argument about points of contact with the Pastorals than the one Vögtle gives is needed if his argument is to be convincing.

nize it. In the sense of reputation honor is given by others to the honorable person (or in this case deity), ideally on the basis of genuine qualities seen in people or genuine deeds done by them. Thus human beings and others are often said to give glory to God (especially in Revelation, Rev 4:11; 5:12-13; 7:12; 11:13; 19:1, 7). It is a mixing up of these two meanings of glory that leads some commentators to say that human beings really cannot give anything to God. In fact, they can give the one thing that he cannot produce for him — free recognition of who he is. They can ascribe to him the honor (i.e., "glory") of which he is indeed worthy.

Along with glory comes majesty.[9] The Greek term first appears in biblical literature as praise to God in the Greek translation (LXX) of the Song of Moses in Deut 32:3 (cf. Sir 39:15); it can refer to God's deeds as well as his being (2 Sam 7:21, 23 LXX). Its first use in a doxology (or a structure very close to a doxology) is in 1 Chron 29:11, "Yours, O LORD, is the greatness and the power and the glory and the majesty and the splendor, for everything in heaven and earth is yours." Majesty is not limited to God, but can also apply to a pagan king (Dan 4:22, 36; 5:18-19). Yet in later Jewish intertestamental literature (e.g., *1 Enoch* 5:4; *T. Levi* 3:9) and the NT (Heb 1:3; 8:1) it is applied only to God and can function as a circumlocution for the divine being. In early Christian literature "majesty" retreats to being an attribute of God rather than a circumlocution for God. Yet "majesty" is attributed only to God (*1 Clem.* 27:4; 58:1), never to Caesar or any other governmental authority of this age, since Christians were well aware that the authority of Christ had supplanted the authority of the empire. It is no surprise, then, that this term was frequently used by these Christian writers in doxologies (*1 Clem.* 20:12; 61:3; 64:1; 65:2; *Mart. Pol.* 20:2; 21:1). Jude will have many successors who knowingly or unknowingly copy his use of the term in his doxology.

The final two virtues attributed to God are power *(kratos)* and authority *(exousia)*. The first simply means "strength," but it is often used to refer to *God's* power.[10] The term is often found in doxologies (1 Tim 6:16;

9. See Walter Grundmann, *"megas ktl.," TDNT* 4:529-44. Since "great" is often applied to God in other contexts, the whole article is relevant, but note the meaning of *megalōsynē* as "majesty." Louw-Nida, *A Greek-English Lexicon*, puts it in two semantic domains, the one (§12.5) translated "majesty" when used as a circumlocution for God, and the other (§87.21) "prominence, greatness, importance." The translation of Kelly, *The Epistles of Peter and of Jude*, 25, "awful transcendence," is attractive but something of an overtranslation based on his belief that the term could be applied only to God.

10. Job 12:16, LXX; Ps 62:12 = Ps 61:13, LXX, "you, O God, are strong"; Isa 40:26; *Pss. Sol.* 17:3, "the strength of our God is forever with mercy"; Luke 1:51; Eph 1:19, "the immeasurable greatness of his power (*dynameōs*) for us who believe, according to the working of his great power (*tou kratous tēs ischyos*)" (NRSV) — note the use of three different terms for strength or power in this verse; Col 1:11.

1 Pet 4:11; 5:11; Rev 1:6; 5:13; *1 Clem.* 64:1; 65:2; *Mart. Pol.* 20:2). The second term is far more common in the NT (108 times versus about a dozen times for the first term), but never appears in a NT doxology (it does appear in the earlier Jewish doxology of *1 Esdr* 4:40). It is applied to God's authority in the Greek OT (Dan 4:17 LXX; Sir 10:4), but this usage is not common. It is more commonly used of God's authority in Philo. In this respect the NT is more like Philo in that it often uses the term of Jesus' authority (e.g., Mark 2:10 and par.; John 5:27) and the authority he delegates (e.g., Mark 3:15) and applies it to God's authority (Luke 12:5; Acts 1:7; Rev 16:9). This application to God's or Jesus' authority is not exclusive, though, since in Ephesians and Colossians it often refers to anti-God spiritual authority (Eph 1:21; 2:2; 3:10; 6:12; Col 1:13, 16; 2:10, 15). The term "authority" itself indicates the right to exercise power, although, since a right without power is in reality a mirage, it often includes the idea of the power one has a right to exercise. Still, the focus is on the authority to use the power.[11] Thus police officers have *power* in their physical training and in their service revolver, but their *authority* is symbolized in their badge. The same power applied in a jurisdiction in which they did not have authority (e.g., on the wrong side of the Canadian-American border) could get them arrested. God has power or strength, but he also has authority, the right to exercise it. Here both are attributed to him, for in him they belong together.

The duration of these virtues ascribed to God is "before all ages, now and forevermore." Jews generally thought in terms of two ages, this age and the age to come (e.g., Matt 12:32). One way of expressing eternal duration, however, was to say "unto the ages," which is the expression translated "forevermore" here. That is how long God's honor is to endure (e.g., Rom 1:25; 9:5; 2 Cor 11:31), so that was the natural time indicator for doxologies (Rom 11:36; 16:27; Gal 1:5; Phil 4:20; 1 Tim 1:17; 2 Tim 4:18; Heb 13:21; 1 Pet 4:11; 5:11). Yet God was also the creator of the ages (e.g., Heb 1:12; 11:3), so before creation was the time "before all ages." Thus in the targumic tradition we find such expressions as the divine name "I AM" expanded into "Who spoke and the world was from the beginning, and shall say again to it, Be! and it shall be."[12] That is, God created this age, and he will create the age to come (sometimes expressed in "first and last" terminology, Isa 48:12; Rev 21:6; Philo, *De plantatione* 93; Josephus,

11. "Since the authority under 2. [i.e., permission conferred by a higher authority] is illusory without real power, the term approximates at times to *dynamis,* but with the distinction that *dynamis* denotes external power but *exousia* has a more inward reference." Werner Foerster, *"exestin ktl.," TDNT* 2:562. Cf. whole article, 562-74.

12. The example is from *Tg. Neof.* Exod 3:14. See McNamara, *The New Testament and the Palestinian Targum to the Pentateuch,* 97-112.

*Ant.* 8.280). Since God is also the one existing now, this easily expands into the formula of the one who was, is now, and will be (Rev 1:4, 8; 4:8; 11:17) or, when applied to Jesus, that he is the same yesterday, today, and forever (Heb 13:8). It is from such expressions of divine transcendence that Jude's expression for the duration of God's honor comes. It is unusual in a doxology, but not unusual in Jewish thought in general (including the thought of the Jesus movement). God is to be honored for creation, for his present being, and in all future ages. He is no mortal king whose kingdom ends (1 Kings 2:15; 11:35; Isa 14:4-20; Dan 2:39-44; 4:31; 5:28), but one whose kingdom and honor last forever (Ps 145:13; Dan 4:3, 34; cf. Ps 72:19).[13]

To this the assembled church listening to this letter being read can have only one response, the response of agreement, "Amen." "Amen" is not simply a rote liturgical response, nor the way a person indicated that a prayer or other liturgical piece was ending, but the response by which the congregation made a prayer or doxology their own. It would be equivalent to modern readers shouting, "Yes!" It ends the other doxologies to which we have referred to, and so here it ends Jude, not as something read aloud by the messenger but as a response of the congregation, affirming the honor of the God whom they served in Jesus Christ.[14]

To this we can only add our own "Amen," perhaps best done as a song:

*Jude Doxology*[15]

And now all glory to him who alone is God,
Who saves us through his Son,
Jesus Christ our Lord,
For he is able to keep us from falling away.
He brings us into his presence
With love and joy.

13. This attitude again contrasts with that of the teachers, who are viewed as dishonoring God. They in turn receive eternal dishonor in the blackness of darkness and more. God himself receives eternal honor from true believers, reaching back to the past and continuing through the present.

14. We note the lack of greetings, an indication of a letter carrier or scribe, a health wish, and other features of a normal Greek letter ending. One suspects that Jude, realizing that the letter would be read in the gathering of the various house churches, chose to end in a manner appropriate to the worship setting rather than that of a typical letter ending. This may also indicate that he had not had significant contact with the Pauline letters, that is, that the collection had yet to reach him. See further the discussion of the letter form in the Introduction to Jude in this volume (pp. 23-25).

15. Randy Butler and Terry Butler, "Jude Doxology," ©1991 Mercy/Vineyard Publishing (ASCAP) CCLI# 919781. Used by permission of the authors.

All power, authority, all splendor,
And majesty are his from the beginning
And evermore and evermore.

And now all glory to You;
You alone are God.
You saved us through Your Son,
Jesus Christ our Lord.
For You are able to keep us
From falling away.
You bring us into Your presence
With love and joy.
Forevermore. . . . Forevermore. . . .

# The Letter of 2 PETER

# *Introduction to 2 Peter*

## I. INTRODUCTION

2 Peter has been termed the "ugly stepchild" of the NT. It is not just that the extended prophetic denunciation is unpalatable to some people and the apparent description of the destruction of the universe in ch. 3 is disturbing, but that many readers wonder whether the book is genuine and belongs in the canon at all.[1] Furthermore, whether or not one determines that the work is or is not by Peter, it is often ignored. As John Elliott writes, "Down to the present day its canonical status and theological significance seem to have remained more a theory than a fact."[2]

This uncertainty about the book is not just the product of modern biblical criticism. The same uncertainty about the book existed in antiquity. While the work found some relatively early acceptance at the eastern end of the Mediterranean, as witnessed to by its presence (1) in Greek in 𝔓⁷² (early A.D. 200s), (2) in Coptic translation (about A.D. 200), and (3) in quotations in some of the church fathers,[3] it was rarely used in the western part of the Mediterranean (e.g., Rome, Carthage) from the second to the fourth century.[4] In the fourth century Jerome reported that many re-

1. For instance, Kraftchick, *Jude, 2 Peter,* 75, states, "The fictive 'farewell testament' suggests that 2 Peter is pseudonymous, as acknowledged by almost every modern New Testament scholar." Kraftchick, however, explicitly states that he does not believe that this implies that the book should not be in the NT canon.

2. Elliott, *I-II Peter/Jude,* 119.

3. For example, Clement of Alexandria and Cyprian apparently knew it, although they do not mention it by name.

4. It was possibly known by Irenaeus, and certainly at least some phrases from it were known by the churches of Lyons and Vienne. Cf. the *Apocalypse of Peter*'s use of the work — this is an apocalypse that was known in Vienne.

jected it, a principal reason being its difference in Greek style from 1 Peter.[5] By that time it was also out of favor in the East, with Origen (*Commentary on John* 5.3) pointing out that it was a disputed work (although he quotes from it) and Eusebius (*Eccl. Hist.* 3.3.1-4; 25.3) treating it as inauthentic. It was not until the second half of the century when the Alexandrian bishop Athanasius listed it in his Festal Letter (A.D. 367) that it started to gain general acceptance. Thus it first found acceptance in Alexandria (i.e., southeastern Mediterranean area), while continuing to be rejected in Antioch (northeastern Mediterranean). After this first indication of final acceptance in Alexandria, 2 Peter appears in the Latin canon of the Synod of Carthage (A.D. 397), showing that it had gained some acceptance in the West. The Antiochene tradition (i.e., Syria) did not accept it until the sixth century.

Some of the same concerns have continued throughout church history. Erasmus, Luther, and Calvin[6] all voiced concerns similar to Jerome's, although none of them tried to remove 2 Peter from their canon and all of them quote it quite freely. In more recent times the canonical

5. Jerome, *Lives of Illustrious Men* 1: "He [Peter] wrote two epistles which are called Catholic, the second of which, on account of its difference from the first in style, is considered by many not to be by him."

6. Calvin, for instance, starts his commentary on 2 Peter by stating his concerns: "The doubts respecting this Epistle mentioned by Eusebius, ought not to keep us from reading it. For if the doubts rested on the authority of men, whose names he does not give, we ought to pay no more regard to it than to that of unknown men. And he afterwards adds, that it was everywhere received without any dispute. What Jerome writes influences me somewhat more, that some, induced by a difference in the style, did not think that Peter was the author. For though some affinity may be traced, yet I confess that there is that manifest difference which distinguishes different writers. There are also other probable conjectures by which we may conclude that it was written by another rather than by Peter. At the same time, according to the consent of all, it has nothing unworthy of Peter, as it shews everywhere the power and the grace of an apostolic spirit. If it be received as canonical, we must allow Peter to be the author, since it has his name inscribed, and he also testifies that he had lived with Christ: and it would have been a fiction unworthy of a minister of Christ, to have personated another individual. So then I conclude, that if the Epistle be deemed worthy of credit, it must have proceeded from Peter; not that he himself wrote it, but that some one of his disciples set forth in writing, by his command, those things which the necessity of the times required. For it is probable that he was now in extreme old age, for he says, that he was near his end. And it may have been that at the request of the godly, he allowed this testimony of his mind to be recorded shortly before his death, because it might have somewhat availed, when he was dead, to support the good, and to repress the wicked. Doubtless, as in every part of the Epistle the majesty of the Spirit of Christ appears, to repudiate it is what I dread, though I do not here recognize the language of Peter. But since it is not quite evident as to the author, I shall allow myself the liberty of using the word Peter or Apostle indiscriminately." *The Catholic Epistles.* http://www.ccel.com.

debate has shifted from authorship to content, with Ernst Käsemann arguing that the work is sub-Christian.[7] Thus we have a book that made it into the canon with some difficulty and since then has been neglected by some, judged canonical but also pseudepigraphical by others, and rejected by still others. We need to examine some of these issues before we look at the text in detail.

## II. AUTHORSHIP

2 Peter states that it is written by "Simon Peter, a servant and apostle of Jesus Christ," by which is meant none other than Simon Bar-Jonah (Matt 16:17), a fisherman from Galilee, whom Jesus had chosen as a member of his apprentices and nicknamed "Rock" (Cephas in Aramaic or Peter in Greek). There is some uncertainty in the tradition as to which town in Galilee he actually came from, for John 1:41 says that he was from Bethsaida, while Mark 1:21, 29-30 indicates that he lived in Capernaum and that both Simon's brother Andrew and Simon's mother-in-law lived in the same house (presumably Simon's wife also lived there, but she never appears in the narratives about Peter). Mark 1:16 presents Peter and Andrew with a cast net, which was used by poorer fishermen to catch small fish and could indicate that Peter and Andrew were not wealthy, but Luke 5:3 states that he owned a boat, which would indicate that he (or they, if Andrew was part owner) had somewhat more money, like most artisans and shop owners. Luke further indicates that Peter did not have a theological education (Acts 4:13), which would not necessarily mean that he had no education. Learning to read and write in the village synagogue would not qualify one as a theologically educated person in the eyes of the Sanhedrin.[8]

After Peter became an apprentice of Jesus, he must have distinguished himself, for all the Gospels agree that Jesus selected him first for his core group of twelve (which he sent out as his representatives or delegates, a fact that 2 Peter indicates in the term "apostle," meaning "one who is sent" or "a delegate") and then for his inner circle of three (which

7. Ernst Käsemann, "An Apologia for Primitive Christian Eschatology," in *Essays on New Testament Themes,* trans. W. J. Montague (SBT 41; London: SCM, 1964), 169-95.

8. We are citing the gospel narratives without examining their historical reliability, for that would take us into gospel criticism, a topic that is beyond the bounds of this commentary. However, these narratives are how Peter was remembered in the Jesus movement at the time the Gospels were written, so it is not unreasonable to say that this is the Peter that the readers of 2 Peter would think of when they heard the name.

appears when Jesus did not want the whole group of Twelve present, but did want two or three witnesses). We also learn that he was not a particularly punctilious Jew, for the story in Mark 2:23-27 indicates that Jesus' apprentices as a whole did not follow Pharisaic interpretations of the law. The general picture that we get of this man is that he was willing to take risks, but his very willingness to step forward could get him into trouble. Thus, on the one hand, he risks proclaiming Jesus the Messiah, risks stepping out of the boat, and risks following the group who arrested Jesus right into the courtyard of the high priest, but, on the other hand, he also risks correcting Jesus' perception of his messianic office, and in both his stepping out of the boat and his following Jesus after his arrest he ends up in some difficulty. Nevertheless, he is often the spokesperson for the Twelve.

According to Acts, after Easter Simon Peter continued as a leader among the group of Jesus' apprentices and family. Whether it is accurate to speak of him as *the* leader (certainly not in a hierarchical sense) or whether he simply remains the most outspoken and thus says what others have been discussing, he is certainly the focal point of Acts. He takes the lead in the appointment of Matthias, the apology on Pentecost, the healing of the lame man at the temple, and the two defenses before the Sanhedrin, among other events. Even his shadow was perceived to be healing (Acts 5:15). Then he disappears from the Jerusalem narrative and appears only outside Jerusalem (e.g., Acts 8:14-25, then 9:32–11:48). When he is again in Jerusalem, it is to defend his actions before the other leaders of the Jesus movement vis-à-vis Pharisaic conceptions of purity that many, if not most, of the community accept (Acts 11:1-18). This is significant, for the narrative of Acts has presented Peter as a much more observant Jew (in the Pharisaic sense) after Pentecost than Luke pictures him as being before. He attends the daily prayer services in the temple (the narrative implies that he was there three times daily), and he can say that he has never eaten ritually impure food.[9] It is his risk-taking at the baptism of the uncircumcised Gentile Cornelius, in particular that he enters Cornelius's house and then eats with Cornelius and his friends (quite likely a postbaptismal celebration of the Lord's Supper) that brings down the criticism of other leaders of the Jesus movement in Jerusalem. Were they shocked at behavior they did not expect from him? What was the re-

9. One wonders how Peter would square this assertion with the fact that he was staying at the house of Simon the Tanner, for a tanner was not viewed as having a ritually pure profession and thus his food should have been considered impure. For later Jewish attitudes see *b. Ketubot* 77a; *b. Pesahim* 65a; *b. Hagigah* 4a; *b. Baba Batra* 21a. Since *b. Ketubot* is citing the Mishnah and since the negative attitude toward tanners was so widespread, there is no reason to think that it was not present in the first century.

sult of this confrontation? The text says that the critics shut up and glorified God, but it does not say whether unanswered questions remained and whether they still trusted Peter the way they had previously done. When Peter next leaves Jerusalem, fleeing from Herod Agrippa I (Acts 12), James the brother of Jesus seems to be the main leader of the Jerusalem community of the Jesus movement. James's primacy is clearly evident in Acts 15, for it is James, not Peter, who sums up the decision of the leaders of the Jesus movement. After this incident Peter will not appear again in Acts. Later (i.e., postbiblical) tradition explains this as Peter's starting to travel outside the Palestinian area, travel that would eventually take him to Rome, where tradition has it that he was martyred (if true, then it was probably between A.D. 64 and 68, i.e., between the great fire in Rome and the death of Nero).[10]

The Pauline picture of Peter complicates the one we find in Acts and the Synoptic Gospels. Paul certainly agrees with the Synoptic Gospels that Peter was married, for Paul assumes that the Corinthians knew that Peter's wife traveled with him (1 Cor 9:5), although we still do not learn her name or whether the couple had children. It is no surprise that Paul cites the example of Peter when writing to the Corinthians, since earlier in 1 Corinthians Paul indicates that some of the Corinthians followed what they perceived to be the way of Peter (1 Cor 1:12). Unfortunately, we never learn what the distinctives of this way were or whether this group had been sparked by a visit of Peter to Corinth (which is quite possible, assuming that he did go to Rome, but not absolutely certain, even though *1 Clement* believes that Peter visited Corinth). The only other significant things that Paul says about Peter are (1) that he was one of the three leaders (Paul refers to them as "pillars") of the Jerusalem Jesus community (implied in Gal 1:18 but stated explicitly in 2:1-10), and (2) that Peter's ministry was the "sending to the circumcision" (NIV, "apostle to the Jews") in contrast to Paul's to the Gentiles. This differing perspective on ministry is reflected in a later clash in Antioch, where Peter, reacting to the perceptions of a delegation from Jerusalem, withdrew from celebrating the Lord's Supper with Gentile believers (i.e., from table fellowship, for at that time the Lord's Supper was a full meal), apparently out of con-

10. J. Ramsey Michaels, "1 Peter," *DLNT*, 916, "Only later traditions make Peter into a martyr (e.g., Origen, Tertullian, Eusebius and, above all, *Acts of Peter* 30–41; *1 Clement* 5:4, written from Rome near the end of the first century, is far from clear on the subject). The fact is that there is no clear tradition of Peter's dying in Rome before the second half of the second century A.D. See Pheme Perkins, *Peter: Apostle for the Whole Church* (Minneapolis: Fortress, 2000), 138-40." Such late-second-century tradition could be true, but it also could be constructed out of John 21:18-19 and how the interpreter of that passage thought it must have been fulfilled.

cern for ritual purity (Gal 2:11-14). (Eating and especially drinking with Gentiles were among the easiest ways for a Jew to contract ritual impurity.) While we learn that Paul confronted Peter, we never find out how Peter reacted to that confrontation. One would think that if his immediate reaction had been to agree with Paul and thus to repent, Paul would have reported it, but all we know for sure is that, whatever Peter's response was, it did not fit Paul's rhetorical purpose in Galatians.[11] The problem with this Pauline picture is that we are not sure how to fit it together with the picture of Peter in Acts. In particular, we do not know how to answer two questions: how much of Paul's narrative about Peter comes chronologically before the conversion of Cornelius (assuming the general historicity of the Acts narrative) and whether any of Paul's narrative (or even the writing of Galatians) postdates the gathering in Jerusalem in Acts 15, a gathering often called the Apostolic Council (again, assuming that it is historical). The answers to these questions would help us clarify whether later developments in Peter's life should make us modify Paul's picture of Peter as a leader focused on evangelizing Jews, who was himself sensitive to Jewish purity regulations.

All of this has relevance to our letter. One can, of course, take the designation of authorship at face value and be done with it. Whatever the problems, the inspired text says that Simon Peter wrote this work, so somehow he was able to do it. John Calvin and others appear to have adopted this stance, so it has significant pedigree. But if one wishes to assemble evidence concerning authorship, in the light of the historical information we have assembled one has to work with some troubling data.

First, there is the fact that 2 Peter (as well as 1 Peter) appears to have been written to a Gentile audience, while Paul's perception of Simon Peter was that his ministry was to Jews and Jewish Christians. When it comes to 1 Peter, we have demonstrated that repeated references to his readers indicate that before their conversion they had been typical Greco-Roman pagans rather than Jews.[12] When it comes to 2 Peter, even if it is not addressed to the same group (see our comment on 2 Pet 3:1), there is little evidence that these readers were Jews and plenty of evidence that they were very much at home in the Greco-Roman world. We will present these data when we discuss the recipients below, but in general they concern the fact that these readers were not only conversant with Greco-

11. Possibly Paul felt that a report of Peter's repentance would have shamed Peter more than was necessary and thus lost Paul favor with the Galatians. It is also possible that Peter did not repent and that he and Paul remained unreconciled. We simply do not know the final outcome of this incident.

12. Peter H. Davids, *The First Epistle of Peter* (NICNT; Grand Rapids: William B. Eerdmans, 1990), 7-9.

Roman philosophy (unless 2 Peter misjudges them) but also liable to the vices that Jews felt characterized Gentile life. Thus we have a Peter who is apparently focused on a different group from that on which Paul has him focused. Does that mean that Peter changed over the intervening fifteen years or so between Galatians and his putative martyrdom? That is possible but the question for most scholars is not whether such a change is possible, but whether it is probable.

Second, there are the thematic differences between 2 Peter and 1 Peter. 1 Peter is written to address the situation of cultural dislocation ("homelessness" as a result of commitment to follow Jesus) and persecution in a group of communities of the followers of Jesus in northwest Asia Minor. It uses basic instruction common in the Jesus movement (so much so that it has at times been thought of as a catechism or baptismal homily) and is full of scripture citations. 2 Peter is written to an unidentified group or groups to warn them about teachers who appear to be teaching ethical deviation from the standard that other followers of Jesus accepted. The teachers appear to support their lifestyle with a denial of the return of Christ and the last judgment, perhaps based on Epicurean philosophy. Thus the eschatological tension that is so much a part of 1 Peter (e.g., the judgment is already beginning with the church [1 Pet 4:17]; "the end of all things is near" [1 Pet 4:7]) is relatively absent in 2 Peter (where the sureness and suddenness of the "Day of the Lord" is stressed, but not its imminence). Likewise 2 Peter focuses on judgment, while 1 Peter focuses on the reward of the righteous. When it comes to evidence to support his arguments, 1 Peter cites the example of the suffering Jesus, while 2 Peter refers only to the glorified Jesus (and then mostly as judge). 1 Peter is almost totally devoid of self-references, while 2 Peter contains more than one personal reference. 1 Peter bases his argument of the Jewish scriptures, while 2 Peter bases his on Jude (see below on this and on his use of Scripture). Now it is clear that an author changes his choice of theme depending on his audience and subject, but the extent of this difference is surprising to many scholars.

Third, there is the style of 2 Peter, both its quality of Greek and its mastery of Greco-Roman concepts. While the Greek of 2 Peter is good Greek (although somewhat bombastic), it does not approach the excellence of the periodic sentences found in 1 Peter 1.[13] Thus one wonders

13. One can easily overstate the excellence of 1 Peter. Karen H. Jobes, "The Syntax of 1 Peter: Just How Good Is the Greek?" *BBR* 13:2 (2003) 159-73, argues that 1 Peter, while showing less Semitic interference than Hebrews, is more similar to 1 Thessalonians in terms of the degree of Semitic interference than to Josephus. This, of course, is only one aspect of style, but it does show that the author of 1 Peter probably had a Semitic language as his mother tongue.

whether the same person could be responsible for the Greek of both books. A common solution to this problem has been to assign the Greek of 1 Peter to an amanuensis (secretary), which is, of course, possible, although the favorite evidence for this theory, namely, 1 Pet 5:12, which names Silvanus (or Silas) as the person "though whom" Peter wrote, is *not* referring to Silas's role as an amanuensis. E. Randolph Richards has shown convincingly that the formula 1 Peter uses designates the letter carrier, not the amanuensis.[14] Still, even though 1 Peter is not naming Silvanus as the secretary, it was quite common during the first century to use a secretary to write a document, and so it would be a reasonable assumption that 1 Peter was written by one. However, at least in the case of Paul the amanuensis was probably normally a contracted worker, not a part of the team responsible for the writing of the various letters. If it were otherwise with 1 Peter (i.e., the author of 1 Peter did not follow the normal procedures for letter writing but had as a secretary a person he could also trust to compose the letter) and the secretary is responsible for not just the physical writing but the style, then in 1 Peter we are not hearing the voice of Peter or words of Peter, but at best only the ideas of Peter. This argument, although significant for 1 Peter, would have little bearing on the authorship of 2 Peter, if that were considered the authentic voice of Peter.[15]

The main problem is that the differences between 1 Peter and 2 Peter go beyond the issue of Greek style, for 2 Peter uses a significant number of Greco-Roman concepts, such as the series of ideas in 2 Pet 1:3-4, culminating in the idea of participating in the divine nature. While 1 Peter is not unaware of Greco-Roman culture, he does not demonstrate the same concentration of such ideas. What 1 Peter does demonstrate is a concentrated use of allusions to the Hebrew Scriptures (which he probably knew in Greek). For instance, look at the concentrations of quotations

14. E. Randolph Richards, "Theological Bias in Interpreting *Dia Silvanou . . . Egrapsa* in 1 Peter 5:12?" 1999 (paper read at the Annual Meeting of the Evangelical Theological Society in Danvers, MA, November 18, 1999), later published as "Silvanus Was Not Peter's Secretary: Theological Bias in Interpreting *dia Silvanou . . . egrapsa* in 1 Peter 5:12," *JETS* 43:3 (2000) 417-32. See also his *Paul and First-Century Letter Writing: Secretaries, Composition and Collection* (Downers Grove, IL: InterVarsity Press, 2004), 33-35.

15. 1 Peter (or 2 Peter, for that matter) is just as much "by Peter" whether he dictated every word or whether he told a co-worker, "Write a letter to x to combat y — you might use argument z, as well as any others you can think of." In either case an ancient would think of the letter as being "by Peter," even if in the latter case we would lack any certain knowledge of how Peter himself thought. On how Paul wrote letters (and thus how the author[s]of 1 and 2 Peter probably did), see the careful examination of the process of letter writing in the Greco-Roman world in Richards, *Paul and First-Century Letter Writing*.

and allusions in 1 Pet 2:4-10 or 2:21-25. Yet when we turn to 2 Peter, the reader could not be blamed for wondering whether the author knows the Hebrew Scriptures at all.[16] Except for the references to OT and intertestamental narratives that he took over from Jude (see the discussion below [pp. 136-43] on its relationship to Jude), there is virtually no direct contact between 2 Peter and the Hebrew Scriptures. Could the same author be so full of Scripture when he wrote one letter and then so empty of it when he wrote a second? This issue would be especially problematic if one believed that the two letters were written to the same group of people (i.e., if 2 Pet 3:1 refers to 1 Peter), since in that case one could not explain the difference between the letters as being due to differing audiences that the author knew to be more or less acquainted with the Hebrew Scriptures.

The truth is that while one ought to raise these issues, there is in the end no conclusive way to respond to them. Descriptively we can examine the writing strategies in 1 and 2 Peter, but we can only speculate as to whether Simon Peter could have been the author of one or both of these letters. Why is that the case? First, these two letters are the only possible sources we have for the writing of Simon Peter. Unlike Paul, whose group of letters almost everyone believes to be genuine and against which one can compare the others, Peter has only these two short letters. Thus there is no external literary basis for determining whether he could or could not have written them. Second, we lack anything like a complete biography of Simon Peter. We know nothing about his youth. We do not know whether he could read and write at all, nor whether he had significant contact with Greek thought (living in Galilee, he certainly had a command of at least enough Greek to handle commercial conversations). He may have had no education or he may have had as good an education as anyone from a Galilean village would have had. He may have had almost no contact with Greek philosophy or he may have learned quite a lot about it (there were many Greek schools and institutions, not only in Galilee but also in Jerusalem itself). We do not know what he learned or what his experiences were after he disappears from Acts. Did he have an experience that reoriented his ministry toward the Gentiles? Or did he remain focused on the Jews, assuming that our perception of Paul's presentation is accurate and that Paul is referring to an ethnic division of ministry and not a geographic one?[17] Certainly one can mount a good defense

16. See the discussion in Peter H. Davids, "The Use of Second Temple Traditions in 1 and 2 Peter and Jude," in Jacques Schlosser, ed., *The Catholic Epistles and the Tradition* (BETL 176; Leuven: Peeters, 2004), 451-60.

17. Some scholars have argued, as N. T. Wright has done orally, that when it comes

of Petrine authorship, as Michael Green has done,[18] or one can decide that 2 Peter must have been composed later than the life of Peter, as Richard Bauckham has done.[19] Both Green and Bauckham are British evangelical scholars,[20] but in either case we are working with incomplete evidence and so cannot have a conclusive answer. But we will reconsider the matter afresh after we have evaluated Bauckham's arguments about literary genre.

## III. DATE, LANGUAGE, AND STYLE

The date of 2 Peter is clearly influenced by one's decision about authorship. If it was written by Simon Peter (even if an assistant was primarily responsible for the composition of the letter),[21] and if one accepts the tradition that Peter was martyred in Rome under Nero, then the work must have been written by A.D. 68 (the death of Nero), and most probably between A.D. 64 (the Great Fire in Rome, which marked the start of Nero's persecution of Christians) and A.D. 68. If one rejected the tradition that Peter was martyred under Nero, then one could still hold to Petrine au-

---

to territory, Paul's concern was always with geographical rather than ethnic territory (e.g., Rom 15:19-20) and that, wherever he went, Paul evangelized Jews and not just Gentiles. Thus what Paul means in Gal 2:8-10 is that Peter's sphere of ministry was the eastern end of the Mediterranean, specifically Galilee and Judea, while Paul's was those areas to the north and west on which Jews had never laid any claim.

18. E. M. B. Green, *2 Peter Reconsidered* (London: Tyndale, 1960). This is a published lecture. See also his *The Second Epistle of Peter and the Epistle of Jude.*

19. Bauckham, *Jude, 2 Peter.*

20. While Bauckham believes that 2 Peter is pseudepigraphical, he also believes that it is written in a testamental form and that that genre would have been recognized by any contemporary reader as being written in the spirit of Peter rather than having been written by Peter. Thus, he argues, the document was neither intended to deceive nor did it in fact deceive its first readers. They would have thought of it as being about Peter rather than by Peter. Bauckham may be right or wrong on this, but the position he holds is fully compatible with evangelical affirmations about the trustworthiness of the canonical Scriptures in all that they truly affirm (versus what we may misread them as affirming).

21. If one pictures Peter being in prison at the time of composition, then it would be highly likely that an assistant was primarily responsible for the writing, given that prison conditions were not conducive to that activity (unless one were under relatively lenient house arrest, as Paul apparently was when he first arrived in Rome, Acts 28:16). The fact is that most amanuensis theories (whether for 1 or 2 Peter or for some of the Pauline letters) end up portraying the assistant/secretary as being responsible for much of the letter, with Peter (or Paul in the case of the Pauline letters) responsible only for the general ideas.

thorship and date the work into the 80s.[22] If what we have stated leaves us with some lack of clarity, we can say that it is absolutely clear that 2 Peter was written before A.D. 140 and most likely before A.D. 110 since that is the probable range of dates within which the *Apocalypse of Peter* was written, a work that borrows from 2 Peter.[23] Thus we have the period A.D. 64-110 as the range within which the work was probably written, whatever one holds about its authorship.

Some attempts have been made to define this range more closely. For instance, the vocabulary of 2 Peter has fifty-seven words not found elsewhere in the NT, of which only twenty-five occur in the LXX.[24] That leaves thirty-two words that do not occur elsewhere in biblical literature. Fifteen of these are found in Hellenistic Jewish writers such as Philo and Josephus, which may give some indication of the thought world to which 2 Peter belongs (i.e., Hellenistic Judaism). It is also interesting that of the fifty-seven words not found elsewhere in the NT, seventeen appear in the apostolic fathers, especially *1 Clement, 2 Clement,* and the *Shepherd of Hermas,* which again is taken by some to be an indication of 2 Peter's thought world and therefore date. However, while the overlap in vocabulary is interesting, in order to establish 2 Peter's relationship to the period of these other works, one needs to show that earlier Greco-Roman writers did not normally use these words and thus that they are not indications that both 2 Peter and the various apostolic fathers were well-educated Hellenistic writers who used appropriate language from their world. What is clear is that very few of his more unusual words come from Jude (there are only four words that the two books share exclusively in the NT). It appears that 2 Peter's vocabulary is his own, stemming from his own education and therefore wide vocabulary, and not from his borrowing from other works.

There are no real indications of date in 2 Peter's style. Watson, following many others, points out that 2 Peter is written in "the grand style" (one of three possible Greek styles), but that it has the faults that that style can lead to as well, being both "swollen" (inflated language, new and/or archaic words) and "frigid" (compound and strange words).[25] While it is

22. If Peter were about 30 in A.D. 29, the approximate date of the death and resurrection of Jesus, an age that would be consistent with his apparent leadership (thirty was the age at which one was considered ready for such responsibility), then it would be possible that, if he were not martyred, he could still be alive in the A.D. 80s, although he would have been a very old man, especially for that age.

23. Likewise, it must for the same reason be earlier than the *Acts of Peter,* but this work was probably written around A.D. 180, much later than the *Apocalypse of Peter.*

24. Bauckham, *Jude, 2 Peter,* 135-37, 149-50, gives the details of the Greek terms involved.

25. Duane Frederick Watson, *Invention, Arrangement, and Style: Rhetorical Criticism of Jude and 2 Peter* (SBLDS 104; Atlanta: Scholars Press, 1988), 144-45.

often attributed to Asian rhetoric (as opposed to Attic rhetoric, which tried to copy classical models),[26] the Asian style was described by Quintilian (*Institutiones oratoriae* 12.10.16) as "empty and inflated" and by Cicero (*Brutus sive de claris oratoribus* 13.51; cf. 95.325) as "redundant and lacking conciseness." One would hardly describe 2 Peter as "empty" even if his language might seem "inflated" and "redundant and lacking conciseness" to some (e.g., the author of 2 Peter loves to put two near synonyms together for rhetorical effect). Watson puts it well when he says, "[2 Peter] is characterized by weight of thought, but also by a swiftness and impetuosity combined with refined and ornate words. 2 Peter is not the best example of Asian style, but does possess several of its characteristics."[27] Thus there may be indications of social location in 2 Peter (the author was neither aristocratic nor schooled in the Attic form of rhetoric more in favor with the upper classes in Greece and Rome, yet he did possess considerable learning, given his wide vocabulary and rhetorical ability) or of physical location (Asian rhetoric was naturally more common in Asia, but one who had learned rhetoric in Asia might carry his style somewhere else, and one who was culturally sensitive and knew Asia might adopt Asian rhetoric in order to influence readers in Asia), but it does not indicate date since both the Asian and Attic styles were used during the first century.

## IV. RECIPIENTS AND OPPONENTS

We have very little information about the recipients of 2 Peter, unless we believe that 2 Pet 3:1 indicates that 2 Peter was written to the same communities of believers to which 1 Peter was addressed. If that is what 2 Pet 3:1 means, then the letter was written to communities of followers of Jesus who were situated in the northwest quadrant of Asia Minor, that is, Pontus, Galatia, Cappadocia, Asia, and Bithynia. If one rejects this identification,[28] then the only thing we know about the recipients is that

26. Bauckham, *Jude, 2 Peter,* 137. See also Reicke, *The Epistles of James, Peter and Jude,* 146-47, who compares the Asian style to European baroque in its degree of ornamentation. This attribution of 2 Peter to Asian rhetoric is far more culturally sensitive than the comments of many earlier scholars who simply blasted the style of 2 Peter since it did not fit classical or neoclassical standards.

27. Watson, *Invention, Arrangement, and Style,* 145-156.

28. The difference in style from 1 Peter would make one tend to reject the identification (either because one did not expect the same author to write two letters in such different styles or because one would not expect the same author to send two such different

they probably were not located in the eastern end of the Mediterranean (Syria, Palestine, and Babylon) nor were they predominantly Jewish (2 Peter expects them to be very familiar with Greco-Roman ideas, but it does not expect them to know a lot of Jewish literature). Some teachers among them have influenced them (or have attempted to influence them — we do not know how effective the teachers have been) in a moral direction of which 2 Peter disapproves. One basis for these teachers' rejection of traditional moral boundaries is their belief that the Parousia of Jesus and its concomitant final judgment will not happen. We do not know what they substituted for this belief, whether they believed that death ended human existence (perhaps the less probable alternative, although some Greek philosophers held this position) or whether they believed that death released the soul/spirit to live an eternal bodiless existence, but in either case the deeds done in the body belonged to the body and would not be judged in a final judgment. They are presented as stating (1) that there has been no apocalyptic divine intervention since the creation, (2) that there has been no return of Jesus within the time frame that the first generation of leaders of the Jesus movement expected, and (3) that Jesus would therefore not return and bring that judgment (probably with the underlying assumption that to return to the physical world in bodily form would be impossible for him in his present glorified state).

This position has often been called Epicurean. The Epicureans argued that the chief human good was "pleasure," which they defined as the "absence of trouble" and/or "freedom from pain and fear." If this is indeed the chief good, then the deity, who embodies the chief good, must be perfectly without trouble, and what could be more troublesome than punishing or blessing human beings? Therefore, the Epicureans denied that there was a provident deity — God does not interfere in human affairs.[29] Neyrey cites four basic arguments that the Epicureans used: (1) the world is made of chance occurrences of passing atoms, (2) a doctrine of providence would destroy freedom, (3) since the world came about by chance, there can be no prophecy and such prophecies that have been made are largely unfulfilled, and (4) injustice in the world shows that there cannot be a provident deity. From the above, one would rightly conclude that the Epicureans did not believe in an afterlife: at death the body returned to its various elements, and that was it.

---

letters to the same group), but many committed to pseudepigraphy, for example, Bauckham, *Jude, 2 Peter,* 286, do, for they view 2 Peter as a different author writing in the name of Peter and consciously referring to 1 Peter as part of the testamental genre.

29. Diogenes Laertius 10.128-39.

But since they have no feeling at all, the dead are perfectly free from pain and fear and certainly experience the absence of trouble.[30] Notice the connection between their denial of providence in this life and their denial of an afterlife.

Epicurean doctrine was not limited to Greco-Roman philosophical circles. Josephus attributes it to the Sadducees, who certainly did not believe in an afterlife and resurrection (Mark 12:18):

> But the Sadducees are those that compose the second order, and take away fate entirely, and suppose that God is not concerned in our doing or not doing what is evil; and they say, that to act what is good, or what is evil, is at men's own choice, and that the one or the other belongs so to every one, that they may act as they please. They also take away the belief of the immortal duration of the soul, and the punishments and rewards in Hades.[31]

While we cannot be sure that the Sadducees would have put their belief in this manner (they may have had a more fundamentalist argument that no afterlife is mentioned in the Pentateuch), Josephus clearly expresses their belief in terms of Epicurean philosophy, which may well have been part of their thinking, since they were involved in the Greek culture in Jerusalem. Nor is Josephus the only Jewish reference to Epicurean ideas. *Tg. Ps.-J.* Gen 4:8 reads, "Cain answered and said to Abel: 'I can see that the world was created[32] in love, but it is not ordered by the issue of good works, because there is partiality in judgment; . . .' [then, after Abel's orthodox response] Cain answered and said to Abel: 'There is no judgment and no judge and no world hereafter; there is no good reward to be given to the righteous, nor any account to be taken of the wicked.' "[33] Thus in the first part of the argument Cain complains about the issue of theodicy, namely, that in his eyes God is partial and does not respect his righteous deeds, but in the second part of the argument Cain resolves the issue by taking the classic Epicurean position that there is neither final judgment nor reward (presumably because God is not in-

30. Neyrey, *2 Peter, Jude,* 122-23.

31. Josephus, *War* 2.164.

32. Geza Vermes, "The Targumic Versions of Gen 4:3-16," in Geza Vermes, *Post-Biblical Jewish Studies* (Leiden: Brill, 1975), 96-100, follows *Targum Neofiti,* which reads, "The world was not created by love." See Martin McNamara, trans., "*Targum Neofiti* 1: Genesis," in *The Aramaic Bible,* vol. 1A (Collegeville, MN: Liturgical Press, 1992).

33. Trans. John Bowker, *The Targums and Rabbinic Literature* (Cambridge: Cambridge University Press, 1969), 132-33; but it is in essence identical to Michael Maher, trans., "*Targum Pseudo-Jonathan:* Genesis," in *The Aramaic Bible,* vol. 1B (Collegeville, MN: Liturgical Press, 1992).

volved in the affairs of the world). Of course, in *Targum Pseudo-Jonathan* that position explains how he could then kill his brother — there is no judgment to be feared.

This Jewish variant of Epicurean philosophy is often referred to by the Aramaic term *'apīqōra'* (often transliterated *apikoros*), which many scholars translate "Epicurean,"[34] while others prefer a more general term such as "sceptic" or "infidel."[35] Thus we see that there are divergent opinions as to the accuracy of the belief that this word refers to Epicurean ideas. That these teachings continued to be an issue in late-first-century Judaism is clear in this saying attributed to R. Akiba in *m. Sanh.* 10:1:

> C. And these are the ones who have no portion in the world to come: D. (1) He who says, the resurrection of the dead is a teaching which does not derive from the Torah, (2) and the Torah does not come from Heaven; and (3) an Epicurean. (Neusner's translation)

In the light of increasing evidence for the currency of Hellenistic ideas in Jerusalem itself, not to mention other areas of Roman Palestine, we are inclined to see real Epicurean influence in these ideas, although those representing the ideas might not have known that they originated with Epicurus. It seems too coincidental that such similar ideas arose in two different parts of the empire, an empire in which there was a free flow of ideas. However, even if one does not grant this much influence to the Epicureans, at the least we must observe that both the Epicureans and some first-century Jews held a position that (1) God does not intervene in the world, and (2) therefore there is no reward for good or punishment for evil, (3) including no resurrection of the dead, and (4) no final judgment. The evidence for God's nonintervention was the classic issue of theodicy: we do not observe that the righteous prosper while the wicked

34. For instance, the Soncino Mishnah translates *m. Abot* 2:14, "Mishnah 14. R. Eleazar said: Be eager to study the Torah; and know what answer thou shouldst give to the Epicurean [Danby translates "unbeliever," but in his note says, "Lit. 'Epicurean'"], and know before whom thou toilest, and who is thine employer and who will pay thee the reward of thy labour." Notice that answering the Epicurean is connected to being aware of rewards and punishments from God.

35. For example, Herbert Danby, *The Mishnah* (Oxford: Clarendon, 1933), 397, n. 4, says that this term (which he later says means literally "Epicurean" in *m. Abot* and which he translates "Epicurean" in *m. Sanhedrin*) is "A frequent epithet applied both to Gentiles and Jews opposed to the rabbinical teachings. It is in no way associated with teachings supposed by Jews to emanate from the philosopher Epicurus; to Jewish ears it conveys the sense of the root *pakar*, 'be free from restraint', and so licentious and sceptical." Marcus Jastrow, *A Dictionary of the Targumim, The Talmud Babli and Yerushalami, and the Midrashic Literature* (New York: Judaica, 1975) argues that it is only coincidental that the term sounds something like Epicurean.

suffer. These observations could and did lead to the conclusion that God does not in fact intervene and that this nonintervention means no final judgment. Such "Epicurean" thinking is espoused by 2 Peter's opponents. However, as we have seen, this does not help in locating the readers, for such "Epicureans" could have been part of a gathering of the followers of Jesus in Palestine as easily as in Athens. In the light of the paucity of references in 2 Peter to nonnarrative portions of the Hebrew Scriptures (i.e., they knew some of the stories from the OT, at least as mediated through later narrative traditions, but they had not had a lot of contact with the OT itself), we would suspect that the recipients were Gentiles and probably lived in Greece or Asia Minor, but that cannot be an absolutely sure conclusion. After all, if the "Epicurean" teachings had already taken some root (i.e., if 2 Peter is being charitable in his tone, which separates his readers from the teachers of "Epicurean" ideas), then it might not have been wise to use arguments from the Hebrew Scriptures (since they portray a God who does intervene) and the historical examples might have come along with his adaptation of Jude. But that brings us to another topic.

## V. JUDE AND 2 PETER

There is clearly a relationship between Jude and 2 Peter. One only has to look at the following passages in order to determine that much:

---

| **Jude 3** | **2 Peter 2:1–3:3** |
|---|---|
| "Dear friends, although I was very eager to write to you about the salvation we share, I felt I had to write and urge you to contend for the faith that was once for all entrusted to the saints." | |

**Comment on Jude 3**

There are parallels here to 2 Pet 1:1-2, 5.

---

| **Jude 4** | **2 Peter 2:1-3** |
|---|---|
| "For certain men whose condemnation was written about long ago have | "But there were also false prophets among the people, just as there will |

secretly slipped in among you. They are godless men, who change the grace of our God into a license for immorality and deny Jesus Christ our only Sovereign and Lord."

be false teachers among you. They will secretly introduce destructive heresies, even denying the sovereign Lord who bought them — bringing swift destruction on themselves. [2]Many will follow their shameful ways and will bring the way of truth into disrepute. [3]In their greed these teachers will exploit you with stories they have made up. Their condemnation has long been hanging over them, and their destruction has not been sleeping."

### Comment on Jude 4 // 2 Peter 2:1–3:3

The basic charge is identical: they have denied "the sovereign Lord" and they have introduced licentiousness. Both authors mention that they did something secretly. Cf. *1 Enoch* 21.

---

### Jude 5-7

"Though you already know all this, I want to remind you that the Lord delivered his people out of Egypt, but later destroyed those who did not believe. [6]And the angels who did not keep their positions of authority but abandoned their own home — these he has kept in darkness, bound with everlasting chains for judgment on the great Day. [7]In a similar way, Sodom and Gomorrah and the surrounding towns gave themselves up to sexual immorality and perversion. They serve as an example of those who suffer the punishment of eternal fire."

### 2 Peter 2:4-9

"For if God did not spare angels when they sinned, but sent them to hell, putting them into gloomy dungeons to be held for judgment; [5]if he did not spare the ancient world when he brought the flood on its ungodly people, but protected Noah, a preacher of righteousness, and seven others; [6]if he condemned the cities of Sodom and Gomorrah by burning them to ashes, and made them an example of what is going to happen to the ungodly; [7]and if he rescued Lot, a righteous man, who was distressed by the filthy lives of lawless men [8](for that righteous man, living among them day after day, was tormented in his righteous soul by the lawless deeds he saw and heard) — [9]if this is so, then the Lord knows how to rescue godly men from trials and to hold the unrighteous for the day of judgment, while continuing their punishment. [10]This is especially true of those who follow the corrupt desire of the sinful nature and despise authority."

### Comment on Jude 5-7 // 2 Peter 2:4-9

The order in Jude is Egypt — Angels — Sodom, while the order in 2 Peter is Angels — Noah — Sodom/Lot.

Note that 2 Pet 2:10 picks up the Sodom theme from Jude 7 and then bridges to Jude 8. Cf. Jude 16.

2 Peter has expanded the Sodom material by discussing Lot, the positive example.

---

**Jude 8-10**

"In the very same way, these dreamers pollute their own bodies, reject authority and slander celestial beings. [9]But even the archangel Michael, when he was disputing with the devil about the body of Moses, did not dare to bring a slanderous accusation against him, but said, "The Lord rebuke you!" [10]Yet these men speak abusively against whatever they do not understand; and what things they do understand by instinct, like unreasoning animals — these are the very things that destroy them."

**2 Peter 2:10-12**

"Bold and arrogant, these men are not afraid to slander celestial beings; [11]yet even angels, although they are stronger and more powerful, do not bring slanderous accusations against such beings in the presence of the Lord. [12]But these men blaspheme in matters they do not understand. They are like brute beasts, creatures of instinct, born only to be caught and destroyed, and like beasts they too will perish."

### Comment on Jude 8-10 // 2 Peter 2:10-12

Cf. 1 Pet 3:20 and *Jub.* 7:20ff. for other descriptions of the fallen angels/Noah motif.

The Michael — devil dispute from *Testament/Ascension of Moses* is omitted from 2 Peter, but it is referred to in a general way.

Jude 10 par. 2 Pet 2:12; cf. Wisd 10:6.

---

**Jude 11**

"Woe to them! They have taken the way of Cain; they have rushed for profit into Balaam's error; they have been destroyed in Korah's rebellion."

**2 Peter 2:13-16**

"They will be paid back with harm for the harm they have done. Their idea of pleasure is to carouse in broad daylight. They are blots and blemishes, reveling in their pleasures while they feast with you. [14]With eyes full of adultery, they never stop sinning; they seduce the unstable; they are experts in greed — an accursed brood! [15]They have left the straight way and wandered off to follow the way of Balaam son of Beor, who loved the wages of wickedness. [16]But he was rebuked for his wrongdoing by a donkey — a beast without speech — who spoke with a man's voice and restrained the prophet's madness."

### Comment on Jude 11 // 2 Peter 2:13-16

2 Pet 2:13 is paralleled in Jude 12; thus 2 Peter has the reverse order of Balaam and the behavior of the false teachers at the Lord's Supper. This is the only time that the order of the topics changes.

---

### Jude 12-13

"These men are blemishes at your love feasts, eating with you without the slightest qualm — shepherds who feed only themselves. They are clouds without rain, blown along by the wind; autumn trees, without fruit and uprooted — twice dead. [13]They are wild waves of the sea, foaming up their shame; wandering stars, for whom blackest darkness has been reserved forever."

### 2 Peter 2:17

"These men are springs without water and mists driven by a storm. Blackest darkness is reserved for them."

### Comment on Jude 12-13 // 2 Peter 2:17

Parallels do not need comment.

---

### Jude 14-16

"Enoch, the seventh from Adam, prophesied about these men: 'See, the Lord is coming with thousands upon thousands of his holy ones [15]to judge everyone, and to convict all the ungodly of all the ungodly acts they have done in the ungodly way, and of

### 2 Peter 2:18

"For they mouth empty, boastful words and, by appealing to the lustful desires of sinful human nature, they entice people who are just escaping from those who live in error."

all the harsh words ungodly sinners
have spoken against him.' [16]These
men are grumblers and faultfinders;
they follow their own evil desires;
they boast about themselves and flat-
ter others for their own advantage."

### Comment on Jude 14-16 // 2 Peter 2:18

2 Peter leaves out the *1 Enoch* 1:9 citation, but then continues with the accusation of boasting.

---

**2 Peter 2:19-22**

"They promise them freedom, while they themselves are slaves of depravity — for a man is a slave to whatever has mastered him. [20]If they have escaped the corruption of the world by knowing our Lord and Savior Jesus Christ and are again entangled in it and overcome, they are worse off at the end than they were at the beginning. [21]It would have been better for them not to have known the way of righteousness, than to have known it and then to turn their backs on the sacred command that was passed on to them. [22]Of them the proverbs are true: 'A dog returns to its vomit,' and, 'A sow that is washed goes back to her wallowing in the mud.'"

### Comment on 2 Peter 2:19-22

While there is a partial parallel to 2 Pet 2:19-22 in Jude 5, Jude never admits that the teachers he opposes were part of the Christian community. They were among them, like unbelievers among the people coming out of Egypt, but they sneaked in secretly and are devoid of the Spirit. In this section 2 Peter looks on the false teachers as people who did really escape from the world, but have now returned and been reenslaved.

**Jude 17-19**

"But, dear friends, remember what the apostles of our Lord Jesus Christ foretold. [18]They said to you, 'In the last times there will be scoffers who will follow their own ungodly desires.' [19]These are the men who divide you, who follow mere natural instincts and do not have the Spirit."

**2 Peter 3:1-3**

"Dear friends, this is now my second letter to you. I have written both of them as reminders to stimulate you to wholesome thinking. [2]I want you to recall the words spoken in the past by the holy prophets and the command given by our Lord and Savior through your apostles.

[3]"First of all, you must understand that in the last days scoffers will come, scoffing and following their own evil desires."

**Comment on Jude 17-19 // 2 Peter 3:1-3**

The paragraph in 2 Peter is not in the same order as that in Jude.

What we see in even such a comparison of the English text — the verbal similarities would be more striking in Greek — is that the same topics are covered in largely the same order, often using the same or almost the same words. There are topics missing in 2 Peter that are found in Jude (the out-of-chronological-order reference to the people coming out of Egypt, the reference to Korah, and the citations of *Testament of Moses* and *1 Enoch*), and there are also topics added by 2 Peter (the reference to Lot and the long section on the false teachers having fallen away), but in only one case is there a change in order. It is this combination of virtually identical order with pieces of similar and at times identical wording that is so striking.

There are three logical ways to explain this similarity.[36] First, Jude may have used 2 Peter. However, the question that arises if this were the

36. One could, of course, deny that any relationship exists between the two works and claim that the similarity is either a coincidence or due to the direct inspiration of the Holy Spirit. However, nowhere else in the world would we make the assumption that such similarity was simply coincidence. For instance, if I had two students who turned in a paper or wrote an essay exam in which I found this degree of similarity, I would certainly conclude that either both had memorized (or used notes from) the same lecture or textbook (which could therefore be easily checked) or that one had copied the work of the other. When it comes to the thesis that the Holy Spirit created the similarity, it would be saying that God was not working through incarnational methods, that is, through human agents, but rather was intervening directly in the world (not much differently than if he had shown Peter and Jude the same golden parchment inscribed by his hand). Such an assumption is different from God's usual methodology (except in rare situations, such as the Decalogue), which is more incarnational. Furthermore, it makes little sense given the personal reflections contained in 2 Peter.

case is why Jude did not use any of the material in 2 Peter 1 and only parts of 2 Peter 3. One would think that there would be at least a trace of the rest of 2 Peter in Jude had he been using it, but, other than items that belong to the framework of many NT letters (e.g., letter greetings), such traces are missing. If Jude has used 2 Peter, there is no evidence that his copy included ch. 1.

Second, both may be dependent upon a common source, oral or written. This is a hypothesis that cannot be disproved in that by definition we do not have the common source. If it is an oral tradition, it is impossible to recover, and if it is a written source, we have yet to find it. Such a hypothesis adds a third work to the two that we have and thus is more complex than the other two solutions. As such, while not impossible historically (Ockham's razor should be applied only to logical situations, not to historical situations, since history is by nature unique and does not necessarily follow the laws of logic), it should be accepted only if no other solution is less problematic. Furthermore, when one describes that hypothetical common source (i.e., one describes a source that includes only the material common to 2 Peter and Jude), it turns out to be virtually identical to Jude, and that raises the question as to why one would have written Jude if something virtually identical already existed?

Finally, 2 Peter may have used Jude. If 2 Peter has used Jude, he has clearly adapted it rather than simply incorporated the letter. (We shall see this adaptation of Jude in more detail as we move through the commentary and look at the various differences.) It is this last solution that appears to the majority of scholars to be the most satisfactory one. As we shall see in the commentary, this solution can explain the differences between 2 Peter and Jude by pointing to a consistency in 2 Peter's editing: he adds the point of view that the teachers he opposes were at one time true members of the community; he removes direct references to *1 Enoch* and the *Testament of Moses;* he also simplifies some of Jude's examples by not taking over all three examples that are in some of Jude's groups of three.[37] Finally, he drops the ending of Jude (although aspects show up in his own closing) and instead integrates the last part of Jude before the ending into his own apologetic for the Parousia, for, unlike the false teachers in Jude, the people whom 2 Peter labels false teachers use a de-

37. Some scholars think that this simplification gains 2 Peter the space that he needs to add his new material. However, in order to assert this we would have to know that he was working with a scroll of such a length that without compressing Jude he could not fit everything he wished on the scroll. Since we do not know this, we can say only that he does edit Jude, leaving out material, and that he does add his own new material. We may discern editorial reasons in the text, but we cannot know whether scroll length had any influence.

nial of the Parousia to support their practices. This, then, appears to be the best explanation of the data that we find in both Jude and 2 Peter.[38]

## VI. LITERARY FORM

2 Peter clearly starts out as a letter. For instance, it begins with the usual "x to y" address formula, "Simon Peter . . . to those who . . . have received a faith as precious as ours." This address formula is followed by a typical Christian letter greeting, "Grace and peace be yours. . . ." We notice, however, that no specific recipients are named, either by name or by locality, so it is far more general than most letters that we have in the NT. Furthermore, after the greeting there are no more letter characteristics. Unlike most NT letters, 2 Peter has no thanksgiving (which should start in 2 Pet 1:3). In the conclusion there are no personal greetings or references to the letter carrier. There is a summary (2 Pet 3:17-18a) and a final doxology (2 Pet 3:18b), but no prayer for or blessing of the recipients. Thus, while it was composed to be sent as a letter, the work is not at its core a letter, but more a sermon or speech within a letter structure. In this it is comparable to Hebrews (which is opposite to 2 Peter in that it is a sermon with a letter ending but no letter beginning, while 2 Peter is a speech or sermon with a letter beginning and no letter ending). While we will follow conventional terminology and refer to 2 Peter as a letter and to its intended audience as addressees, we need to keep in mind that the addressees are general and the letter structure limited, that the work is indeed a speech in letter clothing.

The structure of 2 Peter, like that of many NT letters, is rhetorical. Watson classifies it as deliberative rhetoric with embedded sections of judicial (1:16–2:10a; 3:1-13) and epideictic rhetoric (2:10b-22).[39] That is, as Watson comments, 2 Peter basically looks to the future, but it does judge the past actions of those being opposed and does call for decisions in the present. More significant for our present discussion is the way that rhetorical requirements structure the work. One recognizes that in the letter format (even a limited letter format, as is the case with 2 Peter) adherence to rhetorical structures was looser than when giving a speech before a court, but those structures can often be discerned nevertheless. That is in-

38. See further Lauri Thurén, "The Relationship between 2 Peter and Jude — A Classical Problem Resolved?" in Jacques Schlosser, ed., *The Catholic Epistles and the Tradition*, 451-60.

39. Watson, *Invention, Arrangement, and Style*, 85-86.

deed what we see in 2 Peter. We noted above that we lose the letter structure after the first two verses.[40] Neyrey has pointed out that the opening thanksgiving of a letter has been replaced by a solemn decree that may imply thanksgiving, but he does not state it.[41] The decree rhetoric has been adapted to the letter context, but the argument that it underlies 2 Pet 1:3-15 is persuasive, or at least more persuasive than Watson's argument that 1:3-15 is a homily.[42]

However, more interesting than the underlying rhetorical form is how this section functions rhetorically in the letter, for within the letter this section functions as the *exordium,* that is, that part of the speech that introduces the topics to be discussed in the speech, asks the hearers to pay attention, and sets out the intention of the speaker. This, of course, would be followed by a *probatio* (1:16–3:13), in which the speaker defends his thesis with various proofs. There appear to be five different proofs, along with a digression on the character of the false teachers. Finally, there is a *peroratio* (3:14-18), in which the speaker gives a recapitulation and final appeal. This gives a rhetorical shape to the letter that looks something like this:[43]

Salutation (letter framework, not part of the discourse proper) (1:1-2)
*Exordium* (1:3-15)
- Implications of Divine Goodness (1:3-11)
- Testamental Purpose (1:12-15)

*Probatio* (1:16–3:13)
- Proof 1 — Apostolic Eyewitness (1:16-18)
- Proof 2 — Prophetic Witness (1:19-21)
- Proof 3 — Certainty of Judgment (2:1-10a)
- *Digressio* — Denunciation of False Teachers (2:10b-22)

40. It is possible that 2 Pet 3:17 functions as a purpose statement, which is often found at the end of an ancient letter, but the personal greetings, health wish, and other elements often found at the end of a Greek letter are missing. In this 2 Peter differs from James, which has a general beginning but ends with typical letter elements, although lacking personal greetings.

41. Neyrey, *2 Peter, Jude,* 111. See F. W. Danker, "2 Peter: A Solemn Decree," *CBQ* 40 (1978) 64-82, for a detailed elucidation of this thesis.

42. Watson, *Invention, Arrangement, and Style,* 96-101. As Neyrey, *2 Peter, Jude,* 111, points out, Peder Borgen, *Bread from Heaven: An Exegetical Study of the Concept of Manna in the Gospel of John and the Writings of Philo* (NovTSup 10; Leiden: E. J. Brill, 1965), 28-58, has pointed out that a homily normally began with a text, and in 2 Peter 1 a text is conspicuously missing.

43. This outline is drawn from a combination of Neyrey, *2 Peter, Jude,* 113-18; Bauckham, *Jude, 2 Peter,* 135; and Watson, *Invention, Arrangement, and Style,* 81-146.

*Transitio* — Recapitulation and Introduction to the Rest of the *Probatio* (3:1-2)
Proof 4 — Mocking of Prophecies Unfounded (3:3-7)
Proof 5 — Delay Does Not Mean Uncertainty (3:8-13)
*Peroratio* — Final Encouragement to the Readers to Remain Stable (3:14-18)

The rhetorical purpose of each of these sections should be relatively clear. In the *exordium* 2 Peter makes clear that divine goodness should lead to an ethical lifestyle and that those who depart from such a lifestyle are also departing from their commitment to Jesus. The false teachers, however, defend their lifestyle by arguing that there is no final judgment, so this is what the proofs are about. The *digressio,* or digression, is a purposeful section impugning the honor of the false teachers. They are not honorable men and women, but shameful ones and thus (in an honor — shame society) should not be listened to. Having rejected the position of the false teachers, 2 Peter ends by appealing to his readers to remain stable in their ethical lifestyle. That is, he brings them back to the first part of the *exordium* and urges them not to be moved from such a stance.

Clearly, then, this letter is at root a speech. It is a speech with a letter opening. Furthermore, while it is dependent upon Jude, Jude has been integrated into it, starting in Proof 3 and continuing through to Proof 4. 2 Peter has not simply patched Jude on but rather has utilized Jude as part of an ongoing argument.

The outline above (in that one section is labeled "Testamental Purpose") and the discussion on authorship have both raised the issue whether 2 Peter might be a testament. This hypothesis has been strongly defended by Richard Bauckham. To him it is clear that 2 Peter was not written by Peter, but it is equally clear to him that the author did not *intend* the reader to believe that 2 Peter had been written by Peter; instead he intended that it had been written in the spirit of Peter. The author signals this literary intent by using the testamentary form; thus the pseudepigraphical nature of the work is not in any way fraudulent. The idea that Peter actually wrote the work is, according to Bauckham, a creation of later readers who were not familiar with the testamentary form and what it signaled.[44] How shall we evaluate this argument?

The testamentary or farewell speech was indeed a literary genre known in the first century. Bauckham rightly cites the *Testament of Moses,* the *Testament of the Twelve Patriarchs,* and the *Testament of Job* as freestanding works in this genre, all of which were written by the end of the first

44. Bauckham, *Jude, 2 Peter,* 131-35, 161-62.

century. One could add to this list the *Testament of Abraham,* although there is a difference in this work in that it is about getting Abraham to give up his soul rather than his making a farewell speech upon the realization that he is about to die.[45] Furthermore, Bauckham is correct in arguing that there are parts of other writings that are testamental in nature, for example, Job 14:3-11; *1 Enoch* 91–104 (or perhaps through 107); *4 Ezra* 14:28-36; 2 *Apocalypse of Baruch* 77–86; *Jub.* 21:1–23:7; 35; 36:1-19; Pseudo-Philo, *Liber Antiquitatum Biblicarum (Bib. Ant.)* 19.1-5; 24.1-5; 28.3-4, 5-10; 33; *Life of Adam and Eve* 25–29; Josephus, *Ant.* 4.309-19. One could add to this the farewell speech of 1 Macc 2:49-70.

What can we say about these works or parts of works? First, all the embedded testamental sections are in historical or pseudo-historical works. Second, each of the testamental parts of the works and the works that are entirely testaments reports a final charge that the hero (they all concern some patriarch or other famous person) gives to his or her children, followers, or retainers prior to his or her death. Third, the charge usually contains prophecies about the future of the individuals addressed, and, related to that prophecy, a charge to remain faithful in the light of the coming events. Fourth, after the speech concludes, there is usually a deathbed scene: a final blessing, a going to sleep or dying of the person giving the charge, the grief of those who were addressed, and the burial of the person who gave the charge, often including a summary of his or her length of life or other brief obituary (2 *Apocalypse of Baruch* is different in this regard in that the letter ends without any reference to the death of Baruch, as does *1 Enoch* 91–107, although it may imply Enoch's death; the *Testament of Moses* ends with the grief of Joshua, but the actual death of Moses is found in a missing end of the manuscript). Fifth, all of the works are considered pseudepigraphical in that they were written centuries, even millennia, after the putative life of the worthy who speaks in them. They appear designed to address issues contemporary with the date of their writing. So they are in that respect not only pseudepigraphical but also prophecy *ex eventu.* What we do not know is how the first readers of these works understood them. It is clear to us that they are pseudepigraphical, but was it as clear to those first readers? It would be helpful to have a series of reports that indicated that they did indeed understand them to be relatively recent works drawing on the revered status of the ancient hero.

45. In fact, Abraham in the *Testament of Abraham* never gets a chance to make a farewell speech since he resists death and has to be tricked into giving up his soul. See further Dale C. Allison, Jr., *Testament of Abraham* (CEJL; Berlin/New York: Walter de Gruyter, 2003), 42, who points out that the work sets one up to expect a testament, but seems to mock the testamental genre by Abraham's never producing one.

Later in church history similar works would be written about the apostles: *Acts of Peter* 36–40; *Acts of John* 106–15; *Acts of Thomas* 159–70. Two of these are martyrdoms, with the focus of the discourses being on (1) the apostle's persuasion of his followers not to intervene, (2) the final prayers of the apostle, and (3) his dialogue with the ruler who executed him. The execution is described in some detail. The *Acts of John* is different in that John orders the digging of his grave (which his followers did not know was a grave), gives a final speech, and lies down in his grave and dies.

The farewell speeches/letters in the NT, for example, Acts 20:17-34 and 2 Timothy, differ from the testamentary literature in that they anticipate the death of Paul but do not describe his death. In fact, it is clear from Acts that Paul lives for several years after his farewell speech in Ephesus; indeed, Acts ends with Paul still living. The closest that we get to an apostolic death scene in the NT is John 21, where many scholars believe that the author implies that the informant, the beloved disciple, has died and that this does not contradict Jesus' statement. However, even if this is the correct interpretation of this passage, we do not get any details of this death, nor do we get a final testament like Paul's speech in Ephesus. In fact, in the whole Gospel we hardly get a single word from the beloved disciple.[46]

Bauckham boils the testamentary genre down to two characteristics: (1) ethical admonitions and (2) revelations of the future, both given in light of the impending death of the speaker/writer. Thus he sees in 2 Peter (1) a miniature homily in 2 Pet 1:3-11 (similar to *4 Ezra* 14:28-36 and *Acts of John* 106–7) forming the core of the work, (2) typical language of farewell speeches in 2 Pet 1:12-15 (e.g., his knowledge of his death and his wish that his teaching be remembered), (3) the prediction of the future rise of false teachers in 2 Pet 2:1-3a and 3:1-4, (4) the Transfiguration account perhaps presented as another prediction of the future, (5) the combination of the farewell with the letter genre as in 2 *Apocalypse of Baruch* 76–86, and (6) the "pseudepigraphical character" of the work. He thinks

46. The only words that we get are: "Lord, who is it?" (John 13:25; 21:20) and "It is the Lord" (John 21:7). Furthermore, if Howard M. Jackson, "Ancient Self-Referential Conventions and Their Implications for the Authorship and Integrity of the Gospel of John," *JTS* n.s. 8:1 (1999) 1-34, is correct, both the anonymity and the silence of the "beloved disciple" are deliberate as lending authenticity to the work, and the "beloved disciple" refers to himself in the plural "we" of John 21:24 is self-referential and so is very much alive. He anticipates that a problem could be caused by his death due to eschatological speculation based on the assumption that he would not die before the Parousia. However, it would take us away from the focus of the present work to discuss Jackson's argument fully.

that of these six, the section in 2 Pet 1:12-15 is decisive due to its reference to Peter's impending death.[47]

Now 2 Peter does have some of the characteristics of a farewell speech. 2 Pet 1:12-15 does point to the book as reminding its readers of "these things" (presumably 2 Pet 1:3-11) in the light of his impending death ("I will soon put [the tent of this body] aside"). Clearly it is this that characterizes the work as a farewell letter or, better, farewell speech, since revelations of the future can occur in more than one genre, as can ethical admonitions (both appear in gospels, for example, and both can appear in an apocalypse, such as Revelation). The problem is that while 2 Peter is similar to 2 Timothy (although 2 Timothy has far more implied narrative in that it has a letter closing with greetings and requests, not just a letter opening as 2 Peter has), it is not really similar to *2 Apocalypse of Baruch.* The latter work has a narrative framework in which Baruch is given an apocalyptic revelation that ends by telling him, like Moses, to go up onto a mountain and prepare for death. But before he does this, the people come to him and request that he write a letter. The farewell letter, then, is appended to the narrative framework and ends without any reference to Baruch's dying. Turning to 2 Peter, we find that the partial letter form is the only narrative framework there is; it is not embedded in a larger framework. Furthermore, 2 Peter differs from the majority of the testamental literature in that it reports neither the death of Peter nor the response of his followers to that death. As a result, we wonder whether it would be recognized as a testament in the sense of the testamentary literature. Furthermore, not all farewell speeches found in Greek literature are testaments. Acts 20:17-34, for example, is quite different from the various Jewish testaments Bauckham lists. There is no reason to suppose that a first-century reader would recognize 2 Peter as different in genre from the type of farewell speech found in Acts.

Thus our conclusion is that Bauckham has shown that 2 Peter is a farewell speech. He has not shown conclusively that 2 Peter is a testament like the various Jewish testaments that he cites. To me, it does not share enough of the characteristics of those testaments, in particular the death of the writer/speaker.[48] It may have been read that way by some readers, but Bauckham has not shown that it *obviously* would have been read in that way by *most* readers. Furthermore, he has not shown that first- century readers read testamentary literature as fictive. Possibly they read it this way in light of the permission that was granted historical

47. Bauckham, *Jude, 2 Peter,* 132-33.

48. The Fourth Gospel shows that this is possible within a genre, for in John 21 the narrator breaks in, commenting on the death of the beloved disciple in the third person; a similar narrative comment at the end of 2 Peter was certainly possible.

writers to make up speeches that accorded with what a speaker might have or should have said on a given occasion, but we do not know that they read it with such a historical consciousness instead of as a tradition that had been miraculously preserved and only recently written down (or rediscovered — assuming that most readers were aware that the testamentary literature was comparatively recent). Thus, while the fictive nature of the literature is clear to us as readers, we do not know how clear or unclear it was to its first readers. Therefore, we do not know whether they would have recognized 2 Peter as fictive (pseudepigraphical) even if they had believed it to be a testament.

It is not unreasonable to believe that 2 Peter is pseudepigraphical, although Bauckham assumes the pseudepigraphical character of 2 Peter as being incontrovertible, which in our mind goes beyond the evidence. While it is not unreasonable to believe that 2 Peter is pseudepigraphical, one comes to this conclusion by making assumptions about Simon Peter that, while they are reasonable, are not the only reasonable assumptions that one could make.[49] The fact is that we do not know enough of Simon Peter's history to know whether or not he could have written 2 Peter (and, if so, whether he could also have written 1 Peter). Given that we cannot be fully convinced one way or the other, one wonders how the first-century reader (or second century, if one dates 2 Peter that late) could be clear that it was pseudepigraphical, that it was a testament, and that therefore it did not intend to be anything other than pseudepigraphical? Perhaps they could; one cannot rule out Bauckham's hypothesis as totally out of the question. But to me it is not proved. 2 Peter is a farewell letter. It does show characteristics that differentiate it from 1 Peter. It does show a significant knowledge of the Greco-Roman world, including the use of key philosophical terms. But in the absence of a biography of Simon Peter and in particular knowledge of his education and his activities after A.D. 44, one cannot really know whether or not he was capable of writing it (or of inspiring a disciple to write it for him). We do not deny the problems. We do not claim that one can show that he did write it (such an argument would be built on another set of unprovable hypotheses). In the end we have to conclude that the salutation claims that this letter was written by Simon Peter and that we by the nature of the case cannot know *from historical investigation* whether this is in some sense actual or is a pseudepigraphical attribution.

49. These assumptions are that as a fisherman he would not have been educated, or, if educated, that his Greek education would not have been sufficient to write 2 Peter, that 2 Peter shows too much familiarity with Greco-Roman philosophy for a Galilean fisherman, and so on.

## VII. THEOLOGY

It is necessary in a work of this type to discuss the theology of 2 Peter, but one does this with a certain amount of fear that abstracting theology from its context in the letter tends to make the theology abstract and thus to distort it. Yet with this danger in mind, we can see that 2 Peter contributes to our theological understanding in a number of ways, which we can summarize under a series of headings.

### A. God

God the Father remains in the background in 2 Peter. He is the Creator of the world (3:5), the inspirer of the prophets (1:21), the unseen Majestic Glory who affirms Jesus (1:17),[50] and the ruler of angels and human beings (at least in the OT [2:4-9; 3:6; and assumedly 2:11]).[51] The final judgment is "the day of God" (3:12). It is likely that he is presented as patient and merciful (3:8-10, the other alternative being to refer this to Jesus). None of this teaching is unusual, although the expression "day of God" is unique in the Bible (Rev 16:14, "the great day of God the Almighty," is conceptually similar although grammatically different). What is unusual is that God the Father recedes into the background. He is clearly there, but only in the narratives from the OT is his presence front and center.

### B. Jesus

Jesus is the one who is front and center in 2 Peter. Look at the expressions in the chart on page 151. To this we could add at least some of the six instances in which "Lord" *(kyrios)* appears without a modifier or coordinate noun, especially the phrase "day of the Lord" (3:10, which appears in Acts 2:20 and then six times in Paul's letters, each time referring to the coming of Jesus to reign, including to judge).

50. It is in 1:17 that 2 Peter uses the term "Father God" (also used, among other places, in Phil 2:11; Col 3:17; Phlm 3; 1 Pet 1:2; 2 John 3; Jude 1 — it is most common in letter salutations). While that is the source of Jesus' honor, the voice comes "from the Majestic Glory," which means that 2 Peter feels it appropriate to use a circumlocution for his own personal experience. He shies away from saying that he comes in direct contact with God, while he has no problem in saying that Jesus received honor from God.

51. We are deliberately using the word "ruler" rather than "judge," for while the functions are separate in many contemporary cultures, in that culture they were joined, and "ruler" rather than "judge" is the overarching concept. The latter is a function of the former.

| | *Expression* | *Comment* |
|---|---|---|
| 1:1 | our God and Savior Jesus Christ | Single article = God + Jesus refer to the same thing |
| 1:2 | of God and of Jesus our Lord | Could be understood as 1:1 is to be understood, but that is far from certain |
| 1:8 | our Lord Jesus Christ | |
| 1:10 | our Lord and Savior Jesus Christ | See below on "Savior." |
| 1:14 | our Lord Jesus Christ | |
| 1:16 | our Lord Jesus Christ | |
| 2:1 | the sovereign Lord who bought them | Sovereign Lord = *despotēs* |
| 2:20 | our Lord and Savior Jesus Christ | See below on "Savior." |
| 3:2 | our Lord and Savior | See below on "Savior." |
| 3:18 | our Lord and Savior Jesus Christ | See below on "Savior." |

What conclusions can we draw about Jesus from these data? First, while "Jesus" appears eight times in this letter, it never appears by itself, but only, with one exception (1:2), as part of the phrase "Jesus Christ" (this includes the stereotyped use in 1:1, "a servant and apostle of Jesus Christ"). "Christ" is no longer a title, "Messiah," but part of the name. In other words, our author does not normally allow Jesus to be cited without giving the full name, and for him or his community "Messiah" or "Anointed" is not a meaningful term.[52] These data could, of course, imply that Simon Peter was not the author of this language (given that in Mark 8:29 Peter is identified as the one saying, "You are the Messiah [Christ]," expanded in Matt 16:16 to "the Messiah, the Son of the living God" — thus the term "Messiah" was meaningful to Peter). At the least it implies that he has abandoned his earlier language for Jesus and has fully identified with the Gentile world.

Second, Jesus is consistently identified as "Lord." This term identifies his authority as a ruler, as one to whom one submits. If there were any doubt that it is the sovereignty of Jesus as the regent of God's kingdom that is being referred to, 2 Pet 2:1, which does not use the term *kyrios* but the term *despotēs,* should set it to rest, for while *kyrios* can mean "sir"

52. This certainly means that the context is a Gentile one, for in the Greco-Roman world, unlike the Jewish world, anointing was used only for medicinal or cosmetic purposes, not as part of placing one in a position of authority.

or (in some contexts) "husband," *despotēs* always refers to a ruler, whether on the household level (and so it is used of God in Luke 2:29) or on the national level. It is true that the term has been picked up from Jude 4, but Jude has *despotēs* and *kyrios,* while 2 Peter picks up only the clearer term, apparently not feeling that the double term is needed. Jesus, then, is seen primarily as the ruler of the household of God or kingdom of God (the two concepts are overlapping), as the one who is to be submitted to and obeyed. Those reject his authority over their lives (including his moral teaching) have denied him.

This also means that Jesus has taken over the functions of Caesar (and any client king) for these people. This letter contains no statement or implication that there are other lords alongside Jesus. There is one sovereign Lord, namely, Jesus. That this would be experienced as a threat by the Roman authorities is not surprising. The idea that such a statement could have been only religious or that the religious and the political were separate would not have occurred to anyone during this period, since it came about only with the marginalization of religion during the Enlightenment. Jesus, then, is the ruler of a real kingdom, a kingdom that subsumes all other kingdoms and relativizes the authority of all other rulers. In this respect 2 Peter is fully in line with the Gospels.[53]

Thirdly, Jesus is viewed as Savior. The term itself was primarily applied to deities, both Greco-Roman (from Zeus to the deities of the mystery religions) and Jewish (e.g., Pss 24:5; 26:9, 27:1; 62:2), and it is this usage that appears to be primary in the NT (Luke 1:47; 1 Tim 2:3; 4:10; Titus 2:10; 3:4; Jude 25). Particularly in the OT God is the one who delivers from death and destruction, whether the one being delivered be an individual (usually a king) or the whole nation. (One needs to be careful not to read this term within the context of the focus on sin in Western Christianity, for in most cases it does not occur in a context referring to sin but rather in a context that refers to a much more comprehensive deliverance.) Secondarily it was applied to the ruler, who was often deified, from Ptolemy I Soter to the Roman emperors.[54] This application of the term to Roman emperors, particularly its relationship to their bringing

53. See N. T. Wright, *Jesus and the Victory of God* (Minneapolis: Fortress, 1996), or *The Challenge of Jesus* (Downers Grove, IL: InterVarsity Press, 1999), for a further discussion of this theme in the Synoptic Gospels and in Paul.

54. *"Sōtēr,"* BAG 800-801: ". . . beginning with Augustus, the Roman emperors were given the titles 'lord' and 'savior' in the emperor cult, which particularly prevailed in the cities of Asia Minor. In the case of rulers, their power as savior was evident in ending war and serving as the great benefactor *(euergetēs)* in bringing peace and prosperity (the news of this peace was frequently called *euangelion,* 'good news')." A. Boyd Luter, Jr., "Savior," *DPL,* 867.

peace and prosperity (i.e., "good news"), means that the term has a political implication as well. These implications are particularly important in that there was no tradition of the term being applied in the OT and intertestamental literature to either David and his successors or the Coming One (whether or not he was identified as Davidic), Zech 9:9 being about as close as one gets to such an attribution (in Isa 49:6 the salvation is *God's,* and the Servant the one God uses to bring it).

When Paul applies the term to Jesus, it has to do with his rule (Eph 5:23; Phil 3:20).[55] Of course, in the Pauline literature it appears most frequently in the Pastoral Letters, where it mostly refers to God (three times in 1 Timothy), but at times it also refers to Jesus as the cosmic victor ("who has destroyed death and has brought life and immortality to light through the [good news]" — 2 Tim 1:10; "the glorious appearing of our great God and Savior, Jesus Christ" — Titus 2:13).[56] This world (or cosmic) rulership is also consistent with the application of the term to Jesus in Luke 2:11 ("a Savior . . . Christ the Lord"); Acts 5:31 ("Prince and Savior"), Acts 13:23 (although in this passage national deliverance is the focus, but still with a reference to rulership).[57]

Thus it is not surprising that 2 Peter combines "Lord" and "Savior," for the two fit together when applied to a ruler. Jesus is the ruler who is also the benefactor of his people. As a ruler he is owed obedience (thus the association with "kingdom" in 2 Pet 1:11 and with "command" in 3:2), and this is even more so because he is a benefactor (alluded to in 2 Pet 2:20). Not to submit to his directions is to deny him (as noted above; cf. 2 Pet 2:2), an act of impiety that is all the worse because it shows lack of gratitude.

In other words, there are two competing narratives informing 2 Peter. The first is the implied narrative[58] of the Roman Empire (see the diagram at the top of p. 154).

55. In Philippians the reference is to citizenship and the place of citizenship, this being the place from which the Savior comes, whose power "enables him to bring everything under his control." In Ephesians the term is used in the context of Christ as head, to whom submission is owed.

56. Titus is interesting in that its six usages form three pairs, the first of each pair using the term for God and the second for Jesus.

57. John 4:42 and 1 John 4:14 both refer to the world, but, while fitting with the observations made for Paul and Luke-Acts, do not have enough information in the context to add to the discussion.

58. In the Greimasian narrative diagrams the narrative functions are: top row = sender, object, receiver; bottom row = helper, agent, opponent.

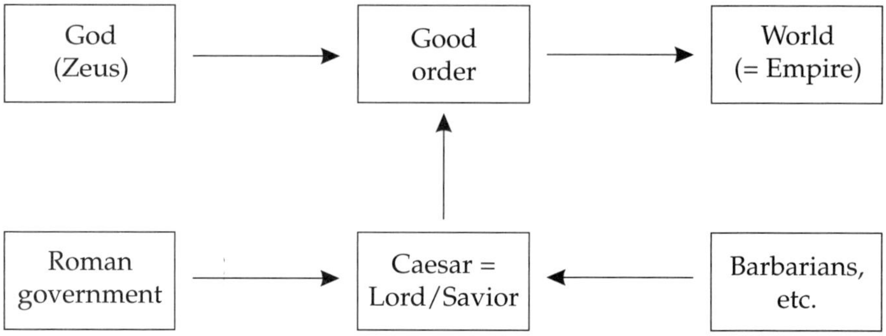


This implied narrative is challenged and replaced by an alternative implied narrative in 2 Peter:

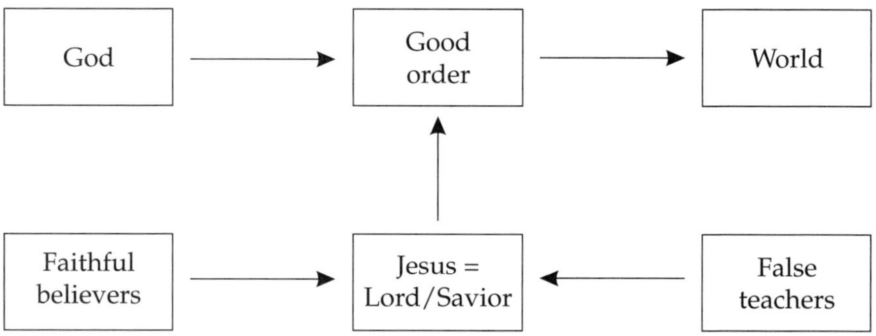


Naturally, the narratives implied in 2 Peter 2 refer to a wider range of opponents, such as the fallen angels and the people of Sodom, but the underlying issue in 2 Peter is the narrative implied above. If this were a situation of persecution, then the opponent would become the persecutors. What is clear is that even though the relationship of the believers to the Roman state is not under discussion in 2 Peter, his whole implied narrative structure is subversive of the implied narrative of the Roman Empire and thus we are not at all surprised that there was conflict between the Roman Empire and the followers of Jesus.

Fourthly, 2 Peter appears to refer to Jesus as God. Partly this is seen in his changing Jude's "To the only God our Savior be glory . . . through Jesus Christ our Lord" (Jude 25), which appears to subordinate Jesus to "the only God," to "our Lord and Savior Jesus Christ. To him be glory . . ." (2 Pet 3:18). Partly this is seen in his frequent transfer of the title "Savior" to Jesus.[59] After all, it is in Titus, a book that parallels Jesus with God in using the term "Savior," that we find "our great God and Savior, Jesus Christ" (Titus 2:13). But primarily it is in the phrase "our God and Savior Jesus Christ" (2 Pet 1:1). As with Titus, we cannot be sure that our author is fully conscious of what the grammar should mean (i.e., the single article before the two titles indicating that they are a single entity). However, 2 Peter differs from Titus in that "our" follows "God" rather than being part of the phrase "Savior Jesus Christ," so while it may be argued that Titus means "the Great God and our Savior Jesus Christ," only the single article pointing to the NIV translation, in 2 Peter the analogous wooden reading would be "our God and [a or the] Savior Jesus Christ," which is awkward to say the least, especially in that "our" goes most naturally with Savior. Thus it is probable that our author thinks of Jesus Christ as the divine Savior. How far he is conscious of his attribution of divinity and how much he has thought through its implications we cannot tell — he certainly does not have a developed trinitarian theology — but he clearly shows the direction that Christian thinking was taking at the time of his writing.[60]

## C. The Holy Spirit

2 Peter is remarkable for how little it mentions the Holy Spirit. 1 Peter has four to six references to the Spirit, in which the Spirit is responsible not only for the inspiration of the prophets but also for the empowering of evangelists, the sanctifying of believers, and the presence of God in believers undergoing persecution. Jude refers to the Spirit twice, once as the mediator of prayer ("pray in the Holy Spirit" — Jude 20) and once as what is lacked by those he opposes (Jude 19). 2 Peter has only one reference to the Spirit, and that is as the one who inspires prophets (who "spoke from God as they were carried along by the Holy Spirit" — 2 Pet 1:21). Having only a single reference to the Spirit is not unique to 2 Peter, for Paul, who normally is not shy about mentioning the Spirit, displays a similar phenomenon in Colossians (Col 1:8 is the only reference to the Spirit), but we are surprised that he neither picks up Jude's reference to the false teachers as being devoid of the Spirit nor refers to the Spirit's action in sanctification, as 1 Peter does.

59. "Lord" is not as specific a title, for it is used for all types of household heads and rulers in the LXX as well as the NT, and thus, without something in the context to indicate the fact, it would not be read as equivalent to YHWH.

60. On the issue of how both Jews and Christians thought about God, particularly how monotheism did not preclude reflection upon the inner nature of God, see Wright, *The New Testament and the People of God*, 245-59, especially 259, and 471-76.

## D. The Human Condition

Humanity, according to 2 Peter, is entrapped by "the corruption that is in the world caused by" desire (the NIV has added "evil" in 2 Pet 1:4, but that misunderstands 2 Peter). This corruption is so real that even those who have previously escaped can become re-entrapped, should they turn back. 2 Peter does not describe or categorize desire (i.e., he lacks a vice list), but it is clear that the main result in the teachers he opposes is licentiousness along with greed and despising authority. While these are stock vices, early Christian vice lists are varied enough that there is good reason to believe that these are in 2 Peter's sight actual issues in the teachers he opposes. His main point, however, is that they are *re-entrapped* and thus have returned to a state of bondage. Furthermore, they are enticing less stable believers toward the same entrapment.

## E. Deliverance

The deliverance that God has brought about is that his goodness has enabled believers to escape from the corruption described above. This escape includes the ability to live godly lives, an ability that comes from being in a proper relationship with Jesus Christ. Furthermore, this escape also includes sharing in the divine nature.

On the other hand, this deliverance is reversible. The false teachers are described as individuals who have escaped the corruption that is in the world but are now "again entangled in it and overcome" and so are in a worse situation than if they had never experienced deliverance (2 Pet 2:20-21).

It is interesting to note that salvation or deliverance is thought of in such strongly ethical terms. This flies in the face of the primarily religious terms (i.e., salvation from sin without a concrete expectation that one thereby ceases sinning) of post-Reformation Christian thought.

## F. Eschatology

As believers continue in their commitment to Jesus Christ and live out the godliness that God has enabled, they may expect to be welcomed into the kingdom of Jesus Christ. For that to happen all that is required is being on one's guard so that one does not "fall from [one's] secure position" (2 Pet 3:17). That is, they are to keep on doing what they are already doing.

On the other hand, those who have forsaken obedience to God face judgment. This judgment may be both proximate (such as the imprisonment of the angels who sinned and the destruction on Sodom and Gomorrah) and ultimate (on "the day of the Lord" or "the day of God"). Between the proximate and ultimate judgments there is an ongoing punishment of some type. For the angels 2 Peter borrows the Greek Tartarus, where the Titans were imprisoned in Greek mythology, but for human beings no place of imprisonment is mentioned. Still, "the Lord knows how to rescue godly men from trials and to hold the unrighteous for the day of judgment, while continuing their punishment" (2 Pet 2:9).

The ultimate judgment does not appear to have a fixed time. On the one hand, believers can speed up the coming of that day, presumably by their holy and godly lives. On the other hand, God has delayed it because he is patient. He does not will the destruction of any human being; his desire is repentance for all. However, it is clear that for 2 Peter God's desire will not come to pass, for the final day will come suddenly, all the secrets of this world will be exposed, and this world will be purified. That day will be a day of judgment and destruction for the ungodly as well as, apparently, for the fallen angels. But on the positive side it will produce a renewed world that is totally righteous. This picture is consistent with the teachings of both Jesus and Paul on the final judgment, namely, that it will come suddenly, that it will result in the judgment of the ungodly, and that it will result in a renewal of this world, a universal kingdom in which God's type of justice and peace will be experienced.

There is, of course, some debate as to whether this day of judgment will also bring about the destruction of the space-time universe (or at least the earth) and the creation of a new universe (or earth). Our conclusion in the commentary is that what 2 Peter is talking about is the exposure and expunging of evil (i.e., what is done in the world "will be disclosed" [2 Pet 3:10], following what appears to be the better manuscripts); thus the "elements" are "melted" and "destroyed" only insofar as is required for the exposure and destruction of evil, a renewal of the world rather than a destruction and re-creation of the world. In this 2 Peter appears to follow the application of cosmic terminology to historical events that is found in Old Testament prophecy.

## G. Scripture

2 Peter has two things to say about Scripture. First, referring to the OT prophets (presumably including such works as *1 Enoch* and *Testament of Moses,* which are cited in his source Jude), he argues that these prophetic statements are of divine origin. God was speaking in the prophets via the

Holy Spirit. In saying this he maintains the transcendence of God, since it is the Spirit who brings the words of God to the prophets. Furthermore, he believes that both the prophetic vision and its interpretation were Spirit-inspired (assuming our exegesis is correct, "no prophecy of Scripture came about by the prophet's own interpretation [of his vision, dream, or other form of revelation]." The passages in the Scriptures that he seems most concerned with are those prophetic passages that refer to divine judgment.

The words of these prophets are confirmed by (1) the personal experience of the exaltation of Christ that Peter experienced at the Transfiguration (thus personal religious experience), (2) the teaching of Jesus transmitted to the believers by the missionaries who had come to them (i.e., "your apostles"), and (3) Paul's writings. From this it sounds as if the community does not yet have written Gospels, or, if it does, values the oral testimony of the missionaries over the more recently produced gospels. Paul's writings have begun to circulate, but we do not know how complete the Pauline collection is. While the command of Jesus is clearly parallel in authority to the words of the holy prophets, for Jesus is Lord and Savior (2 Pet 3:2), it is not as clear what status 2 Peter is giving to the Pauline collection. He does refer to these works in parallel to the Hebrew Scriptures ("the other Scriptures"), but it is not clear to what extent he thinks of these other "Scriptures" as a closed body. First, given that he never cites the Hebrew Scriptures directly, but only through the mediation of Second Temple writings and tradition,[61] it is not certain how conscious he was of an OT canon as such. Second, the term for "Scriptures" in 2 Pet 3:16 is a general one that can refer to any writing, so we are not sure whether he has only the Hebrew Scriptures in view or whether the term includes contemporary writings as well, such as early forms of the Gospels, not to mention various Jewish writings. What is clear is that a sense of canon as such developed in the second century only as a reaction to individuals such as Marcion who would exclude works such as Matthew from being read in the church and groups such as the Gnostics who wished to read in church works that deviated from standard church teaching. Those disputes and thus any developed sense of canon (including a sense of Paul's writings as canon rather than as helpful writings from a major leader of the early Jesus movement) will arise only after 2 Peter is already in circulation (in fact, his letter will be excluded by some from being read in church).

None of the writings that he is referring to is so perspicuous that it cannot be distorted by "ignorant and unstable people" (2 Pet 3:16).

61. Davids, "The Use of Second Temple Traditions in 1 and 2 Peter and Jude," in Jacques Schlosser, ed., *The Catholic Epistles and the Tradition*, 409-31.

# *Commentary on 2 Peter*

## I. SALUTATION (1:1-2)

Our opening section is in the form of a Greek letter opening, but it also serves as a proper opening to a speech. Aware of appropriate rhetoric, our author gains the interest and favor of his readers by establishing his own reliability and honoring them. This, in the view of Greek rhetoric, establishes the appropriate rapport so that they are prepared for the rest of the letter.[1]

> [1]*Simon Peter, a servant and apostle of Jesus Christ, To those who through the righteousness of our God and Savior Jesus Christ have received a faith as precious as ours:* [2]*Grace and peace be yours in abundance through the knowledge of God and of Jesus our Lord.*

1 The letter we know as 2 Peter starts in the way a typical NT letter begins. First, the sender of the letter is named: Simon Peter. The name Simon Peter or a variant of it (e.g., "Simon, who is called Peter") appears over sixty-five times in the Gospels and Acts (e.g., Matt 16:16; Luke 5:8; John 6:68; cf. Mark 3:16; Acts 10:5), so the person intended is not difficult to determine. What is surprising is the spelling of "Simon" (*Symeōn* rather than *Symōn*),[2] for it appears only seven times in the NT, sometimes for the tribe of Simeon (Rev 7:7), sometimes for another person named

1. Duane Watson, *Invention, Arrangement, and Style: Rhetorical Criticism of Jude and 2 Peter* (SBLDS 104; Atlanta: Scholars Press, 1988).

2. Some manuscripts, most notably 𝔓[72] and B, have the more usual spelling, but it is far more likely that the spelling was regularized in a few manuscripts than that the majority shifted to an usual spelling.

Simeon (Luke 2:25, 34; 3:30; Acts 13:1), and only here and in Acts 15:14 for Simon Peter. In the latter passage James refers to Peter as "Simon," and Luke chooses this spelling (Simeon) rather than his usual spelling for Simon, perhaps indicating a Jewish or even a Palestinian usage. This impression that it reflects a Jewish or Palestinian usage is confirmed when one looks at 1 Macc 2:65, where Mattathias refers to his son Simon Maccabeus as "Simeon" (whereas all other references to him are as "Simon"). That is, "Simon" was a common Greek name, so Jews with the name "Simeon" (the most common Jewish name in the 100 B.C. to A.D. 200 period) were normally called "Simon" in Greek-speaking contexts.[3] To be consistent, since our author is using the Semitic form of the name, he should also have said "Cephas" rather than "Peter" (outside of the Gospels only Paul calls Peter Cephas: 1 Cor 9:5 and Gal 1:18; 2:9, 11, 14), but it may be that he is conforming to typical usage, which was inconsistent on this point. The one thing that this observation supports is that our author knows what Peter was called in Jewish (especially Aramaic-speaking) circles and so is probably a Jew himself, despite his command of Greek.[4]

Peter calls himself "a servant and apostle of Jesus Christ." This particular combination ("servant" plus "apostle") is found only in Rom 1:1 and Titus 1:1, although only in Romans does Paul call himself a servant "of Jesus Christ." In Titus he is named a servant of God and an apostle of Jesus Christ. James and Jude simply call themselves "servant" (in James, "of God and the Lord Jesus Christ," while Jude has "of Jesus Christ" and adds "brother of James"; so also Phil 1:1). 1 Peter has "apostle of Jesus Christ," which is also typical of Paul (1 Cor 1:1; 2 Cor 1:1; Gal 1:1; Eph 1:1; Col 1:1; 1 Tim 1:1; 2 Tim 1:1).[5] Thus, in comparing this title to those in the other letters, it appears that "servant" is the expected title, while "apostle"

3. Cf. J. A. Fitzmyer, "The Name Simon," in *Essays on the Semitic Background of the New Testament* (London: Geoffrey Chapman, 1971), 105-12.

4. Commentators are split as to whether this is evidence for/proof of the authenticity of the letter (e.g., Bigg; Green) or whether it was a deliberate attempt by a later pseudepigrapher to impersonate Peter (e.g., Kelly, Schrage). The latter argument must face the fact that this is not how Peter is named in 1 Peter, the Gospels, and, with one exception, Acts. Thus our "pseudepigrapher" is close enough to friends of Peter that he accurately portrays the name, for he would not have picked this up from reading alone. This moves him closer to Bauckham's member of the Petrine circle. The argument that this usage proves authenticity (noted above) claims too much, for while Peter most likely did call himself "Simeon," so did other Jewish-Christians (including James as portrayed in Acts). The evidence points to cultural awareness (and probably cultural membership) on the part of the author; it does not prove authenticity.

5. Phlm 1 has Paul referring to himself as a "prisoner" of Jesus Christ, which fits the non-commanding tone of the letter, while in 1 and 2 Thessalonians Paul's name is joined with that of others and no title is used.

is added because of the need to assert the authority of the sender. That is, in letters where the congregation accepts the authority of the sender, the title "apostle" is not used. The use of this title marks out this letter as something of an official letter rather than, for example, a friendly letter. At the same time "servant" (better, "slave") is not an expression of personal humility or an indication of "servant leadership," but rather an expression for a person totally "owned by" and devoted to Jesus Christ, whose status is not his own but one derived from his master.[6] A servant of Caesar represented the Caesar and needed to be treated with appropriate respect, not because of who he was as a slave but because what was done to him was done to Caesar's property. More importantly, "servant/slave of God/Yahweh" designated someone who was part of the "royal court" or "royal advisors" of God (see the parallel usage for those in the OT who are referred to as servants of a king, e.g., 1 Sam 18:5, 30). Those called slaves of God in the OT include the patriarchs (Exod 32:13; Deut 9:27; Isa 44:1), Moses (Deut 34:5; Josh 1:1-2; 1 Kings 8:53, 56), Samuel (1 Sam 3:9-10), and David (1 Sam 17:32; 2 Sam 3:18; 7:5, 8, 19-21, 25-29).[7] Thus "servant" (slave) indicates an honorable (if intrinsically low-status) place in the "household" of God/Jesus as his slave; while "apostle" indicates that the person is sent on a mission (in this case, "by Jesus Christ"). This is a person with significant authority, not in himself, but in that he belongs to Jesus Christ.

The recipients are identified by neither name nor location, which is atypical of the Pauline letters or of 1 Peter, but is true of Jude and James (although James's "in the Diaspora" is a generalized location). While 2 Peter addresses a specific congregation or group of congregations (since our author knows details about their situation) that have received another letter from our author (2 Pet 3:1, which does not necessarily refer to 1 Peter), we are not told where they live. They are identified as fellow believers ("who have received a faith as precious as ours"). The term for "as precious as" (or "equally valuable," or, still better, "equally honorable")[8] is found only here in the NT, although it is well known from other Greek literature (Dio Chrysostom 24[41].2; Philo, *Leg. alleg.* 2.18; *De sacrificiis Abelis et Caini* 8; *Spec. leg.* 1.181; Josephus, *Ant.* 12.119). Whose faith is this faith equal to? Is it the faith of Jewish Christians?[9] Yet if this is the case,

6. See further Murray J. Harris, *Slave of Christ: A New Testament Metaphor for Total Devotion to Christ* (NSBT 8; Downers Grove, IL/Leicester, U.K.: InterVarsity Press/Apollos, 1999).

7. See further J. N. Collins, *Diakonia: Reinterpreting the Ancient Sources* (Oxford: Oxford University Press, 1990), 92-95.

8. Compounds of *timē* "invariably borrow their meaning from *timē, honour,* and not from *timē* in the sense of *price.*" Mayor, *The Epistles of Jude and II Peter,* 80, quoting Field.

9. So Mayor, *Jude and 2 Peter,* 81.

why is there no other trace of Jew-Gentile tension in this letter? Is it the faith of the apostles (so the majority of modern commentators)? This is likely the case, for (1) 2 Peter writes from the position of his impending death, thus the comparison between the dying apostolic generation[10] and the continuing postapostolic generation, and (2) the comparison is between "I" (or "we" when referring to more apostles in 1:16-19) and "you" and thus between himself as an apostle and them as believers. The point is to put them on the same level as he is with respect to faith.

Their common faith is honorable, while that of the "false teachers" (2 Pet 2:1) is not honorable. Because it is honorable, it is worth paying a price in terms of discipline and conflict to maintain, for honor is a primary social value. This faith has been "received" by them. 2 Peter again uses a rare word, found elsewhere in the NT only in John 19:24. It means "to receive by lot or divine will," and thus indicates that faith is something that God has given them, a favor from their heavenly patron.[11] It is not entirely clear in our context whether "faith" refers to the ability to commit oneself (so Bauckham) or to a belief system/version of the good news. The former is faith's more normal meaning in Paul, but the latter is not absent from his writings either (see Gal 1:23). It seems to me that the latter meaning fits better here, that is, a version of the good news that they have received from God. However, this good news that demanded commitment (faith) should not be made into a credal formula or system. Such a system would appear only later in church history. In his usage, however, 2 Peter is in general closer to the Pastorals, and their usage of "faith" as a shorthand for the good news, than to the earlier Pauline letters.

This faith is granted "through the righteousness of our God." Again a significant theme of the letter is being introduced. The false teachers do not know "the way of righteousness" (2 Pet 2:21; in contrast to Noah, 2 Pet 2:5) and thus will not inherit the coming world where "righteousness dwells" (2 Pet 3:13). That God's action in granting faith is marked by righteousness means that it is something quite different from that which the false teachers proclaim. This "righteousness" does not mean Christ's redemptive work (so Spicq), but ethical righteousness, as the other uses in 2 Peter show. This ethical quality would be better translated "justice" in that the divine patron granting faith acts justly — with fairness and lack of favoritism — in making his grant. Menander Rhetor (and other

10. Strictly speaking, there were apostles around for more than one generation after Jesus' resurrection, for *Didache* 11 refers to traveling apostles, and that work was written after 100. We are using here the conventional, if inaccurate, identification of the first postresurrection generation as the apostolic generation, i.e., the period when the Twelve (who were apostles, but were far from the sum total of the apostles of their time) were alive.

11. See H. Hanse, *"lanchanō," TDNT* 4:2.

Greeks) viewed justice as one of the four cardinal virtues (courage, wisdom, and temperance were the others). The aspect of justice that is important in this context is "mildness towards subjects, humanity towards petitioners, . . . [including] benefaction, impartial treatment, just law, fairness to all."[12] It is out of this character that God has granted to these believers faith equal in honor to that of the apostles themselves.

Finally, this justice is attributed to "our God and Savior Jesus Christ." While some commentators read this "our God and [our] Savior Jesus Christ," bringing it into line with 2 Pet 1:2 (which is, however, a very stereotyped expression) and the usual distinguishing of Jesus from God in the NT,[13] the Greek more naturally implies that one person is being intended. While the fact that a single article is used is not absolutely conclusive, it is highly suggestive.[14] More important, there is only one "our," and that comes after "God" and before "and." "Our" certainly is intended to include "Savior" as well as "God," thus also indicating that one person is being discussed. There are other compound terms referring to Jesus in this book (1:11; 3:18), and in the last of these ("our Lord and Savior Jesus Christ") the parallel to our text is unmistakable. Furthermore, as the last verse in the book, this final reference to Christ forms a lovely *inclusio* with our phrase. Thus, while the NT rarely refers to Jesus as God (John 1:1-3; 20:28; Heb 1:8-9; and probably Titus 2:13 are some of the rare examples), this is one of those few places.[15] (The title was not at all uncommon by the second century.) What 2 Peter means by calling Jesus God we do not know; certainly he is not indicating a fully developed trinitarian theology, but it is also surely not just a casual comment.

That Jesus is called God is surprising, but we must not overlook the title "Savior." While common in the second century and even more com-

12. Neyrey, *2 Peter, Jude,* 147. See Menander Rhetor 375.8-10; cf. 363.17-20.

13. So Neyrey, *2 Peter, Jude,* 147-48. He also notes that only in Phil 1:11 is "righteousness" said to be from Christ rather than from God. Of course, if the sense here is "justice," then any text that viewed Christ as judge would imply such righteousness.

14. We are referring to the Granville Sharp rule that states that a single article followed by two nouns joined by "and" refers to a single object. Don Carson comments in a note to the author, "The most sophisticated treatment of that rule, by far, is by Daniel B. Wallace, in a book-length work to appear shortly in the Studies in Biblical Greek series (Peter Lang). In my view, he has conclusively shown that Greek grammar here must be taken to mean that in this instance 'God' and 'Savior' both refer to Jesus Christ." We would have said this in the text of commentary had the book already been published and we had therefore had the chance to examine the argument. For now we say "highly suggestive" in anticipation that a later edition will be able to say "conclusively proven."

15. See further Raymond E. Brown, "Does the New Testament Call Jesus God?" in *Jesus, God and Man* (Milwaukee: Bruce, 1967) 1-38, and Vincent Taylor, "Does the New Testament Call Jesus 'God'?" in *New Testament Essays* (London: Epworth, 1970), 83-89.

mon in Christian language today, it was not that common in the NT: Luke 2:11; John 4:42; Acts 5:31; 13:23; Eph 5:23; Phil 3:20; 4:14; 2 Tim 1:10; Titus 1:4; 2:13; 3:6; 2 Pet 1:1, 11; 2:20; 3:2, 18. While salvation in the OT is from God (e.g., Deut 32:15; 2 Sam 22:3, 47; Ps 3:8[9 in the LXX], note that "deliverance" and "salvation" are translations of the same word; 18:46), in the NT the preponderance of references to Jesus as Savior come in later books: the Pastorals and 2 Peter. In fact, the term is far more common in 2 Peter than in any other book. Could this be because of the prevalence of "saviors" in pagan religions and especially in the Caesar cult?[16] If so, our author is showing sensitivity to his Gentile environment: Jesus is the true Savior-God (as opposed to Caesar and others as bogus savior-gods), who has granted his readers the honor of a faith equal to that of the apostles. That, of course, he would say to the modern reader as well.

**2** Our author wishes his readers the traditional "grace and peace" (Rom 1:7; 1 Cor 1:3; 2 Cor 1:2; Gal 1:3; and all other NT letters [except James, 1 John, and 3 John], including Rev 1:4). The greeting arises from the typical Hebraic greeting of "peace" (*shalom,* meaning "total well-being") plus the typical Greek greeting of *chairein* (as in Jas 1:1), morphed into the Judeo-Christian "grace" *(charis).*[17] The wishing of "grace" or "favor" fit with the biblical climate. In the OT finding favor before God (or before a noble or ruler) was often critical to survival (Gen 6:8; Exod 33:13). In the NT we find God's favor resting on some people (Luke 2:40; Acts 4:33). Thus this term, which normally refers to a ruler's favor,[18] is quite naturally applied to the divine king's favor. These readers have already received favor from God in that they have received a faith equal to that of the apostles. Now they are wished further favor from their divine patron, indeed multiplied favor. This is at once formal (i.e., one normally started a letter wishing good to come to the recipient) and an introduction to a central topic in that the next verse will indicate both what God has given us and how that favor can be developed.

Grace and peace come "through the knowledge of God and of Jesus our Lord." The term for "knowledge" here is a less usual term *(epignōsis),* which, while not rare in the NT (Rom 1:28; 3:20; 10:2; Eph 1:17; 4:13; Phil 1:9; Col 1:9-10; 2:2; 3:10; 1 Tim 2:4; 2 Tim 2:25; 3:7; Titus 1:1; Phlm 6; Heb 10:26), is characteristic of 2 Peter (1:2, 3, 8; 2:20). Peter can also use the

16. Werner Foerster, *"sōzō ktl.," TDNT* 7:1004-12.

17. While characteristic of NT letters, the combination of "grace" and "peace" is found in some Jewish works. See Gerhard Friedrich, "Lohmeyers These über das paulinische Briefpräscript kritisch beleuchtet," *TLZ* 81 (1956) 158-64. This is a response to Ernst Lohmeyer, "Probleme paulinischer Theologie, I: Briefliche Grussüberschriften," *ZNW* 26 (1927) 158-64.

18. Hans Conzelmann, *"charis," TDNT* 9:373-76.

more common term (*gnōsis;* 1:5-6; 3:18). Two questions arise from this vocabulary: (1) why the emphasis on knowledge, and (2) is there a difference between the two terms? As for the emphasis on knowledge, some commentators argue that the emphasis exists because those whom 2 Peter opposes claimed some special knowledge or revelation.[19] This claim is the result of mirror-imaging the work, not the result of direct statements 2 Peter makes about his opponents; thus, while this was possibly the case, we must evaluate the claim as unproved. What we do know is that 2 Peter thinks that knowledge is very important for his readers. While in some contexts the meanings of the two words for knowledge (and their respective verbs) overlap, recent study indicates that sometimes the term for knowledge that 2 Peter uses here *(epignōsis)* can mean "coming to know" and thus is appropriate for knowledge that leads to or is gained in conversion.[20] This is certainly the case in Heb 10:26, and it fits here in 2 Peter. If this distinction holds, then where the author of 2 Peter uses this term he is thinking of that knowledge gained in conversion rather than that which one may develop on one's own (as in 1:5-6).

Furthermore, of the five meanings for our term distinguished by Picirelli, this usage here in 2 Peter 1:2 may well be the first, coming to know someone for who they really are, although Neyrey[21] argues for the fifth meaning (to give acknowledgment to someone or something). That is, grace and peace come to the readers in abundance in the context of their acknowledgment of or coming to know "God and Jesus our Lord."[22] The fact that persons are named as objects makes me favor "coming to know" as what 2 Peter really means, although certainly that would have to include acknowledgment of the persons, so perhaps this distinction is finer than our author would wish to make. What is clear is that this knowledge implies an ethical lifestyle. Therefore the knowledge is not simply intellectual (knowing things about God and Jesus), or even personal in the sense of having met someone, but knowledge that results in

19. Green, *2 Peter and Jude,* 62-63; Kelly, *Peter and Jude,* 299; Reicke, *James, Peter, and Jude,* 151; Schrage, *Der zweite Petrusbrief, der Judasbrief,* 129.

20. Robert E. Picirelli, "The Meaning of 'Epignosis,'" *EvQ* 47 (1975) 85-93, is the most thorough study, but R. Bultmann, *"ginōskō ktl.," TDNT* 1:707, had previously developed the basic idea. Cf. also J. Dupont, *Gnosis: La connaissance religieuse dans les épîtres de Saint Paul* (Louvain/Paris: Nauwelaerts/Gabalda, 1949).

21. Neyrey, *2 Peter, Jude,* 149.

22. The more probable reading is "Jesus our Lord" rather than "Jesus Christ our Lord," for this is supported by the oldest manuscripts, including $\mathfrak{P}^{72}$ and B (as against א and A), as well as a multitude of later manuscripts, and this is a shorter reading that would more likely be expanded by later scribes than would a longer reading be shortened. While "Christ" was used in the Gentile world, it was not a meaningful term as it was for Jews, where its sense of "Messiah" was appreciated.

committed living. That will become clearer in the next verse. In our present verse the conversion aspect is more the focus, for if these Christians were Gentiles, it was in conversion that they came to know both God and Jesus. The names of the two persons are quite conventional (e.g., 1 Cor 1:3; 2 Cor 1:2; 1 Pet 1:3). Here Jesus is designated "our Lord," a common Christian title (Rom 10:9-10 indicates that it was a basic Christian confession as well), and is paired with "God," who is clearly a distinct person. Thus it is in the context of their having come to know these two for who they really are that they are in a position to receive multiplied favor and well-being. It would not be too much to assert that everything else in the letter assumes this foundation.

## II. LETTER OPENING (1:3-15)

The letter opening consists of two parts, an opening sermon (1:3-11) and a purpose statement (1:14-15). The purpose statement is linked back to the opening sermon and thus belongs with it. Right after the purpose statement the letter shifts gears: 2 Peter addresses the issue of the return of Christ and the judgment associated with it. This will be his subject for most of the rest of the letter, so it forms the body. That, however, is coming later. At this point our author is dealing with more general instruction. This part functions rhetorically as an *exordium,* that part of a classical rhetorical composition that introduced the topic at hand and won the favor of the audience. In 2 Peter the central topic of the letter is hardly touched upon in this *exordium,* but the sympathy of the audience is certainly won.[1]

### A. Opening Sermon (1:3-11)

This section of 2 Peter 1 conforms in structure to a miniature sermon in the early Christian style. That is, it begins with (1) a historical-theological section recounting the divine acts (1:3-4), then continues to (2) an ethical exhortation (1:5-10), and ends with (3) an eschatological conclusion (salvation promised/judgment threatened; 1:11).[2] This sermon surprises us,

1. Watson, *Invention, Arrangement, and Style,* 87-94.

2. Klaus Baltzer, *The Covenant Formulary,* trans. David E. Green (Oxford: Basil Blackwell, 1971), and Karl P. Donfried, *The Setting of Second Clement in Early Christianity* (NovTSup 38; Leiden: Brill, 1974), 41-48, were the first to note the sermonic structure,

for most NT letters have a blessing or thanksgiving at this point; while the sermon does point to the benefactions God had given (and thus has something of the tone of a thanksgiving), the normal address to God ("thanks be to God" or "blessed be God") is missing here. Watson is probably correct in arguing that 2 Peter finds it necessary to catch the attention of his audience and underline for them the importance of the themes he is discussing. Thus the sermon functions rhetorically as an *exordium,* an introduction to a speech. This would indicate that our author has already moved from a strict letter form to a speech form.[3]

### 1. *Historical Introduction: The Divine Benefaction (1:3-4)*

> [3]*His divine power has given us everything we need for life and godliness through our knowledge of him who called us by his own glory and goodness.* [4]*Through these he has given us his very great and precious promises, so that through them you may participate in the divine nature and escape the corruption in the world caused by evil desires.*

3 English commentaries and translations have difficulty with vv. 3 and 4, for their introduction is strange. That is, they are introduced with an "as" or "since" *(hōs)* that either presupposes a following main verb ("Since God has done this, we make every effort to do that"), which the "for this very reason" of v. 5 makes grammatically awkward at best, or depends upon the previous verses. From a grammatical point of view the latter makes more sense, although letter salutations usually stand on their own. There are, however, some examples of grammatical dependence upon the salutation in Ignatius's letters (*Eph.* 1:1; *Rom.* 1:1; *Philad.* Greeting and 1:1; but the often cited *Smyrn.* 1:1 does not follow this pattern). What is clear from these examples is that the dependence is grammatical. A new section is clearly starting with 2 Pet 1:3, but our author

---

which can also be seen in such farewell discourses as *4 Ezra* 14:28-36 and the much later *Acts of John* 106–7. This thesis has been accepted and supported by Bauckham, *Jude, 2 Peter,* 173-74; Vögtle, *Der Judasbrief, der zweite Petrusbrief,* 136; and especially Watson, *Invention, Arrangement, and Style,* 96. This contrasts with the earlier theory of F. W. Danker, "2 Peter 1: A Solemn Decree," *CBQ* 40 (1978) 64-82 (also in his *Benefactor* [St. Louis: Clayton, 1982], 453-67), that this section is modelled on a "decree of honor to patrons and benefactors" (Neyrey, *2 Peter, Jude,* 151, who follows Danker). While the section starts off appropriately for such a decree (a "whereas" introduction), vv. 5-10 do not really inform us as to how to honor the patron, and v. 11 is quite out of place in this structure. One could speak of the loose influence of such decretal language on our passage, especially since it is very Hellenistic, but the major influence appears to be the sermonic form.

3. Watson, *Invention, Arrangement, and Style,* 87-94.

has let it flow grammatically from 1:2.[4] This also explains the shift from "you" at the beginning of v. 2 to "us" in this verse, in that the "our" in "our Lord Jesus" has already made the transition to the common faith of the author and the readers.

The focus of this section is on what God has given us: "everything we need for life and godliness," with the "everything" taking a prominent early position in the sentence. Pairs of words like "life and godliness" are common in 2 Peter, and often function as a hendiadys, two terms standing for a single entity. Thus, while it is possible that our author is talking about eternal life (2 Peter does not use the term "life" again; it is more characteristic of 1 Peter or the Johannine literature) and godliness as separate entities (i.e., future and present life), more likely he is talking about a godly life, for that will be the emphasis of the rest of the letter. In other words, there is no excuse for not living a godly life, for believers have already received everything that is necessary to do so. While the term "godliness" *(eusebeia)* and its cognates are common in 2 Peter (1:3, 6-7; 2:9; 3:11), they are common in the rest of the NT only in Acts (3:12; 10:2, 7) and the Pastorals (1 Tim 2:2; 3:16; 4:7-8; 6:3, 5-6, 11; Titus 1:1; 3:5). In fact, they are not common in the LXX, but only in 4 Maccabees, Philo, and Josephus, that is, later works that are very Hellenistic in character. This is an indication that our author tends to select vocabulary taken from and appealing to his Hellenistic audience. In this case "godliness" or "piety," a term that, when applied to "life," indicates a life that the deity would approve of,[5] is the focal word. This godly lifestyle is quite possible for the believer.

The source of what is necessary for such a life is "his divine power." That God has power is clear in the NT (e.g., Matt 10:28; 22:29 [= Mark 12:24]; Luke 1:35; Rom 1:16, 20; cf. Matt 26:64 [= Mark 14:62], where "the power" is a circumlocution for God), and that Jesus manifested divine power is also clear (e.g., Matt 14:2 [= Mark 6:14]; 24:30 [= Mark 13:26]; Mark 5:30; 6:2; Luke 4:14, 36; 5:17; 6:19; Acts 2:22; 10:38; Rom 1:4; cf. Acts 3:12). The grammar of our passage seems to attribute this divine power to Jesus, the nearest antecedent to "his" (cf. 2 Pet 1:12), but since the NT often talks of God's power being manifested through Jesus (see the Acts passages above), that simply points to the focus, not the nature, of the power. Thus there is nothing in this idea of divine power that is unusual.

4. The other option is that he intended an "as . . . then" construction but for some reason chose to change grammatical structures when he got to 1:5 and so left us with an anacoluthon.

5. On "godliness" in general, and especially in the Pastorals, see Philip H. Towner, *The Goal of Our Instruction: The Structure of Theology and Ethics in the Pastoral Epistles* (JSNTSup 34; Sheffield: Sheffield Academic Press, 1989), 147-54.

What is unusual is how it is expressed. The adjective "divine" occurs only three times in the NT (Acts 17:29 ["the divine being"]; 2 Pet 1:3, 4; cf. a related term in Rom 1:20). It is rare in the LXX (only nine times) and in early Christian literature (once each in *1 Clement, 2 Clement,* Ignatius and Papias, but nine times in Hermas, mostly in *Mandate* 11). Where the term "divine" is common is in the Hellenistic works of 4 Maccabees (twenty-five times), Philo (*Quod deterius . . .* 83; *De Abrahamo* 26; *Spec. leg.* 2.2; *De confusione linguarum* 115), and Josephus (*Ant.* 19.69).[6] This usage in Hellenistic Judaism is right in line with pagan Greek usage, which often referred to the term "divine power,"[7] but most Jews and Christians apparently avoided this term until the time of Justin (e.g., *1 Apology* 32). Thus while the idea expressed is not unusual for the NT, the language is, and it reveals that 2 Peter uses Hellenistic language rather the more usual language of the rest of the NT. It is the language of his pagan environment, indicating either his own linguistic context or else the background of the people to whom he was trying to communicate.

This power is released to believers "through our knowledge of him who called us by his own glory and goodness." If we were correct above that the divine power is the power belonging to Jesus, then one would think that here the person "we" know and "who called us" is also Jesus. While grammatically logical (and accepted by Bauckham[8]), this has been disputed by, among others, Vögtle[9] on the basis that (1) "his own" is unusually emphatic wording and so signals a shift from Jesus to God, and (2) the idea of calling is always referred to God in the NT except in the case of Jesus calling the disciples.[10] Now it is certainly true that in the NT (including 1 Pet 1:15; 2:9) God is normally said to be the one calling us. On the other hand, in later early Christian literature there was no prob-

6. See C. R. Holladay, Theios Anēr *in Hellenistic Judaism* (SBLDS 40; Missoula, MT: Scholars Press, 1977), 177-83, 57-66, for Philo and Josephus respectively.

7. Mayor, *Jude and 2 Peter,* 82-83.

8. Bauckham, *Jude, 2 Peter,* 178.

9. Vögtle, *Der Judasbrief, der 2 Petrusbrief,* 138-39.

10. Because of this and the fact that "knowledge" in 2 Peter is normally knowledge of Christ, some commentators, notably Kelly, *The Epistles of Peter and of Jude,* 300-301, argue that the "divine power" is God's, that the knowledge is that of Christ, and that when it comes to the calling there has been a shift in the referent of "we"/"us" to refer to Jesus' calling of the apostles, who of course included Peter. However, this interpretation does not fit well rhetorically in that "his own glory and goodness" were not significantly involved in the *call* of the apostles (Kelly refers the "glory" to the Transfiguration), and this interpretation would limit the "very great and precious promises" to the apostles as well. This would seem to interrupt the stream of the argument and distance readers from the very advantages that our author wants to hold out to them as reasons for maintaining the orthodox position.

lem in referring calling to Jesus (2 *Clem.* 1:8; 2:4 [= Mark 2:17], 7; 5:1 ["do the will of him who called us"]; 9:5), nor is the idea entirely absent in the NT (Mark 2:17, "I have not come to call the righteous, but sinners," quoted in 2 *Clem.* 2:4 and therefore influential on his thought).[11] Furthermore, "knowledge" or "acknowledgment" (see the discussion of this term in the comment on 2 Pet 1:2) in 2 Peter usually has Jesus as its personal object (2 Pet 1:8; 2:20; cf. 3:18, which expresses the same idea using a slightly different term). Thus the knowledge of Jesus (i.e., coming to understand and acknowledge his significance), which was the basis of the reception of the equally honorable faith, is the means by which he, by his divine power, gives one all that is needed for a godly life.

This "knowledge" of Jesus did not come through their personal investigation, but because Jesus himself "called us." He took the initiative. And this call came "by his own glory and goodness." "Glory" is closely related to "honor" (*timē*), and in fact is paired with it in 1:17. As with many word pairs in 2 Peter, the word pair here is traditional and something of a hendiadys. That is, "glory and goodness" *(doxa kai aretē)* appears frequently in Greek literature (e.g., Pausanius, *Arcad.* 52.6; Dionysius of Halicarnassus, *Ant. Rom.* 5.62.4; Diodorus of Sicily 2.45.2; 3.70.5).[12] *Aretē* has a range of meanings from wealth and achievements to virtue or excellence and the fame, reputation, and praise that they bring (Phil 4:8, where it is paired with "praiseworthy"). In this word pair in 2 Peter it indicates that Jesus' own glorious or honorable achievement or excellence led to their calling.[13] That raises the question whether this action was done *by* his glorious excellence or *for* his glorious excellence (or glorious praise). The grammatical construction (Greek dative) could bear either meaning. That is, God's glory is to be "declared among the nations," according to the OT (1 Chron 16:24; Ps 96:3); his excellence is celebrated in the Psalms. Was that the goal of his calling us? Such a display of one's excellence would not have been thought at all inappropriate in the

11. It is surely Christians rather than apostles who are called in this passage in 2 Peter, for their calling is again referred to in 2 Pet 1:10.

12. Reference the article in *TDNT* 1 and discover more examples of the pair. Bauckham references J. J. Wettstein, *Η ΚΑΙΝΗ ΔΙΑΘΗΚΗ: Novum Testamentum Graece editionis receptae cure lectionibus variantibus codicum MSS, editionum aliarum, versionum et Patrum, nec non commentario pleniore ex scriptoribus veteribus Hebraeis, Graecis et Latinis Historiam et vim verborum illustrante opera et studio Joannis Jacobi Wetstenii,* Vol. 2 (Amsterdam, 1752).

13. "Goodness" is not the best translation, for it has too much of a moral tone and lacks the sense of honor intrinsic in this usage of *aretē.* Similarly, Bauckham's translation of "might," meaning "manifestation of divine power" (178-79), misses the honor context. Neyrey (*2 Peter, Jude,* 156) translates it "excellence," which fits if one understands that as honorable excellence.

Mediterranean world of that day. Indeed, it was thought that a truly honorable person would display his wealth and honor and receive the appropriate acclamation. On the other hand, a person who was excellent would naturally act accordingly, so it would also make sense to say that Jesus called us by his own ("his own" being emphatic in contrast to "us") glorious excellence or glorious achievement. Since both interpretations make sense, it is difficult to decide which is more likely correct. However, the following verse tips the balance toward the latter interpretation. That is, through or by means of these virtues he has given us promises, so very likely the thought in v. 3 is already that they are the basis of our calling. That is, the achievement in our calling was all Jesus' doing. We were called into our knowledge of him; it was not really our discovery. And this calling came on the basis of his achievement and excellence, his honorable nature, not ours. Yet because of his honor we have been called into an honorable status.

4 It is through his glory and honor ("these") that Jesus has given "us very great and precious promises." The term "very great" is found only here in the NT, but it is the normal superlative of "great." As frequently happens in 2 Peter, our author has paired two words, "very great" and "precious" (or "valuable" or "honorable" — see the discussion of "precious" in 1:1). "Very great" (which in Greek is actually the second term) serves to underline and heighten the effect of "precious" or "valuable." What is so valuable is the "promises" Jesus has made. The term "promise" itself is unusual, for this word for "promise," which does not appear in the LXX, appears in the NT only here and in 3:13. Thus it stands out and neatly brackets the whole letter.[14] While this rarer term is a near synonym of the more common term, it does focus on the content of the promise more than on the promise itself.[15] What is this content? In

14. The more common word for "promise" also appears in 2 Peter, in 3:4, 9. This is a word that appears fifty-two times in the NT (especially in Luke-Acts and Hebrews) and eight times in the LXX, although there it occurs most frequently in the intertestamental literature (1 Macc 10:15; 4 Macc 12:9; *Pss. Sol.* 12:6).

15. J. I. Snyder, *The Promise of His Coming — The Eschatology of 2 Peter* (San Mateo, CA: self-published, 1986), argues in this published version of his 1983 Basel dissertation that the less common term refers to the Parousia of Christ, while the more common term refers to the OT judgment of God, which is what the opponents reject. Looking at 2 Peter 3, one cannot sustain this distinction. Reicke, *The Epistles of James, Peter, and Jude,* and Spicq, *Les Épitres de Saint Pierre,* argue that the verse as a whole refers to Christian initiation and thus the promises that one receives in conversion–baptism. Yet while there is some truth to this in that the escape from corruption and the participation in the divine nature begin with Christian initiation, the whole tenor of the passage is forward-looking: adding, growing, developing, and having a future rich entrance. Furthermore, the second use of the term in 3:13 is clearly future. Thus these authors overlook the tone of the passage.

3:13 it is a new heaven and a new earth, perhaps the equivalent of the "eternal kingdom of our Lord and Savior Jesus Christ" (1:11) that closes this section (cf. the promise in 2 *Clem.* 5:5, where in contrast to our short "sojourning in the world," "the promise of Christ is great and wonderful, and brings us rest, in the kingdom which is to come and in everlasting life").[16] Here we are not told what the exact content of the promises is,[17] but the focus is on participation "in the divine nature" and the concomitant escape from corruption. Promises that bring such things are significant indeed.

We could, of course, speculate on the content of the promises. For instance, the Holy Spirit is spoken of as "the Father's promise" in Acts 1:4, a promise mediated by Jesus. That would fit well with the results of the promise, but we find only one reference to the Spirit in 2 Peter, and that is in relationship to the OT prophets (1:21). Of course, 1 Pet 1:3-4, 9 speaks of hope, an inheritance, and salvation, all pointing to the future and so fitting the central characteristic of a promise, but none of these, except perhaps the related "new birth," would imply the benefits that 2 Peter says the promises produced, and "new birth," is an already accomplished fact. We could continue noting other promises in other bodies of literature. The fact is that 2 Peter does not state what the promises are but makes a generalized reference to those things promised to believers in Christian initiation, which might well include the Spirit and some of the other benefits we have noted. Yet our author's focus is not on the promises themselves, but on the benefits that result from them.

It is not the content of the promises themselves, then, but "through" these promises that the follower of Jesus gains two benefits, the first positive ("participate in the divine nature") and the second negative ("escape the corruption in the world caused by [evil] desires"). Both of these benefits are interesting, although it is the first that arrests us: if 2 Peter were written today, many orthodox believers would certainly reject him as "new age" because of this benefit. It is to this that we now turn.

The term "the divine nature" was well established in Greek lan-

16. Bauckham, *Jude, 2 Peter,* 179, rightly notes that most promises are referred to God (*1 Clem.* 26:1; 34:7 are the passages he cites). However, while it is less usual to refer to the promises of Christ, he is certainly depicted in the NT as making some (e.g., Matt 18:19-20; 28:20; Luke 23:43; John 20:23 are three that spring to mind).

17. Mayor, *The Epistles of Jude and 2 Peter,* 87, argues that 3:13 gives the content of the promises and that here "Our nature is changed to divine by the moral power of hope and faith kindled in us by the promises." Bauckham, *Jude, 2 Peter,* 179, is surely correct to reject this interpretation as strained, but he then argues that participation in the divine nature is the content of the promises. Yet that would not be the natural reading of *dia toutōn,* which would normally indicate the means by which one obtained the benefit.

guage and literature, as was the idea of "participating" or "sharing" in it, although most Greek speakers used *metechein* rather than *koinōnoi* as here. The first references to the "divine nature" go back to Plato, for example, *Phaedrus* 230A, and they can be documented right down to the period of the NT (e.g., Epictetus, *Disc.* 2.19.26-27).[18] What is important to note is that sometimes this participation in the divine nature was viewed as innate, a divine spark within the human being that simply needed to be recognized or freed, and sometimes it is something to be obtained by effort. Since in Plato the immortal soul is imprisoned in the mortal body, for him all human beings partake of the divine (i.e., immortality) although they may not realise it. Epictetus, on the other hand, is looking for the attainment of the (for him) godly characteristic of *apatheia* (freedom from desire or rising above emotions), which he doubts can be perfectly achieved in this life. In either case, some aspect of the divine is in mind rather than complete divinization.

More important for our purposes is the fact that several Jewish writers also use this expression. As we would expect, they are the Hellenistic writers, especially Philo and the author of 4 Maccabees. Josephus, *C. Ap.* 2.232, refers to a royal advisor, "one that seemed to partake of a divine nature, both as to wisdom and the knowledge of futurities." Philo, *Leg. alleg.* 1.38, notes, "Human intellect would not have dared to mount up to such a height as to lay claim on the nature of God, if God himself had not drawn it up to himself, as far as it was possible for the mind of man to be drawn up." He also wrote in *De decalogo* 104, "They all [the planets] enjoy a divine, and happy, and blessed nature." In a closing panegyric in 4 Macc 18:3 we read, "Those men who surrendered their bodies to suffering for piety's sake . . . were also deemed worthy of the divine portion *(theias meridos katēxiōthēsan)*." Finally, Pseudo-Phocylides (103–4) wrote, "For in fact we hope that the remains of the departed will soon come to light again out of the earth. And afterwards they become gods *(theoi telethontai)*."[19] What we see in each of these writers is that having some characteristic of God (unchangingness or lack of wandering [for the stars], wisdom and knowledge of the future, and especially immortality) is equated with divinization or partaking of the divine nature.[20] This means that what is being thought about is most likely not sharing in the

18. See Mayor, *The Epistles of Jude and 2 Peter,* 87, for a much longer listing of the classical references.

19. P. W. van der Horst, *The Sentences of Pseudo-Phocylides* (SVTP 4; Leiden: E. J. Brill, 1978), 185.

20. J. Gross, *La divinisation du chrétien d'après les pères grecs* (Paris: Gabalda, 1938), 86-94; C. R. Holladay, Theios Anēr in *Hellenistic Judaism,* 155-70. See further literature in Vögtle, *Der Judasbrief, der zweite Petrusbrief,* 136-37.

Holy Spirit or in Christ,[21] nor is the phrase to be read covenantally,[22] but rather as sharing some characteristic of God, something that makes the readers more like the world of the divine (including the beings other than God inhabiting that world) than like the world of human beings.

This leads us to ask what these characteristics may be. Bauckham and Vögtle suggest immortality and incorruption.[23] In that case we are likely talking about something that happens at death, which is what both authors argue. However, one should look at the negative benefit, which is more explicit, before jumping to conclusions about the positive benefit on the basis of non-Christian Greek parallels.

The negative benefit is "escape from the corruption in the world caused by [evil] desires." In Greek cosmology there was a dualism between the divine realm and the world. This was expressed in terms of mortality versus immortality, incorruption versus corruption, unchanging versus changing, and the like. That is, the divine real was above all change, including the changes implied in death and corruption.[24] Furthermore, human souls were sometimes viewed as imprisoned in the mortal, changing world and in need of escape. The question, then, arises, Has 2 Peter imported Greek dualism into Christian thought?[25]

The answer to this question is in the negative. 2 Peter shows awareness that there is corruption in the world, and Paul would have agreed with this. Yet unlike many Greeks, the author of 2 Peter does not believe that this corruption is in the world because the world is material. There is corruption in the world because of "desire" (contrary to the NIV, not only is there no term for "evil" here, but the word "desire" is singular, not plural).[26] "Desire" is one way of translating the Hebrew term *yetser,* meaning

21. So Mayor, *The Epistles of Jude and 2 Peter,* 87-88, citing Heb 3:14; 6:4; 12:10; 1 John 1:3. The problem is that the Holy Spirit is hardly mentioned in 2 Peter, and then only in connection with the OT prophets.

22. A. Wolters, "'Partners of the Deity': A Covenantal Reading of 2 Peter 1:4," *CTJ* 25 (1990) 28-44, and "Postscript to 'Partners of the Deity,'" *CTJ* 26 (1991) 418-20.

23. Bauckham, *Jude, 2 Peter,* 180-11; Vögtle, *Der Judasbrief, der zweite Petrusbrief,* 140-41.

24. The divine was therefore thought to be above all emotion, since emotions change. Thus in Alexandrian Judaism and later in Alexandrian Christianity the emotions attributed to God in Scripture were read as anthropomorphism. This, of course, is an instance of taking Scripture and conforming it to philosophy rather than taking Scripture at face value.

25. This is precisely the accusation of Ernst Käsemann, "An Apologia for Primitive Christian Eschatology," in *Essays on New Testament Themes,* trans. W. J. Montague (SBT 41; London: SCM, 1964), 169-95.

26. Many Greek writers would also have seen desire as a problem in the world, for desire by its very nature is changing. The divine, immortal real is unchanging. Anything that changes is really part of corruption. This type of thought led to the Stoic idea of

"drive" or, in Freudian terms, "id."[27] In Jewish thought human beings were controlled by unbounded drive. In one sense "desire" or "drive" was not evil in itself, for it drove the person to procreate (as sex drive), plant fields (as hunger drive), and the like. But it could and would drive the person to transgress proper boundaries, that is, to sin.[28] Thus "desire" is at the root of the moral corruption in the world and because of moral corruption the world is subject to decay.[29] The dualism in Judaism and in 2 Peter is at root ethical, not ontological. Furthermore, the "escape" is not an escape from the world or from physical existence (the more Greek idea), but "escape from the *corruption* in the world."[30] Thus at the end of 2 Peter (i.e., in the eschatology of ch. 3) one does not find immortal existence free from a body, but a new (or renewed) heaven and a new (or renewed) earth. The picture 2 Peter presents here uses Greek language, but it is far more Jewish than Greek.[31]

There is, however, a difference between at least rabbinic Judaism

---

*apatheia,* in which one transcended change though philosophical understanding. That is, while one still had emotions and drives, through understanding one rose above them and so participated in the unchanging world.

27. Freud obviously came centuries after rabbinic Judaism developed the idea of *yetser.* However, Freud was a Jew and may well have been influenced by such ideas as he developed his theories. For whatever reason, there is a good match in the two ideas.

28. Wisd 2:23-24: "For God created us for incorruption, and made us in the image of his own eternity, but through the devil's envy death entered the world, and those who belong to his company experience it."

29. Hermas would later say (*Man.* 12:1-2), "He said to me, 'Put away from yourself every evil desire, but put on the desire which is good and holy; for by putting on this desire you will curb it as your will. For the wicked desire is cruel and hard to tame, for it is fearful, and destroys men greatly in its cruelty. . . . But it destroys such as have not the good desire as a covering, but are mixed with this world; these then it delivers to death.'" See further Peter H. Davids, "Themes in the Epistle of James That Are Judaistic in Character" (Ph.D. dissertation, University of Manchester, 1974), 1-93, as well as Davids, *The Epistle of James,* 36, and the literature cited there.

30. Philo, *De migratione Abrahami* 7, 9 has both ideas, but the Greek side predominates: "That he means [in Gen 12:1] by Abraham's country the body, and by his kindred his outward senses . . . we have now shown. . . . Depart therefore from the earthly parts which envelop you, O my friend, fleeing [*ekphygōn*] from that base and polluted prison house of the body, and from the keepers as it were of the prison, its pleasures and appetites [*epithymias,* the term translated 'desire' in 2 Peter]." Notice that the body itself is "base" — in fact, Philo also has a person fleeing the "outward senses" for the inward light of the mind.

31. Not all first-century Judaisms expected a resurrection of the dead (e.g., we read that the Sadducees did not [Mark 12:18]), so the immortality of the soul free from the body might be what some hoped for. However, the expectation of a resurrection was typical of rabbinic Judaism and its predecessor, Pharisaism. It was also an expectation of the Qumran community and the Zealots. Thus it appears to have been the most usual Jewish position, at least in Palestine.

and 2 Peter. In rabbinic Judaism the human impulse or drive was to be controlled by the Torah, the law. By meditation on these scriptures one could set the appropriate boundaries and overcome the impulse to evil. Corruption could be controlled. In 2 Peter we hear nothing about the role of Scripture until ch. 3, and there we discover that Scripture can be misused as well as used. Instead, escape from corruption comes through "our knowledge of him," that is, Jesus, and through his "divine power."

Since this escape from the corruption in the world that parallels participating in the divine nature is ethical (i.e,. escape from the corruption caused by desire), the character of the divine nature must also be ethical and not simply another way of indicating immortality. While immortality alone might fit very well in 1 Peter where persecution is the issue, here in 2 Peter the conflict is with teachers whose advocating of practices that our author considers immoral is supported by their rejection of final judgment. The immortal permanence of the divine (as opposed to the earth, which will change) is connected to holiness, purity, and goodness. And these are the virtues that make sense in the context of 2 Peter. And so it is likely that what 2 Peter has in mind when he claims participation in the divine nature is the reception of an ethical nature like God's, which then leads to immortality.

Furthermore, the "escape" is likely an ongoing process, beginning indeed with Christian initiation (as Kelly and others argue), but not ending there (and not limited to attaining immortality at death, as Bauckham and Vögtle argue).[32] Indeed, in the contemporary world we see that those who claim to have escaped from sin/desire once for all usually are self-deceived and often are cultic, controlling others who are not as "perfect" as they are. Recognition that escape is a process brings a healthy humility to the follower of Jesus. It is this process of escape that leads directly to the call to grow in virtue in the next verse.

## 2. *Call to Virtue (1:5-11)*

*5For this very reason, make every effort to add to your faith goodness;*
*and to goodness, knowledge; 6and to knowledge, self-control; and to self-*
*control, perseverance; and to perseverance, godliness; 7and to godliness,*
*brotherly kindness; and to brotherly kindness, love. 8For if you possess*
*these qualities in increasing measure, they will keep you from being inef-*

32. "Escape" is a participle, *apophygontes,* that describes something that happens either along with or before the main verb "become" *(genēsthe).* Thus the escaping can be the process of growing in virtue now that makes up becoming a partaker of the divine nature.

*fective and unproductive in your knowledge of our Lord Jesus Christ. [9]But*
*if anyone does not have them, he is nearsighted and blind, and has forgot-*
*ten that he has been cleansed from his past sins.*
*[10]Therefore, my brothers, be all the more eager to make your calling and*
*election sure. For if you do these things, you will never fall, [11]and you will*
*receive a rich welcome into the eternal kingdom of our Lord and Savior Je-*
*sus Christ.*

**5** The link to the previous verses is clear in the expression "for this very reason"; that is, because of what has been done for the readers (escape from corruption) is being done for them (participation in the divine nature) and will be done for them (those promises that are yet to be fulfilled, to which our author will come in 1:11), they are to grow in virtue. The form of vv. 5 through 7 is that of a chain-saying virtue list. This is not the only one in the NT. Consider the following parallels:

| *2 Peter 1:5-7* | *Rom 5:3-5* | *Jas 1:3-4*[33] | *Gal 5:22-23* |
|---|---|---|---|
| Faith (*pistis*) | Suffering | Testing (of *pistis*) | Love |
| Goodness (*aretē*) | Perseverance | Perseverance | Joy[34] |
| Knowledge | Character | Maturity | Peace |
| Self-control (*enkrateian*) | Hope | Complete | Patience (= perseverance) |
| Perseverance | Love | Not lacking anything | Kindness |
| Godliness (*eusebeia*) | | | Goodness (*agathōsynē*) |
| Brotherly kindness | | | Faithfulness (*pistis*) |
| Love | | | Gentleness |
| | | | Self-control |

The two most extensive lists are those in 2 Peter and Galatians. Of the eight terms in 2 Peter three and the synonym for a fourth are found among the nine terms in Galatians, although Galatians is different in form in that it is a list rather than a chain-saying. Two of four unmatched terms in 2 Peter are unusual in the NT outside of 2 Peter, although common enough in other Greek writings. These two plus knowledge (of Christ) all appeared previously in 2 Pet 1:3.

33. We could add 1 Pet 1:6-7 here, for it has several formal and verbal similarities to Romans 5 and James 1, but it is not really a virtue list nor a fully formed chain saying. It is its outcome that is most similar to 2 Peter.

34. Romans, James, and 1 Peter all speak of joy in the context of suffering, which parallels the joy mentioned here in Galatians.

What we note in these lists plus others that we could add (e.g., Phil 4:8) is that the virtues do not come in any definite order. While here as elsewhere there is a schema in which some virtues are developed out of others (see Hermas, *Vis.* 3:8:7, where each virtue is a "daughter" of the previous one), this seems more a form for presentation than a logical development.

Looking at the virtues themselves, we can benefit from comparing them with various Jewish lists:

| Philo, *Sacrif. Abel.*[35] | Philo, *Leg. alleg.*[36] | *Wisd* 8:7 | *m. Sot.* 8.15 | 1QS 4:2-6 |
|---|---|---|---|---|
| Virtue *(aretē)*<br>Piety *(eusebeia)*<br>Holiness<br>Truth<br>Right<br>Purity<br>Six others<br>Temperance<br>Sixteen others<br>Gentleness<br>Courtesy<br>Love of one's kind<br>Magnanimity<br>Happiness<br>Goodness *(agathotēs)* | Virtue *(aretē)*<br>Prudence *(phronēsis)*<br>Temperance *(sōphrosynē)*<br>Courage *(andreia)*<br>Justice *(diakiosynē)* | And if anyone loves righteousness *(dikaiosynēn)*, her labors are virtues *(aretai)*; for she teaches self-control *(sōphrosynēn)* and prudence *(phronēsin)*, justice *(dikaiosynēn)*, and courage *(andreian)*; nothing in life is more profitable for mortals than these. | R. Pinhas b. Yair says, "Heedfulness leads to cleanliness, cleanliness leads to cleanness, cleanness leads to abstinence, abstinence leads to holiness, holiness leads to modesty, modesty leads to the fear of sin, the fear of sin leads to piety, piety leads to the Holy Spirit, the Holy Spirit leads to the resurrection of the dead, and the resurrection of the dead comes through Elijah, blessed be his memory, Amen."[37] | Meekness<br>Patience<br>Generous compassion<br>Eternal goodness<br>Intelligence<br>Understanding<br>Potent wisdom<br>Knowledge<br>Justice<br>Purity<br>Truth |

While Philo in *Legum allegoriae* and *Wisdom of Solomon* are limited to the four cardinal virtues, both get in a fifth by making the four flow out of virtue itself. When we compare these with 2 Peter, we see that he overlaps in three items out of twelve with the Dead Sea Scroll (patience = perseverance, goodness [perhaps, for we are equating a Hebrew idiom with a Greek term], knowledge), in one to two items with the Mishnah (piety =

35. Philo, *De sacrificiis Abelis et Caini* 27. Virtue is the chief "lady," and she is attended by the others as by bodyguards.

36. Philo, *Leg. alleg.* 1.64 (1.19/56).

37. Jacob Neusner, *The Mishnah: A New Translation* (New Haven and London: Yale University Press), 1988.

godliness, abstinence if it = self-control), in three of the five items in the four cardinal virtues (although not in the same words), and in at least four items with Philo's more extensive list. His language, then, belongs to the Hellenistic world rather than to the Hebrew/Aramaic world.

The importance of these virtues is clearly underlined by 2 Peter. "Make every effort" is unusual language (the verb occurs only here in the NT and is rare elsewhere in Greek literature), but the meaning is clear. Growth in virtue is of utmost importance and deserves utmost effort. The verb translated "to add" is far more colorful than that translation might indicate. In secular usage it meant "to provide at one's own expense." Here it serves as the chaining verb as if one spent the one virtue to gain a supply of the next. So perhaps "to supply" would be more accurate than "to add." It again notes the expense, the effort involved in this growth in virtue. We do not automatically become more virtuous as if God infused virtue into us intravenously; we need to make plans and expend effort.

The terms themselves are common enough. The term for faith would be translated "faithfulness" if it were in a non-Christian ethical list, for loyalty to friends and family was an esteemed virtue. That is probably what 2 Peter means here, for in typical Christian fashion faithfulness and love bracket the list. This Christian structure indicates that it is not faithfulness in general that our author is concerned about but faithfulness or commitment to God in Jesus, that is, specifically Christian commitment.[38] The next item in the list is "goodness," which does not mean what one would mean in saying that a person is good. Rather, it refers to moral excellence (as in 1:3). We note that in Philo's and Wisdom's lists this term included the four cardinal virtues, which it may well do here. Such a person is an honorable person indeed, for he or she takes part in God's own moral excellence.

To this is added "knowledge" (also found in virtue lists in 2 Cor 6:6; 8:7), which in our context is surely the knowledge of Christ (see 1:2, 3 above). Bauckham distinguishes it from the knowledge found in 1:2, 3 in that the term here *(gnōsis)* is a synonym for the term used there. He explains that the term here is "the wisdom and discernment which the Christian needs for a virtuous life and which is progressively acquired. It

38. Neyrey, *2 Peter, Jude,* 158-59, notes how important fidelity or faithfulness was in patron-client relationships, the patron in this case being God. Often the word is referred to faith in the gospel (so Bauckham, *Jude, 2 Peter,* 185, and J. Daryl Charles, *Virtue amidst Vice: The Catalog of Virtues in 2 Peter 1* [Sheffield: Sheffield Academic Press, 1992], 140), but this expression is misleading, for while one can be called to believe the gospel, the gospel does not call one to faith in itself but to faith in God or Jesus. Thus even the term "faith" can be misleading, if faith is understood to mean belief. Rather commitment to Jesus or fidelity to Jesus is what is indicated.

is practical rather than purely speculative wisdom."[39] While *epignōsis* stresses coming to the awareness of the significance of Christ, it should not be divorced from *gnōsis,* first, because one cannot demonstrate a sharp differentiation in Greek as a whole, and, second, because in both the OT (e.g., Prov 1:7) and the NT (Jas 1:5) wisdom and discernment come from knowing God/Christ and adopting his character. However, our author is clearly not talking about knowledge of Scripture *per se,* which is often the assumed meaning in the contemporary world. Knowledge, including knowledge of Scripture, that is not turned into practical action, that does not produce the character of God/Jesus in one's life, is worse than useless, for it can blind one to his or her true sorry state.

**6** Along with knowledge comes "self-control" *(enkrateia).* While not usually one of the four cardinal virtues for Greek writers, they view this virtue extremely seriously.[40] To narrow our field, we shall simply look at the (Hellenistic) Jewish writers. In a section headed "self-control" starting in Sir 18:30 this virtue is contrasted with desire *(epithymia),* which is made more specific as feasting (which is the vice that is stressed) and sexual indulgence (referenced by one word, "women"). Philo says, "The opposite of desire (here *hēdonē,* as in Jas 4:1) is temperance [self-control], which one must endeavor, and labor, and take pains by every contrivance imaginable to acquire, as the very greatest blessing . . . temperance, being a pure and unblemished virtue, neglecting everything which relates to eating and drinking, and boasting itself as superior to the pleasures of the belly, may be allowed to approach the sacred altars . . ." (*Spec. leg.* 1.149-50). Similar praise of self-control and similar contrasting of it with desire can be found in Josephus (e.g., *War* 2.120 [about the Essenes]; 4.373, "We ought to esteem those that do what is agreeable to temperance and prudence, no less glorious than those that have gained great reputation by their actions in war"). While common in Hellenistic writers, this term is not frequent in the NT. It occurs here, in Acts 24:25 (Paul, speaking to the Roman procurator),[41] and in Gal 5:23 (part of the fruit of the Spirit).[42] For 2 Peter this is a very important virtue because (1) the teachers our author opposes are in no way self-controlled but rather given to desire,[43] and

39. Bauckham, *Jude, 2 Peter,* 186.

40. See further Walter Grundmann, *"enkrateia," TDNT* 2:339-42.

41. Felix would certainly have recognised the theme of self-control even if he were not particularly self-controlled. What surely upset him was not the typical ethical teaching, but the idea of a divine judgment where his self-control would be evaluated.

42. Related terms appear in 1 Cor 7:9; 9:25; Titus 1:8.

43. Neyrey, *2 Peter, Jude,* 160, rightly points out that all of the "windows of the soul" in ancient thought were uncontrolled in themselves: eyes (2:13), mouth/ears (2:2, 10, 12-13, 22), and genitals (2:2, 14, 18).

(2) it fits the general Hellenistic ethical milieu in which he is writing. Given that this commentary is being written in a culture of growing obesity, in which consumption and self-indulgence are virtually viewed as human rights, we would do well to pay more attention to Peter's emphasis on this virtue.

Self-control brings our author to "perseverance," which is a more typically Christian virtue. It is not that this virtue was not valued by non-Jewish Greek writers as well. It was indeed valued, for it was, among other things, a military value (endurance in battle). However, it was also valued in the Jewish world, especially after the persecution under Antiochus Epiphanes (168/9-164 B.C.). Whole books, such as the *Testament of Job,* were written on the theme. In the Christian world the term appears thirty-two times in the NT, for example, in Pauline virtue lists (Rom 5:3-4; 1 Tim 6:11; 2 Tim 3:10; Titus 2:2), James (Jas 1:3, 12; 5:11; cf. 5:7-8, 10, which use a synonym), and in a list in Rev 2:19 (plus six other times in Revelation). It indicates endurance, but in a spiritual battle rather than in a physical battle or an athletic contest. It is the virtue needed to stand firm in one's commitment to Jesus over the long haul in the face of persecution (thus its prominence in James and Revelation) or other hardships. In 2 Peter the need is to stand firm in their commitment in the face of the enticements of the teachers whom our author opposes.

In our list "godliness" or "piety" comes after self-control. While rare in Christian ethical lists (only here and in 1 Tim 6:11 in the NT), this is another favorite Hellenistic virtue. In the Greek world this virtue pointed to appropriate relationships toward the authorities in one's life: the gods, dead ancestors, and family/parents. Or, as Foerster puts it, "In addition to the gods, relatives, rulers, judges, oaths, the law, and the good may all be objects; enjoying divine protection, they must be respected and upheld."[44] Thus in the Jewish *Letter of Aristeas* this virtue indicates not only respect toward God but also respectful conduct toward others. Both *Aristeas* and Philo relate it to justice, a virtue exercised toward others. "There are, as we may say, two most especially important heads of all the innumerable particular lessons and doctrines; the regulating of one's conduct toward God by the rules of piety *(eusebeias)* and holiness *(hosiotētos),* and of one's conduct toward men by the rules of humanity *(philanthrōpeias)* and justice *(dikaiosynē)*" (*Spec. leg.* 2.63). The point is that this virtue indicates appropriate respect and reverence toward the deity and those associated with him or her (something that is decidedly lacking in the teachers opposed in ch. 2; cf. 2:10-12); which is also expressed in respect to those relationships that he has sanctioned.

44. W. Foerster, *"sebomai ktl.," TDNT* 7:176-78.

Thus it forms an excellent bridge into the more horizontally oriented virtues that follow in v. 7.

7 The first of the clearly horizontally focused virtues is "brotherly kindness" *(philadelphia)*, which would be better translated as "familial affection." This virtue would also not have sounded strange in the Greco-Roman world. The term indicated acts of affection and generosity among physical kin, which were quite important in that world and yet which did not extend beyond kin (for one was in competition with non-kin). One of the prime examples in the Hellenistic Jewish world is found in the story of the seven brothers in 4 Maccabees:

> You are not ignorant of the affection of family ties, which the divine and all-wise Providence has bequeathed through the fathers to their descendants and which was implanted in the mother's womb. [20]There each of the brothers spent the same length of time and was shaped during the same period of time; and growing from the same blood and through the same life, they were brought to the light of day. [21]When they were born after an equal time of gestation, they drank milk from the same fountains. From such embraces brotherly-loving souls are nourished; [22]and they grow stronger from this common nurture and daily companionship, and from both general education and our discipline in the law of God.
>
> [23]Therefore, when sympathy and brotherly affection had been so established, the brothers were the more sympathetic to one another. [24]Since they had been educated by the same law and trained in the same virtues and brought up in right living, they loved one another all the more. [25]A common zeal for nobility strengthened their goodwill toward one another, and their concord, [26]because they could make their brotherly love more fervent with the aid of their religion. [27]But although nature and companionship and virtuous habits had augmented the affection of family ties, those who were left endured for the sake of religion, while watching their brothers being maltreated and tortured to death. (4 Macc 13:19-27)

There are several variants on our term here, although the term itself appears in vv. 23 and 26. The point the author of 4 Maccabees makes is clear: this virtue is the bond of natural affection among family members. (So also Philo, *Joseph* 218; Josephus, *Ant.* 2.161 [both concerning Joseph's brothers]; *War* 1.275 [Herod for his brother], 485 [Herod for his relatives in general].) Thus this virtue itself is not unique to the Christian setting. What is unique in that setting is the fact that this familial love was extended to the whole Christian family; that is, all believers were treated as if they were physical kin (and unbelieving physical kin were treated as outsiders, Mark 3:31-35). This is not as evident in the one use of this term in a NT virtue list (1 Pet 3:8) or in Heb 13:1, but is clear in context in 1 Pet 1:22 ("Now that you have purified yourselves by obeying the truth so that you have sincere love for your brothers, love one another deeply, from the heart"), 1 Thess 4:9, and Rom 12:10 ("Be devoted to one another in brotherly love. Honor one another above yourselves"). This is the basis for exchanging the kiss (Rom 16:16; 1 Cor 16:20; 2 Cor 12:12; 1 Thess 5:26; 1 Pet 5:14), which was normally not exchanged except among family and close friends, and for the sharing of goods, for functioning families shared with members in need.

According to the apologists, pagans noted this characteristic of Christians and despised them for treating each other as family (Lucian, *Peregrinus* 13; Minucius Felix, *Oct.* 31.8 ["Thus we love one another, to your regret, with a mutual love, because we do not know how to hate. Thus we call one another, to your envy, brethren: as being men born of one God and Parent, and companions in faith, and as fellow-heirs in hope"]; Tertullian, *Apology* 39 ["But it is mainly the deeds of a love so noble that lead many to put a brand upon us. See, they say, how they love one another, for themselves are animated by mutual hatred; how they are ready even to die for one another, for they themselves will sooner be put to death. And they are wroth with us, too, because we call each other brethren; for no other reason, as I think, than because among themselves names of consanguinity are assumed in mere pretense of affection. But we are your brethren as well, by the law of our common mother nature, though you are hardly men, because brothers so unkind. At the same time, how much more fittingly they are called and counted brothers who have been led to the knowledge of God as their common Father, who have drunk in one spirit of holiness, who from the same womb of a common ignorance have agonized into the same light of truth! But on this very account, perhaps, we are regarded as having less claim to be held true brothers, that no tragedy makes a noise about our brotherhood, or that the family possessions, which generally destroy brotherhood among you, create fraternal bonds among us. One in mind and soul, we do not hesitate to share our earthly goods with one another. All things are common among us but our wives"]).

Yet for the Christians this was, as we have seen, the logical consequence of being born from above, of partaking of the nature of God. Thus while in a non-Christian context this would be the Greco-Roman virtue of familial love, in our context it is that same familial love extended to the whole Christian community. As a result, the NIV translation "brotherly kindness" is unfortunate and restricting, and "familial love" or "kinship affection" would be better, as long as we understand that "family" and "kin" mean fellow Christians rather than blood relatives.

The final item in our list, "love" *(agapē),* flows naturally from "kinship affection." This term is frequent in NT ethical lists (2 Cor 6:6; Gal 5:22; Eph 4:2; 1 Tim 4:12; 6:11; 2 Tim 2:22; 3:10; Titus 2:2; Rev 2:19) and more frequent in the NT in general. In Gal 5:22 it heads the list, in 1 Cor 8:1-3 it is contrasted with knowledge (Paul is not against knowledge, but is against knowledge without love), and in 1 Corinthians 13 it is presented as the chief virtue, even greater than faith (which heads our list here) and hope (1 Cor 13:13). The important point to keep in mind is that love is a virtue, not an emotion. Christians are not encouraged to feel warmly about each other or even to like one another; they are instructed to act lovingly toward one another. Thus Paul's description of love in 1 Corinthians 13 speaks about what love does, how it acts, not how it feels. Furthermore, it is a divine virtue that is passed on to human beings: the Father loves the Son (Mark 1:11; 9:7), and the Father (Rom 1:7) and Jesus love people (e.g., the rich young man in Mark 10:21), so Jesus' apprentices are to love God and others (Mark 12:30, 31). Here is a virtue firmly rooted in the Jesus tradition and carried forward in the epistolary tradition. Thus this is a distinctly Christian virtue.[45]

**8** Having climaxed his virtue list in a very Christian way with love, our author goes on to describe the Christian life as a process. Many Christians wish that their growth in Christ were a series of crises in which holiness and other virtues were suddenly infused into them. That is not 2 Peter's point of view. Instead our author talks about *growth* in virtue, process instead of crisis. Thus he says, "If you possess these qualities in increasing measure" you will get a result. The result is not so much "they will keep you from" (followed by a list of negative consequences) as "you will be" neither "ineffective" nor "unproductive." These two terms, "ineffective" and "unproductive," mean similar things. The first indicates uselessness, such as faith without works, which is not saving faith (Jas 2:20; cf. Matt 12:36), or idleness (Matt 20:3, 6; 1 Tim 5:13; Titus 1:20[?]). The second also indicates uselessness, but employs an agricultural metaphor. The tree that does not bear fruit is cursed or cut down (Matt 3:8, 10; Mark 11:13, 20 and parallels; Luke 13:6-9). It is the deeds of darkness that are fruitless (Eph 5:11), and they contrast with doing what pleases the Lord (Eph 5:10). It is the word that is choked that bears no fruit (Matt 13:22; Mark 4:19), whereas by doing good works one makes sure that one is not fruitless (Titus 3:14). Christian virtues are fruit of the Spirit (Gal 5:22), and good fruit is the result of the wisdom from above (Jas 3:17; cf. the harvest of peace in 3:18).[46] In other words, put positively,

45. E. Stauffer, *"agapaō ktl.," TDNT* 1:35-55, particularly the last half of the article.

46. Bauckham, *Jude, 2 Peter,* 188, argues that 2 Peter is not thinking of Jude 12,

what 2 Peter is saying is that growth in these virtues will make the readers grow in Christian virtue or good works (both being covered by the metaphor) with respect to "your knowledge of our Lord Jesus Christ."

Yet that brings up an issue: is "your knowledge of . . . Christ" the basis of growing in virtue and thus one's conversion knowledge that is not unfruitful,[47] or is this knowledge of Christ a deeper knowledge of Christ that is the result of growing in virtue?[48] The decision between these interpretations turns on two factors. First, what is the meaning of the term "in" *(eis)*? Does it mean "with reference to" or "with respect to," which would indicate the first interpretation, or does it mean "into" or "resulting in," which would indicate the second interpretation? If we were talking about Classical Greek the answer would be clear, for the first meaning was carried by *en* and the second by *eis*.[49] However, in the Koine period this distinction blurred (eventually *en* will disappear from the language), so that commentators agree that *eis* could carry either meaning even if the first meaning is less common.[50] Second, how technical is the term for knowledge *(epignōsis)*? Does it mean only the coming to know Christ that occurs at conversion, or can it also indicate coming to know Christ more deeply? While not convinced that knowledge must be only the knowledge of Christ gained in conversion, the fact that 2 Peter does use "in" with the sense of "with respect to" and the type of contrast that the first interpretation makes over against v. 9 weighs our decision toward that first interpretation. Thus 2 Peter is pointing out that if one grows in virtue, the knowledge of Christ referred to in v. 3, that is, the coming to know Christ that happens in Christian conversion/initiation, will not be unproductive or unfruitful.

---

where the teachers Jude opposes are described as "autumn trees, without fruit." Since 2 Peter does know Jude, it is not impossible that this text may influence him. However, it will not be until the next chapter that he starts following Jude closely, so if there is influence here, it is oblique and anticipatory. No other words or images in the context point to Jude.

47. E.g., Bigg, *Epistles of St. Peter and St. Jude,* 259; Kelly, *The Epistles of Peter and Jude,* 307-8; Bauckham, *Jude, 2 Peter,* 188-89; Neyrey, *2 Peter, Jude,* 161; Charles, *Virtue amidst Vice,* 149.

48. E.g., Mayor, *Epistles of Jude and 2 Peter,* 94-95; Vögtle, *Der Judasbrief, der zweite Petrusbrief,* 151-52 (and virtually all other German commentators).

49. In 2 Peter *en* appears forty-three times and *eis* eleven times.

50. Of the eleven uses of *eis,* eight point forward in time or forward to results and are thus traditional, while in 1:17 and 3:9 we have uses that are close to what is claimed for the first meaning here. Significantly, in contrast to all of the Gospel narratives (Matt 3:16; 17:5; Mark 1:9; Luke 3:22), in 1:17, 2 Peter quotes the divine voice using *eis* rather than *en.*

**9** Such fruitfulness, however, is not always the case. Our author quickly points to the other alternative, an alternative that he will discuss in some detail in ch. 2: "if any of you do not have [these virtues], you are nearsighted and blind, and you have forgotten that you have been cleansed from past sins." The use of the term "blind" for those not "seeing" the truth, including moral truth, is relatively common in the NT (Matt 15:14 [Pharisees]; 23:16, 24 [Pharisees]; Luke 6:39; John 9:39-41 [Pharisees]; 12:40; Rom 2:19 [moral blindness]; 2 Cor 4:4 [blind = unable to "see" the gospel]; 1 John 2:11 [moral blindness]; Rev 3:17 [the moral blindness of Laodicea]). Likewise enlightenment was at times used for the process of Christian initiation (Heb 6:4; 10:32). Here 2 Peter uses a rare word, "nearsighted," along with the term for "blind." It is rare in Greek in general and occurs only here in biblical literature. Most translations take it as a parallel term to "blind," but that ignores the grammar. The text reads, "They are blind, being nearsighted," or, more colloquially, "so short-sighted that they cannot see" (GNB). They are focused on the present, probably with the implication that they are focused on their present desires (in the light of the teachers of ch. 2) and cannot see the past (nor, it will turn out, future judgment).

That the past is what they cannot see comes out in their forgetting their cleansing from past sins. In the ancient world one significant duty of a client toward his or her patron was the remembrance of past benefits received from the patron. People who do not grow in virtue are failing in that important duty.[51] Here the benefaction being forgotten is that of cleansing from past sins. While the image of cleansing from sin is found throughout Scripture (e.g., Lev 16:19 [cleanse from uncleanness], 30 [cleanse from sins]; Ps 51:2 [LXX Ps 50:4]; Ezek 36:33; Zech 13:1; Heb 1:3; 1 John 1:7 cf. Titus 2:14; Heb 9:14; 1 John 1:9), our image here refers, not to ongoing cleansing but to initial cleansing, that is, that accomplished symbolically in baptism: Acts 22:16 ("And now what are you waiting for? Get up, be baptized and wash your sins away, calling on his name"); 1 Cor 6:11; Eph 5:26 ("cleansing her by the washing with water through the word"); Titus 3:5 ("He saved us through the washing of rebirth and renewal by the Holy Spirit"). That is, in the act of Christian initiation, by which we mean that complex of repentance from our past independence of God (including our specific acts of rebellion), commitment to Christ as Lord, the expression of this commitment in baptism, and God's sealing of this commitment through the gift of the Holy Spirit, the sins of our pre-

51. Danker, "2 Peter 1: A Solemn Decree," 64-82. This is reprinted in his *Benefactor* (St. Louis: Clayton, 1982), 453-67. While the whole article is relevant, this particular point is made on p. 463. See also Neyrey, *2 Peter, Jude,* 161-62.

Christian life are forgiven. (For the initial readers of this letter our author assumes a pagan pre-Christian life.) This is a benefit that we should be grateful for, and out of this gratitude arises the desire to grow to be more like the one who cleansed us. If we neglect this growth and instead turn back to our former lives, then we have forgotten what was done for us and are, so the speak, slapping our divine patron in the face (cf. Paul's expression of this idea in Rom 6:1-14; 1 Cor 6:9-11).

**10** Our author is ready to draw a conclusion: "Therefore, my brothers and sisters, be all the more eager to make your calling and election sure." In addressing these readers as "brothers and sisters" (Greek *adelphoi*), he uses a term that occurs frequently in early Christian letters (although only here in the Petrine correspondence) to designate members of the Christian community. It is especially common in James. As noted in the comment above on v. 7, Christians considered each other members of a large extended family and thus siblings with God as Father. That means that this expression is not simply a form of address indicating a fellow believer, but one that indicates that they considered fellow believers as kin, resulting in treating them as kin by sharing possessions and the like. Here the use may be influenced by the family thinking engendered by the virtue list. Naturally, when Peter later turns to those he considers false teachers, he has no temptation to speak of them as "kin."

What these brothers and sisters are to do is to "make your calling and election sure." The phrase "be . . . eager" is the main verb, one liked by 2 Peter (also in 1:15; 3:14) and related to the term for "effort" in v. 5 (indicating that vv. 5-11 are all one unit). It is a term for zeal, effort, and the expenditure of energy. For example, Timothy is to make an effort to come before winter (2 Tim 4:21), and, more to the point, Christians are to make an effort to enter into God's rest in Heb 4:11 or to keep the unity of the Spirit in Eph 4:3. Thus this term indicates making something a high priority for which one will expend physical or moral effort. Given the dire consequences (as noted in v. 9) of neglecting the virtues cited above, our author underlines the importance of the effort involved, "make all the more effort" or "make it the highest priority." This effort is to be expended with respect to their "calling and election." That these believers were called by Christ our author has already indicated in v. 3. Here "calling" forms a synonymous word-pair with the term "election" or "state of being chosen," with no real difference between them (notice the interplay of "called" and "chose" in 1 Cor 1:26-31 and 1 Pet 2:9).[52] 2 Peter likes such

52. The Reformed distinction between God's unconditional election of a person, which is part of his eternal counsel, and his effective calling of a person, in which the person is historically called to faith, is a later development. As far as I know, it first occurs af-

word-pairs, and this one also occurs in Rev 17:14, "with him [i.e., Christ] will be his called, chosen and faithful followers." It is this calling to be a Christian that they need to "make . . . sure" or ratify (*bebaian*).[53] This root appears sixteen times in the NT and "means 'firm,' 'steadfast,' 'steady,' 'reliable,' 'certain.'"[54] While in other places in the NT God is said to make the Christian steadfast or firm (1 Cor 1:8; 2 Cor 1:21), here the Christian is to confirm his or her own calling and election. The way that this is done is through growing in virtue. In other words, this passages states "that the ethical fruits of Christian faith are objectively necessary for the attainment of final salvation."[55] Or, as Wisdom of Solomon puts it,

> 17The beginning of wisdom is the most sincere desire for instruction,
> and concern for instruction is love of her,
> 18and love of her is the keeping of her laws,
> and giving heed to her laws is assurance (*bebaiōsis*) of immortality,
> 19and immortality brings one near to God;
> 20so the desire for wisdom leads to a kingdom. (Wisd 6:17-20, NRSV)

This teaching may sit uncomfortably with some people's theology, but it is the other side of the coin that has on one side that God makes us firm and on this side that we make our own salvation firm. And it is our side of the coin that the believers 2 Peter addresses need to hear, for they have among them some who think that their salvation is firm enough without their pursuing any of the virtues that our author recommends.

The author of 2 Peter does not leave his readers only with the command. He adds a two-part promise. The first part is negative, "For if you do these things, you will never fall." The "these things" that one is supposed to do are either the virtues in particular (the same term appears in vv. 8 and 9 referring to the virtues of vv. 5-7) or the sense of the passage in general, although grammatically a reference to the virtues is preferable. It is in the *doing* (the Greek reader will note the use of alliteration, for "doing," "fall," and "never" all begin with *p*) that one will never "fall." This last term means to "stumble" or "fall," which can mean to stumble ethically, that is, sin (Rom 11:11; Jas 2:10; 3:2). That meaning, however, would

---

ter the Reformation, and thus may appear in Reformed commentaries on this text, although it is a distinction that arose from later theological reflection on the text rather than being part of the author's thought.

53. Vögtle, *Der Judasbrief, der zweite Petrusbrief*, 153, notes that "make" is in an emphatic position and that the imperative "give more effort to the process" is present, indicating ongoing activity. Thus this passage underlines the active involvement of the Christian in confirming his or her salvation.

54. H. Schlier, *"bebaios ktl.," TDNT* 1:600.

55. Bauckham, *Jude, 2 Peter*, 190.

yield a tautology: if you practice virtue, you will never sin.[56] And this idea is so obvious as hardly to need expressing. It is therefore more likely that our author is thinking ahead to the second part of his promise that has a journey metaphor in the "welcome" or "entrance" into the kingdom. In this case the term has a more literal meaning. That is, it means, "Stumble (and fall) on the path to God's kingdom and thus fail to arrive." This is the meaning of the same root in Jude 24 ("keep you from falling"), and it makes more sense in this context.[57] Virtue will keep one from the disaster of stumbling and never arriving at the eschatological home.

**11** The second part of the promise is positive. In this promise we are moved to the end of this life or, perhaps more likely in 2 Peter, to the coming of Christ. If you do these things, "you will receive a rich welcome into the eternal kingdom of our Lord and Savior Jesus Christ." More literally this would read, "Your entrance will be richly provided for." The picture is that of a patron who lavishly celebrates the arrival of a friend or faithful servant at his home. Vögtle suggests as an alternative to the patron-friend picture the picture of a victor returning to his home city after the Olympic Games and being received with a triumphal welcome.[58] The two pictures both present the same general metaphor of reception. That one is richly provided for in this entrance suggests the richness of divine generosity (Rom 10:12; Eph 1:7; 1 Tim 6:17; Titus 3:6), although here we must remember that it reciprocates the provision that one has already made for oneself in growing in virtue (the main verb in v. 5 is the same as the main verb here, making a neat closure of the section with divine wealth rewarding temporal exertion).

The focal point of this lavishness is an "entrance . . . into the kingdom." The image is common in the NT, and it is a gospel image found in the teaching of Jesus: Matt 5:20 ("not enter the kingdom of heaven"); 7:21 ("Not everyone who says to me, 'Lord, Lord,' will enter the kingdom of heaven, but only he who does the will of my Father who is in heaven" could be a paraphrase of our section); 18:3 ("enter the kingdom of heaven"); 19:23 ("enter the kingdom of heaven"); Mark 10:23-25 ("enter the kingdom of God"); Luke 18:17, 24-25 ("enter the kingdom of God"); John 3:5 ("no one can enter the kingdom of God unless he is born of water and the Spirit"), Acts 14:22 ("We must go through many hardships to enter the kingdom of God"). While Jesus could talk of the kingdom of God

56. Spicq, *Les Épitres de Saint Pierre;* Schelkle, *Die Petrusbrief, der Judasbrief;* Schrage, "Der zweite Petrusbrief, der Judasbrief," in *Der "Katholische Brief";* Sidebottom, *James, Jude, and 2 Peter,* 108; Neyrey, *2 Peter, Jude,* 162.

57. Bigg, *St. Peter and St. John,* 261; Kelly, *The Epistles of Peter and Jude,* 309; Bauckham, *Jude, 2 Peter,* 191; Vögtle, *Der Judasbrief, der zweite Petrusbrief,* 154.

58. Vögtle, *Der Judasbrief, der zweite Petrusbrief,* 154.

as already present in his presence, in these expressions he is talking of the full realization of his eschatological kingdom, or what is sometimes called final salvation. The question that 2 Peter, following Jesus, has answered is, "Who will enter, and what will enable that person to enter?" In 2 Peter the positive picture is of people arriving, and finding themselves honorably, even lavishly received. This is one side of the final judgment that will be discussed in ch. 3.

This kingdom is "the eternal kingdom of our Lord and Savior Jesus Christ." There are very few references to Jesus' kingdom as eternal. The idea of an eternal kingdom appears in the OT (e.g., Dan 7:27) and is mentioned in the NT (Luke 1:33; Rev 11:15), but the actual wording "eternal kingdom" does not appear elsewhere in the NT. However, parallels are found in the Caesar cult,[59] and it may be that the wording here intends (without being too obvious) to point to the contrasting kingdom of Christ that is truly eternal. It certainly intends to point to the new (renewed) heaven and new (renewed) earth of 3:13 that contrasts with this earth, which is soon to be burned (purified).

While in the teaching of Jesus the kingdom is the kingdom of God, here, in keeping with the images in Luke and Revelation, it is the kingdom of the Christ. In 2 Pet 1:1 our author referred to Jesus as "our God and Savior." Here in a parallel expression it is "our Lord and Savior Jesus Christ," which will be repeated at 3:18 and appears in slightly shorter forms in 2:20 and 3:2. In this title the soteriological titles of Christ are combined. That is, the confession "Jesus is Lord" (Rom 10:9-10) joins with the references to Jesus as Savior to form a single title. (That the Caesar was at times referred to as Savior as well as Lord gives a political aspect to this title — the kingdom of our Lord and Savior versus the kingdoms of this world.) The kingdom to be entered at the end of our road is his kingdom. The one who provides a triumphal welcome is the one we have served as Lord and are experiencing as Savior as he delivers us from the powers of this world. Such an encouragement should serve as a major impetus to develop the virtues that flow from commitment to (i.e., faith in) him (so 1:5).

59. Vögtle, *Der Judasbrief, der zweite Petrusbrief,* 155, cites the inscription from Stratonicea in Karien that dates to the early period of the Caesars, cited in G. A. Deissmann, *Bibelstudien* (Hildesheim, New York: Olms, 1977), 277-81; E.T. G. A. Deissmann, *Bible Studies* (Edinburgh: T&T Clark, 1901), 363. E.g., "the eternal rule of the Roman lords."

## B. Purpose Statement (1:12-15)

*[12]So I will always remind you of these things, even though you know them and are firmly established in the truth you now have. [13]I think it is right to refresh your memory as long as I live in the tent of this body, [14]because I know that I will soon put it aside, as our Lord Jesus Christ has made clear to me. [15]And I will make every effort to see that after my departure you will always be able to remember these things.*

In the final section of the letter opening our author gives us some personal details that would favorably dispose his readers toward him. This section serves a number of purposes. First, it refers back to the previous mini-sermon, underlines its importance, and yet also makes the charitable assumption that the readers are only being reminded. Second, it sets up the whole letter as a testament, the final words of an author to those reading the letter. And third, it forms a bridge into the body. While it does not actually refer to the themes of the body (e.g., there is no mention of Christ's return or of the resurrection), it does give the purpose of the whole work, sets the tone of personal testimony, and as such serves along with the Transfiguration narrative as the body opening.

In setting up the work as a testament, our author follows in a significant Jewish tradition. There are the ancient testaments of Jacob (Gen 49:1-28),[1] Moses (Deut 33:1-29), and Joshua (Josh 24:1-28, which is also a covenant renewal ceremony), and David (1 Kings 2:1-9). Then there were the intertestamental testaments, such as the *Testaments of the 12 Patriarchs* (the twelve sons of Jacob), *2 Apocalypse of Baruch* 78–87, and *Jub.* 22:1-30 (a testament of Abraham).[2] While Josephus's testament of Moses in *Ant.* 4.177-93 may not have been known to 2 Peter, there was also a testament tradition in the early church, seen in Jesus' final words in Luke 22:14-36 and John 13–17, and in Paul's farewell in Miletus (Acts 20:17-35). What are the common features of these testaments or farewells?[3]

- Prediction of death
- Prediction of future crises for those the dying person leaves

1. Isaac's blessing of Jacob is also a type of testament, but it comes in two parts, Gen 27:1-29 and 28:1-5. Both blessings are given in the face of Isaac's death (Gen 27:2).

2. There is also a much more modern Jewish testamental tradition. See Lawrence W. Raphael, "The Teaching of Writing an Ethical Will," *Judaism* 48 (1999) 174-80. He cites Israel Abrahams, *Hebrew Ethical Wills* (Philadelphia: Jewish Publication Society, 1926), and Jack Riemer and Nathaniel Stampfer, *Ethical Wills: A Modern Jewish Treasury* (New York: Schocken, 1983).

3. Adapted from Neyrey, *2 Peter, Jude,* 164.

- Exhortation to virtue
- Blessing or commission
- Reference to the legacy the departing dying person leaves behind

While some of these are rather obvious (e.g., one would not know that something was a testament without some reference to the proximity of death), the list brings the salient features to our attention. We have already seen 2 Peter's exhortation to virtue. Our present section focuses on the prediction of Peter's death.

**12** The purpose of 2 Peter is to "remind you of these things," although the author admits that "you know them and are firmly established in the truth you now have." It is because of the critical importance of what he has been talking about ("so" [NIV] might be better translated "therefore") that he wants to remind them. The construction "I will always remind you" is difficult. It reads literally "I will always be reminding you" and is a construction for the future paralleled only in Matt 24:6 ("You will hear of wars and rumors of wars").[4] Does 2 Peter mean that he is ready to write again in the future to remind them, or does he take the perspective of their receiving this letter in the future with respect to his writing? Most likely he means the latter, for he does speak of his own death and thus is unlikely to be thinking about future communication. At the same time, he knows that the letter will arrive sometime in the future and that it will be a constant reminder as it is repeatedly read in the community.

To refer to the letter as a reminder is part of politeness. It was thought appropriate in classical rhetoric to assume that the persons addressed were already knowledgeable and that one was simply reminding them.[5] Paul states that Romans is a reminder of what the Romans presumably know (Rom 15:15), and in 1 Cor 15:1 he reminds the Corinthians of his past teaching. In 2 Tim 1:6 Timothy is reminded about a gift he knew about. Likewise Jude 5 reminds his readers of OT narratives. Whether in any of these cases the author really thought that the reader(s) already knew the information and thus needed only a reminder or whether the author was simply being polite, following the guidelines of classical rhetoric, we cannot know. Likewise we cannot know whether 2 Peter here is being polite or actually thinks that his readers already know this information. Naturally the idea of reminder is especially im-

4. For further discussion of the grammar see Bauckham, *Jude, 2 Peter,* 195-96. He rightly points out that Mayor's (*Jude and II Peter,* 99) conjectural correction to "I shall take care to remind you" is unnecessary despite 2 Peter's construction being unusual. It makes less sense in that when someone is facing death, they do not conceive of themselves as being around to "always" take care to remind someone of something.

5. Watson, *Invention, Arrangement, and Style,* 100.

portant in a farewell statement such as this, for memory is all that will be left.[6] Thus the idea of reminding will be mentioned four more times in this letter (1:13, 15; 3:1, 2).

The idea of reminder is carried further in that our author admits that his readers "know" "these things," referring back to the content of 1:3-11, and probably more particularly to the importance of growing in virtue. Does this mean that he knows the readers personally? This is unlikely if we are talking about a letter written in Rome and sent to Asia Minor. Yet it does indicate that what 2 Peter is about is the common teaching of the Jesus movement, teaching that was Peter's core message, teaching that he believes Paul has also supported in his letters (3:15), and so teaching that they should know. Since these Christians are probably in established communities of followers of Jesus, he also assumes that they "are firmly established in the truth" (cf. Rom 16:25; 1 Thess 3:2; 1 Pet 5:10). He will refer to the word group of being established three more times, twice negatively (2:14, the victims of the false teachers are unstable; 3:16, the unstable warp Scripture) and once positively (3:17). Stating that they are established is a positive way of restating what he said in 1:10, namely, that by pursuing virtue they will make sure that they do not fall. That they are established in "the truth" that they "now have" again underlines the aspect of reminder. These followers of Jesus have received the teaching of the true good news ("the faith that was once for all entrusted to the saints" in Jude 3), the one that Peter represents in his homily in 1:3-11, and the one that includes the eschatological teaching that will take up much of the rest of the letter. They do not need to be taught it again, but the legacy Peter will leave to them is a reminder, an underlining of this truth. (For examples of the good news as truth or word of truth, see Gal 2:5, 14; 5:7; Eph 1:13; Col 1:5; 2 Thess 2:12-13; 2 Tim 2:15; Jas 1:18; 2 John 4.)

**13-14** With a second reference to reminder ("I think it is right to refresh your memory"), our author moves on to state his grounds for doing this. The need to refresh the memory is not, as some scholars assume, simply a characteristic of a postapostolic time that was trying to conserve the apostolic teaching. We have already seen that Paul and others viewed their letters as reminders, for memory fades fast when the pressure is on or when new and attractive teaching comes along. This is especially true in an oral-mnemonic culture in which each home does not contain a Bible or other Christian literature. The phrasing of this description of the need

6. John 14:26 is often cited, but it is less relevant in that the reference is to a future reminder by the Holy Spirit. Acts 20:31 is a good example of reminder, as is 2 Tim 2:8, 14, all of which are found in farewell addresses. Many examples of course are found in the extrabiblical literature cited above.

to refresh the memory may indeed be dictated partly by what was thought to be more appropriate to the literary genre and the modesty needed to influence people, and it may indeed be part of the testamental genre (e.g., 2 *Apoc. Bar.* 84:1), but it is also, as any pastor knows, something that needs constant doing even in modern comfortable church situations in which homes are often filled with literature that could do the job if it were only read.

In the situation in which 2 Peter was written, our author indicates that he knows that he has a limited time to accomplish his goals: "as long as I live in the tent of this body" or, more literally, "as long as I am in this tent" (the NIV has expanded the "tent" metaphor to make its reference clear). Rooted in their previous nomadic life (many of the peoples of the Mediterranean world had once been nomadic) and the present use of tents as temporary shelters, the image of a tent for this mortal life is found in the OT (Isa 38:12, although only as an analogy for how it is being taken from him), but it is more common in Hellenistic Judaism. For instance, in Wisd 9:15 we read, "For a perishable body weighs down the soul, and this earthy tent burdens the thoughtful mind," a clear indication of both the tent = body imagery and body-soul dualism (which is rarely seen in the OT). While appearing frequently in later Greek literature (e.g., *Diogn.* 6:8, "The soul dwells immortal in a mortal tabernacle [the same word as 'tent' in our passage], and Christians sojourn among corruptible things, waiting for the incorruptibility which is in heaven"; cf. *Paral. Jer.* 6:6-7; *Sentences of Sextus* 320; *Apocalypse of Paul* 15; Eusebius, *Eccl. Hist.* 3.31.1-2),[7] the image was current in the NT period, for it is used by Paul in 2 Cor 5:1, 4:

> Now we know that if the earthly tent we live in is destroyed, we have a building from God, an eternal house in heaven, not built by human hands. Meanwhile we groan, longing to be clothed with our heavenly dwelling, because when we are clothed, we will not be found naked. For while we are in this tent, we groan and are burdened, because we do not wish to be unclothed but to be clothed with our heavenly dwelling, so that what is mortal may be swallowed up by life.

Certainly the image of "tent" in 2 Peter as in Paul indicates mortality. Is there also some indication, as in Paul, of the "tent" being temporary while the "building" is eternal? That idea is not necessarily in the image of "tent" per se, but surely the temporary nature of the tent cannot be far from our author's mind (even though he never mentions the resurrection

7. See further references in W. Michaelis, *"skēnē ktl.," TDNT* 7:368-94, especially 381-84.

and any eternal incarnation), for he goes right on in the next verse to say, "because I know that I will soon put it aside."

While several of the passages cited above speak of the separation of the soul or heart from the "tent" as a metaphor for death, in our passage, as in 2 Corinthians, there is a mixed metaphor, for to "put . . . aside" is a picture of taking off clothing. While this certainly would have been considered poor style,[8] the image of taking off and putting on clothing was traditional Christian language. It is used in Col 2:11; 3:9-10 for the moral death and resurrection of the Christian associated with baptism as part of Christian initiation. Paul uses it for physical death and resurrection in 1 Cor 15:53-54 and, as we have seen, in 2 Corinthians. Our author uses only half of the metaphor, that of taking clothing off, for his focus is on his own death.

He knows that his death is "soon," a feature that is common in testamental literature, as one would expect. (If one were not anticipating death, why would one be giving one's last instructions?) He believes that his death will be "soon" not just because of illness or advancing age (as in the case of Isaac, Jacob, and David), nor because of a prophetic saying (Acts 20:23; cf. 21:11) or a vision (*Acts of Paul* 10) or an angel (Acts 27:24, where the prediction is that Paul would not die; the angel of death figures in several intertestamental farewells), but because of a word from Jesus ("as our Lord Jesus Christ has made clear to me"). The Greek terms translated "as" mean "as also" (cf. Luke 11:1; Acts 15:8; Rom 1:13; 15:7), so our author assumes that there is some evidence from sources other than Jesus that his death is approaching, and that this has been confirmed by a word from "our Lord Jesus Christ." Assuming that this prediction is one that we know from preserved sayings of Jesus, it must refer either to John 13:36 ("Where I am going, you cannot follow now, but you will follow later")[9] or to 21:18-19 ("'I tell you the truth, when you were younger you dressed yourself and went where you wanted; but when you are old you will stretch out your hands, and someone else will dress you and lead you where you do not want to go.' Jesus said this to indicate the kind of death by which Peter would glorify God." [This quotation includes the Johannine commentary with the word of Jesus]). All other possible sayings come from later literature that is probably dependent on either John

8. Watson, *Invention, Arrangement, and Style,* 100.

9. Bauckham, *Jude, 2 Peter,* 200, points out that some scholars feel that this was created by Johnnine reflection on "Matt 26:35; Mark 14:31; Luke 2[2]:33, in the light of Peter's martyrdom." This is not the place to discuss Johannine criticism, but while this saying is in a similar context to our saying (Jesus would "go" = die, and Peter will "follow" = die, but only later), it is so enigmatic that it would be surprising if an author created it after the death of Peter.

or 2 Peter itself.[10] Either of the Johannine passages would be sufficient (and each has the obscurity typical of prophetic sayings), although the latter is more specific. That neither of the sayings has a specific time reference in it and that Peter did not die "quickly" after the time of Jesus are not the problem some scholars believe they are.[11] If our letter places Peter in Rome, and especially if it places him there after the writing of 1 Peter, then it assumes that he is an old man (in an age when the average life span was forty years or less, a man who was at least in his 60s was old indeed). Even if one thinks of our author as writing in the name of Peter, it would be clear to him that such a man as Peter would likely die relatively soon. If it was written after A.D. 64, everyone knew of the anti-Christian feelings unleashed by Nero after the great fire. Neither a pseudepigrapher nor the author himself would need revelation to think that death might be near. That would be the first evidence that his death was "soon." But there was something else that our author knows about (the "as also"). Jesus in at least one saying had indicated that Peter would die (and thus not experience the Parousia), and would not die a natural death (at least so both sayings were interpreted), so clearly his death must be close. This verse does fit the testamental genre, and one reason it fits is that that genre reflects the experience of some people as they see death approaching. Yet form alone cannot determine whether 2 Peter is the work of a pseudepigrapher who knew testaments and projected himself into Peter's setting, or a reminiscence of Peter himself. (See the Introduction to 2 Peter [pp. 145-49] for a fuller discussion of this issue.)

**15** At this point we get to the core purpose of the letter. With another reference to Peter's death ("after my departure") the purpose is given as making it possible that "you will always be able to remember these things." In other words, this letter is to serve as his testament, not in the sense that it would stand as a monument to Peter and his thought, but in the sense that it would enable the churches to whom the letter is addressed to remain true to the position that our author takes on the issues of concern. It would keep on working after Peter was gone.

The language that expresses this is somewhat unusual. The phrase "I will make every effort" is in the future tense. We have already noted that this root is something of a favorite with 2 Peter (1:5, 10, 15; 3:14), so it is not the term, which we have already discussed, that is unusual but the tense. Is the author thinking of the letter as that future effort in that it will arrive long after it is sent and so be continuing his effort? Or is the author

10. Bauckham, *Jude, 2 Peter,* 200-201.

11. Although it is discussed at length by Vögtle, *Der Judasbrief, der zweite Petrusbrief,* 159-61.

referring to some future Petrine work? Candidates for the latter include various suggestions about future letters, which by their nature make the suggestion hypothetical since we have no other indication of any such letters, and especially Mark's Gospel.[12] There is the tradition that Mark is the preaching of Peter. Eusebius (*Eccl. Hist.* 2.15.1) writes that ". . . the hearers of Peter . . . besought Mark, whose Gospel is extant, seeing that he was Peter's follower, to leave them a written statement of the teaching given them verbally. . . ." He then states that both Clement and Papias have this tradition. Irenaeus, *Adv. haer.* 3:1:1, states, "After their departure [*meta tēn toutōn exoudon,* referring to Peter and Paul], Mark, the disciple and interpreter of Peter, did also hand down to us in writing what had been preached by Peter." The problem is that only Clement (via Eusebius) suggests that this writing took place during Peter's lifetime; all the others place Mark's writing after Peter's lifetime. Moreover, Mark does not seem to focus on "these things," namely, the topics of 2 Pet 1:3-11 (which is what our author has referred to several times). Thus it seems unlikely that Mark is the work being referred to. This brings us back to the other suggestion, that the reference is to 2 Peter itself viewed as future with respect to its arrival. While the use of the future to indicate that aspect of writing is quite unusual, this is the most satisfactory (or least unsatisfactory) interpretation of this phrase.

Peter's death is referred to as "after my departure" *(meta tēn emēn exodon).* The term *exodos* can carry a variety of meanings, and the question here whether it means the conclusion of life ("after my end") as it does in Luke 9:31,[13] or "departure." It is not that our author knows about the reference in Luke 9:31, for that verse is Luke's thematic summary of a conversation, not a term that anyone claims was actually said on the mountain of Transfiguration. The question revolves around the fact that this type of expression, while not extremely common, was used throughout the Jewish and Hellenistic world (e.g., Sir 38:23 ["his spirit has departed"]; Wisd 3:2 ["their departure ('end' would be better in this context) was thought to be a disaster"]; 7:6 ["there is for all one entrance into life, and one way out"]; *T. Naph.* 1:1 ["at the time of his death"]; Josephus, *Ant.* 4.189 ["I am going out of the world"]). Thus the issue is whether our author was thinking of the departure of the soul from the body (his not being in "this tent" of 1:13) or simply the end of his life. Does he think in terms of the more Hellenistic body-soul dualism or in terms of the more

12. E.g., Bigg, *St. Peter and St. Jude,* 264-65; Mayor, *Jude and II Peter,* cxlii-cxliv; Green, *The Second Epistle of Peter and the Epistle of Jude,* 80-81.

13. "In Lk. 9:31 and 2 Pet. 1:15 it means the end of life in the sense of 'conclusion' rather than 'departure.'" W. Michaelis, *"hodos ktl.," TDNT* 5:107.

Hebraic death of the person? While he does not say enough to definitively determine the answer to this question, the evidence that we do have leans toward the former[14] rather than the latter.[15]

Our author, then, views himself as departing from "this tent." In the light of that he is writing a letter that they will be able to keep after his death so as to be continually remembering the important truths that he wishes to impress on them.

## III. LETTER BODY (1:16–3:16)

Having stated the purpose of his letter, i.e. to serve as a testament or witness after his death, our author now turns to the central issue of this letter: the return of Christ and the concomitant final judgment. The main issue that he is dealing with is formally stated in 3:4, "Where is the promise of his coming?" In this first section of the letter body this question is assumed and hovers as a shadow lying behind the argument.

### A. The Implications of the Transfiguration (1:16-21)

> 16 *We did not follow cleverly invented stories when we told you about the power and coming of our Lord Jesus Christ, but we were eyewitnesses of his majesty.* 17 *For he received honor and glory from God the Father when the voice came to him from the Majestic Glory, saying, "This is my Son, whom I love; with him I am well pleased."* 18 *We ourselves heard this voice that came from heaven when we were with him on the sacred mountain.*

The Transfiguration narrative itself serves two functions. First, it is the *narratio,* that part of a rhetorical argument that states the facts and introduces the point to be proved. Second, it is itself an argument, for it produces witnesses to facts that prove the point. Thus in some ways this section closes the argument before it starts, although ch. 3 will include theological and biblical arguments that by their nature cannot be found here.

The topic of this section is the Transfiguration. This account is clearly not dependent upon any of the Synoptic accounts, as a comparison of some of the key elements will show.

14. Argued by Neyrey, *2 Peter, Jude,* 167-68.
15. Which Bauckham, *Jude, 2 Peter,* 202, argues.

| | *Introductory description* | *Description of glory* | *Content of voice* |
|---|---|---|---|
| 2 Peter 1 | the power and coming of our Lord Jesus Christ | Majestic Glory | This is my Son, whom I love; with him I am well pleased. |
| Mark 9 | the kingdom of God come with power | none | This is my Son, whom I love. Listen to him! |
| Matthew 17 | The Son of Man coming in his kingdom | a bright cloud | This is my Son, whom I love; with him I am well pleased. Listen to him! |
| Luke 9 | the kingdom of God | his glory . . . a cloud appeared | This is my Son, whom I have chosen; listen to him. |

When we look at these parallel accounts we see that 2 Peter is closest to the Matthean redaction or version of the narrative. That is, (1) his interpretation of the event is focused on Jesus and his coming, (2) his description of the voice originating in glory is closest to Matthew's "bright cloud" (probably alluding to the glory of God in the cloud in the wilderness), and (3) his report of the content of the voice has three of four elements in common with Matthew (versus one of three in common with Luke and two of three with Mark). There is no need to argue that 2 Peter has imported the "with him I am well pleased" from the baptism of Jesus (Matt 3:17; Mark 1:11; Luke 3:22), for at least one Gospel tradition already has it in the Transfiguration narrative.[1] While not found in Mark's version, the presence of this combination of statements in both Matthew and 2 Peter is certainly not coincidence. Most likely both are drawing independently on a similar tradition.[2]

1. Even here 2 Peter is closest to Matthew, for while the other two Gospels have the voice at the baptism addressing Jesus, "You are my Son . . . with you I am well pleased," Matthew has the voice addressing the onlookers, "This is my Son . . . with him I am well pleased."

2. After a long discussion Bauckham, *Jude, 2 Peter,* 205-10, concludes, "We may conclude that the evidence is strongly in favor of the view that in his account of the Transfiguration the author of 2 Peter was not dependent on the synoptic Gospels but on independent tradition." The reason for this is that while the content of 2 Peter is parallel to that of Matthew's account, the Greek wording of 2 Peter is independent of Matthew. In

The purpose of this tradition is to defend one of the "very great and precious promises" (1:4), namely, that of Christ's rule and return (including his final judgment of all people). The issue for 2 Peter is not simply that this teaching was a foundation of Christian morality. Something more fundamental is at stake: the honor of the God who made the promise and the honor of the prophets and teachers (including our author) who have relayed it.

**16** The apologetic tone that characterizes this section is struck immediately: "We did not follow cleverly invented stories (*sesophismenois mythois*)." The issues involved in this phrase were already well known by Philo, who in *Fuga et inventione* 121 writes, "Thus he says that 'Lot's wife turning backwards became a pillar of salt'; not here inventing a fable (*mythoplasteō*), but pointing out the proper nature of the event." In *Somn.* 1.172 he asserts about a dream reported in Scripture, "These statements are not fables (*mythos*) of my own invention, but are the oracle written on the sacred pillars." And in *Opificio mundi* 2 he states, "But Moses, rejecting both of these methods, the one as inconsiderate, careless, and unphilosophical, and the other as mendacious and full of trickery, made the beginning of his laws entirely beautiful, and in all respects admirable, neither at once declaring what ought to be done or the contrary, nor (since it was necessary to mould beforehand the dispositions of those who were to use his laws) inventing fables (*mythou plasma*) himself or adopting those which had been invented by others." In fact, in at least a dozen different works Philo defends Scripture as not being "fables." The reason for this apologetic is that in the Greek-speaking world many stories about the gods and heroes were considered "fables" or "myths" (two translations of *mythos*). While this term can simply mean a story as distinguished from reason or argument (*logos*), for some (e.g., some Stoics) this meant that myths were useful insofar as they could be allegorized into supporting positive values, while for others (e.g., Epicureans) who valued reason above all else the term often carried the implication of stories that were untrue or inappropriate. This was especially true when the stories were about the gods and the afterlife and the rewards and punishments to be found there.[3] This term is used uniformly in this negative sense elsewhere in the NT (1 Tim 1:4; 4:7; 2 Tim 4:4; Titus 1:14), and in our passage the negative sense of the term is reinforced by the participle *sesophismenois*, "cleverly invented," where the idea of cleverness is nega-

---

our opinion, independent redactions of the oral tradition to Greek could account for the differences. Given the popularity of a story such as this, the likelihood that multiple versions of the story existed is very high.

3. C. K. Barrett, "Myth and the New Testament: The Greek Word *mythos*," *ExpT* 68 (1957) 345-48. G. Stählin, "*mythos*," *TDNT* 4:762-95, discussing our passage on 789-90.

tive rather than positive.[4] Following such myths would certainly be a mistake, a mistake that Josephus says Moses did not make,

> Now when once he had brought them to submit to religion, he easily persuaded them to submit in all other things; for, as to other legislators, they followed [same verb as in 2 Peter for following] fables, and, by their discourses, transferred the most reproachful of human vices unto the gods, and so afforded wicked men the most plausible excuses for their crimes; but, as for our legislator, when he had once demonstrated that God was possessed of perfect virtue, he supposed that man also ought to strive after the participation of it; and on those who did not so think and so believe he inflicted the severest punishments. (*Ant.* 1.21-23)

The context of not following cleverly invented stories is "when we told you about the power and coming of Lord Jesus Christ." Here is the clue as to what the whole issue is about. In 2 Pet 3:4 the "scoffers" say, "Where is the promise of his coming?" In our present passage our author says that it is that "coming" *(parousia)* that they (the apostles) told these followers of Jesus about. Two things are clear from this statement. First, the charge 2 Peter is refuting is that all of the prophetic promises about Jesus' "coming" are stories and nothing more, with the implication that they are stories invented by the leaders of the church to control the behavior of the believers (that, at least, is how many Greeks viewed stories about the afterlife and especially retribution in the afterlife). Second, our author interprets the Transfiguration not simply as a vision of the power or glory of Jesus, but as a vision of his coming. The two terms "power" and "coming" are probably a hendiadys for "his powerful coming." The Transfiguration was for 2 Peter, so to speak, a proleptic second coming. The use of "coming" or *parousia* for the second coming of Jesus is common in the NT (Matt 24:3, 27, 37, 39; 1 Cor 15:23; 1 Thess. 3:13; 4:15; Jas 5:7-8; 1 John 2:28), although, as Bauckham correctly notes, it is not the language of 1 Peter.[5] That power is associated with this coming is also clear in the NT: Matt 24:30 ("They will see the Son of Man coming on the clouds of the sky, with power and great glory"); Mark 13:26 ("At that time men will see the Son of Man coming in clouds with great power and glory"); Luke 21:27 ("At that time they will see the Son of Man coming in a cloud with power and great glory"); cf. Mark 9:1.

4. For example, in *Barn.* 9:4 we are told that the Hebrews "erred because an evil angel was misleading them." The term translated "misleading" is the same verb found in our participle here.

5. Bauckham, *Jude, 2 Peter,* 215. 1 Peter normally uses "revelation" for the second coming (1 Pet 1:7, 13; 4:13).

It is also clear that our author is giving us an interpretation of the Transfiguration. Sometimes this event is interpreted in both modern and ancient works as a revelation of the glory of Jesus, as if the veil were pulled back and the readers get to see who Jesus really is. Sometimes it is viewed as a reassurance to Jesus, God reassuring him that he really is on track and really is God's loved Son. 2 Peter, however, says that the Transfiguration was a view into the future of the coming exaltation of Jesus, a view of his second coming with power and glory.[6]

This view of the future was not something made up, but "we were eyewitnesses of his majesty." There are probably two references for "we" in this text. The first "we" is that of the teachers or evangelists who instructed these believers about the Parousia of Christ ("when we told you"). If 2 Peter is written to the same people as those addressed in 1 Peter (see the Introduction, pp. 132-33), then it is unlikely that our author was among these teachers/evangelists. However, he identifies with them, for their story is the same as his story. The second "we" in this verse is that of the apostles ("we were eyewitnesses"). We are not told how many apostles were eyewitnesses or their names — or even that the eyewitnesses were apostles — for the readers are expected to remember the story. Besides, the issue of who and how many is not the point. The point is that the group including the author were "eyewitnesses" as contrasted to their having made the story up.

The point of the eyewitness testimony is not that of proving the authenticity of the letter or of defending the integrity of the apostles. That is not the issue under discussion.[7] The reality of the hope of the Parousia of Christ is the issue. So the testimony is introduced in the rhetorical function of an "inartificial proof" of the reality of Christ's investiture and thus of his coming reign.[8] The factuality of the Transfiguration is not being de-

6. Howard Clark Kee, "The Transfiguration in Mark: Epiphany or Apocalyptic Vision?" in J. Reumann, ed., *Understanding the Sacred Text* (*Festschrift* for M. S. Enslin) (Valley Forge, PA: Judson, 1972), 137-52. See especially p. 149, "The transfiguration scene is not a theophany *to,* nor an epiphany *of,* Jesus, but a proleptic vision of the exaltation of Jesus as kingly Son of Man granted to the disciples as eschatological witnesses."

7. While it was not the issue under discussion in the original context, it is for us. Certainly our author expects the eyewitness testimony to be accepted as genuine, not as a "myth." If Peter were not an eyewitness to the event, then our author is being deceptive in that what he is presenting as "eyewitness" is a myth. Conceivably the testamental genre might allow an author to so cite Peter without believing himself to be inauthentic, but it would be easier to defend the idea that our author does intend to identify himself as Peter.

8. Watson, *Invention, Arrangement, and Style,* 102. Inartificial proofs are "not manufactured by the rhetor and include witnesses, evidence extracted by torture, informal agreements, contracts, laws, decisions of previous courts, rumors, documents, and

fended, but rather the event is being introduced as evidence of Jesus' investiture with majesty.

The majesty of which they were eyewitnesses could be the royal majesty of earthly kings (e.g., Jer 40:9: "And this city shall be to me a name of joy, a praise and a glory [in the LXX "glory" is the same word as "majesty" in our text]"; Dan 7:27: "The kingship and dominion and the greatness of the kingdoms under the whole heaven"; 1 Esdr 1:5 [4 in the LXX]: "in accordance with the directions of King David of Israel and the magnificence of his son Solomon"; 4:40: "To [truth] belongs the strength and the kingship and the power and the majesty of all the ages"). But because divine majesty was viewed as a superlative version of royal majesty, this term was commonly applied by Jewish and Christian writers to that as well, whether the majesty of pagan gods (e.g., Acts 19:27, referring to Artemis/Diana of the Ephesians) or of the one true God (e.g., Josephus, *Ant.* 1.24: "there is nothing [in these books] disagreeable either to the majesty of God, or to his love to mankind"; 8.111: "O Lord, to other animals by thee, it becomes us to bless thy Majesty"; *C. Ap.* 2.168: "these notions are just, and agreeable to the nature of God, and to his majesty"; Luke 9:43: "they were all amazed at the greatness [majesty] of God"). What type of majesty does 2 Peter refer to here? Is it the majesty of the kings of the earth coming to the Son of Man in the spirit of Dan 7:27? Perhaps, yet it is also clear that there is a divine element, for the next verse will explain this as honor and glory from God. Thus we can safely say that the eyewitnesses are eyewitnesses of the bestowal of some form of divine majesty on Jesus, a majesty that he will fully exercise in his coming judgment.

**17** The investiture itself is now cited: "he received honor and glory from God the Father when the voice came to him from the Majestic Glory." For 2 Peter the point of the Transfiguration is not that the divinity or glory of Jesus was revealed, but that "he received honor and glory from God the Father." That is, a status ("honor and glory") was given to Jesus by the source of honor, namely, God himself. It is this honor (and therefore also the honor of the one granting it to Jesus) that our author is defending.[9] The word-pair "honor and glory" appears thirteen times in the NT, always in epistolary literature (Rom 2:7, 10; 1 Tim 1:17; Heb 2:7, 9 [in reverse order]; 1 Pet 1:7; 2 Pet 1:17; Rev 4:9, 11; 5:12, 13; 7:12; 21:26; cf. the parallel expression in Heb 3:3). In the LXX it appears in Exod 28:2, 40;

oaths. . . . Artificial proofs are those constructed from propositions and supporting material gathered from the facts of the case, and include ethos, pathos, and logos" (*Invention*, 14). Watson will go on to show that 2 Peter 1:16ff. also uses artificial proof, namely, ethos.

9. Neyrey, *2 Peter, Jude*, 172.

2 Chron 32:33 [in reverse order]; Job 37:22 [in reverse order]; 40:10 [in reverse order]; Pss 8:6 [in reverse order]; 28:1 [in reverse order]; 95:7 [in reverse order]; 1 Macc 14:21. The fact that the terms appear so frequently together and that in other contexts they are related (e.g., one may be used in one sentence, and the next sentence may pick up the idea with the other term) indicates that they are not to be separated. They are the dual designation of the status that God grants to Jesus.

God is called "Father" here (rather than some other title) because he will in the voice from heaven call Jesus "Son," yet the following phrase is unusual in that it says "the voice came [lit. "was conveyed to him"] from the Majestic Glory." Clearly, our author is designating a divine voice, but why does he do it in such a way? The term for "majestic" appears only here in the NT, but the root as a characteristic of God is common enough in the LXX (Deut 33:26; Pss 8:2; 20:6 [21:5]; 28:4 [29:4]; 67:35 [68:34]; 70:8 [71:8]; 95:6 [96:6]; 110:3 [111:3]; 144:5, 12 [145:5,12]). While the exact combination with "glory" does not appear there, majesty is associated with glory in Pss 20:6 [21:5]; 67:35 [68:34]; 70:8 [71:8]; 145:5, 12, the last two verses being very close to the structure found here. Our author, then, is using a circumlocution for the divine presence. Rather than say, "God spoke from his throne," 2 Peter avoids speaking of the throne/abode of God and guards the divine transcendence by saying that a voice was brought to Jesus from "the Majestic Glory." While many places refer to God's voice as "a voice from heaven" or the equivalent (Dan 4:31; John 12:28; Rev 4:4; 11:12; 16:1), here, perhaps reflecting a reticence among some Jews (Matt 5:34; 23:22), the throne or abode of God is not directly mentioned. This also serves to tie in the glory given to Jesus with the source of glory, that is, God, and heightens the solemnity of the investiture, giving it a regal tone.

The comparison with the Synoptics is instructive. Mark refers to a voice from a cloud (Mark 9:7; Luke 9:34-35) or a "bright cloud" (Matt 17:5), which draws out the parallel with Moses and the cloud of God's glory on the mountain.[10] Here that parallel is not important, and instead we have a scene of investiture. Thus the words are also slightly different:

Mark: "This is my Son, whom I love. Listen to him!"
Luke: "This is my Son, whom I have chosen; listen to him."
Matthew: "This is my Son, whom I love; with him I am well pleased. Listen to him!"
2 Peter: "This is my Son, whom I love; with him I am well pleased."

10. Bruce D. Chilton, "The Transfiguration: Dominical Assurance and Apostolic Vision," *NTS* 27 (1980-81) 120-21.

All four passages agree that the words are addressed, not to Jesus (as in the voice at his baptism), but to his apprentices. All agree that the voice spoke in terms of Ps 2:7, "I will proclaim the decree of the LORD: He said to me, 'You are my Son; today I have become your Father.'" Luke then adds a phrase from the Servant Songs of Isaiah, "My chosen one" (Isa 42:1, "Here is my servant, whom I uphold, my chosen one in whom I delight; I will put my Spirit on him, and he will bring justice to the nations." This reference fits Luke's interest in with that of the nations), while the others refer to "my beloved," similar to the phrase found in places like Gen 22:2.[11] Thus far all the terminology speaks of status. Then the Synoptics give the command, "Listen to him!" and thus fit a Mosaic context (i.e., how one was to treat the prophet like Moses; Deut 18:5), while 2 Peter leaves that out.

What has happened in 2 Peter is that by leaving out the reference to the cloud and the command to listen to Jesus, our author drops the Mosaic references. Instead, Ps 2:7 comes to the fore.[12] This stresses the point of divine investment, the inauguration of Jesus, so to speak. In one sense, the Transfiguration is for 2 Peter what the baptism of Jesus is for the Synoptic Gospels. In another sense there is a difference even here in that the voice at the baptism is more a private event: it addresses Jesus alone (even if it is quite possible in Synoptics — and clear in John — that the voice was heard by others) without any outward signs to attract attention. Here in 2 Peter the voice addresses the apprentices of Jesus, who have been suitably prepared by the dramatic change in Jesus' appearance. The language emphatically (through use of *egō,* "I," in Greek) states that God's approval rests upon Jesus.

To the extent that our author is aware of the background in Psalm 2, he is surely also aware that in that psalm the king is said to conquer/rule over the nations. This fits the purpose of the inclusion of this narrative excerpt quite well. If the teachers 2 Peter opposes deny final judgment, this narrative stresses that already Jesus has been invested with the authority to judge the nations. And if those teachers are dishonoring Jesus by their behavior, then this passage points to the most honorable status that Jesus has already been given.

**18** Now our author underlines the veracity of this information:

11. Either the phrase, "whom you love" or "your only son," found in Gen 22:2, 12, 16, etc., could be the reference, for in the LXX both are translated as "love," although it is the latter that is translated "beloved."

12. That Psalm 2 was already interpreted in a messianic sense in some of the Judaisms of the first century is clear. For example, see 4QFlor 1:18–2:1; *Pss. Sol.* 17:23-24. There are also rabbinic references, which E. Lövestam presents in *Son and Saviour: A Study of Acts 13, 32-37* (ConNT 18; Lund: C. W. K. Gleerup/Copenhagen: E. Munksgaard, 1961), 17-21.

"We ourselves heard this voice that came from heaven." As stated above, one of the purposes of the *narratio* in an argument is to establish matters of fact. Here the Transfiguration is pointed to as such a matter of fact. One of the bases for establishing a fact was testimony, which broke into two parts, the testimony of ancient sources and that of eyewitnesses. Here we clearly have the use of an eyewitness, which, said Aristotle, is useful for establishing "whether a thing has occurred, or not occurred."[13] There is a further piece of artistry in this verse in that in v. 16 we have reference to being an eyewitness and here to having heard the voice. This serves not only to tie vv. 16-18 into a unit but also to involve a second area of sensation: seeing plus hearing, thus again underlining the value of the testimony.[14]

When we learn that this event happened "when we were with him on the sacred mountain," there is no surprise in the first part of this statement, for in "when we were with him" we have a closure statement that sums up what was implied in the previous two verses. The statement "on the sacred mountain/hill" is unusual, however. This could be a reference to Mt. Sinai in that in Exod 19:23 the people were instructed to set the mountain apart and sanctify it, but Sinai is never called a holy mountain. Instead, in the OT it is Mt. Zion that is so designated (Ps 2:6; Isa 11:9; 27:13; 56:7; 57:13; 63:18; 65:9, 11; Jer 38:23; Ezek 20:40; 43:12; 48:10; Obad 16; Zeph 3:11; Zech 8:3). Of particular importance is the use of the phrase in Ps 2:6, "I have installed my King on Zion, my holy hill." This precedes Ps 2:7, in which the king is declared God's son. That such a declaration happens "on my holy hill" is surely no coincidence. Our author is pointing to the Transfiguration as the fulfillment of the psalm. While neither 2 Peter nor any other tradition identifies the Mount of Transfiguration with Mt. Zion in any literal sense, by referring to it as the "holy hill" (NIV, "sacred mountain") our author gives us a picture of the sacred investiture that by rights took place in Zion.

> [19]*And we have the word of the prophets made more certain, and you will do well to pay attention to it, as to a light shining in a dark place, until the day dawns and the morning star rises in your hearts.* [20]*Above all, you*

13. Aristotle, *Rhetoric* 1375–76a, divines nonartistic proofs into five types, the second of which is witnesses. These are further divided into ancient witnesses and recent witnesses. The quotation pertains to recent witnesses, even if they are involved in the matters before a court.

14. In antiquity there was a perception of three interrelated zones of human behavior: hands–feet, eyes–heart, and mouth–ears. See Bruce J. Malina, "Hands–Feet," in John J. Pilch and Bruce J. Malina, eds., *Biblical Social Values and Their Meaning* (Peabody, MA: Hendrickson, 1993), 92. This means that the testimony also comes from two different zones of human behavior.

*must understand that no prophecy of Scripture came about by the prophet's own interpretation.* [21]*For prophecy never had its origin in the will of man, but men spoke from God as they were carried along by the Holy Spirit.*

Having stated the facts of the matter, 2 Peter now goes on to explain the relevance of those facts.

**19** The main relevance is that "we have the word of the prophets made more certain." The problem is that this phrase itself is unclear. First, what does it mean to "have something . . . more certain/more firm/more reliable"? Two meanings have been proposed: (1) "to have a firm grasp on something" (Bauckham), (2) "to have something made (more) certain" (Neyrey). Of these two the weight of evidence appears to point toward the latter.[15] That is, while Bauckham's meaning exists (he gives examples of it), so does the other, and it is the second that appears more commonly and fits our context better. In our verse the comparative is used, so we are not talking about making something certain or reliable, but more certain/more reliable. Given that in Koine Greek the comparative was frequently used as if it were a superlative, the meaning could also be "most certain/reliable" or "completely certain."

What is said to be made more certain or reliable is "the word of the prophets." This has bothered some commentators in that it places experience ahead of the word, so they argue that the prophetic word makes the Transfiguration more certain, citing later Jewish opinion that even a voice *(bat kol)* from heaven could not overrule a scripture.[16] That, however, is not what the grammar of the text indicates. Instead, in the text we see that "the word of the prophets" is what is made more certain/reliable.

What could this prophetic word be? There have been various suggestions, and they fall into two categories: (1) OT prophecies and (2) NT prophecies (sometimes including the OT as well, and sometimes viewed as quite specific; thus 2 Pet 1:20–2:19 is one such prophecy and the Transfiguration is a prophetic event).[17] While all of these meanings are in theory possible, the fact is that the phrase "word of prophecy" or "prophetic word," when found in Christian writing through the second century, is used only for OT scripture. (Since all of Scripture was considered prophetic in the eyes of many of the Judaisms of the first century, the equivalence of "word of prophecy" with "Scripture" was quite natural.) It is un-

15. Heinrich Schlier, *"bebaios ktl.," TDNT* 1:600-603. See especially the examples on 600.

16. For example, E. M. B. Green, *2 Peter and Jude* (TNTC; Grand Rapids: Eerdmans, 1987), 97.

17. See Bauckham, *Jude, 2 Peter,* 224, for details on the various positions.

likely, then, that here it suddenly refers to an NT scripture or event. But if it refers to the OT, does it refer to a specific OT passage? It could if one were mentioned in the context, but since there is no clear reference, it more likely refers to OT prophecy in general and especially that prophecy that was interpreted to refer to the Parousia of Christ, since that is the issue under dispute.

What this means, then, is that the apostolic preaching on the Parousia is here based on two things. First, it is based on eyewitness experience of seeing Jesus invested with honor by none other than God himself. Second, it is based on Scripture, which, as 2 Peter will go on to argue, stems from God, and thus has God's honor behind it. Thus our author is arguing that to reject the Parousia is to impugn the honor of both Jesus and God.

One "does well" to pay attention to Scripture. This is a mild exhortation, like those found in Acts 15:9; Jas 2:8 (although in James there is an ironic twist); 3 John 6 (in the past tense as a commendation it appears in Acts 10:33; Phil 4:14). Why is it good to pay attention to Scripture? It is good because it is "a light shining in a dark place." (The word for "dark place" is found only here in the NT or the LXX and is rare elsewhere in Greek, but its meaning is clear.) Since God's word is often compared to a lamp or light in Jewish tradition (Ps 119 [118]:105 ["Your word is a lamp to my feet and a light for my path"]; Wisd 18:4 ["through whom the imperishable light of the law was to be given to the world," NRSV]), it is not surprising to find the metaphor used here. Interestingly enough, in *4 Ezra* 12:42 we read of Ezra, "For of all the prophets you alone are left to us, like a cluster of grapes from the vintage, and like a lamp in a dark place, and like a haven for a ship saved from a storm." While independent of 2 Peter, this passage does show that the imagery readily sprang to mind for both God's word and the bearer of that word, particularly a prophet. Naturally, given the fact of problems and persecution in this age, it was a natural image for other reasons than that biblical and extrabiblical precedent suggested it. The point is that the prophetic word provides guidance, and the one about the Parousia is more certain than some, for it has been confirmed by the experience of the apostolic eyewitness.[18]

18. Neyrey, *2 Peter, Jude,* 180, points out that a contemporary Jewish writer, Philo, argued that prophecies with eyewitnesses are sure to be authentic (*Quod deterius potiori insidiari soleat* 124; *De migratione Abrahami* 139; *Quis rerum divinarum heres* 4; *Spec. leg.* 1.272, 342; 4.32), with God being the best witness (*De migratione Abrahami* 115; *Somn.* 2.22). Personal experience is the most certain testimony (*De ebrietate* 97–98; *De congressu quarendae eruditiones* 73; *Vit. Mos.* 2.280). Thus here we have prophecy that is confirmed by eyewitness testimony, and also has God standing behind it. This must be the most certain of prophecies in the eyes of a Hellenistic Jew following Philo's thinking.

The prophetic word is the guidance that one has until "the day dawns and the morning star rises in your hearts." Part of this imagery most likely comes from Num 24:17 ("I see him, but not now; I behold him, but not near. A star will come out of Jacob; a scepter will rise out of Israel"), a passage already interpreted messianically in various contemporary Judaisms (*T. Levi* 18:3 [regarding "a new priest" it is said, "And his star shall rise in heaven like a king"]; *T. Jud.* 24:1 ["And after this there shall arise for you a Star from Jacob in peace: And a man shall arise from my posterity like the Sun of righteousness . . . and in him will be found no sin"]; CD 7:18-20 ["And the star is the Interpreter of the law, who will come to Damascus. . . . The scepter is the prince of the whole congregation . . ."]; 1QM 11:6-7; 4QTest [4Q175] 9–13), although here in our passage the star is specifically referred to as the "morning star" (i.e., Venus) in line with the dawning of the day.[19] The dawning day is surely the coming of the eschatological age (the night-day imagery is used elsewhere in the New Testament, e.g., in Rom 13:12; 1 Thess 5:4-9).[20] Along with the dawning of the coming age, then, is the return of Jesus (who is called the "bright morning star" in Rev 22:16).

But why does the star arise "in your hearts"? Is this not a reference to the Parousia at all, but rather to inner enlightenment (Mayor, Spicq)? Or does it mean that the coming of Christ has been made into an individual spiritual experience rather than an apocalyptic event (Schelkle, Kelly). To answer this we must remember the context. 2 Peter clearly states the apocalyptic nature of the Parousia (2 Pet 3:10-13), so it is unlikely that he is speaking out-of-character here and talking about inner enlightenment or an individual experience. The unusual language is explained by the more proximate context. We are speaking about prophetic Scripture. This shines as a light until the coming of the "dawn." After the "dawn" there is no need of Scripture, for the rising of Christ in our hearts gives us full knowledge (Bauckham; Lucas and Green; and apparently

19. Hans Conzelmann, *"phōs," TDNT* 9:312. While Venus normally appears before dawn, the star imagery from Numbers plus the association with the dawn appear to have determined the choice of "morning star." However, since the *Testament of Judah* reference associates the star with the "sun of righteousness" in Mal 4:2, this association may be something that 2 Peter is taking over from Judaism, not something that he has created himself.

20. There is some evidence that Origen knew a Greek text of the Song of Songs 2:17 ("Until the day breaks/and the shadows flee, turn, my lover, and be like a gazelle or like a young stag/on the rugged hills") that used the same expression as is found here. So J. Smit Sibinga, "Une citation du Cantique dans la Secunda Petri," *RB* 73 (1966) 107-18. If this text existed as early as 2 Peter, and if our author knew it, then it is possible that an allusion is intended, but, given the prevalence of night-day imagery and the number of "ifs," that is a distant possibility.

Vögtle). This is what Paul said in 1 Cor 13:8-10, "But where there are prophecies, they will cease; where there are tongues, they will be stilled; where there is knowledge, it will pass away. For we know in part and we prophesy in part, but when perfection comes, the imperfect disappears." Now the prophetic word (in Paul the reference is to the prophecies of contemporary prophets, while in 2 Peter it is to the OT) is a light in the darkness, but when the darkness disappears with the coming of the dawn, we will know even as we are known. Then the light of Christ will be in our hearts, and we will no longer need the Scriptures. One treasures a love letter while the beloved is absent, but once he or she is present, the letter is laid aside and exchanged for the personal contact.

**20** But why should we value this particular set of prophecies, these particular "love letters," now while we are in the darkness? The answer to this comes in two parts: (1) prophecy is not a product of the prophet, and (2) prophecy is a product of God through the Holy Spirit. In other words, the "love letters" are genuine — they come from God.

In setting forth this argument 2 Peter first "clears the decks" by saying, "No prophecy of Scripture came about by the prophet's own understanding." However, this translation is disputed, with many arguing that we should translate this sentence, "No prophecy of Scripture is a matter of one's own interpretation." Why such different understandings of this clause? The answer lies in the ambiguity of the terms used. This sentence is a reason for the previous sentence: you should pay attention to the word of the prophets, "since you know this first of all" (to give an overly literal translation). What they know concerns "prophecy of Scripture" (in other words, our author is not talking about the many and various prophecies — and such abounded in both the Greek and Jewish worlds — that are not found in the Scriptures). So far all is clear. Then our author states, "is of its own interpretation." The critical term here is "its own" *(idias)*: does it refer to the prophet's own interpretation or to the contemporary reader's own interpretation?

Three basic interpretations commend themselves: (1) no scriptural prophecy may be interpreted as one will since its origin is divine (this assumes that the teachers he opposes are, as in 3:16, making novel interpretations of Scripture),[21] (2) no scriptural prophecy may be interpreted as one will, and "we" have the divine word on its meaning (i.e., the statement of God at the Transfiguration),[22] and (3) no scriptural prophecy

21. For example, Mayor, Kelly, and most German commentators, the latter viewing this as a contest between the orthodox church interpretation and that of the teachers opposed by 2 Peter.

22. Vögtle, *Der Judasbrief, der zweite Petrusbrief,* 175-78.

came due to the prophet's own interpretation, for it comes from God (this assumes that Scripture is a second witness to the Parousia alongside the Transfiguration).[23] One's choice among these three interpretations rests on (1) the interpretation of the individual words and grammar, and (2) the contextual flow of the passage.

When it comes to the grammar, it is clear that "its own" can refer to the prophet's own interpretation of his visions, as one sees very clearly in Philo (*Quis rerum divinarum heres* 259, "for a prophet says nothing of his own (*idion*), but everything which he says is strange [i.e., belongs to another] and prompted by some one else"; *Vit. Mos.* 1.281, "for I [Balaam] am saying nothing of my own (*idion*), but whatever the Deity prompts me to say"; 1.286; *Spec. leg.* 4.48-49, "[soothsayers etc. are] a mere bare imitation of the real inspiration and prophetic gift; for a prophet does not utter anything whatever of his own (*idion*), but is only an interpreter, another Being suggesting to him all that he utters, while he is speaking under inspiration . . ."). Other Greek writers express similar opinions (cf. Jer 23:16; Ezek 13:3). There is, however, one place where our term does indicate the interpretation of prophecy, *Clem. Hom.* 2:22 (although this is much later than 2 Peter). Thus the use of this word is not in itself decisive.

The term for "interpretation" appears only here in all of biblical literature. However the word does appear in nonbiblical Greek literature and means "the solution or explanation for a dream, riddle, parable, omen, vision or the like."[24] The term appears in Gen 40:8; 41:8, 12 in Aquila's Greek translation of the OT, and refers to the interpretation of a dream. It also shows up repeatedly in Hermas (ca. A.D. 100; *Sim.* 5:3:1-2; 5:4:2-3; 5:5:1; 5:6:8; 5:7:1; 8:11:1; 9:10:5; 9:11:9; 9:13:9; 19:16:7), where the angelic "shepherd" is giving Hermas interpretations of his similitudes (parables), which are usually visions that Hermas does not understand. This type of language should not surprise us in relation to either the prophet or the interpreter of prophecy. In the OT "the prophet is given a sign (e.g., Amos 7:1; Jer 1:11, 13), a dream (e.g., Zech 1:8; Dan 7:2) or a vision (e.g., Dan 8:1), and then its interpretation."[25] When it comes to non-Jewish prophecy, the technical diviner (who could be called either a *prophētēs* or a *mantis*) also frequently interpreted dreams or signs, although this was not true of the inspired diviner, who nonetheless occasionally had a *prophētēs* between him or her and the inquirer, the latter interpreting or polishing the ora-

23. Bauckham, *Jude, 2 Peter,* 229-33.

24. See Liddell and Scott or J. T. Curran, "The Teaching of 2 Peter 1.20," *Theological Studies* 4 (1943) 347-68, especially 351-52.

25. Bauckham, *Jude, 2 Peter,* 231.

cle.[26] In other words, from neither a Judeo-Christian nor a pagan viewpoint would it be surprising to discover that a prophet needed to interpret the revelation that he or she received. Indeed, even today prophetically gifted Christians speak of the need to distinguish "revelation," "interpretation," and "application," and argue that a major source of problems in Christian prophecy is the failure to do just this (as well as a failure of "timing"). Naturally, one reading a scriptural prophecy clearly needs to interpret that prophecy. Examples of such interpretation in the NT period are abundant in the Dead Sea Scrolls (1QpHab; 4QpNah; etc.).

In terms of context we need to follow the logic of the passage. V. 21 is grammatically subordinate to v. 19 (it is introduced by a participle, not an independent verb), which means that we are expecting a reason for or some other support of the statement in v. 19. The Transfiguration testimony makes the prophetic word of the OT (about the Parousia of Christ) more certain (i.e., because of it there are now multiple streams of testimony). One should pay attention to this prophetic word *since* (grammatically more accurate than the independent sentence construction in the NIV) you understand that no prophecy came into being/presently exists *idia* interpretation (we use the Greek to preclude making a premature decision). *For* no prophecy ever came though human will, but. . . . We can diagram it as follows:

We have the prophetic word made more sure
*which* you do well to pay attention to
*since* no prophecy is . . . interpretation
*for* prophecy . . .
*but* men spoke

At no place in the discussion surrounding our verse does the interpretation of Scripture/a prophetic word come into the discussion. It is true that in 2 Pet 3:16 there is a reference to the teachers whom 2 Peter opposes having distorted Paul "as they do the other Scriptures," but that is two chapters later than our passage and even there we find no discussion of the Scriptures they are said to distort. Furthermore, not until the time of Justin Martyr, much later than 2 Peter, would Paul be said to be among the "prophetic Scriptures." So our focus here is on the interpretation of the Hebrew Scriptures.

Thus since the preponderance of the uses of *idia/idion* have to do with

26. David E. Aune, *Prophecy in Early Christianity and the Ancient Mediterranean World* (Grand Rapids: William B. Eerdmans, 1983), 35, 39. Contrary to Neyrey's claim (*2 Peter, Jude,* 180-81), Aune does not support the idea that a *prophētēs* normally came between a *mantis* and the inquirer, although that sometimes happened. See Aune, *Prophecy,* 28-32.

the prophet's own interpretation, since the term for interpretation fits well with discerning the significance of dreams, visions, and other prophetic phenomena, and since our author seems to be at pains to give two types of testimony to the Parousia of Christ, that of the eyewitness experience of his investiture and that of Scripture, Bauckham's interpretation appears the most fitting. Why should one pay attention to the prophetic word in Scripture (and in particular those having to do with the Parousia)? Because not only the prophetic phenomena (dreams, visions, etc.) were not invented by the prophets, but also the interpretation of those phenomena was not their invention. In both the phenomena and the interpretation of those phenomena we have a testimony independent of human testimony, and that is what the final verse of this chapter underlines.

**21** One should understand that no scriptural prophecy came about by the prophet's own interpretation of the prophetic phenomena that he received because of two things: (1) the prophecy did not originate in the human will, and (2) the prophets spoke from God as the Holy Spirit "carried them along." Several points are worth noting in this regard.

First, while the English translation cannot make it clear, the same verb is used to speak of what did not happen and what did happen: "no prophecy was carried out by the human will, but human beings were carried along by the Holy Spirit." This is the same verb used to describe the voice that "was carried to him [Jesus]" in v. 17. Thus our author is clearly negating one source of prophecy and affirming another, which is heavenly just as the voice that came to Jesus was heavenly.

Second, the fact that prophecy did not come from the human will, which is stated emphatically, would have been clear to anyone with a background in the Scriptures. In fact, the characteristic of a false prophet was that he prophesied out of his own mind (Jer 14:14; 23:16; Ezek 13:3). This is also how Deuteronomy describes a false prophet: "But a prophet who presumes to speak in my name anything I have not commanded him to say, or a prophet who speaks in the name of other gods, must be put to death" (Deut 18:20). Even the relatively innocent presumptive prophecy (just saying something that God had not said, presumably knowing full well that God had not said it) was to be punished, not just those speaking in the name of (and presumably inspired by) other gods. This denial that prophets spoke on their own may have been a counterstatement to the claims of the teachers 2 Peter opposes. We do know that there was an Epicurean attack on Greek prophetic oracles as people speaking their own ideas.[27] We also know that the Sadducees reportedly accepted only the

27. See Jerome H. Neyrey, "The Form and Background of the Polemic in 2 Peter" (Ph.D. dissertation, Yale University, 1977), 196-99.

authority of the Torah and not the authority of the *Nevi'im* (prophets). This would also be true of the Samaritans. Furthermore, there is evidence that some later Ebionite groups criticized the OT prophets.[28] Finally, there is the evidence of the *Ascension of Isaiah,* which comes from the end of the first century, which states that

> afterwards . . . his [the Beloved's = Jesus'] disciples will abandon the teaching of the twelve apostles . . . everyone will speak whatever pleases him in his own eyes. And they will make ineffective [set aside] the prophecy of the prophets who were before me [Isaiah], and my visions also . . . they will make ineffective [pay no attention to], in order that they may speak what bursts out of their heart." (*Asc. Isa.* 3:21, 30-31)[29]

Each of these citations shows that there were some groups in the church before the time of Marcion that rejected the prophets for one reason or another. (In the *Ascension of Isaiah* the charge is that Isaiah was lying, speaking his own ideas as prophecy.) We do not know if our author is facing such a group that rejected prophecy, but it is clear from the next chapter that those he opposes certainly were not taking the OT as seriously as he did. We also note that our author uses Jude, who specifically says that some scriptural prophecies (and Jude includes those of *1 Enoch* in this category) were aimed against such teachers. So to point out that prophecy did not come about because the prophet wanted to say this or that (i.e., that it was not his ideas that he was proclaiming) and that the prophet did not even interpret his own prophetic phenomena (visions, dreams, etc.) is to rule out any such attack on the validity of prophecy.

Third, the way that prophecy does come is through men and women speaking "from God as they [are] carried along by the Holy Spirit." The concept of being carried along by God or the Spirit occurs in Hellenistic Jewish literature. It is used in Philo of Balaam (*Vit. Mos.* 1.283, "He [Balaam], as soon as he was by himself, was again suddenly filled by divine inspiration, and, without at all understanding the words which he uttered, spoke everything that was put into his mouth, prophesying in the following manner . . .") and of the prophet predicted in Deuteronomy

28. E. Molland, "La thèse 'La prophétie n'est jamais venue de la volonté de l'homme' (2 Pierre I, 21) et les Pseudo-Clémentines," in *Opuscula Patristica* (BTN 2; Oslo: Universitetsforlaget, 1970), 64-77 (= *ST* 9 [1955] 67-85).

29. The material in brackets (other than the identification of Isaiah) is from J. Flemming and H. Duensing, "The Ascension of Isaiah," in E. Hennecke, *New Testament Apocrypha,* vol. 2 (London: Lutterworth, 1965). The main translation is from Charlesworth.

18 (*Spec leg.* 1.65, "Some other prophet will appear to them on a sudden, inspired like himself [i.e., like Moses], who will preach and prophesy among them, saying nothing of his own (for he who is truly possessed and inspired, even when he speaks, is unable to comprehend what he is himself saying), but that all the words that he should utter would proceed from him as if another was prompting him; for the prophets are interpreters of God, who are only using their voices as instruments, in order to explain what they choose"), as well as by Josephus, *Ant.* 4.119, also of Balaam ("[Balak] canst thou suppose that it is in our power to be silent, or to say anything, when the Spirit of God seizes upon us? — for he puts such words as he pleases in our mouths, and such discourses as we are not ourselves conscious of"). The language used is the language of being carried (i.e., some compound of the same verb found here is used). While the language used in the passages we have cited is relatively mechanical and beyond the control of the prophet, it does illustrate the use of the "carried along" type of language to indicate divine inspiration of prophecy. Our author, however, has talked about interpretation of prophetic phenomena that, even though inspired, appears understandable to the speaker (i.e., it is interpretation). Paul, in his discourse on prophecy (which he presumably would have attributed to the earlier canonical prophets as well as to contemporary prophets of the Jesus movement), speaks of revelation, but he also says that "the spirits of the prophets are subject to the control of the prophets" (1 Cor 14:32), so he apparently did not view prophecy as a totally passive activity.[30] We do not know whether our author would go as far as Paul in speaking of the prophet being under conscious control, but we do know that both would agree on the inspiration of the prophetic word.

Up to this point the author of 2 Peter has concerned himself with setting the groundwork for his coming denunciation of the teachers he opposes. It is not that he has failed to hold them in view. Already he has been busy cutting the ground from underneath them. In particular, he has established what he believes to be two facts. The first is the eyewitness fact of the Transfiguration, an event that revealed that Jesus had been inaugurated as the eschatological ruler and thus implied the Parousia, when he will openly exercise that rule. The second is the fact of prophecy, which the eyewitness data supported. Since OT prophecy was not the product of human desires but of divine inspiration, it was also a

30. Paul apparently sees relative passivity as the mark of tongues rather than of prophecy ("no one understands them; he or she utters mysteries in the Spirit"; 1 Cor 14:2), but even then the activity is not totally passive in that the tongues speaker can shut up if no one is present to interpret (1 Cor 14:28).

trustworthy source of information. Thus there are two witnesses, his own eyewitness account and God's witness in Scripture, to the truth of what he is saying. Having established these facts, our author is now ready to move on to his main argument. On the basis of Jesus and OT words he is going to show that the teachers he opposes are wrong. Furthermore, he will argue that they stand under divine condemnation.

Naturally, for us as readers another set of questions is raised. Are our commitments based on the trustworthy basis of the testimony about Jesus and the Scriptures? Often Christian faith is focused more on doctrine and ideas than on Jesus, preferring Paul to the Gospels. Our author focuses our eyes back on Jesus and the events of his life. At other times Christians have tended to neglect the prophetic portions of the OT (which for the Jews included what we would call history as well), not seeing how they relate to the story of Jesus. Our author is clearly reading the OT christologically in that he sees the prophets speaking, not of a Jewish commonwealth, but of the universal rule of the Christ. Yet he does view the OT, when read in this way, as instructive, as we shall see in the next section.

We in the church today are heirs of the whole narrative of God's dealing with human beings, the OT narrative as well as the OT. If we neglect any part of the story, we end up with gaps in our own story.

## B. Condemnation of False Teachers (2:1-22)

Our author has set the stage in the previous section. Now he is ready to directly address his main concern, a group of teachers whom he opposes. It is this next section of 2 Peter, 2:1–3:3, that appears to have borrowed heavily from Jude. It is not that 2 Peter 2:1–3:3 is simply a copy of Jude, but that 2 Peter has taken Jude and adapted his material to the situation and the audience that 2 Peter is addressing (which is also the reason for his being able to divide the material and include it in two parts of his letter). This editorial work will become evident as we discuss the passage in detail.

### *1. Introduction to the False Teachers (2:1-3)*

*[1]But there were also false prophets among the people, just as there will be false teachers among you. They will secretly introduce destructive heresies, even denying the sovereign Lord who bought them — bringing swift destruction on themselves. [2]Many will follow their shameful ways and will bring the way of truth into disrepute. [3]In their greed these teachers will ex-*

*ploit you with stories they have made up. Their condemnation has long been hanging over them, and their destruction has not been sleeping.*

1 The section 2:1-3 is the introduction to a prophetic denunciation of those Jude calls "false teachers." The transition from the previous chapter is smooth, without the nouns of address that our author will use in 3:1 and 3:14. 2 Peter makes the transition structurally, that is, by using a chiastic (ABBA) structure. First he discussed the apostolic witness in 1:16-18 (the plural "we" indicates that he is grouping himself with the other apostles), then he goes on to discuss the (true) OT prophets in 1:19-21. Now in quick succession we have the false OT prophets and then the false teachers of the present. (Notice that 1:16 mentions following "invented stories" and 2:3 mentions following "shameful ways," using the same Greek verb for "following" in each case.) This structure has been diagrammed as follows:

A. NT apostles (1:16-18)
B. OT prophets (1:19-21)
B. OT false prophets (2:1a)
A. NT false teachers (2:1b-3)[1]

The transition works because it moves through the known phenomena of the OT to bridge the two contemporary phenomena (apostles — false teachers) and because the false teachers are contradicting the apostolic tradition and thus in a sense functioning as false apostles.

The term "false prophet" appears in the Greek OT (LXX; e.g., in Jer 6:13; 33:7-16 [= MT 26:7-16]; 34:9 [27:9]; 35:1 [28:1]; 36:1, 8 [29:1, 8]; Zech 13:2),[2] always as an expansion of the simple term "prophet" in the Hebrew text. That is, it is because these prophets were critical of or criticized by Jeremiah or other prophets that they were false prophets. The concept, however, is far more widely attested in the OT than the word is. In the two pentateuchal passages on prophetic activity (Deut 13:1-5; 18:15-22) prophets speaking in the name of Yahweh but not sent by him are distinguished from prophets truly sent by Yahweh. The former group of prophets is to be stoned, while the latter is to be heeded. The historical narratives know of many prophets who were prophets of Baʿal or who otherwise did not accurately report the words of Yahweh. For example,

1. F. Marín, "Apostolícidad de los escritos neotestamentarios," *Estudios Eclesiaticos* 50 (1975) 226. Bauckham underlines this thesis.

2. Notice that the chapter and verse numbering and arrangement in the Hebrew OT, or Masoretic Text (MT), differs from that in the Greek.

1 Kings 22:5-12 reports a group of prophets who proclaimed victory in the name of Yahweh. They are depicted by Micaiah, the (true) prophet, as being influenced by a "lying spirit" that did indeed come from Yahweh, but only to deceive those prophets and lead Ahab to his death. Whatever the other prophets may have thought they were doing, the text obviously regards Micaiah as the true spokesperson for Yahweh and the other prophets as unreliable at best, yet it never uses the term "false prophet." The same phenomenon recurs many times in the OT, for the text simply calls those who prophesy prophets and lets the content and results of their prophecy and the character of their behavior indicate whether they are true or false. However, once the term "false prophet" was used in the LXX, it was repeated in the NT (Matt 7:15; 24:11, 24; Mark 13:22; Luke 6:26; Acts 13:6; 1 John 4:1; Rev 16:13; 19:20; 20:10) and was used by Josephus (writing contemporarily with the later NT writers) for OT false prophets.[3]

Given the fact of the existence of false prophets in the OT period, our author instructs his readers that "there will be false teachers among you," although from the context we gather that the future tense is rhetorical: the false teachers are already among them. The term "false teacher" is found only here in the NT and is not found in the LXX at all. Indeed, while "false teaching" will be mentioned by Polycarp, *Phil.* 7:2, the term "false teachers" will not appear again until Justin Martyr (*Dial.* 82:1), where he says, "For the prophetical gifts remain with us [Christians], even to the present time. And hence you [Jews] ought to understand that [the gifts] formerly among your nation have been transferred to us. And just as there were false prophets contemporaneous with your holy prophets, so are there now many false teachers amongst us, of whom our Lord forewarned us to beware. . . ." Many scholars view this passage as dependent upon 2 Peter, since it reintroduces his vocabulary (previous writers had continued to use only "false prophet," while Justin also uses "false teacher") in an identical contrast with false prophets. Thus Justin Martyr may be a witness to 2 Peter's concepts living on.

At this point in the argument 2 Peter has labeled his opponents "false teachers," but he has not forgotten the comparison with false prophets. As Bauckham says, "It is relevant to note . . . three prominent characteristics of the OT false prophets which can also be applied to the opponents in 2 Peter: (1) unlike the true prophets (1:20-21) they did not speak with divine authority (Deut 18:20; Jer 14:14; 23:21, 32; Ezek 13:2-7); (2) frequently their message was one of peace and security in contrast to the

3. It also appears in the Greek version of *T. Jud.* 21:9 and in the Greek *Mart./Asc. Isa.* 2:12, 13; cf. 3:1, 7.

prophecies of future judgment uttered by the true prophets (Jer 4:10; 6:14; 14:13, 15; 23:17; 27:9, 16-18; Ezek 13:10; Mic 3:5, 11); (3) they were condemned to punishment by God (Jer 14:15; 23:15; 28:16-17; cf. Deut 18:20)."[4] All of these characteristics will be mentioned in the following denunciation. Also notice that the false teachers are "among you." Unlike the opponents in Jude (Jude 4), these are not people who have "secretly slipped in among you" but people who already existed "among you." Jude never considers those he opposes part of the Christian community. They are interlopers in his eyes, although they may have passed themselves off as Christians. 2 Peter views the false teachers as indeed part of the community, but a part that has left the true faith. This contrast in attitude will recur several times throughout 2 Peter's section that parallels Jude.

What we are told about the false teachers is that (1) "they will secretly introduce destructive heresies," (2) they will deny "the sovereign Lord who bought them," (3) their destruction will come quickly, (4) many will follow their shameful ways, (5) they will bring dishonor to the way of truth, and (6) they will exploit the church out of greed. Three of these have to do with the behavior of the false teachers, two with the results of that behavior for others, and one with the results of that behavior for the teachers themselves. Let us look at these statements in order.

The first thing that we learn is that these teachers will "secretly introduce destructive heresies." The term translated "secretly introduce" is unique in the NT. Its meaning is "to bring in," and while it often does indicate a secretive action, only the context can indicate whether or not the bringing in is secretive or not.[5] Thus Louw-Nida defines the word as "to cause something to happen by introducing factors from outside."[6] The emphasis, then, is not on the secretiveness of the behavior, but that something was brought into the community from the outside (which is also the emphasis of the adjectival form of the word in Gal 2:4).

What these teachers brought in was a foreign teaching. The term "heresy" simply means a school of thought or a teaching. (In translating the term "heresies" the NIV introduces an anachronistic meaning into the text.) When used negatively in the NT it indicates a division or clique in the church (1 Cor 11:18; Gal 5:20), not a false teaching. When used by Josephus it means a school of thought among the Jews: "At this time there were three sects among the Jews, who had different opinions concerning human actions; the one was called the sect of the Pharisees, another the sect of the Sadducees, and the other the sect of the Essenes"

4. Bauckham, *Jude, 2 Peter*, 238.
5. BAG, "*pareisagō*."
6. Louw-Nida, "13.132 *pareisagō*." This is a division of words of happening.

(Josephus, *Ant.* 13.171). Josephus himself was a Pharisee, so he hardly viewed the term "sect" (our word "heresy") as negative. In fact, Acts can use our word neutrally of Christians being viewed as a clique or school of thought within Judaism (Acts 24:5, 14; 28:22). In our passage the emphasis is more on the idea that this is a school of thought than that this teaching forms a division in the body, for the perpetrators are said to be teachers. Yet at the same time, the fact that it is brought in from the outside indicates that it is not part of the tradition that the church has received and should raise suspicions. In order to make it clear that these ideas were not acceptable, our author modifies the term for "teaching" with "destructive" (i.e., this is a teaching or school of thought that is not helpful or godly, but rather destructive). 2 Peter uses this term five of the eighteen times it appears in the NT, three times in this section and twice in the following chapter (2 Pet 3:7, 16). His classic use is in 3:7, in which he speaks of the "day of judgment and destruction of ungodly people." This sense of eschatological judgment is its more usual meaning in the NT (Matt 7:13; John 17:12; Acts 8:20; Rom 9:22; Phil 1:28; 3:19; Heb 10:39; Rev 7:8, 11). The implication is that these teachings are destructive in that they lead those who follow them to destruction, meaning in colloquial terms that they "send them to hell."

Interestingly enough, the term for school of thought is plural. Bauckham, citing Justin, *Dial.* 35:3, which contains an otherwise unknown teaching of Jesus ("For he [Jesus] said, 'Many shall come in my name, clothed outwardly in sheep's clothing, but inwardly they are ravening wolves.' And, 'There shall be schisms and heresies.' And, 'Beware of false prophets, who shall come to you clothed outwardly in sheep's clothing, but inwardly they are ravening wolves'"), believes that our passage may be alluding to this saying of Jesus, which is also plural.[7] In other words, it is a deliberate allusion to a teaching of Jesus. This is certainly possible, although unprovable;[8] we should not dismiss too quickly the idea that several schools of thought are represented among the false teachers (the characteristics 2 Peter describes being, perhaps, their main unifying features) or that they have selected their teachings from more than one school of thought. Whatever the case, 2 Peter's conclusion is

7. Bauckham, *Jude, 2 Peter,* 239-40. He cites Joachim Jeremias, *Unknown Sayings of Jesus,* trans. R. H. Fuller (London: S. P. C. K., 1957), 59-61; 1 Cor 11:18; Justin, *Dial.* 51:2 ("heresies and false prophets would arise in his name"); and *Asc. Isa.* 3:22 ("there will be many heresies") in support. While in 1 Cor 11:18 the issue is more the divisions within the church than any teachings associated with the divisions, certainly both Justin and *Ascension of Isaiah* indicate a belief that false teaching would enter the church, although in the case of Justin we are far later than 2 Peter.

8. So Vögtle, *Der Judasbrief, der zweite Petrusbrief,* 184.

that the end result is a series of teachings from outside the apostolic stream that will lead those following them to damnation.

The second thing we learn about these teachers is that they deny "the sovereign Lord who bought them." This statement is very close to Jude's "deny Jesus Christ our only Sovereign and Lord," but it also has its unique features. First, 2 Peter does not include the title "Jesus Christ," although he uses this title eight other places in his work. Perhaps this omission is to further stress the titles that he does use. Second, he drops the title "Lord" but retains the title "Sovereign" or "Master" (again the NIV translation is misleading in that it views "Lord" as being implied). "Sovereign" is a far less usual title, which refers either to a sovereign power, such as the Roman emperor or God, or to the head of a household, who held life-and-death power over his family, including his slaves. While the Jude reference might lead us to suspect some type of divine overtone (in line with Gen 15:2; Isa 1:24; Jer 4:10; Luke 2:29; Acts 4:24; Rev 6:10 and the sentiments of Josephus in *War* 7.418-19), the qualifying phrase seems to point in the direction of the ruler of a household (also seen in Luke 2:29 in that it requests an order to be given to a servant; 1 Tim 6:1-2; 2 Tim 2:21; Titus 2:9; 1 Pet 2:18). Third, this Master is the one who purchased them, which is precisely how a householder did acquire slaves.[9] Jude never sees those whom he opposes as belonging to the Lord, so they are said to deny "*our* Lord and Master," who is never said to have had a relationship with them. Here in 2 Peter our author picks up the common theme of purchase (without mentioning "with his blood," which is sometimes added) to point out that these people *did* belong to Christ and had been purchased by him and thus owed him obedience.

Although they did belong to Christ, these teachers now deny him. From a modern context we immediately imagine them to be rejecting some statement in the creed, for example, the Apostolic or Nicene Creeds. This is reinforced if we have already imported a modern concept of heresy into this passage. But in fact in this passage our author never accuses these teachers of doctrinal error, but rather of behavioral aberrations. Their problems are not so much heterodoxy as heteropraxy. Their heterodoxy, which will show up in ch. 3, is in support of their aberrant lifestyle. This lifestyle is the root of the problem. They deny their sovereign Lord in that they do not obey him. Far from being his apprentices, they are living in contradiction to his life and teaching.

9. Neyrey, *2 Peter, Jude,* 191-92, suggests that the idea is that of the purchase of slaves for freedom, thus making Jesus their patron, "to whom his clients owed an eternal indebtedness, so that failure to remember this and repay loyalty and honor to the Patron would mean shameful behavior on the part of the clients."

The result is disastrous, for they are "bringing swift destruction on themselves." There is a rhetorical structure called an inclusion (or *inclusio*) here, for first their teachings or schools of thought are described as "destructive" and now that destruction comes back upon them. It is "swift" not in that it happens quickly, but in that it is "coming soon" or "imminent" (BAG). There is double irony in this statement. First, their teachings are destructive to others, so destruction is coming upon them. Second, looking forward to ch. 3, they deny coming judgment and stress how long the world has continued in the present disorder, but in fact judgment will soon come upon them. One wonders whether the author smiled at his own black humor.

**2** The problem is that "many" will follow them, and in particular will follow their "shameful ways." Teachers are role models to their students, in many periods of history deliberately so, and not just conveyors of information. These teachers are accused of having "shameful ways," which parallels the accusation in Jude 4 (see the comment there) and will appear twice more in this chapter (2:7, 18). As one can tell from the terms that appear along with it in the vice lists in Mark 7:22, Rom 13:13, Gal 5:19, and 1 Pet 4:3, the term is sexually toned (see BAG or Lowe-Nida),[10] so the NRSV's and NAB's translation "licentious ways" is quite appropriate (NLV, "shameful immorality"; TEV, "immoral ways") and preferable to the NIV's "shameful ways." In other words, the sexual license of these teachers is catching, and as it becomes apparent in the Christian community, "the way of truth" will be "brought into disrepute" or slandered. 2 Peter more than once uses "way" (2:15, 21) as the OT does for "way of life" or "lifestyle." The early groups of followers of Jesus were referred to as followers of "the way" (Acts 9:2; 19:9, 23; 24:14, 22) or the "way of the Lord/God" (Acts 18:25, 26). Christianity is not so much a set of propositional truths to be believed as a way of life to be lived,[11] that is, an apprenticing of oneself to Jesus as one's master. That this way of life was the true way went without saying for the early Jesus cells, so we are not surprised that both here and in Jas 5:19 they borrowed the phrase "way of truth" from Ps 118:30 (119:30) to describe their "way." When those who were identified with this "way" lived in ways that the society around them considered immoral, it reflected on the whole group. So, for example, referring to another group that claimed to follow God, Isa 52:5 was interpreted in Rom 2:24, "God's name is blasphemed among the Gentiles be-

10. Otto Bauernfeind, *"aselgeia," TDNT* 1:490. "In the NT only the older and sensual sense of 'voluptuousness' or 'debauchery' is relevant."

11. Thus in rabbinic texts Jewish teaching is termed *halakha,* or "walk" = way of life.

cause of you." The charges were slanderous (blasphemous means slanderous), not in that they were not true accounts of the behavior of the group in question, but in that this behavior was not the way God desired nor did it accord with the directives of "the way of truth." But people who observed such dishonorable behavior readily believed and spread the word that this behavior was characteristic of those who followed Jesus. In a society where an honorable reputation was of the highest value and shame the worst thing that could happen to one, this was indeed a serious result. Furthermore, this reputation reflected on Jesus, who was the leader of "the way." Apparently this has not yet become the reputation of the community that our author addresses, for he puts in the future the danger of slander spreading, but it is nevertheless a real issue for him.

Neyrey argues that such charges as we find here in 2 Peter were stereotyped polemics in the ancient world; thus what we read here is "less . . . actual statements of what the author's opponents did or said than projections of what their errors lead to."[12] Certainly he is right that the language is stereotyped, for we see similar language in a variety of vice lists. He is also right that the language covers the behavior of the teachers our author opposes as much as reveals in that 2 Peter never explains the details of what he considers "immoral ways." (But then he might well have considered that it was shameful and inappropriate to go into detail.) However, that does not necessarily mean that these charges are projections. The fact is that in this book the main charges against the false teachers are ethical. In ch. 1 we have escaping corruption caused by evil desires contrasted with a list of virtues that will bring eschatological reward. In this chapter all of the charges brought against the false teachers are ethical (sexual or financial or being proud). In ch. 3 the scoffers are led by their "evil desires." Thus throughout this book the root problem is ethical, and often sexual impropriety is stated or implied. Therefore, if this is only stereotyped language of where the behavior of the false teachers is headed, then the author of 2 Peter presents no real charge against them, or else he has been consummately poor in communicating what he opposes. It is far better to assume that stereotyped language developed from what were in truth common problems and that our author uses the stereotyped language because it fits the actual situation of his opponents.

3 The false teachers have apparently accused the apostles of making up "cleverly invented stories" about the return of Christ (1:16, *mythos* = stories). Now Peter turns the table on them and says that the false teachers themselves use "stories they have made up" (the expression *plastois logois* indicates words that have something to do with deceit, forg-

12. Neyrey, *2 Peter, Jude,* 192.

ery, fiction, or pretending, judging from its use outside biblical literature, for it never appears elsewhere in biblical literature).[13] They make these stories up out of greedy motives, greed being one of the major vices spoken against in the NT, whether by Jesus (Mark 7:22; Luke 12:15), Paul (Rom 1:29; Eph 5:3; Col 3:5), who equates it with idolatry, or 2 Peter (here and at 2:14). Their goal is to "exploit" or "make merchandise of" (the term appears neutrally in Jas 4:13, but here it means "to take advantage of someone by implying that what is offered is more valuable than it is"[14]) the believers. This contrasts with their having denied the Lord who bought them (and their fellow believers). Thus the metaphor is that of their using falsehood to make merchandise of believers whom the Lord has bought; they are, so to speak, operating a business selling someone else's property.

It is not that they will get away with this. With biting irony our author adds the couplet, the first part of which is that their condemnation (a legal term for a sentence in a court) was pronounced long ago (*ekpalai* = *palai* in Jude 4), and it is "not idle." It is still in effect, and in fact, as we learned in verse 1, it is imminent. The second part of the couplet restates the first, that their destruction is not sleeping. Here destruction is personified. Since this destruction comes from the God of Israel, it is not like that of Baʿal, who might sleep (1 Kings 18:27), but like that of God, who does not sleep (Ps 121:4; cf. Isa 5:27). We are not told when or where this judgment was pronounced, whether in the OT condemnation of false prophets (Mayor), in the OT examples we find cited later (so Bauckham), or in some decree that 2 Peter knows about from other literature (such as *1 Enoch*). He is not that specific. His purpose is rhetorical. The teachers he opposes claim that everything is going on as before and that no judgment is coming. Our author, by way of contrast, asserts that the judgment has been hanging over their heads for a long time and that, far from sleeping, it is imminent. The use of the twin negatives here ("not idle," "not sleeping") to express the positive statement of 2:1 is biting irony indeed.

### 2. *Argument for the Judgment of the False Teachers (2:4-22)*

*4For if God did not spare angels when they sinned, but sent them to hell, putting them into gloomy dungeons to be held for judgment; 5if he did not spare the ancient world when he brought the flood on its ungodly people,*

13. Neyrey, Jerome H. "The Apologetic Use of the Transfiguration in 2 Peter 1:16-21," *CBQ* 42:2 (1980) 507-9, shows that in Philo the *plasm-/plast-* root was connected to *mythos* in a parallel argument to what we find in 2 Peter.

14. Louw-Nida, "13.132 *pareisagō*."

*but protected Noah, a preacher of righteousness, and seven others; [6]if he condemned the cities of Sodom and Gomorrah by burning them to ashes, and made them an example of what is going to happen to the ungodly; [7]and if he rescued Lot, a righteous man, who was distressed by the filthy lives of lawless men [8](for that righteous man, living among them day after day, was tormented in his righteous soul by the lawless deeds he saw and heard) — [9]if this is so, then the Lord knows how to rescue godly men from trials and to hold the unrighteous for the day of judgment, while continuing their punishment. [10]This is especially true of those who follow the corrupt desire of the sinful nature and despise authority.*

Having asserted that the judgment of the false teachers is certain, 2 Peter now supports this assertion with four analogies from Scripture: (1) angels, (2) the prediluvian world/Noah, (3) Sodom, and (4) Lot. In terms of scriptural narratives they fall into two pairs. The whole paragraph is an "if — then" construction running from v. 4 to v. 10a, but the grammar breaks down along the way because the excursus about Lot in v. 8 interrupts the structure. This type of "if *x* is true . . . then how much more is *y* true" construction is referred to in the exegetical rules of Hillel as *qal wahomer* and in our Latin terminology as *a fortiori.*

4 The first example refers to Gen 6:1-4 as it was passed on in Jewish tradition in *1 Enoch.* In Gen 6:1-4 we have a reference to the "sons of God" *(beney ha-elohim)* mating with human women.[15] While the text clearly does not approve of this act, it gives few details and says nothing about what happens to these beings. In *1 Enoch* 6–10 the beings are clearly identified as angels rebelling against God, and the results of their copulation and their judgment are described in detail. Then in *1 Enoch* 15–16 and 21 their prison and final judgment are described.[16] Since this tradition is already found in Jude, it is possible that 2 Peter is simply adapting that information rather than independently citing *1 Enoch,* although he is elsewhere aware enough of *1 Enoch* to remove Jude's direct citation of that work.

The sin of the angels is that they mated with human women. In

15. Bruce K. Waltke, *Genesis: A Commentary* (Grand Rapids: Zondervan, 2001), 115-17, argues that the idea that Genesis 6 refers to intermarriage between human groups (i.e., the "sons of God" are a race or group of human beings) "must be rejected for philological reasons" in favor of divine beings. Then he argues that rulers who claimed divine status might fit, despite the difficulties, if they were viewed as demon possessed.

16. *Jub.* 5:1-11 has in essence the same story, as does other Jewish literature. Since Jude shows elsewhere that he is acquainted with *1 Enoch,* and since 2 Peter uses Jude, whether or not he knows *1 Enoch,* it is more likely that 2 Peter gets the story at least indirectly from the Enochian tradition.

other words, it is sexual and wrong because it crosses species lines.[17] The author of 2 Peter mentions neither this issue nor the sins of the other sinful people he mentions, although he alludes to them in v. 10. The main point here is the certainty of judgment, not the reason why the angels were judged. These angels were sent to Tartarus, which in Greek mythology was the lowest part of the underworld where the Titans were imprisoned.[18] It is not necessary that our author knew the myth of the Titans, although given his familiarity with Hellenistic ideas and terminology he may well have. He is also not necessarily dependent on the Jewish writers who compared the myth of the Titans to the story of the fallen angels (Josephus, *Ant.* 1.73, "these men [the offspring of the fallen angels] did what resembled the acts of those whom the Grecians call giants"; Jdt 16:6 identifies the angels as Titans), although again this is quite possible. What 2 Peter certainly knew is that Tartarus is at times used in the LXX (Job 40:20; 41:24 [Tartarus of the abyss]; Prov 30:16) for the netherworld (apparently parallel to Hades in Prov 30:16). However, if the reading "gloomy dungeons" is correct,[19] then 2 Peter does reveal independent knowledge of *1 Enoch,* for *1 Enoch* speaks of deep valleys in which the fallen angels are kept (which is not mentioned in *Jubilees*), which detail is missing in Jude, but present in the term "pits" or dungeons here.

The point of the verse is that these fallen angels await eternal judgment. Our author assumes that his readers know and accept this story, so it forms a good analogy for him. The eschatological judgment of the angels who sinned is sure. They are already in prison. How much more sure is the judgment of those who have denied the Christ who purchased them.

**5** The reference in the previous verse to the beings of Genesis 6 as viewed through the lens of later Jewish tradition that identified them

17. That the crossing of species lines rather than sexuality per se is the issue is very clear in *Jubilees* 5, for after this incident God makes a decree that beings mate within their species. In *1 Enoch* the sin is also connected with crossing the species barrier, but there it is known in advance that it is a sin. *1 Enoch,* however, puts less emphasis on the crossing of the species barrier by putting more emphasis on the resulting violence on the earth and on the teaching of heavenly secrets (including curses and divination) to the wives of the angels. So sexual relations per se are not the issue in *1 Enoch,* nor even that angels engage in sexual relations, but that they engage in sexual relations with human beings, another species.

18. Edith Hamilton, *Mythology* (New York: New American Library, 1942), 39.

19. While $NA^{27}$ and $UBS^4$ along with $\mathfrak{P}^{72}$, read *seirais* ("fetters"), for it is in one sense the harder reading (What is a "fetter of gloom"?), the major uncials read *sirois,* "pits." It appears likely that "pits," a rare word, appeared in the text and that, since Jude 6 mentions "chains," it was consciously or unconsciously shifted to "fetters" without noticing that the reference to deepest darkness or gloom was different in 2 Peter.

with fallen angels leads naturally to a reference to Noah and the flood, which story follows the story of the "sons of God" in both Genesis and *Jubilees* and is referred to in *1 Enoch*.[20] Noah brings 2 Peter closer to the teachers he opposes, for it was not angels but "ungodly people" who were judged in the flood, and these teachers are described as ungodly by 2 Peter. That Noah, his wife, his sons, and their wives were saved, that is, Noah plus seven other persons, is clear in the biblical narrative and in several of the later Jewish versions of the tradition,[21] but it is only in various later Jewish versions that we discover that Noah was a preacher of righteousness. "For many angels of God accompanied with women, and begat sons that proved unjust, and despisers of all that was good, on account of the confidence they had in their own strength; for the tradition is, that these men did what resembled the acts of those whom the Grecians call giants. But Noah was very uneasy at what they did; and being displeased at their conduct, persuaded them [better, urged them] to change their dispositions and their acts for the better: but seeing they did not yield to him, but were slaves to their wicked pleasures, he was afraid they would kill him, together with his wife and children, and those they had married; so he departed out of that land."[22] The point in our work is that Noah was not just righteous, but a preacher of righteousness. This righteousness is apparently assumed for his family as well. (Since in that culture it was expected that a family would follow the religion of the head of the family, this assumption was a culturally appropriate one.) The contrast is, of course, between the righteous remnant that was delivered and the "ancient world of the ungodly" (to give a more formally equivalent translation) that was not spared. The implication is that God can bring the final judgment upon this world and spare the righteous while destroying the unrighteous. Indeed, the presence of the righteous is no safety for the unrighteous, for God can save the former in the midst of judgment, just as he did Noah.

20. *1 Enoch* does not discuss the flood in detail in the section cited in Jude, but it does refer to it in *1 Enoch* 10:1-3 (an angel is commanded to warn Noah about the flood), in the Similitudes at 54:7–55:2 (without mentioning Noah) and 65:1–67:13 (significant because Noah is called righteous), and in the Dream Visions in ch. 89. The stories are also connected in CD 2:17–3:1; *T. Naph.* 3:5 (both using "Watchers" for the beings of Genesis); *Tg. Ps.-J.* Gen 6:1-8 (which intertwines the two narratives); *Tg. Neof.* Gen 6:2-3.

21. Kraftchick, *Jude, 2 Peter,* 128, argues that the mention of eight persons is a symbolic reference to eschatological deliverance since Christians (e.g., *Barn.* 15:8-9) referred to the resurrection as the eighth day. There does not appear to be any reason to import this symbolism into 2 Peter, for his point appears to be fewness, not a symbolic eight.

22. Josephus, *Ant.* 1.74 (1.3.1); *Sib. Or.* 1:125-98, has God initiating the preaching; it also includes the narrative reaction by the other human beings to Noah's preaching, which was to sneer at him.

**6** Our author moves on from Noah to Sodom and Gomorrah. This is a significant step forward for him, for he moves from water to fire as the means of destruction. Jude did not include the example of Noah, jumping directly from the fallen angels to Sodom and Gomorrah, but 2 Peter does, for it is important to his later argument,[23] for in ch. 3 there is also movement from water to fire,[24] but there it is movement from the deluge as something that has happened to the coming destruction of the world through fire rather than the more limited past judgment of Sodom and Gomorrah. Here 2 Peter follows Jude in moving from the flood narrative (although Jude cites only the cause, the sin of the angels) to Sodom, but here again he edits Jude so as to make a different point. The point in Jude for both the fallen angels and Sodom is that God has in the past punished unrighteous behavior, and he will do the same in the future. Here in 2 Peter the point being made with respect to both Noah and Sodom is that God can appropriately punish the ungodly while at the same time saving the righteous, which may indicate that one argument that the teachers had advanced against final judgment was that it could not mean both salvation and judgment but must be indiscriminate: either the righteous would endure judgment or the wicked must be saved, neither of which was morally acceptable. 2 Peter counters with this second example of judgment, this one through fire, in which a righteous individual is delivered despite the annihilation of the unrighteous.

Sodom and Gomorrah had become proverbial for judgment long before 2 Peter. Not only do we have the references in the latter books of the OT (Isa 1:9-10; Jer 23:14; 50:40; Ezek 16:46-56; Amos 4:11; Zeph 2:9), but we also find references in the Apocrypha, such as this one from 3 Macc 2:4-5: "You destroyed those who in the past committed injustice, among whom were even giants who trusted in their strength and boldness, whom you destroyed by bringing on them a boundless flood. You consumed with fire and sulfur the people of Sodom who acted arrogantly, who were notorious for their vices; and you made them an example to those who should come afterward" (cf. 2 Esdr 2:8). Likewise the "Q" tradition of Jesus' words uses

23. Noah and Sodom-Gomorrah were clearly linked in Jewish tradition, for we find the connection made in *T. Naph.* 3:4-5; Philo, *Vit. Mos.* 2.52-65 (2.10) (where he also comments that fire and water are God's two means of destruction); and several places in Greco-Roman literature. The reference to Josephus, *War* 5.566, found in some authors, is not really germane, for while it does refer to the potential of destruction by fire or water, it also adds that of the ground opening up, as in the case of Korah. Furthermore, it names Sodom, but it does not name Noah with respect to destruction by water. So it appears to be more a catalogue of types of destruction than a specific connection of the two events.

24. The connection is reinforced by the choice of two words starting with *kappa* to describe both the deluge and the destruction of Sodom and Gomorrah.

Sodom proverbially (Matt 10:15 par. Luke 10:12), as do other Jesus sayings (the judgment on Capernaum in Matt 11:23-24 and the warning of the suddenness of judgment in Luke 17:29). Paul in Rom 1:29 cites Isa 1:9 on how thoroughly Sodom had been destroyed. The point in all of these passages is clear: Sodom and Gomorrah were indeed proverbial for cities that had been condemned and burned to ashes.[25]

This destruction serves as "an example of what is going to happen to the ungodly." This point had already been made by 3 Maccabees, and a similar term is found in Jude 7. The point for 2 Peter is that God has already shown what happens to the ungodly (so much for the theory of the teachers that there is no final judgment), but that is not his only point, for just as he added Noah to the story of the fallen angels that had been mentioned in Jude, so he now goes on to add Lot to the story of Sodom and Gomorrah.

**7-8** For Jude the point of the example of Sodom was that it suffered *eternal* destruction. That is not the concern of 2 Peter,[26] as we see in his use of the example of Lot. For 2 Peter Lot is a "righteous man." In Genesis Lot, viewed against the background of the high value that his culture put on treating foreigners well, is indeed presented as relatively righteous in that he offers hospitality to the foreigners (not knowing that they are angels), while the rest of the population attempts to abuse them, but he does not seem otherwise distressed by Sodom, nor does he appear eager to leave. In fact, the covenant loyalty of Lot toward Abraham, if not his righteousness, is put in question in the narrative of Gen 13:8-13 by Lot's choice of the Jordan plain and his moving toward Sodom. The righteousness of Lot is far clearer in later Jewish literature. Wisd 10:6 states, "Wisdom rescued a righteous man [the same Greek term as in 2 Peter] when the ungodly were perishing; he escaped the fire that descended on the Five Cities" (NRSV; so also Wisd 19:17) Philo is a bit more restrained, but he still argues that he did not join in with the Sodomites in pursuit of evil (Philo, *Vit. Mos.* 2.58).[27] Thus even if Genesis implies only narratively

25. The verb that 2 Peter uses for burning to ashes is not used elsewhere in the NT, but is the one used by Philo, *De ebrietate* 222–23, for his allegorical interpretation of Sodom.

26. This is probably not because 2 Peter is either "focused on preliminary punishment in the intermediate state" or "prefers to see the fate of the wicked at the day of judgment as annihilation," as Bauckham suggests, but more because it does not suit his theme of deliverance from judgment.

27. One should note that the reference in Philo joins Lot to Noah, who, rather than simply avoiding evil, "never committed any intentional or voluntary wickedness." Thus he was positively righteous, while Lot was simply not a participant in evil. *Gen. R.* 49.13 also compares Noah to Lot, assuming in both cases that they were righteous. In Lot's case the basis for this assumption is Abraham's prayer.

that Lot was relatively righteous, the writers of 2 Peter stands in a solid Jewish tradition in making that implication explicit. And he certainly does make it explicit, for not only is Lot called righteous in 2:7, but this is repeated in 2:8 and then amplified by referring to his having a "righteous soul." If James can talk about the patience of Job, which is not apparent in the biblical text, but is the theme of the *Testament of Job,* 2 Peter talks about the righteousness of Lot, a theme also amplified more outside the Hebrew Scriptures than within. One strongly suspects that like James 2 Peter is dependent on some first-century "haggadic" tradition, although in the case of 2 Peter it is one that we have yet to document.[28]

The issue for 2 Peter is that Lot was rescued. This issue of rescue is an important enough point for 2 Peter in that it is repeated in 2:9.[29] It is not that Lot needed to be rescued from the Sodomites. They are described as "lawless people" (a term used in the NT only by 2 Peter, here and in 3:17, but parallel to the more common term that 2 Peter uses in 2:9) with a "licentious lifestyle" (or "indecent conduct," BAG), but while this is said to have "oppressed" or "worn [him] out" (a term used elsewhere in the NT only in Acts 7:24), it is the behavior that he is said to find distressing rather than that he was himself the object of oppression and in that sense in need of rescue. The next verse makes this clear. It was not what was happening to him that "tormented" him, but his "living among them day after day" led to his hearing and seeing (a term that is used only here in biblical literature) "lawless deeds." The rescue has to do with something other than any danger Lot faced from the inhabitants of Sodom, just as the rescue of Noah had to do with something other than any danger that he may have faced from the other inhabitants of the earth. The trials of neither man are said to be from their personal danger of attack or oppression by the people surrounding them, but from their observation of (and perhaps vain protest against) the evil they saw around them.

**9** The point of both the Noah and Lot examples is: "the Lord knows how to rescue [the] godly [. . .] from trials and to hold the unrighteous for the day of judgment." The term for "rescue" is less usual in NT Greek, but it is not unusual in Greek as a whole. It is another indication of the wide vocabulary of 2 Peter. Thus it is not necessarily correct to argue

28. *1 Clem.* 11:1 puts this tradition, "For his hospitality and piety Lot was saved out of Sodom when the whole countryside was judged by fire and brimstone. . . ." This comes in a section in *1 Clement* that stresses hospitality as a cardinal virtue, so he does not use the term "righteous" for Lot. Thus this appears to come from another stream of thought than that used by 2 Peter.

29. *Test. Abr.* Resc. B, 6:13, mentions Lot as needing protection or preservation (the verb is different from the one used in 2 Peter) from the Sodomites, although the nature of the protection is not spelled out.

that the term always points to a "dramatic situation,"[30] although this can be the case and although the deliverance can be eschatological.[31] Eschatological deliverance is certainly the meaning in 1 Thess 1:10, but at least some of the word's meaning in 2 Tim 4:18 is focused on dangers within this age. What is clear is that such deliverance is often from the powers of evil that hold sway in this age, as we see in Matt 6:13 and Col 1:13. In our passage the deliverance is from "trials," a term that normally refers to tests that one experiences as a result of his or her commitment to Christ and his mission.[32] According to Luke Jesus looked on his whole life as characterized by these trials (Luke 22:28), and they are referred to frequently in the NT (e.g., Jas 1:2; 1 Pet 1:6). This fits the context of 2 Peter, for if Lot is the immediate reference (with a parallel in Noah), his suffering came from his observing the evil around him. The inbreaking of God in judgment was a deliverance for him, not something that he needed to be saved from.[33] It was the trial of living among the ungodly that was the issue, according to 2 Peter, as also in the case of Noah. In his own time our author is probably thinking of the trials engendered within the community of the followers of Jesus by the activities of the teachers he opposes. In our own age there are trials to be endured due both to the evil and injustice within the church and that outside it in the general culture. Indeed, one of the characteristics of our age is that there appears to be no discernible difference between the lifestyles of those inside and those outside the church. Would 2 Peter think that the teachers he opposes have won?

2 Peter underlines the unity of this paragraph by repeating the term "rescue" or "deliver" from 2:7 and then, when it comes to the ungodly, repeating the term "held" ("hold" or "keep") from 2:4, which will again appear in 3:7 with respect to the present world being kept for a final judgment by fire. "Rescue" and "holding" are the two sides of the same coin. The godly are rescued and the ungodly are held or bound over for judgment. The question arises, however, whether our author is thinking only of final judgment or also of an intermediate state while awaiting final judgment. If the angels are his paradigm, in 2 Peter and all the traditions that we know about they are presently being held in "gloomy dungeons" awaiting a final end.

30. Vögtle, *Der Judasbrief, der zweite Petrusbrief,* 192.

31. Wilhelm Kasch, *"ryomai," TDNT* 6:998-1003, especially p. 1003.

32. Kraftchick, *Jude, 2 Peter,* 131, "the afflictions which the righteous suffer in an evil world."

33. Referring this discussion to the Tribulation (Thomas R. Edgar, "Robert H. Gundry and Revelation 3:10," *Grace Theological Journal* 3 [1982] 19-49, especially 44-49) is therefore incorrect, for other terms are used for the affliction of the eschaton.

But did not Sodom and Gomorrah suffer their final end as Lot was delivered? The discussion revolves around the meaning of the present participle underlying the phrase, "while continuing their punishment." On the one hand, there is (1) a Jewish belief in the punishment of the wicked between their death and final judgment (*4 Ezra* 7:79-80, "And if [the spirit of a person who has died] is one of those who have shown scorn and have not kept the way of the Most High, and who have despised his Law, and who have hated those who fear God — such spirits shall not enter into habitations, but shall immediately wander about in torments, ever grieving and sad, in seven ways"; see also Jesus in Luke 16:23-24), (2) the fact that the participle underlying our clause is a present participle, and (3) 2 Peter's assertion that the angels referred to are being kept in an unpleasant place. On the other hand, (1) the angels, while not in a comfortable situation, are said to be being kept for a future judgment, (2) the future participle occurs only thirteen times in the NT and only one of these is passive, so the present participle is sometimes used for the future participle (as in Matt 26:25; Luke 1:35; John 17:20; Acts 21:2-3), and (3) the verb for punishing (and its related noun) are normally used in an eschatological sense for final judgment, not the intermediate state.

Furthermore, the author of 2 Peter is not threatening the death and immediate judgment of the teachers he opposes, but rather the coming of the Parousia and final judgment. Indeed, that is the sense of 3:7, that this present time is a time when the heavens and earth are being "held" for a future final judgment. Thus, while grammar alone might predispose us to the NIV translation, on the basis of the context in 2 Peter we agree with Bauckham, Vögtle, and Kraftchick, among others, when they argue that the translation should be "to hold the unrighteous for the day of judgment, when they will be punished." The present is a time of trials for the righteous, either because of the deeds that evil people do to them or because they must live in a world filled with evil, but this state is not permanent. The time is coming when the Lord will deliver the righteous, while those practicing evil will be held for the coming judgment. The histories of Noah and the angels and Lot and the cities of Sodom and Gomorrah point to a far more awesome and fearful destiny for the world than any intermediate judgment, yet this is a destiny filled with hope for the righteous.

**10a** Our author stops the argument abruptly to insert a phrase that brings his readers back to the present danger to their community and sums up this section: "This is especially true of those who follow the corrupt desire of the sinful nature and despise authority." While expressed as a full clause in English, it is in fact a participial clause in Greek, an interjection that underlines the point of the examples. In both the sin of the angels in the time of Noah and the attempted assault on the angelic messengers in Sodom species boundaries were transgressed or attempted to be transgressed. Thus we have the first summary charge against those who, to give a woodenly literal translation, "in desire of defilement go after flesh." To "go after flesh" is the expression used in Jude 7 as a partial description of the sin of Sodom. 2 Peter has modified this description in two ways.

First, rather than using the verb Jude uses in parallel to "going after flesh," that is, "to give oneself to fornication," and rather than underlining the breaking of the species boundary by describing it as "going after *other* flesh," 2 Peter uses an adverbial phrase to describe how they went after flesh, that is, "in desire of defilement." Desire itself, whether sexual or other, was not viewed as evil in many Jewish circles, although it was often seen that way in Greek circles. However, both agreed that when desire started to run one's life, it broke acceptable boundaries and thus became evil. Here the situation clearly deals with desire that has broken acceptable boundaries, for it is a "desire of defilement" or a "defiling desire" that is the driving force behind their "going after flesh."

Second, 2 Peter has conformed the term for "going after" to the language of the Greek OT, language that is used for going after other deities (Deut 4:3; 6:14; 28:14; 3 Kgdms 11:10 [1 Kings 11:10]; Isa 65:2; Hos 11:10). This implies that, like Mammon, desire in the NT can function as a pagan deity did in the OT. The first charge against the teachers he opposes, then, is that they, like the fallen angels and like Sodom, have defiled themselves due to following, perhaps deifying, their desire, and specifically their sexual desire. We are not told how this expressed itself, although the language in Jude, which 2 Peter surely knows, hints that it was expressed in fornication. Could anything be more characteristic of postmodern society, inside or outside the church?

The second charge is that they "despise authority," or, more literally, "despise lordship." While this probably forms a transition and points forward to the despising of angelic authority, that is not the primary referent of the term since it is singular. While it could pick up the despising of "the Master who bought them" of 2 Pet 2:1 (a parallel to Jude 4, where Jude clearly refers to Christ), the closer referent is God (2 Pet 2:4), who after all is the being who sets the boundaries for human behavior. In practice it does not matter whether the term refers to the rule of God or the rule of Christ, for in the eyes of the followers of Jesus they were (and are) identical. The fact is that when one ignores the teaching of Jesus or the instruction of his Father, one is in practice despising their lordship. Such persons may still be honoring Jesus or his Father with their lips. They may be energetic worshipers, but their actions betray them in that they have thrown off all authority over their lives. Reflection on Matt 7:21-23 will show that this is not a good situation in which to be.

> *Bold and arrogant, these men are not afraid to slander celestial beings; [11]yet even angels, although they are stronger and more powerful, do not bring slanderous accusations against such beings in the presence of the Lord. [12]But these men blaspheme in matters they do not understand. They are like brute beasts, creatures of instinct, born only to be caught and destroyed, and like beasts they too will perish.*

**10b-11** The second part of v. 10 belongs, along with vv. 11 and 12, to our next paragraph, the next set of charges. These people disregard the authority of God, so it is not surprising that they also arrogantly reject the authority of heavenly beings. Adapting the root that he found in Jude 9, our author accuses these teachers of being "bold and arrogant."[34] These two terms occur together with some frequency (e.g., *1 Clem.* 30:8); the first term indicates people who claim rank, authority, or ability to which they are not entitled (Rom 15:18; 2 Cor 10:12; Philo, *Somn.* 1.54), while the second indicates a similarly unfounded arrogance (Prov 21:24; Titus 1:7; Josephus, *Ant.* 1.189). In other words, they are challenging the honor of God. "They extend themselves beyond what God assigned, thus infringing on God's honour and that of his agents."[35]

In breaking the boundaries of their status and making such an honor challenge, they fail to show the proper respect to those higher in rank than they are; that is, they "are not afraid" ("fear" indicating respect and "not being afraid" indicating an arrogant disrespect) to slander (*blasphēmountes,* which one recognizes as the source of "blaspheme," although in the first century it indicated any type of slander, not just religious slander)[36] "the glorious ones" (or "the majestic ones"). It is at this point that the interpretation runs into difficulty. These glorious ones are clearly some type of angelic being (*contra* Luther, Calvin, and some modern commentators), for (1) the contrast is with the behavior of angels, and (2) the parallel in Jude 8-9 has to do with Michael's behavior toward an angelic being, even if a fallen one. But who are these angelic beings to whom our author refers?

One line of argument is that if 2 Peter is following Jude 9 closely, then he must be thinking of Satan or some similar being (misunderstand-

34. The noun for "bold" *(tolmētai)* is similar to what Michael did not do *(etolmēsen)* in Jude 9.

35. Neyrey, *2 Peter, Jude,* 207.

36. Neyrey, *2 Peter, Jude,* 207, defines it as "injuring the reputation of another by speech," citing Titus 3:2; Josephus, *Life* 232; Philo, *Spec. leg.* 4.197.

ing the meaning of "glorious ones" in Jude according to our evaluation in the commentary section on Jude 9). In that case the passage would mean that these teachers speak disrespectfully of Satan and evil angels (perhaps because they believe that they will neither share their fate nor come under their sway), even though the (holy) angelic beings who are higher in strength and power (both honorable qualities) than they are, and thus their betters, do not bring a slanderous judgment against the "glorious ones" (i.e., fallen or evil angels).[37] This is an entirely possible interpretation if we follow the text behind the NIV, although even then we should notice that 2 Peter (1) ties the contrasting angelic behavior more closely to the behavior of the teachers than Jude does, and (2) has dropped the example of Michael and Satan (although he may imply it in his general statement). If he dropped the citation in order to generalize the statement of Jude to a wider angelic group (not just because he knew that his readers were unfamiliar with the story), he may be implying that the "glorious ones" are not evil like Satan. In that case they may include the angels who, according to Jewish tradition, mediated the law, that is, the "glorious ones" in Jude, whom the teachers may be rejecting in their rejection of boundaries. Unfortunately we have neither Peter nor the teachers here to get the full answer to this question, but on this interpretation 2 Peter is at least following Jude in insisting that human beings have no ground for speaking disrespectfully of angels, whether they be fallen or holy angels. (At the same time Col 2:18 warns followers of Jesus against honoring angels too highly, or, the more likely meaning of the phrase used there, trying to enter into their worship, both of which are activities that distract us from the centrality of Christ.)

Another approach argues that the "glorious ones" are indeed holy angels (which appears to fit better with the normal meaning of the term, as we argued in the commentary on Jude, pp. 56-59) and that the ones whom the angels of 2 Pet 2:11 *do not* slander are the teachers whom 2 Peter is condemning.[38] (In other words, it would be difficult to imagine angels slandering other angels, so if the "glorious ones" are holy angels, either Jude's example has been misunderstood or else the "them" is the human teachers, not the angels.) Related to this interpretation is the textual reading "from the presence of the Lord" rather than "in the presence of the Lord."[39] If this reading is accepted, then the sense is that teachers

37. So Bauckham, *Jude, 2 Peter,* among others.

38. So Vögtle, *Der Judasbrief, der zweite Petrusbrief,* 197-201.

39. Bauckham comments, "The reading *para kyriou* [from the Lord] ($\mathfrak{P}^{72}$ al) must be preferred, as the more difficult reading, to the better-attested *para kyriō̧* [before the Lord] (א B C K P *al*). To avoid attributing the . . . 'slanderous judgment' to the Lord, scribes either changed *para kyriou* to *para kuriō* or omitted the phrase altogether (A *al*). It is true that

arrogantly slander angels, but angels, who would have far more right to accuse them, do not bring against the teachers the charge that the Lord has spoken. For the angels to speak it would be slander, even though it is the Lord's judgment. This would be a warning to Christians not to take over the Lord's place as judge, a theme also found in Jas 4:11-12.[40]

This is one of those issues in biblical interpretation about which one cannot be sure, but we lean toward the second interpretation. Although Kraftchick appears correct at first in arguing that there was more reason for the teachers to dare to slander evil angels than holy angels,[41] this would not necessarily be the case if the teachers felt that the holy angels had foisted ethical rules or even the teaching about the coming judgment on the Jesus movement (or the wider Jewish community of whom they were a branch). Furthermore, there is no support for interpreting the designation "the glorious ones" as being evil or fallen.

The text-critical issue would be decisive if it fell clearly in the direction of "from the presence of the Lord." However, we feel that the more widespread reading has enough support that it may well be original, given (1) the paucity of support for the more difficult reading and (2) the possibility that it could have arisen through mishearing the one dictating the text to a copyist. If the NIV reading is original, then the angels do not slanderously accuse the teachers "before the Lord." They leave all judgment up to God, unlike the arrogant teachers. If the older reading is original, then the angels do not slander the teachers with the judgment "from the Lord," that is, that the Lord has pronounced. Either interpretation should give pause to human beings who accuse and even pronounce judgment on other human beings, an activity that is quite common in the church, even among church leaders.

**12** Whatever the exact meaning of the previous verse, it is clear that these teachers are overreaching their status, for they "slander in matters they do not understand" (the use of "blaspheme" in the NIV is unfortunate in that the issue is not their insulting God or the faith, but their bringing charges against angels, perhaps evil angels, or perhaps "taking authority over" or "throwing down" such angels, to use contemporary

---

*para kyriō* would make good sense: the angels pronounce judgment before God's judgment seat in the heavenly courtroom. But *para kyriou* is explicable as 2 Peter's equivalent of Jude's . . . 'May the Lord rebuke you.'" However, Bauckham does not notice that while Michael does say, "May the Lord rebuke you," in 2 Peter the angels *do not* bring a slanderous judgment "from the Lord."

40. See also the long (if somewhat overly argued) discussion of this theme in Scripture in Gregory A. Boyd, *Repenting of Religion: Turning from Judgment to the Love of God* (Grand Rapids: Baker, 2004).

41. Kraftchick, *Jude, 2 Peter,* 136.

parlance). In response to this overreaching of status 2 Peter makes an insidious comparison. They may claim wisdom or insight, but in fact they are acting like "beasts, creatures of instinct." They are driven by their natural drives and are behaving in a subhuman, not a superhuman manner. In this our author is probably referring to their entrapment by desire. Like many animals, they are "born only to be caught and slaughtered." This attitude toward some of the animals, namely, that they were created for (or their natural use was for) slaughter is known from both Greek and Jewish sources (Juvenal 1.141; Pliny, *Hist. Nat.* 8.81; *b. Mesʿia* 85a ["There was a calf being taken to slaughter, and it broke away and hid under the rabbi's garment and cried out. He said to it, 'Go your way, for this is why you were created.'" However, in this story the rabbi suffers for his lack of mercy.]). The point here is not about animals, but that the common supposition about animals (which 2 Peter has taken over from Jude and adapted to make a different point) was true of these teachers, who were acting like animals driven by instinct. That is, these teachers would be destroyed in the coming judgment.

At this point another interpretive difficulty arises. The clause "like beasts they too will perish" has been variously interpreted. The most common and best-supported interpretations are: (1) "they will be destroyed in their own destruction" (a Hebraism, like Exod 18:18; Isa 24:3; Mic 2:10),[42] (2) "they will be destroyed in the same destruction with them" (either in the suddenness/sureness of the final judgment/slaughter of the animals or in that the final judgment will destroy animals as well as the teachers),[43] or (3) "they will be destroyed in the same destruction [with the evil angels, whom they slander]."[44]

The first explanation is attractive in that Semitisms of this type are found in the NT, but it runs into a problem in that the text reads literally "in their destruction they will be destroyed," and for it to be a Semitism it should read "in destruction they will be destroyed." The "their" breaks the pattern. The third explanation, that of Bauckham, reaches back to his argument that the "glorious ones" whom these teachers insult (or slander) in v. 10b are the fallen angels of v. 4. It would make a lovely pattern of poetic justice, with the teachers caught in the same web of just judgment that the fallen angels that they despise are caught in. However, we have already argued (while acknowledging that the issue is not clear)

42. James, *Second Peter and Jude;* Green, *Second Peter and Jude.* The position of Plumptre, *The Epistles of St. Peter and St. Jude,* appears to be a variation of this explanation. Kraftchick, *Jude, 2 Peter,* 137, mentions this last, but he does not make his decision clear.

43. Vögtle, *Der Judasbrief, der zweite Petrusbrief,* 203, and most commentators.

44. Bauckham, *Jude, 2 Peter,* 264.

that we do not think that Bauckham is correct in that identification, and with that previous decision the interpretation of the clause here stands or falls. That leaves us with our second explanation, "they will be destroyed in the same destruction with them." This could refer to the destruction of the world by fire at the end of the age (2 Pet 3:7, 10), which destruction may include the natural world as we know it (see the discussion below of those passages), or it could refer to a destruction analogous to the surety or perhaps the suddenness of the slaughter of such animals. It is this latter that is preferred by most commentators (and the NIV translators). But if this is what is intended, it could have been put more clearly with an "as" or "like" rather than an "in." We tend to think that our author is focused on the final judgment at the end of the age (it is unlikely that he is simply thinking that such teachers will die suddenly at a young age — both alternative versions of this interpretation argue that the destruction of the false teachers is in the final judgment), which will affect not only the animate creation but also the inanimate, so clearly animals are included. And these teachers who have behaved like animals will die with the animals, their end fitting their lifestyle.

> [13]*They will be paid back with harm for the harm they have done. Their idea of pleasure is to carouse in broad daylight. They are blots and blemishes, reveling in their pleasures while they feast with you.* [14]*With eyes full of adultery, they never stop sinning; they seduce the unstable; they are experts in greed — an accursed brood!* [15]*They have left the straight way and wandered off to follow the way of Balaam son of Beor, who loved the wages of wickedness.* [16]*But he was rebuked for his wrongdoing by a donkey — a beast without speech — who spoke with a man's voice and restrained the prophet's madness.*

**13** The destruction that they will experience will be their reward. This clause is again difficult, with some arguing for "being defrauded [due to their destruction] of the profits of their evildoing" and so paralleling 2 Pet 2:15 (and Acts 1:18), but since their desire for money has not yet been mentioned, it is difficult to imagine that the author would expect his readers to anticipate v. 15. This interpretation does not fit into the flow of thought. Rather, it is more likely that the NIV translation is correct, that the reward of wrongdoing is eschatological (so in this negative sense *Barn.* 4:12; *Diogn.* 9:2; in a positive sense Rev 22:12) and that the passage means (in a rather wooden translation) "suffering wrong as the reward of [their] wrong." The wordplay is intended, for in Greek *adikoumenoi* ("receiving the wrong") and *adikias* ("wrong") are plays on the same root. God's law of retribution holds firm. When the eschatological judgment takes place (a judgment that we will later learn these teachers deny), they will receive a full payback for the wrong they have done. This finishes the discussion that began in v. 10b.

Our author moves on to a further charge, perhaps related to his previous comment on the teachers living like animals (i.e., as creatures of drives and instinct). (It is, however, unrelated to the main theme of the previous section, their boldly speaking about things of which they were in fact ignorant.) The instincts now in question are those of eating, drinking, and sex. In an adaptation of Jude 12 ("These men are blemishes at your love feasts, eating with you without the slightest qualm — shepherds who feed only themselves"), our author comments that these teachers are self-indulgent (the term, which can indicate carousing but does not necessarily do so, is found elsewhere in the NT only in Luke 7:25) in broad daylight. It is this "daylight" aspect that makes such behavior negative in both Jewish and Greco-Roman eyes (Eccl 10:16 ["Alas for you, O land, when . . . your princes feast in the morning!"; Isa 5:11; *Test. Moses* 7:4 ["they will be deceitful men, pleasing only themselves . . . loving feasts at any hour of the day — devouring, gluttonous"]; Juvenal 1.103). Feasting (including appropriate drinking) after a day's work was done could be appropriate, but when it happens during the day, duties and responsibilities are clearly being neglected.

The real problem, however, is not that this self-indulgence is practiced during the day, but that the feasting in which these teachers take part is at the common meal of the community that developed into what we now call the Eucharist or Lord's Supper. At that meal they are "blots and blemishes," language suggested by the use in Jude 12 of a term meaning "reefs" or "spots" (*spilas,* translated "blemishes" in the NIV, but both meanings, "reefs" and "spots," are well established in Greek literature, so the NET Bible translates it "reefs," as do the NLT, NASV, and ASV). Here 2 Peter has chosen two words, one of which is close to that in Jude *(spilos),* to indicate that these people are unfit for the service of God (Lev 1:3; 21:21). They are the opposite of what the people of God as a whole is to be (2 Pet 3:14, where one has the negative of both of these words, a word choice that is hardly accidental). The common meal that was the Lord's Supper (it was a full meal through A.D. 250) was indeed a place for pleasure (note that the Greek word in this passage translated "reveling" in the NIV is used in a good sense in Isa 55:2 ["your soul will delight in the richest of fare"]; Hermas, *Man.* 10:3:1), for Scripture is not against indulging in pleasure under appropriate circumstances. After all, God created the world and created humanity so we could enjoy it. However, what these people do is not appropriate, for it is "deceits" in which they indulge ("deceit" being the most common and basic meaning of *apatē*), a term that Hermas often pairs with the term translated "carousing" above and which in contexts such as this means "deceitful pleasure" or "a pleasure that involves one in sin."[45] While this use is rare in the NT, 2 Peter is making a play on Jude, where the Lord's Supper (termed "love feasts" *[agapais]*) sounds very similar to our term *(apatais)*.[46] Indeed, since they were feasting with believers (a Greek term used only here and Jude 12 in the NT), they were turning the Lord's Supper into something deceitful. They were not there celebrating in the presence of their living Lord, but rather they were there indulging their own selves, having their own agendas, for Jesus was not their Lord. Our author knows that Jesus was not their Lord since they were not apprentices to him, evident in the fact that they refused to follow his ethical instruction.

**14** While 2 Peter does not say it explicitly, part of the agenda of these teachers at the celebrations of the Lord's Supper may have been the women (although we would not want to rule out self-indulgent eating, for that went on in Corinth, although for other reasons, as 1 Corinthians 11 shows), since his next charge is that they have "eyes full of adultery." Whether the context is the Lord's Supper or not, our author's point is that these men are not safe. The expression itself is possibly a play on a saying found in Plutarch, *Moralia* 528E, in which, using a play on words, the shameless person does not have pupils in his eyes but prostitutes,[47] while the virtuous sees the purity of womanhood. Whether or not this or a similar expression is in our author's mind, he clearly views these teachers as sexual predators and thus unsafe for the community, for they are compulsive.[48] Yet he does not dwell on this charge, instead adding that they "seduce the unstable," a charge that he expresses using a verb found in biblical literature only in this chapter (2:14, 18) and in Jas 1:14. The idea of seduction is that of being drawn away from what one should be doing by something that one views as attractive — originally the term indicated attraction by a bait — but this attraction is appealing only to the unstable, for the stable should in 2 Peter's eyes see through the ruse.

Again our author does not answer our question as to whether this

45. BAG 82, *apatē*.

46. There is a textual issue here in that some manuscripts have *agapais* instead of *apatais*. However, these manuscripts are few and late, and they retain the "their" of 2 Peter, which does not fit "love feasts." Thus this is probably a simple error by a scribe who knew both passages.

47. Plutarch, *Moralia*, De vitioso pudore 528E8: *ho mēn rhētōr ton anaischynton ouk ephē* ***korai*** *en toi ommasin echein alla* ***pornai***: the two words in question having been highlighted and underlined.

48. The "never stop sinning" is not an independent statement, but one connected to their "eyes full of adultery." The term for "never ceasing" occurs only here in the NT.

seduction is a seduction to join them in adultery or to other forms of libertine behavior. Instead he hurries on to what is likely a more major concern, "they are experts in greed." A more formally equivalent translation is more vivid: "they have hearts exercised/trained in greed." The unstable whom they seduce are not "trained" enough in the faith, but these teachers are trained, stable individuals. However, their training is in greed. They will happily exploit those whom they have seduced from the truth. One is reminded of a man who lured a woman away from her husband only to live off her wages, which meant that she had to slave at multiple jobs to support them. Clearly this exasperates our author. He interjects a Hebraism, "cursed children." This expression is literally "children of cursing," similar to expressions found in Isa 57:4 ("children of destruction"); Hos 10:9 ("children of wrongdoing"); Eph 2:3 ("children of wrath"); 5:8 ("children of light"); 1 Pet 1:14 ("children of obedience"); *Barn.* 7:1 ("children of gladness").[49] The point is that these individuals are subject to divine judgment ("cursing"), a thought interjected with intense emotion. Our author is a pastor, and he is upset by what he sees happening to unstable individuals in the community.

**15** Having already mentioned the greed of the teachers he is attacking, 2 Peter now discusses this charge in a fuller form, using the negative example of Balaam, which he extracts from Jude 11 as the only one of the three individuals mentioned there (the other two are Cain and Korah) and whose main sin was greed. The constant theme in the charges against the teachers is that they once knew better than to do what they are doing. It is not that they have acted in ignorance, but that they have "left the straight way and wandered off." The idea of wandering *(eplanēthēsan)* is taken from Jude 11, where the reference is to Balaam's error *(planē)*, but the image also reflects the imagery of the Hebrew Scriptures. The "straight way" is mentioned in the Greek translation of 1 Kings 12:23; Ps 106:7; Prov 2:13, 16; Isa 33:15; Hos 14:10, while the idea of wandering from it is referred to in Deut 11:28; Wisd 5:6.[50] The two ideas fall together in Prov 2:13, which speaks of people "who leave the straight paths to walk in dark ways." Naturally many Jewish writers used similar imagery. For our purposes the most interesting use is in a saying of Jesus, who reverses the image in that the way of life is not straight or easy (Matt 7:13), but is still a road to be traveled and from which one should not

49. The exact expression is not found in the Greek OT. Clearly our author is building the expression by analogy to expressions he has read in his OT. That is, he has picked up some biblical language patterns and expresses himself naturally in them.

50. The idea of wandering itself indicates error. Jude 13 refers to wandering stars, and Jas 5:19-20 to people wandering from the way. The concept is that of something out of its place, and this often pictures someone in rebellion to the divine order.

turn. Similarly, Acts 13:10 refers to twisting the way of God ("Will you never stop perverting the right ways of the Lord?"). These teachers castigated by 2 Peter have left the right way (meaning, way of life) to go in another way, so one has the contrast of departing from following Jesus with starting to follow someone or something else. The apostolic group may not have followed "myths" (1:16, the other use of the term for following in 2 Peter), but these people have followed Balaam.[51]

Balaam is known well enough from the Hebrew Scriptures (Num 22–24; 31:8, 16; Deut 23:4-5; Josh 13:22; 24:9-10; Neh 13:2; Mic 6:5) and by the time of the NT he had become proverbial (e.g., Rev 2:14). The point being made here as in Jude is that "he loved the wages of wickedness."[52] In saying that Balaam "loved" the "wages of wickedness" 2 Peter has amplified Jude, for Jude mentions only an error for "wages," and here we are told that Balaam "loved" (one of the negative uses of *agapē*) the "wages of wickedness." In saying this both Jude and 2 Peter reflect the type of traditions that we find in later rabbinic reflection on Balaam.[53] The rabbis also argued that Balaam had received his "wages," "They also killed Balaam son of Beor with the sword. The Israelites paid him his full salary, and did not deprive him because he had come to give them [the Moabites] counsel" (*Sifré Numbers* 157 on Num 31:8; see also *Num. R.* 22.4).

**16** This behavior of Balaam was irrational, and the crowning touch was his being rebuked by an irrational beast. In writing this, 2 Peter is probably following the Targumic tradition, for in the version of the narrative in the Hebrew Scriptures (Num 22:21-35) Balaam's animal only complains of mistreatment and reasons with the prophet as to whether his treatment of his beast was justified. In Numbers it is the angel who rebukes Balaam for his behavior. In three Targumim (*Pseudo-Jonathan/Yerushalmi, Neofiti,* and *Fragment Targum*) the donkey is the one who rebukes Balaam.[54] The allusion to these expansions of the text serves a dou-

51. Balaam is called the son of Beor, but in fact the version of the name found here is the otherwise unattested "Bosor." Many scholars believe that this stems from a Jewish play on the Hebrew word for "flesh," *basar* (the first "a" can be read as a short "o" in some circumstances), and so is punning that Balaam is a "son of flesh." The rabbis would later make a different play in *b. Sanhedrin* 105a in which *Beʿor* was connected with *beʿir,* meaning "beasts," to accuse Balaam of bestiality.

52. Balaam's love of money is also found in Philo, *Vit. Mos.* 1.268, "And Bal, being allured by the gifts which were already proffered to him, and also by the hopes for the future which they held out to him, and being influenced also by the rank of those who invited him, began to yield. . . ." See also *De cherubim* 33–34, a more allegorical treatment.

53. See the "Excursus on Balaam in Rabbinic Literature" at the end of this chapter.

54. Neyrey, *2 Peter, Jude,* 211-12; Bauckham, *Jude, 2 Peter,* 268. The actual quotations from the Targumim are in the "Excursus on Balaam in Rabbinic Literature" at the end of this chapter.

ble purpose. On the one hand, it means that the prophet was warned about his "madness"/"foolishness" (both *Neofiti* and *Pseudo-Jonathan* on Num 22:30 refer to him as "foolish," while Philo, *De mutatione nominum* 203, speaks of Balaam as being "overthrown by his own insane wickedness, and having received many wounds, he perished amid the heaps of wounded"), and, on the other hand, it indicates that this was done by an animal that is by nature speechless (animals were considered dumb or speechless because they did not possess articulate speech) and thus by a subhuman creature, which made it a humiliation. The teachers 2 Peter opposes were, according to him, "unthinking animals." Thus they are also like Balaam, who was rebuked by a dumb animal, which is perhaps one step lower than being such an animal oneself. They have "eyes full of adultery," and Balaam counseled sexual entrapment. The parallels are striking. And the implication is that just as Balaam perished in the divine judgment on Midian (Num 31:8),[55] along with those he persuaded to act immorally (Num 31:15-17), so these teachers will perish when the judgment of God falls upon them.

> [17]*These men are springs without water and mists driven by a storm. Blackest darkness is reserved for them.* [18]*For they mouth empty, boastful words and, by appealing to the lustful desires of sinful human nature, they entice people who are just escaping from those who live in error.* [19]*They promise them freedom, while they themselves are slaves of depravity — for a man is a slave to whatever has mastered him.* [20]*If they have escaped the corruption of the world by knowing our Lord and Savior Jesus Christ and are again entangled in it and overcome, they are worse off at the end than they were at the beginning.* [21]*It would have been better for them not to have known the way of righteousness, than to have known it and then to turn their backs on the sacred command that was passed on to them.* [22]*Of them the proverbs are true: "A dog returns to its vomit," and, "A sow that is washed goes back to her wallowing in the mud."*

**17** Our author passes on from OT examples to a more general condemnation of the teachers he opposes. Here again he is following Jude, specifically Jude 12-13, 16, which he has edited to serve his own purposes. Instead of Jude's "clouds without rain" our author has "springs without water," and instead of "blown along by the wind" he has "mists driven by a storm." The reason for the changes is not entirely clear. While

55. This narrative is expanded in *Targum Pseudo-Jonathan,* but not in *Targum Neofiti.* There is no clear indication in the text as to whether or not 2 Peter knows the expanded form of the narrative.

several scholars suggest that for our author the idea of a "cloud without water" (a more literal rendering of Jude) did not make sense, it is unclear whether he knew that much about the nature of clouds, that is, that they are made up of condensed water vapor and thus always have water in them. What is clear is that the idea of divine instruction being a source of "water" is rooted in Scriptures that he surely knew (Prov 13:14 ["The teaching of the wise is a fountain of life"]; 18:4 ["the fountain of wisdom is a bubbling brook"]; Sir 24:23-31 ["the book of the covenant of the Most High God" = a river]); the Scriptures also make a connection between waterlessness and forsaking God (e.g., Jer 2:19; 14:3). Given that the meaningfulness of the metaphor is rooted in Scripture that is itself rooted in the climatic conditions of Palestine, it is likely the scriptural allusion that controls 2 Peter, given that we suspect that the work was written in Italy, which enjoys a less arid climate. The image of mists is not found in either the Hebrew or Greek versions of the OT, but as a weather phenomenon it indicated the coming of hot weather rather than rain.[56] In other words, both images indicate that these teachers promise something "refreshing," a revelation from God, and in actuality they produce nothing. They are charlatans. Furthermore, the image of a storm ("driven by a storm") suggests that they are in the wrong place, out of God's order. Since this disorder parallels that of the angels who left their place in 2 Pet 2:4, their punishment also echoes the angels' punishment: these teachers have "reserved seats" in "blackest darkness." The storm that they promised and could not fulfill will be one that breaks on them, not with refreshing rain but with eternal gloom.

**18** The theme of promising much and delivering little is continued as the diatribe moves on. Using a term for speaking or proclaiming something that can also be used for the "speech" of animals,[57] our author notes that these teachers speak "inflated things of emptiness" ("empty, boastful words," NIV). The term for "inflated things" ("boastful words," NIV) itself is taken from Jude 16, its only other appearance in the NT. The idea is that the teachers make great promises (2 Peter will later say that they promise freedom) to others and boast about themselves, but these puffed-up words are simply emptiness or futility. In this case the word order is significant, for first one has the great promises and boasts and then one discovers that they are empty, futile, or, as we would say, hot air.

However, even though they pour out hot air, they are not harmless. Indeed, if they were harmless, our author would surely not have bothered with them. What disturbs him is that they "seduce"/"entice" (we

56. Watson, *Invention, Arrangement, and Style,* 120.
57. BAG, 857, *phthegomai.*

have already seen this word in 2 Pet 2:14) others to licentiousness based on the desires of the "flesh," that is, the physical drives. (The NIV translation "sinful human nature" imports Pauline theology into this text.) Anyone coming from a Jewish background recognized the various physical drives, and especially the sexual one, as neutral and necessary, but such a person would also recognize that when these drives become the motivating force in a person's life, they are destructive. Thus we saw in 2 Pet 1:4 that corruption has come into the world through desire (or through our drives) in that proper boundaries were not put on them. These teachers entice people because they do not put boundaries on the physical drives (i.e., they are licentious with respect to them) and thus encourage others to do whatever "feels good" (presumably, but not necessarily, as long as it feels good to anyone else involved as well). Naturally, this is not unlike Western society today, both within and outside the church (within the church some out-of-control drives are criticized, but others are not, so gathering wealth or overeating is more or less acceptable, while at least certain transgressions of sexual boundaries are not).

This enticement is particularly effective on newer believers, those who "are just escaping from those who live in error." The idea of escaping from the corruption that is in the world because of the various (uncontrolled) human drives is the description of redemption in 2 Pet 1:3. "Error" is, of course, the condition of nonbelievers, the pagans around them (so Wisd 12:24; Acts 14:15-17 [here described as ignorance rather than error]; 17:22-31 [also uses ignorance rather than error]; Rom 1:27; Titus 3:3 [using the verb rather than the noun]; 2 *Clem.* 1:7; *Barn.* 4:1; 14:5). The image behind "error" is that they have "wandered" from the right place or right way. They are out of place, which means that they are out of harmony with God. In particular they have wandered morally. These new believers "are just escaping" (which can mean either that they are newly escaped [the more probable meaning] or that they have scarcely escaped in the sense that they are not yet totally free) from these "ways of the world." They have just learned that what is normal in the world (in our age this would include the normal patterns of consumption in the world, as well as sexual mores) is an error, a wandering from God's way. Through God's grace they are newly escaped. But they are not yet stable (2 Pet 1:12). Now these teachers come along with their inflated promises that their old way of life was not really wrong in God's eyes, that there will be no final judgment for them, and by these means they entice these less stable believers back into the lifestyle in which they were once entrapped. This description of the false teachers hooks back to the reference to Balaam, but more importantly it shows the pastoral heart of 2 Peter. His concern with the teachers is not that he is angry at their behavior per se (they will suffer for it, so it should be more a cause for sadness than anger), but that he is upset at the damage that they can do to others. Naturally this is not unknown in the church today, where the emphasis on grace is often so interpreted as to teach, "Free from the law, O happy condition; now I can go and live like perdition." Normally it is not put in those words, but rather what is implied is that if you have "asked Jesus into your heart" (in itself not a biblical phrase) it no longer matters how you live, although lifestyle may affect the reward that you get in heaven. This is a teaching with which our author would have had no patience, just as he would have had little patience with those Christian leaders who through their indulgent lifestyle indicate that living according to the values of the culture around us is fine.

**19** How do these teachers entice the less stable members of the community? "They promise them freedom." This may be part of their inflated words (2:18), if their inflated words are not about themselves and their spiritual insight. Peter will shortly show that this promise of freedom is indeed empty. The nature of the freedom promised is undefined. Bauckham lists four possibilities that have been suggested: (1) freedom from the moral law, (2) freedom from the archons/demiurge (i.e., Gnostic freedom), (3) freedom from perishability ("depravity" in the NIV), (4) political freedom, and (5) freedom from judgment (since the final judgment does not exist).[58] Since there is no convincing evidence of either Gnostic ideation or political concerns in this letter (although, of course, simply referring to Jesus as "the sovereign Lord" or "God and Savior" was a political statement in a world in which those were titles of Caesar — yet 2 Peter does not indicate that this contrast is his special concern), those two suggestions may safely be dismissed. "Freedom from perishability" is attractive in that it is the coordinate to the second part of the sentence, namely, their enslavement to perishability/corruption/depravity. However, this does not fit with the wider context of the letter, which shows no particular concern about perishability or corruption. Rather, Vögtle is surely correct when he concludes about the meaning here, "They were promised freedom from the fear of final judgment and certainly also from conventional moral constraints."[59] That is, if there is no final judgment, then

58. Bauckham, *Jude, 2 Peter,* 275.

59. Vögtle, *2 Peter, Jude,* 206 (English translation ours). Bauckham agrees with this conclusion. Jerome Neyrey, "The Form and Background of the Polemic in 2 Peter," *JBL* 99:3 (1980) 418, notes that in Greco-Roman thought, "Epicurean freedom [free in that they denied the afterlife and the judgment and thus were free from the anxiety that these doctrines caused] is tantamount to antinomianism." He then cites Lactantius, *Div. Inst.* 3.17, where Lactantius makes this very point about Epicurean teaching. Could this have been the root of the teaching that 2 Peter opposes?

those parts of conventional morality that make sense only in the light of final judgment (versus those parts that make sense when viewed with enlightened self-interest with regard to life in this age) would not be binding. The behavior of the teachers demonstrated this.

The promise of freedom, however, is specious since the teachers themselves are not free. They are "slaves of corruption." The NIV follows a number of commentators in translating the Greek term *phthora* as "depravity."[60] Both meanings can be found, not only in Greek literature in general but also in Hellenistic Jewish literature.[61] We have already seen this term twice in 2 Peter (1:4; 2:12). In the first passage this *phthora* is in the world on account of desire (i.e., desire without boundaries) and is contrasted with participation in the divine nature; thus "corruption" seems better than "depravity." In the second passage it is the eschatological destruction that these teachers will endure just as animals experience temporal destruction (meanings close to Paul's use in Rom 8:21; 1 Cor 15:42, 50). In our present passage the sense of corruption/destruction again probably predominates, although moral overtones may be intended as well. These teachers promise freedom from final judgment, but they themselves are under the power of corruption or destruction. That is, they will die and face that very judgment from which they proclaim freedom. In 2 Peter's imagery, "*Phthora* is personified and portrayed in the common imagery of a victor in war who seizes those defeated as slaves and booty."[62] It is not that moral depravity has seized these people — they were not proclaiming freedom from that, but rather justifying it — it is rather that due to their moral depravity they have been enslaved by the corruption toward which all humanity is headed, unless God intervenes in grace (as 2 Peter has pictured in 1:4). The boasts of the teachers to offer freedom were disastrously wrong.

Having made his main point, our author closes his sentence with a common maxim:[63] "a person is a slave to whatever has mastered them."[64] Perhaps the contemporary church should keep this maxim in mind as it looks at its own situation, asking which powers have mastered the

60. E.g., Hillyer, *1 and 2 Peter, Jude,* 205; Green, *Second Peter and Jude,* 117.

61. BAG, 858, which argues that it can mean abortion, seduction, and religious or moral depravity, although these are the second and third definitions, not the primary one. Günther Harder, *"phtheirō ktl," TDNT* 9:93-105, documents this more fully.

62. Watson, *Invention, Arrangement, and Style,* 120.

63. Watson, *Invention, Arrangement, and Style,* 121 n. 271, gives some of the evidence.

64. More literally translated, "to whatever a person succumbs, to that they are enslaved." This reveals the balanced structure, but note that in Greek both verbs end with the same syllable, giving the maxim an almost poetic sound.

church in general and many of its members in particular. Freedom in Christ is one thing to announce but another thing to experience. Often the church is so busy pointing the finger at obvious corruption outside her walls that she does not see rampant enslavement within them.

**20** 2 Peter needs to make one final terrible point about the situation of these teachers, which is that it would have been better for them never to have heard and committed themselves to the good news. "If they have escaped" is a bit misleading as a translation, since "escaped" and "entangled" are participles. We would be following the grammatical structure better if we translated the sentence, "If, having escaped . . . and again being entangled, they are overcome, they are worse off. . . ." Nor is this previous escape and later entanglement a hypothetical condition, since in Greek it is what is called a "real condition" (using the indicative rather than the subjunctive). The point our author is making is, first, that they had been true followers of Jesus Christ, that is, they had escaped the corruption of the world. Look at the following comparison with 1:3-4:

| *2 Pet 1:3-4 (NRSV)* | *2 Pet 2:20 (NRSV)* |
|---|---|
| His divine power has given us everything needed for life and godliness, *through the knowledge* of him who called us by his own glory and goodness. [4]Thus he has given us, through these things, his precious and very great promises, so that through them you may *escape* from *the corruption* that is in *the world* because of lust, and may become participants of the divine nature. | For if, after they have *escaped* the *defilements* of *the world through the knowledge* of our Lord and Savior Jesus Christ, |

In 2 Pet 1:3-4 we have a description of the situation of one who is committed to "our God and Savior Jesus Christ." Beforehand the person was captive to "the corruption" that is in the world because of desire. Then, through the knowledge of Jesus Christ, that person has been enabled to escape from this corruption and becomes a participant in the divine nature. We discussed all of these concepts in our commentary on that earlier passage. Now we encounter these same elements again, although in condensed form. The verb for "escape" is the same, the reference to "the world" is the same, the description of the means of escape is nearly identical (the Greek preposition for "through" differs in that 2:20 is identical to 1:2, not 1:3, but the meaning does not differ substantially), and only the reference to "corruption"/"defilement" differs. Whereas in 1:5 the focus is on corruption, not just in the moral sense but in the sense

that sin and evil bring about death and its consequential corruption, here in 2:20 a term for cultic impurity is used (although it can have a moral and even sexual sense).[65] Used only here in the NT, this term for cultic impurity is rare in the Greek OT, but more common in both Philo and Josephus. Perhaps its use here was suggested by the use of a related term in 2:10 to describe the sexual sin of the teachers 2 Peter opposes.[66] The point is that the choice of the new term here not only connects the teachers back to the defilement in the world but also lays the emphasis on the behavior of the world as separating it from God (i.e., cultic defilement), whereas the term in 1:2 lays the emphasis on the destructive nature of such behavior. In both passages freedom has been experienced through the knowledge of "our Lord and Savior Jesus Christ" (discussed in the comment on 1:11). These two passages (1:3-5 and 2:20) together set the stage for the proverbs of 2:22.

Now these teachers[67] have again become entangled in the web of defilement. The term for entanglement itself occurs elsewhere in the NT only in the analogy of a soldier in 2 Tim 2:4. The term for being overcome just appeared in the previous verse (and appears only in these two verses in the NT), although the concept of being overpowered or mastered by sin is not that unusual in the NT (e.g., Rom 6:12-19; Titus 3:3). The picture that springs to mind is a graphic one, that of a person venturing back to the area of a giant spider's web that he or she has escaped (perhaps believing that they can handle the situation now) only to get entangled and be mastered by the huge spider.[68]

Our author now reaches the conclusion of his "if . . . then" construc-

65. Cf. *T. Benj.* 8:2-3, "He [the person with a mind that is pure when looking at a woman] has no pollution in his heart, because upon him is resting the spirit of God. For just as the sun is unpolluted, though it touches dung and slime, but dries up both and drives off the bad odor, so also the pure mind, though involved with *the corruptions of the earth,* edifies instead and is not itself corrupted." (The underlined terms are all forms of our word or its root, and the italicized phrase uses our term in a phrase like that in 2 Pet 1:5.)

66. Friedrich Hauck, *"miasma," TDNT* 4:646. The related term is *miasmos.* The other reason to change the term is that the term found in 1:5 has just been used in 2:19.

67. Given the connection with 2:10 and the focus of this passage on the teachers, we agree with Bauckham, *Jude, 2 Peter,* 277, and Vögtle, *Der Judasbrief, der zweite Petrusbrief,* 207 (as well as Mayor, Green, and others) that the focus remains on the teachers against such scholars as Kelly, *The Epistles of Peter and of Jude,* 347-48, who argue that it refers to the followers of the teachers. Kelly views it as a hypothetical warning, but, as indicated above, the Greek indicates a real rather than a hypothetical condition.

68. Given the language of the previous verse, in which corruption overcomes a person like a warrior capturing and enslaving a defeated foe, that may be the picture in our author's mind. The image we have suggested fits the language of the text and is more contemporary, at least in terms of contemporary literature and film.

tion: such people "are worse off than they were in the beginning." This is virtually a verbatim quotation of the words of Jesus in Matt 12:45/Luke 11:26 (changing only the singular reference of Jesus to a plural pronoun to fit the context here). In Matthew and Luke it was the return of a demon with seven worse ones that made the situation worse; here people are entangled in the same situation in which they were before they responded to the good news. Apparently what is worse about this situation is that (1) they have willingly entered into it (since they were once rescued from the power of evil), (2) it entails a rejection of the authority of Jesus in their lives, and (3) it is more hopeless than their pre-Christian state (and certainly so if our author is thinking along the same lines as Hebrews 6; cf. Heb 10:26). In the eyes of the NT and the postapostolic church apostasy, including moral apostasy, is very serious indeed.

**21** In case we readers have missed his point, 2 Peter follows up his main point with a so-called *Tobspruch,* one of those many proverbial statements in Hebrew and Jewish literature (including the literature of the early Jesus movement) in a "better . . . than" form.[69] In our verse this "better . . . than" is expressed in a past tense because it does not envision a possible situation, but rather one that has already ocurred and cannot be changed.

"It would have been better," says our author, for them never "to have known the way of righteousness." We have already seen the concept of "knowing" or, better, "coming to know" for conversion/Christian initiation in 2 Pet 1:2, 3 as well as in 2:20. Here it is expressed in Greek by a perfect infinitive, indicating coming to know at a point in the past with the result that one knows, which is precisely how one experiences conversion, that is, coming to know Jesus with the result that one goes on through life knowing him. But since Jesus was already used as the object of knowing in the previous verse, here the roughly synonymous "the way of righteousness" (i.e., the way of Jesus) is used. The messianic form of Judaism that we know as Christianity was already known as "the way" early in its history (e.g., Acts 9:2; 19:9), but Judaism had much earlier referred to itself or its true form as "the way of righteousness" (not just in Proverbs, but also in *Jub.* 23:26 ["in those days, children will . . . return to the way of righteousness"], *1 Enoch* 82:4 ["blessed are all those who walk in the way of righteousness"], the Dead Sea Scrolls, and similar literature), and Jesus had used the phrase in Matt 21:32 ("John came to you to show you the way of righteousness"). It will later show up in the

69. Graydon F. Snyder, "The *Tobspruch* in the New Testament," *NTS* 23:1 (1976-77) 117-20. Examples would be Prov 15:16-17; 16:19, 32; Eccl 7:1-2, 5; Mark 9:42-43, 45, 47; Rom 14:21; 1 Cor 7:9; 1 Pet 3:17.

apostolic fathers and other early church literature (e.g., *Barn.* 5:4, "a man shall justly perish who, having the knowledge of the way of righteousness, holds to the way of darkness"). It fits here well as an alternative to having come to know Jesus since (1) commitment to Jesus as Lord meant following his way of life and thus produced an ethical lifestyle, and (2) the failure of the teachers condemned in this work was primarily ethical rather than doctrinal.

Although these teachers had come to know the way of righteousness and had experienced Jesus' power freeing them from the corruption found in the culture around them, they have "turn[ed] their backs on the sacred commandment that was passed on to them." That is, when they had come to Christ they had received a "holy commandment" (so in 1 Tim 6:14 there is a solemn charge to Timothy to "keep this command [lit. the commandment] without spot or blame until the appearing of our Lord Jesus Christ"). This would have consisted of the teaching of Jesus and the teaching about Jesus. "Jesus is Lord, and this is how one follows him as Lord." This information was therefore "passed on" to them, a term used for the passing on of tradition. Receiving this "commandment" was how one was initiated into the way of Jesus or the way of righteousness: one committed oneself to Jesus as Lord, and one learned what their new Lord called them to. Jesus' call then as now was, "Follow me." It was not that these teachers were ignorant of that teaching — they had come to know it. But knowing perfectly well how Jesus as their Lord called them to live, they had turned from it. As we saw in the comment on the previous verse, in concert with Hebrews our author says that it would have been better for them never to have accepted the good news. Perhaps that evaluation is not as serious as Jesus' saying that it would have been better for Judas never to have been born (Mark 14:21), but it does show how seriously the early community of Jesus took ethical apostasy. There is no hint of, "Well, at least they accepted Jesus as their Savior when Peter preached here ten years ago," but instead the statement that it would have been better if they had not done so. Unfortunately, they had been properly initiated into the way of life of the Jesus movement and had turned away from it.

**22** The chapter closes with two proverbs (Peter appears to present them as one proverb since they make the same point of one returning to the unclean, but in fact they come from two different sources), both about unclean animals. We need to underline this fact of "impurity" when we read these proverbs. While pigs are intelligent and may be thought of as cute in our world where *Babe* is a popular movie, in the ancient world they were not thought of as cute or intelligent and in the Jewish part of that world they were ritually impure (which meant that Jews did not keep pigs at all). And while dogs may be "man's [*sic*] best friend" in our culture, in all ancient Eastern cultures they were despised, even if they were sometimes used. Notice how the two unclean animals are referred to negatively in the saying of Jesus in Matt 7:6 (in this he was typical of his culture). Thus the first proverb is drawn from Prov 26:11 ("As a dog returns to its vomit, so a fool repeats his folly") and expresses an often observed behavior of dogs, that is, their returning to, sniffing, and sometimes eating what they have vomited. The second proverb comes from pagan sources (since, as noted, the Jews did not keep pigs). The sow is washed only to return to the mud.[70] While often attributed to sayings about pigs washing in mud found in Heraclitus and other Greek literature (given that pigs were common and their behavior easily observed, the commonness of such sayings is not surprising), more likely it comes from a source like *Ahikar* 8:18: "My son, thou hast been to me like the swine that had been to the baths, and when it saw a muddy ditch, went down and washed in it, and cried to its companions: come and wash" (Syriac version).[71] It is not clear whether 2 Peter is familiar with *Ahikar* or whether he had at some time (perhaps as a youth) come in contact with a collection of proverbs that included both of these (the version of Prov 26:11 does not follow the LXX, so either it is being recited from memory, or it has been mediated through another source). Whatever the situation in the history of these proverbs, their meaning in this context is clear: both indicate a return to the unclean, and both call the one who so returns an unclean being (animal). This sums up the behavior of the teachers whom our author opposes. Despite having once turned to Christ and been freed from their past, they, like unclean and despised animals, have turned back to and embraced their former uncleanness.

70. We agree with Bauckham, *Jude, 2 Peter,* 279 (and also with the note in the NET Bible), that this proverb contains an ellipsis. The Greek for "A sow that is washed *goes back* to her wallowing in the mud" lacks "goes back," that is, the verb of returning or going back needs to be supplied. (In fact, in Greek there is no finite verb in the proverb.) Otherwise it could read, "A sow that washes herself by wallowing in the mire" (BAG 145, but to be fair to BAG the traditional translation appears in both this article and the reference to a sow on 848). The NRSV tries to get at both the sense and the grammar with "The sow is washed only to wallow in the mud." (This translation adds an interpretive "only" and changes the noun "wallow" into its implied verb.)

71. See Bauckham, *Jude, 2 Peter,* 279, for a discussion of this passage, the Arabic variant, and similar background issues.

# EXCURSUS ON BALAAM IN RABBINIC LITERATURE

## 1. *Talmudic references to Balaam*

There is extensive material on Balaam in *b. Sanhedrin* (the numbering in the abbreviated section below is that of Neusner = *b. Sanhedrin* 105–6 in the more traditional numbering). While this material comes from various dates from the centuries after the NT was written, it illustrates the type of tales that were told about Balaam.

**XI.1**

A. Four ordinary folk: Balaam, Doeg, Ahithophel, and Gehazi [M. 11:2F = *m. Sanhedrin* reference]:
B. [The name] Balaam [means] not with [the rest of] the people [using the same consonants], [who will inherit the world to come].
C. Another interpretation: Balaam, because he devoured the people.
D. "Son of Beor" means that he had sexual relations with a cow [a play on the consonants of the word for Beor].

**XI.2**

A. *A Tannaite statement:*
B. Beor, Cushan-rishathaim, and Laban, the Syrian, are one and the same person.
C. Beor: because he had sexual relations with a cow.
D. Cushan-rishathaim [two acts of wickedness], for he committed two acts of wickedness against Israel, one in the time of Jacob and one in the time of the Judges.
E. But what was his real name? It was Laban the Aramaean.

**XI.8**

A. Said R. Yohanan, "Balaam had one crippled foot, for it is written, 'And he walked haltingly' (Num. 23:3). . . .
C. "Balaam was blind in one eye, as it is said, 'Whose eye is open' (Num. 24:3).
D. "He practiced enchantment with his penis.
E. "Here it is written, 'Falling but having his eyes open' (Num. 24:3), and elsewhere: 'And Haman was fallen on the bed whereon Esther was' (Esth. 7:8) . . ."
H. Mar, son of Rabina, said, "He had sexual relations with his ass."
I. As to the view that he practiced enchantment with his penis, it is as we have just now stated.

J. As to the view that he had sexual relations with his ass:

K. Here it is written, "He bowed, he lay down as a lion and as a great lion" (Num. 24:9), and elsewhere it is written, "At her feet [105B] he bowed, he fell" (Judg. 5:27)."

**XI.9**

A. "He knows the mind of the most high" (Num. 24:16):

B. *Now if he did not know the mind of his own beast, how could he have known the mind of the most high?*

C. *What is the case of the mind of his beast?*

D. *People said to him, "What is the reason that you did not ride on your horse?"*

E. *He said to them, "I put it out to graze in fresh pasture."*

F. [The ass] said to him, "Am I not your ass" (Num. 22:30). [That shows he rode an ass, not a horse.]

G. *"[You are] merely for carrying loads."*

H. "Upon whom you rode" (Num. 22:30).

I. *"It was a happenstance."*

J. "Ever since I was yours, until this day" (Num. 22:30).

K. [The ass continued,] "And not only so, but I serve you for sexual relations by night."

L. *Here it is written,* "Did I ever do so to you?" (Num. 22:30) *and elsewhere it is written,* "Let her serve as his companion." [The same word is used, proving that sexual relations took place as with David and the maiden in his old age.]

**XI.18**

A. "And he looked on the Kenite and took up his parable" (Num. 24:21):

B. Said Balaam to Jethro the Kenite, "Were you not with us in that conspiracy [of Pharaoh, Exod. 1:22]? [Of course you were.] Then who gave you a seat among the mighty men of the earth [in the Sanhedrin]?"

C. *This is in line with what R. Hiyya bar Abba said R. Simai said,* "Three participated in that conspiracy [of Exod. 1:22, to destroy the Israelites in the river], Balaam, Job, and Jethro.

D. "Balaam, who gave the advice, was slain. Job, who kept silent, was judged through suffering. Jethro, who fled, had the merit that some of his sons' sons would go into session [as judges] in the Hewn-Stone Chamber,

E. "as it is said, 'And the families of scribes which dwelt at Jabez, the Tirahites, the Shemathites, the Sucathites. These are the Kenites that came of Hammath, the father of the house of Rehab' (1 Chr. 2:55). And it is written, 'And the children of the Kenite, Moses' father-in-law . . .' (Judg. 1:16)."

**XI.21**

A. "And now, behold, I go to my people; come, and I shall advise you what this people shall do to your people in the end of days" (Num. 24:24):

B. *Rather than saying,* "This people to your people," *it should say,* "Your people to this people." [Freedman, p. 723, n. 4: He advised the Moabites to ensnare Israel through uncharity. Thus he was referring to an action by the former to the latter, while Scripture suggests otherwise.]

C. Said R. Abba, "It is like a man who curses himself but assigns the curse to others. [Scripture alludes to Israel but refers to Moab.]

C. "[Balaam] said to [Balak], 'The God of these people hates fornication, and they lust after linen [clothing, which rich people wear]. Come and I shall give you advice: Make tents and set whores in them, an old one outside and a girl inside. Let them sell linen garments to them.'

E. "He made tents for them from the snowy mountain to Beth Hajeshimoth [north to south] and put whores in them, old women outside, young women inside.

F. "When an Israelite was eating and drinking and carousing and going out for walks in the market, the old lady would say to him, 'Don't you want some linen clothes?'

G. "The old lady would offer them at true value, and the girl would offer them at less.

H. "This would happen two or three times, and then [the young one] would say to him, 'Lo, you are at home here. Sit down and make a choice for yourself.' Gourds of Ammonite wine would be set near her. (At this point the wine of Gentiles had not yet been forbidden to Israelites.) She would say to him, 'Do you want to drink a cup of wine?'

I. "When he had drunk a cup of wine, he would become inflamed. He said to her, 'Submit to me.' She would then take her god from her bosom and said to him, 'Worship this.'

J. "He would say to her, 'Am I not a Jew?'

K. "She would say to him, 'What difference does it make to you? Do they ask anything more from you than that you bare yourself?' But he did not know that that was how this idol was served.

L. "'And not only so, but I shall not let you do so until you deny the Torah of Moses, your master!'

M. "As it is said, 'They went in to Baal-peor and separated themselves unto that shame, and their abominations were according as they loved' (Hos. 9:10)."

**XI.24**

A. "And they slew the kings of Midian, beside the rest of them that were slain . . . Balaam also, the son of Beor, they slew with the sword" (Num. 31:8):

B. *What was he doing there anyhow?*
C. Said R. Yohanan, "He went to collect a salary on account of the twenty-four thousand Israelites whom he had brought down' [Cf. Num. 25:1-9]."
D. *Mar Zutra b. Tobiah said Rab said, "That is in line with what people say: 'When the camel went to ask for horns, the ears that he had they cut off him.'"*

**XI.25**
A. "Balaam also, the son of Beor, the soothsayer, [did the children of Israel slay with the sword]" (Josh. 13:22):
B. A soothsayer? He was a prophet!
C. Said R. Yohanan, "At first he was a prophet, but in the end, a mere soothsayer."
D. *Said R. Pappa, "This is in line with what people say: 'She who came from princes and rulers played the whore with a carpenter.'"*

### 2. *Targumic versions of the donkey's speech in the Balaam narrative*

*Targum Neofiti* reads: "Where are you going, wicked Balaam? You lack understanding! What! If you are not able to curse me who am an unclean beast, and die in this world and who do not enter the world to come, how much less are you able to curse the sons of Abraham, of Isaac, and Jacob, on whose account the world was created from the beginning, and for whose merits it is remembered before them? And with regard to your having taken undue advantage of these men (saying): This is not my donkey; she is borrowed: — am I not the donkey upon which you have ridden from your youth until this day?"

*Targum Pseudo-Jonathan:* "Woe to you, Balaam, (you are) lacking knowledge, for I, an unclean animal, who will die in this world and who will not enter the world to come, you are unable to curse me; how much less the children of Abraham, Isaac, and Jacob, by whose merits the world was created! But you are going to curse them? And so you have deceived these people, to whom you said: 'This ass does not belong to me. It is a loan to me, while my horses are resting in the meadow.' Am I not your ass on which you have ridden from your youth until this very day? Behold, have I profited from you sexually?"

---

## C. Conclusions about the Day of the Lord (3:1-13)

Our author now returns to the theme of the coming of "the day of the Lord" and the concomitant judgment. He has already pointed out that he has seen it in the Transfiguration (1:16-18), that the Scriptures bear witness to it (1:19-21), and that there are numerous historical narratives that show that God can and does judge the wicked while delivering the righteous (2:1-10a). Now, after his denunciation of the false teachers (2:10b-22), he is ready to move back to his argument and deal head-on with the denial of God's judgment that the teachers he opposes are using to justify their lifestyle.

> [1]*Dear friends, this is now my second letter to you. I have written both of them as reminders to stimulate you to wholesome thinking.* [2]*I want you to recall the words spoken in the past by the holy prophets and the command given by our Lord and Savior through your apostles.*

**1** The first section of this concluding part of our author's argument is a transition. 2 Peter signals this transition with an address to his readers: "dear friends" (or "loved ones"). He will use this address three more times in this chapter, in each case signaling that a new section is beginning. In using this address he follows Jude (3, 17, 20), 1 Peter (2:11 and 4:12), and 1 John. Paul also uses this address, but relatively rarely (Rom 12:19; 1 Cor 10:14; 2 Cor 7:1; 12:19; Phil 2:12; 4:1), although both he and James use the address "my beloved brothers and sisters." The use of this address in this verse in 2 Peter is probably influenced by its use in Jude 17:

| *2 Peter 3:1-2* | *Jude 17* |
|---|---|
| Dear friends, . . . I want you to recall the words spoken in the past by the holy prophets and the command given by our Lord and Savior through your apostles. | But, dear friends, remember what the apostles of our Lord Jesus Christ foretold. |

What we see is that 2 Peter and Jude have no fewer than five terms in common. What 2 Peter has done is fill out the more compressed statement of Jude.

Our author informs us that 2 Peter is his second letter to this group. If this is the "second" letter, what was the "first"? There are four theories about the identity of the "first" letter: (1) 2 Peter 1 (with 2 Pet 1:15 promising a second letter and 2 Pet 3 being the second letter),[1] (2) Jude,[2] (3) 1 Pe-

1. Initially proposed in another form by Hugo Grotius, the modern proponent of this form of the hypothesis is M. McNamara, "The Unity of Second Peter: A Reconsideration," *Scripture* 12 (1960) 13-19.

2. T. V. Smith, *Petrine Controversies in Early Christianity* (WUNT 2.15; Tübingen: J. C. B. Mohr, 1985), 74-78.

ter,[3] and (4) a lost letter.[4] The first and second hypotheses fall on the basis that they fail to understand the structure of 2 Peter. The first fails to see the rhetorical unity of the letter, and both fail to see that Jude continues to be used in the first part of 2 Peter 3, not least in 2 Pet 3:1-2. This hurts the first hypothesis in that it splits the use of Jude into two different letters, and it hurts the second hypothesis in that it has a "second letter" referring to a part of itself as the first letter.

The more serious contenders are 1 Peter and a lost letter. One could in all fairness describe 1 Peter as a "reminder to stimulate you to wholesome thinking," although it is a quite different type of reminder than 2 Peter. While, *contra* Green, it is not clear that the author of 1 Peter knows his addressees personally while the author of 2 Peter does not (probably neither letter is addressed to people the author knows personally), the strength of the argument for 1 Peter being the "first" letter is not (a) overlaps in vocabulary and style (there is hardly any), nor (b) the borrowing of ideas from 1 Peter by 2 Peter (there is little evidence of such borrowing), but (c) the idea that a later pseudepigrapher (or the writer of a Petrine testament) would have happily attached his writing to a known writing of the person in whose name he is writing. Bauckham argues that he did this at this place because (1) he was probably from a Petrine circle in Rome and thus Peter was his inspiration, (2) he was probably writing to the same group to which 1 Peter is addressed, and (3) having gone through the long digression at the end of ch. 2, he now needs to refer to Peter again so that he can give a prophecy in his name. The problem with the hypothesis is that Bauckham is not only correct in not discovering direct borrowing from 1 Peter in 2 Peter, but also (1) 2 Peter is far more Hellenistic in style and vocabulary than 1 Peter, (2) 2 Peter makes a very different use of the OT than does 1 Peter (1 Peter quotes texts while 2 Peter refers only to narratives and then only as the narratives were known in Second Temple Judaism), and (3) 2 Peter has a very different topic than 1 Peter (false teachers rather than standing firm under persecution). Thus it is not clear that appealing to 1 Peter would give any support to the authenticity of 2 Peter as Petrine, especially if the reader were a thoughtful person reading both letters in Greek.

Nor is it clear that 2 Peter is written to the same addressees as 1 Peter; it could be, since 1 Peter is written to churches in an area of the Hellenistic world, but many places in the Hellenistic world would fit the type

3. G. H. Boobyer, "The Indebtedness of 2 Peter to 1 Peter," in A. J. B. Higgins, ed., *New Testament Essays: Studies in Memory of T. W. Manson* (Manchester: University of Manchester Press, 1959), 36-39; Neyrey, *2 Peter, Jude,* 229; Bauckham, *Jude, 2 Peter,* 285-86; Vögtle, *Der Judasbrief, der zweite Petrusbrief,* 212.

4. Green, *Second Peter and Jude,* 123-24.

of address we have in 2 Peter. We would never have imagined that 2 Peter was written to the northwest quadrant of Asia Minor unless we had 1 Peter (see the discussion of addressees in the Introduction, pp. 132-33). Thus the hypothesis of the same readership has to assume itself to establish itself. Unless 2 Peter is indeed trying to hook onto the established reputation of an earlier letter of Peter (whether or not he is writing to the same group), it makes little sense to refer to this letter as a second letter to the same audience.

As for the need at this point to give a prophecy in the name of Peter, we will note that the prophecy is not given in the name of Peter, but in the name of an unnamed group called "your apostles." If this were the reason for a reference to 1 Peter, the text should read, "which I spoke to you." Therefore, even if 2 Pet 3:1 reflects a pseudepigrapher trying to gain authenticity, appealing to such a different letter as "his" first letter would seem a poor way to do so since the contrasts would be so obvious and thus would imply inauthenticity rather than support 2 Peter's authenticity (as the modern debate about the authenticity of 2 Peter shows). It seems to us, then, that the most reasonable hypothesis is to admit that we do not know to what letter our author is referring, and that most likely he is referring to a letter that he did previously send to the addressees of 2 Peter, a letter that we do not have.

Whatever the first letter was, the purpose of both letters is to serve as "reminders to stimulate you to wholesome thinking." The concept of reminder has already been discussed in the comment on 2 Pet 1:12-15. The points we made there were that (1) reminding was a polite way of stating a teaching in that it assumed that the reader was already instructed rather than uninstructed and thus ascribed a more honorable status to the reader, and (2) reminding is an important function of oral mnemonic culture in that without having books available that one could read oneself it was important that critical stories and ideas be repeated, whether through having a letter such as this one read aloud in church or through having a teacher frequently repeat a teaching. The recitation of the events of Exodus during the Passover ritual and the recitation of the events of the last supper during the celebration of the Eucharist/Lord's Supper are examples of this repetition. Thus 2 Peter will remind addressees of the truth of the Parousia of Jesus and the final judgment, while the teachers he opposes have willfully forgotten important facts of the story of God's interaction with the world (3:5), which forgetting our author wants to protect the readers from falling into (3:8).

The goal of the reminder is "wholesome thinking." Neyrey argues that this phrase means "correct understanding." It is true that the word translated "thinking" does mean "understanding" or "meaning," that is, the product of the thinking process more than the process itself.[5] But what does "wholesome" understanding or thinking indicate? The term translated "wholesome" means "pure" or "unmixed." It was often applied morally to mean "sincere" or "honest" or "pure" in the moral sense (Phil 1:10). Philo uses it to indicate pure or true knowledge versus the apparent or false knowledge of sense perception (*Leg. alleg.* 1.88-89; *De ebrietate* 101; 189; *De migratione Abrahami* 222). More importantly we find in *T. Benj.* 6:5 that the "good mind" (our word for thinking) has a "pure disposition"; *1 Clem.* 32:1 appeals for "sincere thought." Thus the goal in our passage is that the readers may come to pure or sincere understandings. This will contrast with the thinking of the "scoffers" that is distorted by "evil desires." They "deliberately forget" things, which the readers should instead remember. The sense of "wholesome," then, is moral, but not just moral. It is undistorted thinking, whether the distortion be moral or volitional or simply a lack of information. Most importantly, it is thinking that accords with the teaching of the prophets and "your apostles" rather than that which is characterized by the distortions of the teachers our author opposes.

**2** Therefore, the words that our author wants his readers to remember are those spoken "in the past by the holy prophets" and those spoken more recently by their apostles. What are these words? First, we notice that the same two groups are referred to here as are referred to in 2 Pet 1:16-21, where the eyewitness testimony of the apostles confirms the prophetic word of the OT prophets (who for our author likely included the authors of such works as *1 Enoch*). The "holy prophets," then, are not the prophets active in the Jesus movement[6] but the prophets of Israel, referred to in a way that we also see in Wisd 11:1 (referring to Moses); Luke 1:70 (a general reference to "his holy prophets of long ago"); and Acts 3:21 (Peter's speech refers to the promise of restoration "as he promised long ago through his holy prophets"). It is therefore fitting to refer to their words as spoken "in the past" or "spoken beforehand," for that is just what they were with reference to the time of Jesus and the later Jesus movement. Are there specific prophecies to which this general statement is referring? In an earlier book, but not in his commentary, Vögtle refers to such passages as Isa 5:18-20; Jer 5:12-24; Ezek 12:22; Amos 9:10; Zeph 1:12; Mal 2:17 in which judgment is pronounced on those who mock or

5. Johannes Behm, *"dianoia," TDNT* 4:965.

6. Although the idea is quite attractive and has the support of Sidebottom, *James, Jude, and 2 Peter,* 118, who cites "the holy apostles and prophets" in Eph 3:5 as evidence, it is probably wrong. In Eph 3:5 the apostles are named first, and the apostles and prophets are grouped together, so it is clear that prophets and apostles from the same community are meant.

deny the delayed judgment of God.[7] Quite possibly our author does have some such specific prophecies in mind, but it is also clear that he does not feel it necessary to be more specific than to give his general statement. If one knows the OT, one knows that it prophesies that judgment will eventually come.

The second group referred to are "your apostles" who passed on "the command given by our Lord and Savior." The expression is awkward in Greek, but that is because our author wants to make clear that the command originated with Jesus and that the apostles were giving it in a secondary sense as representatives of Jesus (which, of course, is just what "apostle" means, "one sent as a delegate" — in the first century this term was not a purely religious term). Jesus is presented in authoritative terms, since both "Lord" and "Savior" are titles of sovereignty that he has taken over from Caesar. Again 2 Peter is general and does not make clear which command he is thinking about. The term "command" would predispose us to ethical commands or to the command to "watch" and be prepared for his coming. But it could be that our author is referring to the teaching of Jesus in general as a command, since in other places the good news (or, "the truth") is referred to as something that must be obeyed (e.g., Rom 6:17; Gal 5:7; 2 Thess 1:8; 1 Pet 1:2; cf. Acts 17:30). In Jesus the rule of God became manifest in this world, and this manifestation of the rule of God brings with it a demand that people turn from their way and submit to God's way, that is, obey the good news and submit to the way of life that it proclaims. While often missing from contemporary preaching, this is the message of the New Testament.

Yet who are "your apostles" to whom our author refers? Many commentators assume that this group is the "college" of apostles, that is, the original apostles thought of as a group, who are now being referred to as the apostles of the whole church. That this is a change from Jude's "the apostles of our Lord Jesus Christ" (Jude 17) is viewed as evidence for the post-apostolic date of 2 Peter, as is the pairing of apostles and prophets.[8] However, the wording makes this interpretation suspect. First, it would sound strange for Peter to be referring to the whole group of apostles as "your" apostles, for it seems to separate him from them. Late-first- and early-second-century works refer to "the apostles" and sometimes group them with the OT prophets (2 *Clem.* 14:2; Polycarp, *Phil.* 6:3), but never to "your" or "our" apostles.

7. Anton Vögtle, *Das neue Testament und die Zukunft des Kosmos* (Düsseldorf: Patmos, 1970), 125-26. Note that Vögtle sees his commentary as correcting this earlier book on 2 Peter 3, as he notes in n. 21 on p. 215 of his commentary.

8. E.g., Vögtle, *Der Judasbrief, der zweite Petrusbrief,* 215.

Second, given that (1) the group of apostles was much wider than the Twelve and even than the Twelve plus Paul, including as it did Barnabas, Andronicus, Junia, and others, and (2) the function of apostles according to Paul was to plant churches (e.g., Rom 15:18-20; i.e., they were "missionaries" or "church planters" in our contemporary language), the reference makes the best sense as referring to that group of missionaries (and Paul and other such apostles seem to have traveled in groups rather than as individuals) that had evangelized the area in which the addressees lived and formed the communities of which they were a part. Bauckham thinks that Paul was one of those who had evangelized in their area (due to 2 Pet 3:15).[9]

This is, of course, quite possible, although all that the reference indicates is that Paul had written them a letter and that they knew some of the letters of Paul, which could be true even if Paul had never come near their area (as was the case with the Italian believers in Rome at the time of the writing of Romans). What we do know is (1) that some missionaries ("apostles") had evangelized in the area of our addressees, (2) that in the eyes of our author they had accurately passed on "the command of our Lord and Savior," and (3) that these missionaries were apparently no longer in the area (Paul moved on as soon as a community of followers of Jesus was established, spending only three months to three years doing this, unlike much missionary practice today). The result was that their "command" was something to be "recalled" along with the words of the "holy prophets," the writings of whom they probably read in their gatherings from week to week.

> [3]*First of all, you must understand that in the last days scoffers will come, scoffing and following their own evil desires.* [4]*They will say, "Where is this 'coming' he promised? Ever since our fathers died, everything goes on as it has since the beginning of creation."* [5]*But they deliberately forget that long ago by God's word the heavens existed and the earth was formed out of water and by water.* [6]*By these waters also the world of that time was deluged and destroyed.* [7]*By the same word the present heavens and earth are reserved for fire, being kept for the day of judgment and destruction of ungodly men.*

**3** What aspect of the teaching of the prophets and apostles did these followers of Jesus need to recall? Naturally, one cannot take apart the teaching of Jesus and remember only bits and pieces of it without doing damage to the whole. But in the context in which he was writing,

9. Bauckham, *Jude, 2 Peter,* 288.

2 Peter believes that the most important thing that they need to "understand" or "know" (or, to use his previous terminology, "recall") is the predictions of "scoffers." The time reference for the appearance of these "scoffers" is "the last days," which expresses Jude's "in the last times" in the more standard language of the Jewish Scriptures. It appears in Jer 30:24 (LXX 37:24); Ezek 38:16; Dan 2:28; Hos 3:5; Mic 4:1, in each case indicating the time when God will come in judgment and restoration (although the various OT prophets are not necessarily referring to the same time). It was used by the late-first-century and early-second-century church in a similar manner (*Barn.* 12:9; 16:5), as well as to refer to the time of the manifestation of Jesus (i.e., birth to ascension), a time that was, from their perspective, already past (2 *Clem.* 14:2; Hermas, *Sim.* 9:12:3). Thus for the early Jesus movement they were living in "the last days," since they were living in the age inaugurated by the coming of Jesus, even though there had been other periods of judgment (e.g., A.D. 70) that could also be referred to by this designation. What is common to all of these references is that "the last days" was a time of judgment and salvation, and that precisely in that time "scoffers" would come. They mock the idea that such a "coming" of God in judgment and salvation will happen, but their existence is in itself evidence that his readers are living in the age when that "coming" will take place, a time that the appearance of Jesus had inaugurated.

"Scoffers" are mockers or those who insult others, which means that they are people who challenge the honor of someone or something. In this case the honor challenge will be made against God or, as Neyrey puts it, "the Lord's state visit."[10] What is characteristic of them is their motivation, for they are "following their own evil desires" (more accurately, they are "living according to their own desires," for, as we have noted previously, the issue is not specific "evil desires" but the fact that their life is controlled or directed by their desires in general rather than by God).

**4** The content of the insult or mockery is two-part. The first part is a question, "Where is this 'coming' [Parousia] he promised?" not unlike the question that was thrown at Jeremiah ("Where is the word of the LORD? Let it now be fulfilled!" Jer 17:15) and other OT prophets. The second part is the observation behind the mocking question, "Ever since our fathers died, everything goes on as it has since the beginning of creation."

The theme of promise occurs here for the third time in 2 Peter. In 1:4 we read about "great and precious [or honorable] promises," among which are surely those of the return of Christ and his manifesting his rule

10. Neyrey, 2 *Peter, Jude,* 227-29.

over the earth, promises that motivate his followers to live according to his standards. Our author picks up that reference by using exactly the same word for "promise" here.[11] The promise in question is not the OT promise of God's protection of Israel ("Where is [Israel's] God?" Ps 79:10 [LXX 78:10]; 115:2 [LXX 113:10]; Joel 2:17; "Where is YHWH your God?" Mic 7:10) or of God's just rule ("Where is the God of justice?" Mal 2:17), but the specific NT promise of "his coming" or "his Parousia." While this "coming" could be Jesus' coming (i.e., the promise of his return referred to in Acts 1:11 and multiple times by Paul, although only in Matt 24:3, 27 does Jesus refer to it, whether that passage is viewed as referring to what Paul means by the Parousia in 1 Thess 2:19; 4:15, or whether that passage refers to the "visitation" of God and vindication of the "Son of Man" that came in A.D. 70, as argued by N. T. Wright), more likely our author is thinking of it as God's coming (promised by Jesus in his announcing that the rule or kingdom of God has come), for that fits the focus in our passage on divine judgment in both the time of Noah and the coming final judgment.

This focus on God is, among other things, what has convinced Bauckham[12] that 2 Peter is following a Jewish apocalypse that is partially preserved in *1 Clem.* 23:3 and *2 Clem.* 11:2-4, and to which *2 Clem.* 16:3 may also belong (although its subject matter does not show up until 2 Pet 3:10).[13]

| | |
|---|---|
| *1 Clem.* 23:3 | [In a context of discussing double-mindedness] May this Scripture be far removed from us that says: "How miserable are those who have heard these things from the time of our <u>parents</u>, and look! We have grown old, and none of these things has happened to us." |
| *2 Clem.* 11:2 | For the prophetic word also says, "How miserable are those of two minds, who doubt in their hearts, who say, |

11. The verbal form of the word appears in 2 Pet 2:19 for the empty promising of the false teachers. They promise freedom but are themselves slaves.

12. Bauckham, *Jude, 2 Peter,* 283-85. He suggests that J. B. Lightfoot may have been right in his work on the apostolic fathers in guessing that the Jewish work is the *Book of Eldad and Modad,* which is definitely cited in Hermas, *Vis.* 2:3:4, and thus was in use in the church at the time of the writing of *1 Clement;* but the content of that work is otherwise unknown. Yet Bauckham continues that since we know so little about the content of this book, Lightfoot's guess is just that, an unsupported guess. Note that a version of this hypothesis was suggested first by Daniel von Allmen, "L'apocalyptique juive et le retard de la parousie en II Pierre 3:1-13," *Revue de Théologie et Philosophie* 16 (1966) 255-74.

13. Bauckham includes *2 Clem.* 16:3 only because (1) it is close enough in content to 2 Pet 3:10 to indicate a common source, and (2) economy of hypothesis suggests that hypothesizing Jewish apocalypse in common is more likely than hypothesizing two.

'We heard these things long ago, in the time of our parents, but though we have waited day after day, we have seen none of them.'"

2 Pet 3:4 *They will say, "Where is this 'coming' he promised? Ever since our fathers died, everything goes on as it has since the beginning of creation."*

2 *Clem.* 16:3 But you know that the day of judgment is already coming like a blazing furnace, and some of the heavens and all of the earth will melt like lead in the fire; and then the hidden and secret works that people have done will be made visible.

2 Pet 3:10 *But the day of the Lord will come like a thief. The heavens will disappear with a roar; the elements will be destroyed by fire, and the earth and everything in it will be laid bare.*

What evidence can we find for Bauckham's thesis? First, both *1 Clement* and *2 Clement* are referring to a source that they variously identify as a "Scripture" (i.e., a written document) or a "prophetic word" (which could be either oral or written), so a source is clearly involved. Second, the content of *1 Clem.* 23:3 and *2 Clem.* 11:2 is similar, so they are probably referring to the same source. Third, the general concern of both is that prophecies made to their parents have remained unfulfilled. This is the same concern that we find in 2 Peter. Fourth, there is only one word that these first two passages have in common with 2 Peter, which is "parents." There is more verbal agreement between *2 Clem.* 16:3 and 2 Pet 3:10, but even there few of the key terms are held in common. Our conclusion is that since the topic of unfulfilled promise/unfulfilled prophecy was one that was found as early as the OT and since the verbal overlap is so limited, while it is possible that Bauckham is correct, he does not have enough evidence to prove that there must be a common source.[14]

These teachers, then, argue in common with a number of Jewish precedents that the promise of divine judgment is chimerical in that "Ever since our fathers died, everything goes on as it has since the beginning of creation." The creational reference will be important to our author, for he will pick it up in the next two verses, but the critical time reference is the one made to "the fathers" (unlike the two references in *1* and *2 Clement,* the text of 2 Peter, has no "our," so the NIV translation is to some extent misleading). The usual meaning of "the fathers" in Jewish literature is the OT worthies, that is, the righteous men of the OT period, and particularly the patriarchs. The same usage was normal in the writings of the Jesus

14. This is also the conclusion of Vögtle, *Der Judasbrief, der zweite Petrustrief,* 216.

movement (John 7:22; Acts 13:32; Rom 9:5; Heb 1:1; also *Barn.* 5:7; 14:1) — in fact, Bauckham admits that our passage is the only probable exception to this rule.[15] However, he and most commentators believe that this reference is to the death of the original generation of the followers of Jesus, or at least of the most important leaders of that generation.[16] Bauckham's argument is that for followers of Jesus, including the false teachers, the advent of Jesus had surely made significant change and therefore this term must be being transferred to the leaders of the first post-Jesus generation.

Given that there is no evidence that any other writer through the mid–second century made this transfer of the title "the fathers," this claim can be sustained only if it does not make sense to take this term in the normal Jewish sense. And, in fact, that normal Jewish sense does make sense. The promises being referred to are the promises of judgment. The "coming" is most likely the coming of God in judgment, although of course in the expectation of the Jesus movement the fully vindicated Jesus would also be part of that "coming" and Jesus would become God's regent upon earth. The origin of the promise was in the OT, which is the basis of the previous part of this argument, that found in 2 Pet 1:19-21. Thus it makes good sense to say that "since those OT worthies the prophets ["the fathers"] have died,[17] everything goes on as it has since creation — there has been no final judgment." The next verse will pick up on just such an assertion by providing evidence from the OT that that assertion was not even true within the OT narrative. It is this understanding of "the fathers," therefore, that we will assume in the rest of our discussion.

Parenthetically we should comment that even if one takes the position that the "fathers" are the leaders of the first generation of the Jesus movement, it does not follow that (1) they have died a long time ago, or (2) the writer has made a slip in putting a reference to them as "the fathers" on the lips of Peter. First, there certainly would have been some concern as the first generation died and the words of Jesus that seemed to

15. Bauckham, *Jude, 2 Peter,* 290. He cites 2 *Clem.* 19:4 as a possible exception, but thinks that the usual meaning is the more likely. See Gottlob Schrenk, *"patēr," TDNT* 5:976-77.

16. For example, Bauckham, *Jude, 2 Peter,* 290-91; Vögtle, *Der Judasbrief, der zweite Petrusbrief,* 216, almost without argument other than a footnote that mentions that commentators such as Green, *Second Peter and Jude,* 128-29, who support Petrine authorship, take this to mean the OT fathers.

17. The use of "fallen asleep" as a euphemism for "died" (the NIV drops the euphemism and simply translates it "died") is common in the literature of our period (Matt 27:52; John 11:11; Acts 7:60; 13:36; 1 Cor 7:39; 11:30; 15:6, 18, 20, 51; 1 Thess 4:13-15). See further R. E. Bailey, "Is 'Sleep' the Proper Biblical Term for the Intermediate State?" *ZNW* 55 (1964) 161-67, who points out that this terminology is a euphemism and does not imply any particular theory of the afterlife or resurrection.

put his coming before the death of the first generation were not fulfilled (e.g., Matt 16:28 par. Mark 9:1 par. Luke 9:27; Matt 24:34 par. Mark 13:30 par. Luke 21:32; John 21:22-23), but there is no evidence that this continued to be a problem once the date had clearly passed. As it became clear that few were left of the original generation, expectation naturally built, but once these had died, either one gave up the faith due to "unfulfilled prophecy" or one came up with an explanation and got on with life. The tension would be *before* that time when "the fathers" had died, not *after* it. Thus there is no indication in the reference to their being dead that they have been dead a long time, just that they are dead.

Second, Peter is referring to the death of "the fathers" as his opponents would, and they would naturally refer to them as "the fathers." Such an expression does not mean that everyone from that generation is dead. It simply means that from the perspective of the speaker the bulk of the leaders of that generation are dead, and there is still no indication that anything cataclysmic is about to happen. There is no reason why this charge could not be thrown into the face of an aging, but still alive, member of that generation. And there is no reason why Peter himself could not express it in this way, either as a prophecy (although this is a prophecy that someone else, not Peter, has given, since it is something that he is reminding them of) or as a reference to the words of his opponents. In other words, this expression does not appear to us decisive either way in arguing for either Peter as the author of the letter or a pseudepigrapher, even granting that the reference is to the first generation of the followers of Jesus. However, as we argued above, there is no evidence other than this passage that the expression "the fathers" was ever used in the first century or so of the Christian era for anyone other than the worthies of the OT, and it is that meaning that we believe fits best with the argument of the next two verses.

**5** The charge that the promises of God have gone unfulfilled is a charge against the honor of God. Our author is quick to bring evidence to the contrary. The "scoffers" are forgetting something: they are forgetting their biblical history. But are they forgetting "deliberately," or is their forgetting the result of their maintaining their position (much as we often overlook data to the contrary when we are focused on our own position)? Here there is an interesting split along continental lines, with most North American translations and commentators following the understanding of the NIV, "they deliberately forget,"[18] and most English and Continental commentators (except the French) arguing for "in maintaining this, they forget" (Bauckham) or "for those who want this to be true, the fact is hid-

18. KJV, RSV, NRSV, NIV, TEV, most French versions, Bigg, Mayor, Moffatt, Spicq, etc.

den that" (Vögtle).[19] The grammar is not very clear, but the grammatical indicators that there are seem to favor the participle "willing" ("deliberately" in the NIV) having an object "this" (i.e., the position cited in the previous verse) and therefore the translation, "since they want/desire this [position to be true], they forget these things," which, when smoothed out, is what we have designated above as the English–Continental position. In other words, the forgetting is not deliberate, as if the "scoffers" were conscious that they were suppressing data, but it is a result of their desire that it be true that there is no evidence for a final judgment.

The part of biblical history that they are forgetting is the narrative of creation and the flood. First comes creation. The time is "long ago." The agent is God's word, which should not surprise us since Gen 1:3-30 repeatedly says, "And God said," and then notes that the event happened. This theme is picked up in Ps 33:6 ("By the word of the Lord were the heavens made . . ."); 148:5; Wisd 9:1 ("O God . . . who has made all things by your word"); Heb 11:3 ("the universe was formed at God's command" [NIV] or "the worlds were prepared by the word of God" [NRSV]); and numerous other Jewish and Christian writers stretching out into the second century. Indeed, as Neyrey points out, in Philo's world creative power was seen as one of God's two powers, the other one being executive power, the authority to rule and judge, which we will encounter in our next verse.[20] In other words, our author is defending the orthodox doctrine of God, as it was expressed in his day.

The agent (God's word) creates "the heavens . . . and the earth," which is language describing creation that is straight from Genesis. In fact, most of the references to creation cited above describe the heavens and then the earth (although they do not always name it "earth" but may cite parts of the earth instead), following the Genesis narrative. These two parts of the universe were formed "out of water and by water." Here we again have, not a reference to such Greek philosophers as Thales of Miletus, who argued that of the four elements water is the basic one and everything is therefore made out of water,[21] but a clear reference to the Genesis creation

19. Einheitsübersetzung, revised Elberfelder, Bauckham, Neyrey, Vögtle, Kelly, etc.

20. Neyrey, *2 Peter, Jude,* 233-34. He cites Philo, *Vit. Mos.* 2.99; *De plantatione* 85–89; *De fuga et inventione* 101; *De Abrahamo* 121–22.

21. Rainer Nickel, *Lexikon der antiken Literatur* (Düsseldorf/Zürich: Artemis und Winkler, 1999), 701. Thales' contribution was to argue that everything had a material cause, and the basic matter was water. This position would be reflected after the time of 2 Peter in *Clem. Hom.* 11:24:1, "And now from inferior things learn the cause of all, reasoning that water makes all things, and water receives the production of its movement from spirit, and the spirit has its beginning from the God of all. And thus you ought to have reasoned, in order that by reason you might attain to God, that, knowing your ori-

**Ancient Hebrew Conception of the Universe**

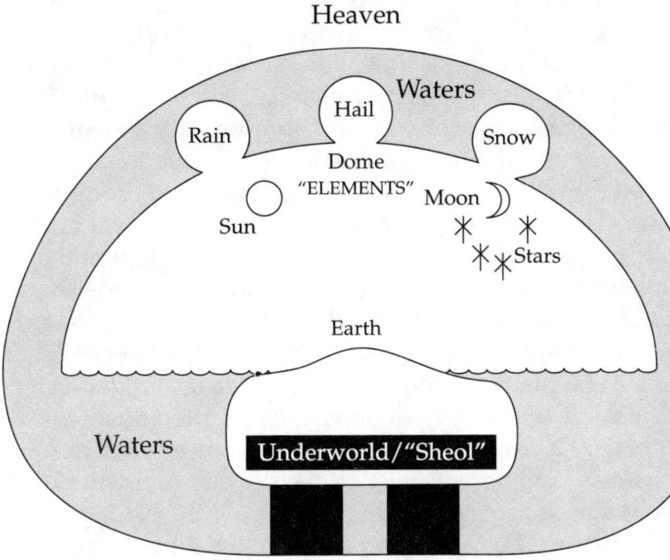


Foundations/Pillars of the Earth

story. That is, in that story we do not start with *creatio ex nihilo* (as, e.g., Heb 11:3 appears to do), but with a title verse (Gen 1:1) and then a description of a watery chaos (Gen 1:2) upon which light breaks (Gen 1:3-5) and from which heaven (by means of the establishment of an "expanse" [NIV], "dome" [NRSV], or "space" [NLV] between the waters above the "sky" and the waters below) and earth (by means of gathering the waters below the sky into seas so that dry land appears) are separated (Gen 1:6-10). The model would look something like the figure above, although we are only dealing with the waters, the firmament, and the heavenly bodies.[22] With this picture in mind, 2 Peter's "out of water" is easy to understand, but his "by means of water" is less easy. Because this is a creation picture, this

---

gin, and being born again by the firstborn water, you may be constituted heir of the parents who have begotten you to incorruption."

22. Adapted from Andy M. Reimer, "In the Beginning . . . Lessons Learned in Teaching Genesis 1 to Evangelical College Students," *Canadian Evangelical Review* 29 (2005) 35, who in turn adapted it from K. I. Parker, *Text and Tradition: A Guide to the Old Testament* (Burlington, ON: Trinity, 1990), 48. Remember that this is only a model that can be pieced together from data in the various texts referring to the Hebrew worldview. It is assumed by many writers of Scripture, but it is never taught. But then our scientific model is also a model pieced together from lots of data. It is assumed by moderns, and may be more helpful to us in going about our business, but that does not make it more than a model.

phrase does not mean that the earth lives from rain,[23] but that in being gathered within its bounds the water was also the means of forming the earth or making it appear. None of this would sound unusual to anyone who was familiar with Genesis's creation narrative. Nor is this part of the story something that the "scoffers" would necessarily dispute, for they too can refer to "the beginning of creation," presumably a creation by God. Their point is that nothing has changed since this creation.

**6** 2 Peter now continues the story of the world, bringing in God's second power (i.e., executive power: rule and judgment), and pointing out that it is the second assumption in the "scoffers'" argument that is out of step with reality. He moves on to the time of Noah and underlines the narrative point that these same waters that had been used by God to form the creation were used by God to destroy the creation. The Greek text reads "by these." The NIV's interpretation, "waters," referring to the waters above and the waters below the sky, is one viable interpretation. Other suggestions have been: "because of which [heaven and earth]," "by means of which [heavens]," and "by means of which [water and word]." Only the last of these is a reasonable alternative to the NIV translation.[24] Bauckham argues that since the Greek text later says "deluged by water," a reference to water alone at this point would be less likely and that a reference to water and the word would mean that the word is referred to in all three verses in our section. This interpretation is not only attractive but the fact that the Greek word order puts God's word last in v. 5 also makes it possible.

On the other hand, Gen 7:11 describes two groups of waters, those above the sky in heaven and those gathered off the earth into "the springs of the great deep," combining to form the deluge (this picture is picked up in the retelling of the story in *1 Enoch* 83:3 in which the heavens collapse onto the earth). Given that our author appears to be following the Genesis narrative rather closely, we are immediately inclined toward this latter interpretation, which would make the second reference to water pleonastic, but useful in that he wants to stress water as the agent of destruction. Yet given that our author wants to stress divine agency, not just the water–fire contrast, it still makes more sense to argue that he is picking up both water and word in the phrase "by these," especially since, as we noted above, "word" is the nearest antecedent. This would explain the later reference to water. Thus we would translate the verse, "By means of this very water and word the world of that time was deluged by water and destroyed."

23. Green, *Second Peter and Jude*, 129-30. Green, however, may be right that part of 2 Peter's target is the Epicurean theory of constant self-sustained evolution.

24. See the discussion in Bauckham, *Jude, 2 Peter*, 298. So also Vögtle, *Der Judasbrief, der zweite Petrusbrief*, 226.

What was destroyed was "the world of that time," which contrasts with "the present heavens and earth" that are mentioned in the next verse. While the focus of the destruction is certainly on the human beings inhabiting that world (as any reader of Genesis would agree), the destruction extended to the whole "world" as the merging waters undid the work of Gen 1:6-10, returning the creation to a watery chaos and concomitantly destroying those living things that were created after Gen 1:10. As our text says, "the world of that time was deluged by water" (the term "deluged" being unique in the NT, but used in both Wisd 10:4 and Josephus, *Ant.* 5.566) and destroyed, not meaning, of course, that it was totally annihilated (our author, like any reader of Genesis, would know that not only the people and animals in the ark survive, but so do fish and at least some plants that are outside the ark, for a fresh-plucked olive leaf (Gen 8:11) indicates that the waters have receded to the treetops), but that it was largely destroyed, sufficient for the purposes of the judgment. This observation of the use of language will be important when we come to looking at the parallel destruction in 2 Pet 3:10.

So the "scoffers" have forgotten something. Yes, there was an original creation, and, yes, the world appears to be running quite well now along the lines laid down in the creation, but, no, there is not a full continuity. We are in the second age of the world, an age that is demarcated from the first age by God's judgment in the flood, just as our age will be demarcated from the next by God's judgment with fire. Things have not continued as they were from the beginning of the creation. There was a great discontinuity, after which God again had to separate the waters, restraining chaos and returning the world to its original order. Forgetting this discontinuity is quite serious, for it has allowed the "scoffers" to forget that there is a precedent for the coming judgment. Their first assumption has proved false.

7 Our author continues his argument, drawing his conclusion but at the same time showing both continuity and discontinuity with creation and the flood. The word of the Lord created the world, that word destroyed it once (certainly the implication of v. 6, and in our view probably the explicit referent of "through these"/"by these"), and that same word (our author makes it very clear that it is the *same* word) is now causing it to be reserved or kept for fire. The thought is similar to that in *1 Clem.* 27:4, "By the word of his majesty he established all things, and by his word he is able to destroy them." In contrast to 2 Peter, Clement does not mention the deluge, and so he also lacks the water–fire contrast. But while his application is different, he, along with 2 Peter, views God's word as the force behind both creation and judgment (mentioned by Clement in *1 Clem.* 27:1).

It is important to our author that God is the cause of both of these aspects. That clearly separates him from Greco-Roman ideas of world conflagration and puts him in the thought world of Jewish concepts of judgment. What the word has done, then, is "reserve" the present heavens and earth (as opposed to "the world of that time" of 2 Pet 3:6, that is, the original creation, and the "new heaven and new earth" — our author is working with a concept of three ages of the world) for fire. The term "reserve" (or "keep" or "treasure up") is somewhat unusual. Usually it is rewards/judgment that is treasured up or reserved for the godly/the world or the ungodly. *Pss. Sol.* 9:5 states that the one who does righteousness stores up life for himself with the Lord, while the ungodly forfeits his life to destruction; *4 Ezra* 7:77 has an angel saying to Ezra, "You have a treasure of works laid up with the Most High," and then goes on to say that the unrighteous will be tortured in a number of ways, one of which is to "see the rewards laid up for" the faithful (7:83) and another that they will "regard the torture that is laid up for themselves in the last days" (7:84). Paul, of course, moves within the same tradition and can write about "storing up wrath against yourself for the day of God's wrath" (Rom 2:5). Philo, in reflecting on Deut 32:34, writes,

> For, just as there are storehouses of good things, so are there also storehouses of evil things with God; as he says in his great song, "Behold, are not these things collected with me, and sealed up in my treasure-houses, against the day of vengeance when their foot shall be tripped up?"
>
> You see then that there are several storehouses of evil things, and only one of good things. For since God is One, so also is his storehouse of good things one likewise. But there are many storehouses of evil things because the wicked are infinite in number. And in this observe the goodness of the true God, He opens the treasure-house of his good things freely, but he binds fast that which contains the evil things. For it is an especial property of God to offer his good things freely and to be beforehand with men in bestowing gifts upon them, but to be slow in bringing evil on them, and Moses, dwelling at length upon the munificent and gracious nature of God, says that not only have his storehouses of evil things been sealed up in all other times, but also when the soul is tripped up in the path of right reason, when it is especially fair that it should be considered worthy of punishment; for he says that, "In the day of vengeance the storehouses of evil things have been sealed up," the sacred word of scripture showing that God does not visit with his vengeance even those who sin against him, immediately, but that he gives them time for repentance, and to remedy and correct their evil conduct. (*Leg. alleg.* 3.105-6)

We could also cite the Targum tradition on Deut 32:34 and Clement of Alexandria, who quotes a tragedy of Pseudo-Sophocles (a Hellenistic Jewish writer) who states, "For there shall come, shall come that point of time,/When Ether, golden-eyed, shall open its store/Of treasured fire; and the devouring flame,/Raging, shall burn all things on earth below,/ And all above." All of these and more refer to a Jewish tradition (although Clement of Alexandria believes his quotation is from a Greek source that stole the idea from Jewish writers) about storehouses of either judgment or reward. It is no wonder, then, that our author, living within this tradition, would use the image of a treasure-house in his choice of verb to speak of the present heavens and earth being reserved for fire.

That fire is the metaphor for the Day of Judgment is also not unusual within the Jewish world, even if the image of world conflagration is unique in 2 Peter in the NT. Just look at Zech 12:6, in which Judah is the fire that judges the nations, and Mal 4:1 (LXX 3:19), in which the Day will be a furnace and the evildoers will be stubble that is set on fire. To these we could add Deut 32:22; Isa 33:11-12; and Zeph 1:18 (and in some manuscripts of the LXX, Isa 34:4). We need to make this point because in Plato's philosophy (and also in that of Seneca and Lucretius) there was the positing of an alternating periodic cycle of the destruction of the world through water and then through fire. Furthermore the Stoics argued (based on Heraclitus) that all matter (and matter is all that there is) was based on fire and would return to fire. Thus the relative stability of the present world will end in conflagration only to regenerate the world again.[25] Now it is quite possible, as we shall see, that 2 Peter, being well educated in the Greco-Roman world, has borrowed some of his language from such philosophers, and from the Stoics in particular. This would make sense if his opponents were influenced by Epicurean philosophy.

On the other hand, it is very clear in 2 Peter that we are not talking about repeating cycles, but about linear history punctuated with divine judgment. We are also not talking about a necessary and natural process (and that is especially the case in Stoic materialism), but about the divine word being the cause of these judgments. Finally, we are not talking about an event that engulfs everyone in the world, but one that affects the ungodly (remember that 2 Peter has argued in the previous chapter that God knows how to spare the godly while judging the ungodly). Whatever the source of his language, our author is moving within the world of Jewish ideas, not that of Platonic or Stoic ideas.[26] If one were to ask why fire

25. On the Stoic theory see Everett Ferguson, *Backgrounds of Early Christianity* (2d ed.; Grand Rapids: William B. Eerdmans, 1993), 335-36.

26. With this judgment both Bauckham, *Jude, 2 Peter,* 300-301, and Vögtle, *Der*

comes after water, he or she should remind themselves that our author has followed the Genesis narratives closely. He is therefore aware of Gen 9:11-16, in which God promises that there will never be another deluge. Yet the prophets speak of judgment by fire. Thus we have here a combination of his knowledge of Genesis and his knowledge of the metaphor of fire as an image of judgment in the prophets and later Jewish tradition.

This impression of the source of his thought is confirmed when we look at the last phrase in the sentence, "being kept for the day of judgment and destruction of ungodly men [*sic*]." The focus of our author is not world history, but the final judgment of ungodly human beings. The heavens and the earth are "kept" (the same verb as that used for the fallen angels in 2 Pet 2:4) for this Day of Judgment. Yet the judgment is not of the creation but of human beings, just as the flood was not about the creation but about human evil. This point needs to be kept in mind as we move through the rest of the passage. Our author is not against the creation since that is something that God made. He does believe that it needs to be purified, but this purification is principally a purification of the human evil that has polluted it. Presumably, as with the deluge, the extent of the destruction by fire will be limited by that needed to wipe out human evil.

> [8]*But do not forget this one thing, dear friends: With the Lord a day is like a thousand years, and a thousand years are like a day.* [9]*The Lord is not slow in keeping his promise, as some understand slowness. He is patient with you, not wanting anyone to perish, but everyone to come to repentance.* [10]*But the day of the Lord will come like a thief. The heavens will disappear with a roar; the elements will be destroyed by fire, and the earth and everything in it will be laid bare.*

Up to this point our author has addressed the issue of whether the world has continued in something of a steady state since creation. He has argued that it has not, that the deluge shows that God has intervened in judgment, and that this fact points to the reality of a coming final judgment. Now our author turns to the second issue raised by the "scoffers," which is the issue of the apparent delay of judgment. This will be his final argument before he draws his conclusions for the community of the followers of Jesus.

**8** Again 2 Peter signals a significant division in the argument with a repletion of the noun of address ("dear friends"; cf. 3:1), an expression underlining a fact that the "scoffers" evidently forget ("this one thing";

---

*Judasbrief, der zweite Petrusbrief,* 227-28, agree. The reader will find more details on the Platonic and Stoic concepts in either of these works, and especially in Bauckham.

cf. "first of all" in 3:3), and another reference to remembering/forgetting ("do not forget"; cf. "reminders," 3:1; "recall," 3:2, "understand," 3:3; and "forget," 3:5). Clearly our author intends to start another line of reasoning in the same general line of thought, another argument that will help his addressees remember what they should not forget. This argument and its implication will last through v. 13, since v. 14 begins a new line of thought with another noun of address.

The data that they are not to forget is Ps 90:4 (LXX 89:4), "For a thousand years in your sight are like a day that has just gone by, or like a watch in the night." In the context of the psalm it has to do with the eternity of God ("from everlasting to everlasting you are God"; Ps 90:2) and the transience of human life ("You sweep men away in the sleep of death . . ."; Ps 90:5). Such a picture of the human condition fits into the ancient view of time in which human time is the now and divine time is the future.[27] This passage was used in a number of ways in the ensuing Jewish (and Christian) tradition: "(1) to define the length of one of the days of creation, (2) to explain why Adam lived for a thousand years after his sin, (3) to calculate the length of the Messiah's day, and (4) to explain the length of the world."[28] Now most of the references to these uses of the passage are in later Jewish literature, but there are some earlier attestations. For instance, *Barn.* 15:4, "Pay attention, children, to what it means that 'he finished in six days.' This means that in six thousand years the Lord will complete all things. For with him a day represents a thousand years. [Then he cites Ps 90:4]." *Barn.* 15:5 then goes on to argue that "the Son [will] come" on the seventh day. Here we see the outlines of uses (3) and (4) above. This interpretation is also found in 2 *Enoch* 33:1-2, although in this case the time period is 8,000 years.[29] Then we also find *Jub.* 4:29-30. The first verse describes the death of Adam, and the next adds, "And he lacked seven years from a thousand years, for a thousand years are like one day in the testimony of heaven, and therefore it was written concerning the tree of knowledge, 'In the day you eat from it you will die.' Therefore he did not complete the years of this day because he died in it." This is clearly usage (2) above.

Some scholars, building on meanings (3) and (4) above (i.e., *Barn.* 15:4 and 2 *Enoch* 33:1-2 plus a number of rabbinic passages), argue that

27. See further Bruce Malina, "Christ and Time: Swiss or Mediterranean?" *Catholic Biblical Quarterly* 51:1 (1989) 1-31.

28. Neyrey, 2 *Peter, Jude,* 238, with references to Jewish and Christian literature removed.

29. Since the basic cycle in 2 *Enoch* is 7,000 years, some scholars think that the addition of the eighth day is Christian, coming from their celebration of the eighth day, the first day of the week, rather than the Sabbath.

our passage is indicating that the Day of Judgment (since that seems to be the reference) will be 1,000 years long.[30] The problem with this interpretation is that, although it has precedent in Jewish materials, it does not fit in our text. In this interpretation 2 Pet 3:8 would have had to be a parenthetic thought tossed in to give extraneous information on the length of the Day. However, the opening words of 2 Pet 3:8 indicate that our author views it as important to the flow of the argument.

Neyrey, building on meaning (2) above, believes that the verse is building on the length of Adam's life, fitting God's promise that he would die in the day he ate the fruit. "This use, while it is not the source for 3:8, contains structural similarities. God's word will surely come true: Adam will die; but God's mercy delayed the punishment. In 2 Peter, God's word will prove true, after God grants mercy to sinners for repentance."[31] While this explanation surely gets into the area of meaning of our text, it seems strained in that no clear reference to Adam is in the text. Thus many commentators argue that 2 Peter has an entirely independent use of Ps 90:4.[32]

Bauckham, however, suggests yet another use of Ps 90:4 that is closer to both the original meaning of Ps 90:4 and the meaning of the larger passage in 2 Peter. He points to a passage in *Pirqe Rabbi Eliezer* 28 that seems to embody a tradition found in the earlier *Apocalypse of Abraham* 28–30[33] that argues that the Gen 15:11 reference to Abraham's driving away the birds from the carcasses of the animals that he had sacrificed was one day and that, therefore, "From this incident thou mayest learn that the rule of these four kingdoms [i.e., the period during which the four kingdoms of Daniel will oppress Israel, which is therefore the time of eschatological delay] will only last one day according to the day of the Holy One" (*Pirqe Rabbi Eliezer* 28). To this he adds Sir 18:9-11, which does not explicitly cite Ps 90:4, but seems inspired by it: "The number of days in their life is great if they reach one hundred years. Like a drop of water from the sea and a grain of sand, so are a few years among the days of eternity. That is why the Lord is patient with them and pours out his mercy upon them." This noneschatological passage is in turn similar to one in *2 Apoc. Bar.* 48:12-13: "For we are born in a short time, and in a short time we return. With you, however, the hours are like times, and the

30. Friedrich Spitta, *Die zweite Brief des Petrus und der Brief des Judas* (Halle an der Saale: Verlag und Buchhandlung des Waisenhauses, 1885); August Strobel, *Untersuchungen zum eschatologischen Verzögerungsproblem*, 93-94; von Allmen, "L'apocalyptique juive et le retard de la parousie en II Pierre 3:1-13," 262.

31. Neyrey, *2 Peter, Jude*, 238.

32. For example, Vögtle, *Der Judasbrief, der zweite Petrusbrief*, 230.

33. Richard J. Bauckham, "The Delay of the Parousia," *TynBul* 31 (1980) 23.

days like generations." In this case a use of Psalm 90 is being applied to an eschatological situation, calling for God to intervene to help Israel. Finally, Bauckham cites an allusion to Ps 90:4 in Pseudo-Philo's *Bib. Ant.* 19.13, "But this age will be in my sight like a cloud which flies quickly by and like yesterday which passes." "This age" is the time between Moses' death and the resurrection of the dead at the end of time, a period that the work indicates will be about 1,500 years. Bauckham's argument is, then,

> These four parallels establish that in Jewish literature Ps 90:4 was used with reference to the contrast between the brevity of human life and God's eternity, that it was so used in apocalyptic contexts, and specifically that it was used with reference to the period of time up to the End, to indicate that although this period may seem long by human reckoning, in God's eternal perspective it is short. The thought of 2 Pet 3:8 may plausibly be regarded as borrowed from a Jewish apocalypse which made this point.[34]

While we have argued above that Bauckham's argument for a Jewish apocalypse underlying this section of 2 Peter is possible, but not proven, his general argument for a Jewish origin of such a use of Ps 90:4 is worth serious consideration whether or not one sees it as embodied in a Jewish apocalyptic source. That is, a use of Ps 90:4 was at the least "in the air" for discussions of the shortness of human life in comparison with the length of God's life, and this use was at times applied to apocalyptic contexts, namely, as the reason for the delay of the final end.

Whether one agrees with Bauckham that this use was traditional or prefers the explanation of Vögtle and others that 2 Peter has invented this application of Ps 90:4 on his own, the point that he appears to be making is that divine time is not human time. Human time is relatively immediate, a single lifetime, while divine "days" can stretch over eons (see the discussion in Bruce Malina's article, referenced above), as the psalm indicates. In critiquing God for his slowness in fulfilling his promises, human beings are making an honor challenge against God that steps over the boundaries of their sphere of present time and invades his sphere of future time. In other words, they are trespassing in God's arena, an arena in which human beings do not know what they are talking about.

**9** The fact that God's time is not our time means that we cannot judge whether or not God is delaying. Yet our author is not content to leave that issue as a mystery, but goes on to argue that "the Lord is not slow in keeping his promise." The promise theme hooks back to the promise of his coming mentioned in 3:4, but also the "great and precious

34. Bauckham, *Jude, 2 Peter,* 308-9.

promises" of 1:4. The idea that "the Lord" is not slow is probably an allusion to Hab 2:3: "For the revelation awaits an appointed time; it speaks of the end and will not prove false. Though it linger, wait for it; it will certainly come and will not delay." In some Greek translations of the OT exactly the same word is used for "delay" that 2 Peter uses. Furthermore, one could understand the Greek as saying, "He will not be slow" or "He will not delay." While a similar thought is expressed in Isa 13:22, Sir 35:19 (LXX; 35:22 in the NRSV) is closer to our thought here, "Indeed, the Lord will not delay, and like a warrior [or "upon them"] will not be patient until he crushes the loins of the unmerciful. . . ." The central issue is not whether the author of 2 Peter depends directly on Hab 2:3 or is instead dependent on Sir 35:19 (LXX),[35] but that he is in fact dependent on a theme that is found in both the Scriptures that he knew and in later Jewish and Christian writings dependent on those Scriptures.

But why might the "scoffers" have used the "delay" argument? In the texts cited the issue is the sureness of God's judgment. It will indeed come, and it will come, at least from God's perspective, promptly. But in the world of 2 Peter the Epicureans were arguing that the delay of the judgment was in fact an argument against the idea of God's providence. Thus Plutarch in his work *De sera numinis vindicta* (*Moralia* 548–68) begins his critique of the Epicureans with, "The delay and procrastination of the Deity in punishing the wicked appears to me the most telling argument by far."[36] Thus this argument of delay was being used against the idea of divine providence. It is no wonder that Matt 24:48 characterizes the *wicked* servant as saying, "My master is staying away a long time," using the same word for "staying away a long time" that the LXX uses for "delay" in Hab 2:3, the point being that he never expects to be called to account for his actions because the delay indicates that the coming will never happen.[37] Whether Matthew was interacting with Epicurean thought or not (Syria and Palestine were certainly not immune to it, so whether we think of Matthew as the redactor or Jesus as the originator of the saying, such ideas could lie in the background) is not a matter for discussion here, but it is likely that such ideas are behind the thought of the

35. Strobel, *Untersuchungen zum eschatologischen Verzögerungsproblem,* 89-90, argues for direct dependence on Habakkuk, while Jacques Schlosser, "Les jours de Noé et de Lot: A propos de Luc, XVII, 26-30," *RB* 80 (1973) 34, argues for dependence on Sirach.

36. Neyrey, *2 Peter, Jude,* 239. See the much longer discussion by Plutarch, especially of the Epicureans, in Gregory Bloomquist, *"The Epicurean Tag in Plutarch: Implications for New Testament Study."* http://www.bloomquist.ca/publications/articles/Epicurean%20Tag%20in%20Plutarch.html.

37. Hab 2:3 is also cited in Heb 10:37, not to mention 1QpHab 7:5-12 and *2 Apoc. Bar.* 20:6.

"scoffers" in 2 Peter. Here they are characterized as "some" in the phrase "as some understand slowness." Our author asserts that delay is emphatically not what is happening.

Instead of delay, what is happening is mercy. God is patient or long-suffering. This is part of his self-revelation in Exod 34:6, "The LORD, the LORD, the compassionate and gracious God, slow to anger, abounding in love and faithfulness. . . ." The phrase "slow to anger" is represented in the LXX by the same Greek root as our term here. Moses calls upon this characteristic in Num 14:18 when he asks God to forgive Israel: "The LORD is slow to anger, abounding in love and forgiving sin and rebellion." Jonah complains about it in Jonah 4:3, "I knew that you are a gracious and compassionate God, slow to anger and abounding in love, a God who relents from sending calamity." And this theme is repeated elsewhere in the Jewish Scriptures: Neh 9:17; Pss 86:15 (LXX 85:15); 103:8-10 (LXX 102:8-10); 145:8-9 (LXX 144:8-9); Joel 2:13; Nah 1:3; Wisd 15:1 ("But you, our God, are kind and true, patient, and ruling all things in mercy"; NRSV). Naturally the same idea is repeated in the Dead Sea Scrolls and in a number of other pieces of literature from the Second Temple Period. Interestingly enough, 1 Pet 3:20 attributes this characteristic to God with relation to the generation of the flood. This divine characteristic also underlies the virtue of patience or long-suffering that is required in followers of Jesus, for they are to be like their Father: 2 Cor 6:6; Gal 5:22; Eph 4:2; Col 1:11; 3:12; 1 Tim 3:10; 4:2; Heb 6:12. One cannot properly claim to follow a Father who is patient and slow to anger if one is herself impatient and quick to anger, which is one reason why the control of anger is such an important topic in the NT, as is the command not to judge.[38]

While the characteristic of patience demonstrates the honorable magnanimity of the divine ruler (over against those who slander him by claiming that the slowness of the coming judgment is a delay or a failure to fulfill his promises), it is not a purposeless magnanimity. The goal of God's patience/long-suffering/slowness to anger is human repentance, as Wisd 11:23 states, "But you are merciful to all, for you can do all things, and you overlook people's sins, so that they may repent" (NRSV). Of course, that is just the point of the Joel and Jonah texts cited above, the former calling on Israel to respond with repentance and the latter complaining that the repentance of the Ninevites is just what he had feared would happen. In this vein Rom 2:4 asks, "Do you show contempt for the

38. It was also a major theme of Greco-Roman ethics. See William V. Harris, *Restraining Rage: The Ideology of Anger Control in Classical Antiquity* (Cambridge: Harvard University Press, 2001).

riches of his kindness, tolerance and patience, not realizing that God's kindness leads you toward repentance?"

Naturally, this desire for repentance rather than judgment applies not only to the intermediate judgments of history but also to the final judgment. In support of this we have, of course, our own passage in the NT but also Revelation, where it appears that the final judgment is held back in the hope that people will repent. There is a repeated lament that instead of repenting people either kept on sinning or cursed God (Rev 9:20, 21; 16:9, 11). (Of course the same reluctance to judge is applied to the church, which is given an opportunity to repent: Rev 2:5, 16, 21, 22; 3:3, 19.) This view of history was also that of Jewish works. *1 Enoch* 60.5-6 quotes Michael as saying, "This day of mercy has lasted until today; and he has been merciful and long-suffering towards those that dwell upon the earth. And when this day [of judgment] arrives . . . it will become a day of covenant for the elect and inquisition for the sinners." The delay of the final judgment, then, is for the purpose of mercy. Since delay of judgment is an important theme in apocalyptic literature, it is also an important theme in other apocalyptic works, such as *2 Apocalypse of Baruch* (1:3; 12:4; 21:20-21; 24:2; 48:29; 59:6; 85:8).

Yet if repentance is the purpose of God's slowness of anger (which, of course, has its downside in that some people take it as an indication that he will not execute justice and that they therefore can do evil and get off free), does that repentance have any influence on the timing of the end? There is a passage in *b. Sanhedrin* 97b–98a that, if authentic, shows a late-first-century rabbinic discussion of this issue of whether repentance actually influences the timing of the end or whether the time is set and repentance does not influence it:[39]

> This matter is disputed by Tannaim: R. Eliezer said: If Israel repent, they will be redeemed; if not, they will not be redeemed. R. Joshua said to him, If they do not repent, will they not be redeemed? But the Holy One, blessed be He, will set up a king over them, whose decrees shall be as cruel as Haman's, whereby Israel shall engage in repentance, and he will thus bring them back to the right path. Another [Baraitha] taught: R. Eliezer said: If Israel repent, they will be redeemed, as it is written, Return, ye backsliding children, and I will heal your backslidings. R. Joshua said to him, But is it not written, ye have sold yourselves for naught; and ye shall be redeemed without money? Ye have sold yourselves for naught, for idolatry; and ye shall be redeemed without money — without repentance and good deeds. R. Eliezer retorted to R. Joshua, But is it not written, Return unto me, and I will return unto

39. See the discussion in Bauckham, *Jude, 2 Peter,* 312-13.

> you? R. Joshua rejoined — But is it not written, For I am master over you: and I will take you one of a city, and two of a family, and I will bring you to Zion? R. Eliezer replied, But it is written, in returning and rest shall ye be saved. . . . (Soncino translation)

Later rabbis seem to side with R. Eliezer, but in 2 Peter we are not in a later period but the period when this topic was still under discussion. In Revelation it looks as if repentance will change God's plans, although the prophet does not hold out hope of repentance (then, neither did Jonah in the word he preached in Nineveh). In 2 Peter it also looks as if the human response can change at least the timing of the end, as we shall see when we get to 2 Pet 3:12.

However one decides the effect of repentance on the final judgment, it is clear that, according to 2 Peter, if God had his way no one would come under condemnation in that judgment. "The Lord" (while in the tradition this refers to God, it is not clear whether or not 2 Peter means it to refer to Jesus in that he often uses "Lord" to refer to Jesus) is patient with "you" (i.e., the addressees), and they can be glad of his patience, for he has freed them from entrapment in desire and enabled them to take part in the divine nature (so 1:3-5). He has done this not wanting (or not willing) "anyone" to perish (as the generation of the flood did; 2 Pet 3:6), but "everyone" to attain repentance (as the addressees of the letter had). There is a play here between the "anyone" or "some" (earlier in our verse) and "everyone" or "all." "Some" (probably the "scoffers") understand God to be slow in keeping his promise, but God does not want "anyone"/"some" (they are the same pronoun in Greek) to perish. What he wants is "everyone"/"all" to come to repentance. It looks as if 2 Peter is saying that God does not wish even the "scoffers" to perish (although our author does not have any expectation that they will repent) but rather wants even them to repent. God's will may not be done, but it will not be for lack of trying on his part.

We see here a concept closely related to Jesus' command to pray for one's enemies (Matt 5:43-48 par. Luke 6:27-28, 32-36): "But I tell you: Love your enemies and pray for those who persecute you, that you may be sons [*sic*] of your Father in heaven." God's will is that no one will perish in whatever form of judgment. Those who are really his children will have a heart or character like his. (After all, we are partakers in the divine nature.) So the followers of Jesus pray for the good of those who persecute them. He or she wants God to turn insurgent leaders like Saul (a self-described zealot who wanted to purify Israel by getting rid of the followers of Jesus, which followers of Jesus thought that the revolution had already happened and so would not join in against the Romans) into great leaders of his people, that is, Paul. They do not rejoice in the death of any evil person, but rather hope against hope for their repentance. This should set them off from the culture around them. Unfortunately, it is often the culture that co-ops the followers of Jesus into sharing their national and cultural hatreds and rejoicing in the destruction of people whom God wished would have repented. The Day of the Lord may indeed come, but the desire of God and of his people is that it finds no one whom God has to judge (even if there is little hope in Scripture that that will actually be the case).

**10** "The day of the Lord" will indeed come, and it will "come like a thief." This image certainly comes from Jesus (Matt 24:43-44 par. Luke 12:39-40), who compares the vigilance that the head of a household should have toward a possible thief to the vigilance that his followers should have with respect to the coming of the Son of Man. In the epistles this metaphor is shifted (as is common with live metaphors) from the vigilance of the head of the household to the unexpectedness of the coming of the Lord (1 Thess 5:2, 4; Rev 3:3; 16:5). In this later use of the metaphor the Day of the Lord or Jesus himself is what comes like a thief in the night, a usage that would be continued in later Christian literature (*Did.* 16:1; *Gospel of Thomas* 21). The expression in our passage is so close to the "you know very well that the day of the Lord will come like a thief in the night" of 1 Thess 5:2 that scholars wonder whether 1 Thessalonians might be one of the Pauline letters that 2 Peter knows (2 Pet 3:15-16) and whether he might have picked up the metaphor from 1 Thessalonians rather than directly from Jesus' saying.[40] Whether this is true or not is difficult to determine, for the wording in 2 Peter is not exactly the same as that in 1 Thessalonians, although the thought is, and the use of the metaphor is widespread enough in the early Jesus movement that one would need other contacts with 1 Thessalonians to be sure that that was the source. On the other hand, Peter does admit that he knows more than one letter of Paul, and he is using the metaphor more as Paul does than as Jesus does, so this proposal is quite possible.

The point that our author is making is that God's patience or slowness to anger and his desire that all come to repentance do not mean that the Day of the Lord is called off. Thus our author says (using Greek word order to show the emphasis), "But *it will come* the Day of the Lord. . . ." While the Day may not be fixed (again, see 3:12), the Lord will eventually decide that the time of delay is at an end and thus the opportunity for repentance will have run out. This will happen without prior announcement — it will take place as suddenly and unexpectedly as a thief in the night.

40. For example, Neyrey, *2 Peter, Jude,* 242.

When this Day comes, three things will occur: (1) the heavens will pass away with a roar, (2) the "elements" will be dissolved by fire, and (3) the earth and all that has been done in it (the NIV leaves out the idea of "the deeds in it" that is clearly in the Greek text) will be disclosed or discovered. We need to look at these three things in order.

While Jesus said that the law would remain until heaven and earth "disappear" or "pass away" (Matt 5:18 par. Luke 16:17), he also said that "heaven and earth will pass away, but my words will never pass away" (Mark 13:31 par. Matt 24:35 par. Luke 21:33). Rev 21:1 (using a slightly different verb) pictures that passing away of the heavens and earth as having already taken place. Naturally, this idea is also found in Jewish sources (e.g., *1 Enoch* 91:16, "The first heaven shall depart and pass away; a new heaven shall appear; and all the powers of heaven shall shine forever sevenfold"), for it depends on OT images, especially the description of the judgment of Edom in Isa 34:4, "All the stars of the heavens will be dissolved and the sky rolled up like a scroll; all the starry host will fall like withered leaves from the vine, like shriveled figs from the fig tree." This is picked up more literally in Rev 6:12b-14: "The sun turned black like sackcloth made of goat hair, the whole moon turned blood red, and the stars in the sky fell to earth, as late figs drop from a fig tree when shaken by a strong wind. The sky receded like a scroll, rolling up, and every mountain and island was removed from its place." Here in 2 Peter the sky simply disappears or passes away. The roar or loud noise (the word for this is unique in the NT) may refer to the Lord's shout (i.e., the thunder of the Lord in 1QH 3:32-36)[41] or to the noise of the heavens passing away. Given its parallel structure to the burning of the elements, it is likely that it indicates the latter.

Along with the passing away of the heavens there is a second event, the destruction of the elements (Greek *stoicheia*). What happens to the elements is clearly pictured in that they will be "broken up" or "destroyed"[42] as they burn. The question is, "What are the elements?" 2 Peter has used various terms for the universe, especially as he has paralleled creation, the deluge, and the coming Day of Judgment (see the table on p. 284). We see that the earth is reserved for fire, but, when the fire comes, it is the elements that burn, not the earth, but then we do not learn of new heavens and new elements, but new heavens and a new earth.

41. Bauckham, *Jude, 2 Peter,* 315. He cites not just Second Temple literature but also the thunder of God in the OT: Ps 18:13-15 (LXX 17:14-16); 77:18 (LXX 76:19); 104:7 (LXX 103:7); Amos 1:2; Joel 3:16 (MT and LXX 4:16). This is a quite attractive option because it puts God directly into the picture and because it is rooted in OT images of God, but, as we note in the text, to accept it would mean to overlook the parallel structure in the text.

42. H. M. F. Büchsel, *"lyō," TDNT* 4:335.

| | *Terms* | *Comment* |
|---|---|---|
| 2 Pet 3:5 | Heavens and the earth | Formed out of water |
| 2 Pet 3:6 | World *(kosmos)* | Destroyed (not the same term as in 3:10) by water |
| 2 Pet 3:7 | Heavens and earth | Reserved for fire; ungodly will be destroyed (the same root as in 3:6) |
| 2 Pet 3:10 | Heavens, elements, earth | Pass away, burned, laid bare respectively |
| 2 Pet 3:12 | Heavens, elements | Both burn and are broken apart (heavens) or melted (elements) |
| 2 Pet 3:13 | New heavens and a new earth | According to the Lord's promise |

Commentators have offered a series of suggestions explaining this language. (1) The elements are the four basic elements, earth, air, fire, and water. This was a normal meaning for *stoicheia.*[43] (2) The elements are the heavenly bodies, the sun, moon, and stars. This meaning for *stoicheia* is clearly found in the second century.[44] (3) The elements are angelic powers, a meaning that many scholars believe is found in Paul (Gal 4:3 ["the basic principles of the world" (*kosmos,* which can mean "universe")]; Col 2:8, 20). All three of these suggestions have a *prima facie* validity and fit the culture in which 2 Peter was written.

The first suggestion fits the cosmology of that day in that many philosophers argued that the whole universe was made up of earth, air, fire, and water, and, as we saw above, in Stoic thought fire was viewed as the chief element into which the others dissolved in periodic cycles. This would fit with the ending of the first age of creation by water in 2 Pet 3:6 (perhaps alluding to an alternative Greek conception of the universe in which the periodic cycles ended with all dissolving in water). More importantly, it seems to parallel Jesus' statement in which heaven and earth pass away, not heaven and the elements. It would also explain why a new heavens and new earth were needed in 2 Pet 3:12. If this is the proper understanding, we are talking about a total dissolution of the creation as we know it.[45]

43. Gerhard Delling, *"stoicheō ktl.," TDNT* 7:672-79.

44. Gerhard Delling, *"stoicheō ktl.," TDNT* 7:681-82.

45. A scholar who takes this position is Neyrey, *2 Peter, Jude,* 243. It is also supported by the listing of the elements in *Sib. Or.* 2:206-7; 3:80-81; 8:337-39, although there is some lack of clarity in these passages.

The second suggestion not only has second-century examples to call upon[46] but also argues that 2 Peter is dependent on Isa 34:4. The Hebrew text differentiates between the "hosts of heaven," which will "decay" or "rot away" (NIV, "dissolve"), and the heavens themselves (NIV, "sky"), which will be rolled up like a scroll. Thus the text clearly differentiates between the heavens (the "expanse" of Gen 1:6-8 that God calls "sky" [NIV], the same word as for "heavens," and created on the second day) and the heavenly bodies (the "lights" of Gen 1:14-19, which are "in the expanse of the heavens" and are assigned to the fourth creative day). The Septuagint (LXX) condenses the Hebrew of Isa 34:4 (which mentions the heavenly bodies in two parts of the verse), dropping the first reference to the heavenly bodies, but still keeps the same distinction. In at least one manuscript of the LXX the first line of Isa 34:4 is translated, "all the powers of the heavens will melt." The author of *2 Clem.* 16:3 appears to know this version, for he writes, "The day of judgment is already coming like a blazing furnace, and some [or, with J. B. Lightfoot and Bauckham, emend to "the powers"][47] of the heavens and all of the earth will be melted as lead melts upon the fire, and then the hidden things will be manifest and the hidden works of people." Interestingly enough, the verb for melting that appears in the LXX manuscript of Isa 34:4 and in 2 *Clement* also appears in 2 Pet 3:12. Thus, it is argued, what 2 Peter is describing is the disappearance of the sky and the destruction of the heavenly bodies.

The third suggestion in a sense builds on the second. It points out that (a) Paul believed in angelic/demonic powers that controlled human beings before conversion and that he called *stoicheia,* (b) many Jewish writings believed that the heavenly bodies either were or were controlled by spiritual beings and that is how at least some of them interpreted Isa 34:4,[48] and (c) the author of 2 Peter also believes in fallen angels, who were, or, perhaps in some cases, are, connected to the stars (2 Pet 2:4, es-

46. Theophilus of Antioch, *Autolycus* 1:4 ("sun, moon, and stars are His elements, made for signs, and seasons, and days"), who clearly focuses on the meaning of these elements in 1:4-6; 2:15, 35; Justin, 2 *Apol.* 5:2 ("God, when He had made the whole world, and subjected things earthly to man, and arranged the heavenly elements for the increase of fruits and rotation of the seasons, and appointed this divine law"); *Dial.* 23:2 ("Do you see that the elements are not idle, and keep no Sabbaths?"). While he does not use the term "elements," Tatian, *Oratio* 9–10, does illustrate the importance of the heavenly bodies for Christian thought.

47. J. B. Lightfoot, *The Apostolic Fathers,* part 1 (London: Macmillan, 1890), 2:250; Bauckham, *Jude, 2 Peter,* 316. Bauckham, of course, believes that 2 *Clement* is following a Jewish apocalyptic source, the same source that 2 Peter is using, and that this, not mutual dependence on Isa 34:4, is what accounts for its close similarity to 2 Peter.

48. For example, the phrase "the unseen spirits are melting" in *T. Levi* 4:1, although the whole passage is not an entirely clear allusion to Isa 34:4.

pecially if he connected it to other OT passages referring to "gods" or "the sons of God"). Thus what our author is talking about is the destruction of these angelic powers.[49]

How shall we evaluate these suggested interpretations? In our view, in the light of the role that "elements" plays as the only thing other than "the heavens" that is to be burned up or melted, and in the light of the fact that the earth is mentioned separately, the second position appears to be the best argument, although we would not want to say that too dogmatically. Is there, then, the possibility of combining it with the third?[50] Given that this is an eschatological judgment and that it is not material things per se that God judges, but people and powers that use or abuse these material things, that is possible. Yet the reference to "the elements" refers primarily to the heavenly bodies, and any beings connected to those bodies remain an unspoken assumption of our author. The point is that to bring about judgment the Lord must peel back all that stands in the way, and this means removing the heavens (or the sky) and burning up the bodies that are in those heavens (or that sky).

The third event of "the day of the Lord" is that "the earth and everything in it will be laid bare." There is a textual problem in this verse that has to do with the term "will be laid bare" or "will be discovered." If, however, our reading makes sense, it is the preferable one, since none of the others has as strong support, nor can they explain how our reading arose.[51] And "will be laid bare" does make sense. The picture is indeed that of stripping off everything that stands between the eye of God and the earth. When the sky and the heavenly bodies are gone, "the earth and everything in it will be laid bare." And that is the goal: to expose all that has gone on and is going on on the earth so that all those things that human beings thought that they were getting away with or thought that that God did not see are suddenly exposed to his unblinking eye. Probably our author believes that this process will do damage to the earth and its structures, but the point is the uncovering and exposing and

49. Schrage, *Der zweite Petrusbrief, der Judasbrief,* 150. He is following and developing Spitta.

50. This is what both Bauckham, *Jude, 2 Peter,* 316, and Vögtle, *Der Judasbrief, der zweite Petrusbrief,* 234, do, although neither with a lot of emphasis on the third.

51. One manuscript (C) has "they will not appear," and several (Alexandrinus, a few uncials, and the so-called "majority text") have "they will be burned up." Neither explains how the reading that is in our text arose. One manuscript ($\mathfrak{P}^{72}$) has what is clearly an error, starting out writing "will be discovered" and then adding "being loosed" or "being dissolved." Two versions have "will not be found," which appears to be an emendation of the text, especially since no Greek manuscript has this reading. The manuscripts Sinaiticus, Vaticanus, several other uncials, as well as much of the Syriac and some miniscules, contain the reading translated by the NIV.

thus the purifying of the earth. This uncovering is similar to the point of the flood, namely, to destroy human evil; in the process of doing that many animals and plants were also destroyed. In this case what is destroyed is the heavens, and perhaps with them spiritual forces that are influencing evil on earth. Yet 2 Peter does not dwell on the spiritual forces, assuming that he believes in them, but rather on the stripping away of the protective covering from earth.[52]

> *[11]Since everything will be destroyed in this way, what kind of people ought you to be? You ought to live holy and godly lives [12]as you look forward to the day of God and speed its coming. That day will bring about the destruction of the heavens by fire, and the elements will melt in the heat. [13]But in keeping with his promise we are looking forward to a new heaven and a new earth, the home of righteousness.*

**11** The apocalyptic scenario that our author has painted is not designed so that the addressees say, "Oh, yes. Now I understand what will happen." And they turn back to whatever they were doing before hearing the teaching. Like many apocalyptic writings and all NT letters, this one (which is both) is designed with a parenetic (i.e., ethical) purpose. Our author has reminded his addressees of the truths (1:12-15; 3:1-2) because the "scoffers" are not theoretical thinkers but teachers who are "following their own desires" (3:3). Their false conception of God's future has led them to make charges against the honor of God and to live in ways that deny "the sovereign Lord who bought them" (2:1). Likewise a proper understanding of God's future should bring about an appropriate lifestyle. It is those implications that 2 Peter addresses here at the end of the letter, just as many NT writers do at the end of their letters.[53]

"Since everything [or "all these things"] will be destroyed in this way" is the assumption. Our author is clearly referring to the destruction of the heavens and the elements in the previous verse. This interpretation is preferable to that of authors who refer back to 2 Pet 3:7 and see this as

52. This interpretation is found as early as W. E. Wilson, "*Heurethesetai* in 2 Pet. iii. 10," *ExpT* 32 (1920-21) 44-45, and is also that preferred by Bauckham, *Jude, 2 Peter*, 317-21, who provides an exhaustive list of other ways in which the verb can be understood. It also enjoys the strength of the parallel in 2 *Clem.* 16:3, which uses the more usual verb to express this thought.

53. Bauckham, *Jude, 2 Peter*, 323, cites both the ethical exhortation at the end of NT letters (1 Cor 15:58; Gal 5:7-10; Eph 5:10-16; Phil 4:5; Col 4:5; 1 Tim 6:14; 2 Tim 4:1-5; 1 Pet 5:1-10) and the ethical exhortations combined with eschatological sanctions in apocalyptic testamentary literature (*1 Enoch* 91:3-19; 94:1-5; *Jub.* 36:3-11; *2 Apocalypse of Baruch* 84–85; Pseudo-Philo, *Bib. Ant.* 33.1-3). This list could be lengthened, but it is sufficient to make the point.

the destruction of the heavens and the earth, for the verb for "destroyed" does not appear in 3:7, but rather appears in the reference to the elements being destroyed (same verb) by fire. Naturally, if one sees the elements as earth, air, fire, and water, as Neyrey does, then in 3:10 one is talking about the destruction of the earth, which would be part of "all these things." Or if, with Bauckham, one feels that 3:10 abbreviates an original Jewish apocalypse and simply fails to mention the destruction of the earth that we find in 2 *Clem.* 16:3, then the earth also has been destroyed.[54] But if we understand 3:10 as we explained above and take it at face value as expressing the vision of the future that our author wishes to communicate, then "all these things" are the heavens and the elements (heavenly bodies), the destruction of which was to expose human evil and lead to "the judgment and destruction of ungodly people" (3:7) or, to give the exact expression in 3:10, to expose "the earth and everything done in it."[55] Naturally, such cosmic destruction would have an effect on the earth, as would the destruction of the ungodly, but that is not Peter's focus. Instead, his focus is the positive vision of the future and what it means for the present. While that positive vision will not appear until 3:13, the practical implication appears immediately.

The practical implication is, "What kind of people ought you to be? You ought to live holy and godly lives." That is, there is no reason to adjust one's life to the values and mores of this age of the world, for this age is coming to an end. In would be like investing in a firm that was about to crash. Rather, one ought to be living now the lifestyle of the promised coming age, a lifestyle that will mark one out as a person who belongs to that age and will make the coming judgment a welcome event rather than a dreaded one. The "scoffers" are living lives run by their desires; those who look forward to the Day of the Lord ought to live lives that are "holy and godly." That holiness does not mean religious acts, but rather a lifestyle (the word for "lives" is the term for "lifestyle" that appears thirteen times in the NT) that reflects the character of God as seen in 1 Pet 1:15-16 (cf. 1 Pet 2:12, a "good lifestyle"). Where would a member of 2 Peter's community have found a model of such a lifestyle? In the portrayals of God in the OT for sure, but primarily in the life and teaching of Jesus. In the rough-and-tumble of the politics of first-century Palestine he showed what being merciful and slow to anger and the like looked like. Thus holiness is not abstract but concrete. And it is the opposite of the lives of the teachers our author opposes, for it reflects lives that are freed from the corruption that is in the world through various human desires (1:4). The reference to a "godly"

54. Bauckham, *Jude, 2 Peter,* 324.

55. Vögtle, *Der Judasbrief, der zweite Petrusbrief,* 240-41.

lifestyle also carries us back to ch. 1, for this term that is common in the Pastoral Epistles (1 Tim 2:2; 4:7; 6:3; 2 Tim 3:5; Tit 1:1)[56] appears in 2 Pet 1:3 (see the comment there). But what this looks like concretely is then worked out in 2 Pet 1:5-7. Both words, then, are defined in terms of concrete virtues.

The life of a follower of Jesus, then, is not to be led in fear of judgment but in hope of a new age. Fear tends to paralyze people rather than to motivate them. Thus, while our author goes to pains to refute the teachings of the "scoffers," his focus is on the new that is coming rather than on the fearfulness of the intermediate judgment. His addressees are to be living the life of the future age no matter how dysfunctional it may seem in this age, for the structures of this age are temporary — we will likely be surprised at how quickly they collapse — and the structures of the coming age are permanent. Given the massive investment of contemporary Christians in the nationalism, materialism, and pleasure orientation of Western culture, this passage should serve as wake-up call. When the Day comes, one's retirement fund will not be important, but rather what one has invested in the kingdom of our Sovereign Lord.

**12** Since followers of Jesus are looking forward to that future age, they want the "day of God" to come soon. Despite the fact that our human experience of time is not God's experience of time (3:8), our author does not imply that his addressees will not be alive at the Parousia. He is not talking about "Parousia delay" in the sense that he has given up the expectation of experiencing the Parousia but in the sense that the "scoffers" are charging that the waiting has been long enough that it indicates that the event will not happen, a charge that he felt he needed to answer. When it comes to this expectation, Jude talked about waiting for "the mercy of our Lord Jesus Christ" (Jude 21), while our author talks about "waiting for" or "looking forward to"[57] "the day of God" (or, more exactly, "waiting for the coming of the day of God"). (2 Pet 3:10 has called this "the day of the Lord," and here it is called "the day of God," so it looks as if "the Lord" in the previous part of the chapter is God rather than Jesus, although in practice it makes little difference. What is clear is that "the day of the Lord" and the "day of God" refer to the same eschatological event, which is also spoken of as the "coming" or "Parousia" of Christ [2 Pet 1:16; 3:4].) This overlapping terminology should make us extremely cautious in trying to separate these terms or in applying them to separate events. For our author they apply to a single event that we are to await.) This "waiting for"

56. Other than these references, it appears in the NT in Acts 3:12 and in 2 Pet 1:3 and 3:11. It does not appear in any of the earlier Pauline letters; it is apparently too Hellenistic a virtue for that.

57. The NIV uses "waiting for" in Jude 21 and "looking forward to" here in 2 Pet 3:12, but the Greek verb is the same.

or "looking forward to" is the stance of the whole end of the letter, for the verb is repeated in 3:13 and 3:14. The connection of this verb to eschatological hope is common in the NT, for the question of whom one is waiting for comes up in Matt 11:3 (par. Luke 7:19; cf. Luke 3:15) and future expectation (or the danger of a lack of it) in Matt 24:50 (par. Luke 12:46). As seen in the teaching of Jesus, this expectation also has the sense of being prepared for the Day. There is a moral side to waiting; it is not merely an intellectual stance. It is, in fact, very similar to the idea of "watching" (often in the teaching of Jesus, and of course also in the letters, and translated "be alert" in 1 Pet 5:8 and a number of other places in the NT). This fits with the likely origin of this idea of waiting, that is, Hab 2:3, "Though [the revelation] linger, wait for it; it will certainly come and will not delay."[58]

But one does not simply "look forward to" or "await" or "watch" passively. The structure of our passage parallels two stances: "looking forward to the coming of the day of God" and "speeding the coming of the day of God" (both verbs parallel participles in Greek). This later phrase indicates that the "day of God"[59] is not a fixed date but something that believers can change by their "holy and godly lives." This idea is based on God's hasting a day in Isa 60:22 ("in its time I will accomplish it quickly"). This was picked up by a number of Second Temple Jewish authors (Sir 36:10: "hasten the day and remember the appointed time"; NRSV [36:7, LXX]; 2 *Apoc. Bar.* 20:1-2; 54:1; 83:1; Pseudo-Philo, *Bib. Ant.* 19.13) as well as some early Christian writers (e.g., *Barn.* 4:3). Now these references, for the most part, refer to God's hastening the day, not to human beings doing it, but, as we saw above when commenting on 2 Pet 3:9, there was a Jewish tradition (we cited *b. Sanhedrin* 97b–98a) in which God hastens or delays the day due to Israel's repentance or lack thereof. Various other rabbis were said to express similar views in *y. Ta'anit* 1:1; *b. Yoma* 86b; or *b. Baba Bathra* 10a. In other words, in the first couple of centuries after Jesus such sentiments are attributed to more than one rabbi.

58. In the LXX "wait for" is translated by a different verb (*hypomeinō,* meaning "wait patiently" or "wait enduringly") than we have here *(prosdokeō),* but, as noted above, in Aquila's translation the same verb is used as here, as happens in the references to this passage in *1 Clem.* 23:5; *2 Apoc. Bar.* 83:4. So 2 Peter may simply be using a different translation than the one we have in the LXX, or he may be referring to a traditional understanding of the passage.

59. This is an unusual expression, for normally it is "the day of Christ" (2 Pet 1:16; 3:4; 1 Cor 1:8; Phil 1:6, 10; 2:16) or "the day of the Lord" (1 Cor 5:5; 1 Thess 5:2; 2 Thess 2:2), although there are texts in which the expression "the day of God" is used (Rev 16:14; cf. 1 Pet 2:12, which implies that God will come to judge on a certain day). That these days are distinct from one another is unlikely, for (1) the phrase "day of the Lord" can refer to either Christ or God, and (2) Rev 6:17 joins Christ (the Lamb) and God in one undifferentiated "day" of their wrath.

That this idea was not a later development is shown in Acts 3:19-20, which ties repentance to the return of Christ ("Repent, then, and turn to God, so that your sins may be wiped out, that times of refreshing may come from the Lord, and that he may send the Christ"). It is also found in 2 *Clem.* 12:6 ("When you do these things [i.e. good deeds, forsaking hypocrisy, sexual purity]," he says, "the kingdom of my Father will come"). A related idea is found at the end of the first century in Hermas, *Sim.* 10:4:4 (or ch. 114:4 in Ehrman's numbering). Thus we see that our author is following a solid Jewish tradition, including one found in the early Jesus movement, in declaring that the coming (Greek *parousia*) of the Day of God is not a fixed date, but that under the sovereignty of God and due to his mercy (mentioned earlier in our chapter) it can be sped up (or, conversely, slowed down) by the behavior of the followers of Jesus. Thus an exhortation to hasten that day was appropriate then (and continues to be appropriate now).

Having exhorted his addressees to hasten that day, our author goes on to repeat what he said in 2 Pet 3:10, namely, that because of that Day[60] there will be "the destruction of the heavens by fire, and the elements [i.e., the planets and other heavenly bodies, as argued in the exegesis of 3:10] will melt in the heat." While this picture does not differ significantly from that found in 3:10 (which is, as we argued, dependent on Isa 34:4), the term for melting is new (and unique in the NT), but has been used previously in the Greek OT for God's melting of the heavens in Isa 34:4 (in some manuscripts) and the mountains in Isa 63:19–64:1. The picture is picked up in *T. Levi* 4:1 and later in 2 *Clem.* 16:3. The apocalyptic day will destroy business as usual on this earth. The heavenly powers (perhaps viewed as those determining the evil going on on the earth or perhaps viewed as covering the evil going on on earth) will be stripped away so that true justice and a new order can come.

**13** Clearly, then, investing in this age is investing in something without a future. The future is the Day of God, and what stretches out beyond that Day. Thus the text puts into the emphatic position "new heavens and a new earth," then adds that we are to expect them "according to his promise," and finally, almost as an afterthought (after all, it could hardly be otherwise if God has fulfilled his promises), "the home of righteousness" (or "where righteousness dwells").

The point is that God's goal and the topic of this text are not primar-

60. Kelly, *The Letters of Peter and of Jude*, 367-68, notes that "the implication in *because of* [is] that the universal disintegration will not be the result of any natural cyclic process, like the periodical conflagration of the universe envisaged in Stoic thought, but the direct effect of God's sovereign will." This causal implication is not expressed as clearly in the NIV translation, but is found in the NRSV and RSV translations.

ily the destruction of evil. The issue that the "scoffers" are raising in 3:4 and that our author returns to in 3:9 is God's promises. His promise to the followers of Jesus is not simply that he will remove evil, but that he will reward and honor them (even make them partakers of the divine nature; 2 Pet 1:4). It is in essence a positive promise, for which the removal of evil is a necessary preliminary.

The actual promise of the new heaven and earth comes from Isa 65:17 ("Behold, I will create new heavens and a new earth. The former things will not be remembered, nor will they come to mind") and 66:22 ("As the new heavens and the new earth that I make will endure before me," declares the Lord, "so will your name and descendants endure"). The need for a renewal of creation was often reflected on in Second Temple Jewish literature.[61] This literature uses the language of "renewal" of creation rather than "new heavens and new earth," although some of the descriptions indicate a renewal as extreme as that in the time of Noah. Such an expectation is not surprising, for while the Jews never saw creation itself as problematic — indeed, they could hardly conceive of life without some type of creation — they did realize that evil had so penetrated it that radical renewal was necessary, especially when it came to human beings. Romans picks up this need, stating in Rom 8:21 that "the creation itself will be liberated from its bondage to decay and brought into the glorious freedom of the children of God." Salvation is for all of creation, according to Paul. Many commentators think that this renewal is what Jesus is speaking about when he speaks of "the renewal of all things" (or "the rebirth"/"regeneration") in Matt 19:28. But it is Revelation that uses the terminology found in Isaiah and 2 Peter, "Then I saw a new heaven and a new earth, for the first heaven and the first earth had passed away, and there was no longer any sea" (Rev 21:1). John's symbolic presentation is stating that the forces of chaos (i.e., the sea in OT thought) have been decisively defeated and the heavens and earth have been decisively renewed (in Revelation there are powers of evil in the heavens as well as on earth, e.g., in Revelation 12). The picture is that of a new city (as opposed to the evil cities of Genesis and, for that matter, the rest of Revelation), which is symbolically presented as the holy of holies (i.e., cubical), a new Garden of Eden with a new river and the tree of life, which is now freely available. In other words, eschatology returns to protology, but this time there will be no fall. The plan of God in Genesis comes to fulfillment in Revelation: humanity rules the fruitful earth in full communion with God.

Now we do not know how much of this picture of Revelation our

61. For example, *Jub.* 1:29; *1 Enoch* 45:4-5; 72:1; 91:16; *Sib. Or.* 5:212; *2 Apoc. Bar.* 32:6; 44:12; 57:2; *4 Ezra* 7:75; Pseudo-Philo, *Bib. Ant.* 3.10. This list is abbreviated from Bauckham.

author is aware of, but he is clearly aware of the essential elements. The earth will be renewed.[62] The renewed heavens and earth will be "the home of righteousness" or "the place where righteousness is at home" or "the place where righteousness dwells." The point is that this renewed creation is not a place where God's will is occasionally done (as in the unrenewed creation) or a place where God's will is done in subversive groups (as in the Jesus movement), but a place where God's will rules, that is, is totally at home. Remember that the teachers 2 Peter opposes do not live righteously — they deny the Lord who bought them by disobeying his teaching. Such people will have no place in this new age of the universe. Instead, it will be the addressees of the letter, who are exhorted to live and assumed to be living "holy and godly lives" who will be at home there, as their present dysfunctional (in terms of the culture around them) lifestyle shows.

Our author points out that it is this renewed creation to which followers of Jesus are looking forward. The problem contemporary followers of Jesus have is not that they are looking forward too much to the future world, but that they are not looking forward enough to it. We tend to conform our lifestyles to this present age, trying to live functionally with respect to it, which is short-sighted since this age is passing away. Instead, 2 Peter exhorts us to have our eyes fixed on the coming age and to let that age determine our present lifestyle. It is to that topic that he turns in the final encouragement of his letter.

## D. Body Closing: Final Encouragement (3:14-16)

> [14]*So then, dear friends, since you are looking forward to this, make every effort to be found spotless, blameless and at peace with him.* [15]*Bear in mind that our Lord's patience means salvation, just as our dear brother Paul also wrote you with the wisdom that God gave him.* [16]*He writes the same way in all his letters, speaking in them of these matters. His letters contain some things that are hard to understand, which ignorant and unstable people distort, as they do the other Scriptures, to their own destruction.*

**14** Our author signals the letter body closing with an inferential conjunction ( "so then" or "wherefore") and the repetition of the noun of address ("dear friends" or "beloved"). A similar pairing of conjunction

62. Bauckham, *Jude, 2 Peter,* 326, says about the Jewish and Christian literature, "Such passages emphasize the radical discontinuity between the old and the new, but it is nevertheless clear that they intend to describe a renewal, not an abolition, of creation."

and noun of address in 3:17 will indicate that the body closing is finished and the letter closing is beginning.

The "so then" refers back to the situation described in the previous section, that is, the end of the second age of the world and the beginning of the third, the new heavens and new earth. This is made clear by the participial phrase "since you are looking forward to this." They are expecting something, and this has consequences for their present behavior, just as brides and grooms approaching their wedding are already changing their financial, social, and other behavior in the light of what they are expecting.

These addressees are exhorted to "make every effort" to be prepared for the new age. The idea of making every effort has already appeared twice in 2 Peter, first with respect to them in 1:10 ("be all the more eager to make your calling and election sure") and then as a commitment of Peter in 1:15 ("I will make every effort to see that after my departure you will always be able to remember these things"). It is the former reference that is relevant here, for holiness is how they make their calling and election sure. Such effort is not foreign to the rest of the NT, for the verb occurs in ethical exhortation in Eph 4:3; 2 Tim 2:15; and Heb 4:11. The appropriate lifestyle of a follower of Jesus does not just happen; it requires effort, especially since the forces of the surrounding culture will attempt to make apprentices of Jesus adjust their behavior back to that of the majority culture.

The effort is directed toward behavior that follows the directives of Jesus, here described in terms of purity: "spotless, blameless." Both terms in this word pair come from sacrificial language and are thus metaphorical. In fact, the word pair is probably expressing a single idea, not two ideas (i.e., we have a metonymy). In the OT it is only pure animals, that is, "unblemished," that are appropriate for sacrifice. For instance, in the Greek OT our second term, "blameless"/"unblemished," is applied to a bull and two rams in Exod 29:1 and two lambs in Exod 29:38 (see also Lev 1:3, 10; 3:1; and many similar passages in the OT). The animal is to be whole or perfect in every way. The best animals are to be offered to YHWH. Likewise, in 1 Macc 4:42 the priest who offers the animals is to be whole or entire, both in the sense that he is a faithful follower of the law (which is the probable idea in 1 Macc 4:42) and in the sense that he is physically whole (Lev 21:17-24).[1] In the NT this metaphorical language is

1. Lev 21:17-18, 21 repeatedly uses the word "blemish" *(mōmos),* which is the positive form of our word "blameless"/"without blemish" *(amōmētos).* On priestly purity see Rodney K. Duke, "Priests, Priesthood," in T. Desmond Alexander and David W. Baker, eds., *Dictionary of the Old Testament: Pentateuch* (Downers Grove, IL: InterVarsity Press, 2003), 646-55, especially 651-52.

applied to Christ in 1 Pet 2:19, where he is viewed as "a lamb without blemish or defect." (Heb 9:14 has a similar use of our second term alone.) Normally, however, the terms are used without explicit sacrificial imagery for moral uprightness,[2] as in 1 Tim 6:14; Jas 1:27 (for our first term) and Eph 1:4; Phil 2:15; Col 1:22; Rev 14:5 (for our second term). In most of these passages our terms appear paired with other synonyms or near synonyms, including the term "holy." The particular use here in 2 Peter is likely influenced by Jude 24 ("To him who is able to keep you from falling and to present you before his glorious presence *without fault* and with great joy"), where a form of our second term appears.

The point our author is making is that purity in the eyes of the Lord (which is not limited to sexual purity, as it often is in contemporary usage) is something to make every effort to gain. It alone has lasting value. It is the lack of this purity that marks the lives of the teachers our author opposes. And this lack of purity will condemn them to destruction since purity is the natural result of submission to Jesus as Lord. Thus, if we need to spend time in spiritual disciplines, perhaps under the direction of a spiritual director, join a recovery group to seek release from compulsive actions, spend time in counseling, or take some other appropriate action to gain this purity, it is well worth the effort. Indeed, the rest of our life may be vitiated without such effort.

Moving on in our passage, we ask, "How does 'at peace' relate to this purity?" Two basic ways of translating this verse bring out the possible relationships. The one, followed by the NIV, relates "at peace" to "him" (i.e., "our Lord," as the next verse makes clear), and the "spotless and blameless" are either parts of a three-adjective series (as in the NIV),[3]

2. In fact, our second term is ordinarily used in Greek for moral purity, and so the NIV's "blameless" is accurate enough. See F. Hauck, "*mōmos, amōmos, amōmētos,*" *TDNT* 4:829-31 and in particular our term *amōmētos* on 831. There are exceptions to this moral use, such as Philo, *Quaest. Gen.* 2.5 (with respect to a person's physical proportions) and *Aet.* 41.5 ("All the works of God are without blemish. . . . But it is consistent with the character of, and becoming to God to give form to what is shapeless, and to invest what is most ugly with admirable beauty"), but most of the forty occurrences in Greek literature from the fifth century B.C. through the third century A.D. are moral in character. The term is not found elsewhere in the Greek Bible, except in some later manuscripts of Phil 2:15, although its positive form *mōmētos* ("blemished," probably in a moral sense) appears in Deut 32:5. While this term in our text seems to have a moral tone, its pairing with "spotless" and its close relationship to the term for "without blemish" that is often used in sacrificial contexts (i.e., *amōmos*), as well as the fact that Philo always uses it with the "without blemish" meaning, make it probable that our author wishes us to recall the sacrificial background here as well.

3. So also the main German translations, following Luther. *Die Gute Nachricht* makes "at peace with him" independent, but then repeats "at him" with "spotless and blameless."

or they expand on the idea of being "at peace with him."[4] The second, as seen in the ASV ("Wherefore, beloved, seeing that ye look for these things, give diligence that ye may be found in peace, without spot and blameless in his sight") relates "spotless and blameless" to "him" and takes "at peace" as a further characteristic of the community.[5]

In our view it is this latter interpretation that fits best into the passage. In 2 Pet 3:10 the "fire" will strip off the heavens, and the stars and planets in them, so that "the earth and the works in her will be found/discovered" (to give our own rather wooden translation), presumably by God or the Lord. Here in our passage we have the other side of the coin, that true followers of Jesus (i.e., the addressees of the letter) are "to be found/discovered by him spotless and without (moral) blemish." Those scoffers who ignore the Lord's Parousia will have their character and works exposed with appropriate consequences, but so will those true followers of Jesus have theirs exposed, also with appropriate consequences. Here in 3:14 we have the flip side of 3:10. This fits with (1) the normal meaning of the verb for finding/discovering, (2) the contrast of the "scoffers" or false teachers with the addressees, and (3) the usual eschatological sense of the "spotless" and "without blemish" metaphors (i.e., in most of the passages this moral state is determined only at the coming of Christ). Finally, it seems the most natural way of reading the Greek word order.[6]

But what about the phrase at the end of the verse, "in peace"? Neyrey relates this to the Hebrew *shalom* in its Semitic root meaning of "complete" or "whole" and thus as a restatement of "spotless and unblemished" in their moral meaning.[7] Bauckham suggests that this is "the state of reconciliation with God which is Christian salvation."[8] Both of these interpretations are possible since in 2 Pet 1:2 it does occur in the stylized greeting that wishes grace and peace *(shalom)* upon the addresses from God (cf. 1 Pet 1:2). But given that the type of issues mentioned in this book could disturb the community and that the references to scoffers and false teachers could leave them hunting for such people and thus damaging the solidarity of the community, one suspects that this add-on phrase is a reference to being at peace in the community, which is a signif-

4. NRSV. So apparently the TEV (although it is not clear).

5. In this it follows the KJV. So also Vg, RSV, NASV, NKJV, ESV, NAB, NLV (although the peace there is clearly "with God").

6. On the concept of purity, see further Neyrey, *2 Peter, Jude,* 247-49.

7. Neyrey, *2 Peter, Jude,* 250-51. He further relates this to Isa 32:17, which links peace to righteousness, and to 1 Thess 5:23, where the "God of peace" is said to sanctify the readers.

8. Bauckham, *Jude, 2 Peter,* 327.

icant Christian virtue (e.g., 1 Pet 3:11; Jas 3:18). In that case peace is not to be taken with "in him" but as a separate thought added to the sentence.

**15** But if 3:14 instructs the addressees how to live while expecting the coming new age, how are they to deal with the delay that they are experiencing. Our author has advice for this as well: "Bear in mind that [or "count" or "consider"] our Lord's patience means salvation." The "scoffers" consider "our Lord's patience" to be an indication that there will be no Parousia, that everything will go on as it has since the beginning of creation (2 Pet 3:4). They consider it to be a myth in the negative sense of that term. Others (perhaps the "scoffers" themselves in the course of their argument) consider "our Lord's patience" to mean that he is slow to keep his promises (2 Pet 3:9); in other words, they attribute a dishonorable motive to the Lord. Our author has already argued that this is not the case. First, he argued that past historical precedents show that the idea that judgment is a myth is unfounded. Second, he has argued that the Lord's slowness is not a moral fault (i.e., human slowness), a dishonorable motive or defect in character, but rather the honorable character trait "long-suffering"/"patience" because the Lord wants everyone to "come to repentance" so that they do not "perish." Now our author picks up on that theme and abbreviates it.

"Consider" or "count" our Lord's "patience" (or "long-suffering" — this is the nominal form of the verb that was used in 3:9 and which we discussed while exegeting that verse) "salvation" (which is a short way of indicating the result of repentance and the opposite of perishing). This salvation is probably eschatological salvation on that final day, which is how Jude 3 use the term and also how 1 Pet 1:5; 2:2 use the term. Salvation is not something that we have in the sense of experiencing it, but something that we have in the sense of a promise, something that will be revealed at the coming of Jesus. It is then that judgment will be given (and that judgment is the main subject of this chapter in 2 Peter), and the followers of Jesus (notice that our author refers to Jesus or perhaps God as "our Lord" and so includes his addressees among the true followers of Jesus) will experience his deliverance and reward in that day of judgment. This salvation, as we have seen (see the comment on 2 Pet 1:1) is from "our God and Savior Jesus Christ" and comes on that final day, for "the Lord knows how to rescue godly men from trials" (2 Pet 2:9), dividing between the righteous and the unrighteous, as examples from history have shown.

So this is how one is to think about the long wait that the church has endured with respect to the Parousia. It is salvation, salvation for many of those whom Peter addresses who had recently come to repentance, salvation for the millions of followers of Jesus who have lived throughout the ages, and salvation for peoples around the world about whom our author is not even dimly aware, but whom we know have come to repentance and thus will not perish, people living from Tierra del Fuego to the Arctic Circle and from the east coast of China right around to the west coast of the United States. And especially in our age we remember the millions of believers in the global South since the average believer today is not Caucasian or Western but black or otherwise colored and probably living in the southern hemisphere, far beyond the worldview of our author. But this is what our Lord's patience has meant: it has meant that salvation has reached them, and it has meant that salvation has reached us.

This interpretation of the delay of the Parousia (a delay for which followers of Jesus are in part responsible since they can "speed its coming"; 3:12) is confirmed by "dear brother Paul." "Dear [or "beloved"] brother" was a way of referring to a colleague in the Jesus movement. We find the complete phrase in Eph 6:21 (Tychicus) and Col 4:7 (also Tychicus), 9 (Onesimus), and the last part of it ("brother") in 2 Cor 2:13 (Titus); Phil 2:25 (Epaphroditus); Col 1:7 (Epaphras); 1 Thess 3:2 (Timothy), Phlm 1 (Timothy) and 1 Pet 5:12 (Silvanus). "Beloved" or "dear" is probably not simply a term of courtesy, but it seems to convey affection since it is also attached to the names of co-workers (e.g., Acts 15:25 [Barnabas and Paul]; Rom 16:12 [Persis]; 3 John 1 [Gaius]). So we note that in the NT "brother" as a type of address is always used for some type of co-worker, and the adjective "beloved" indicates that this co-worker is a valued and honored co-worker, one whom the author views with some affection.

As a title for Paul it should be compared with *1 Clem.* 47:1 ("the blessed Paul the apostle"), Ignatius, *Eph.* 12:2 ("Paul, the holy one who received a testimony and proved worth of all fortune"), *Rom.* 4:3 (Peter and Paul are "apostles" with authority the author does not have), Polycarp, *Phil.* 3:2 ("the blessed and glorious Paul"), and 9:1 ("Paul himself and the other apostles"). What is noticeable in 2 Peter is that our author does not refer to Paul as an apostle, which virtually all passages in the apostolic fathers do, but uses the normal term for a fellow worker in the fictive family[9] of the Jesus movement, "brother," and he uses a term of endear-

9. The Jesus movement, following Jesus (Mark 3:31-35), saw itself as a fictive family (fictive in the sense that it was not a blood family) that took precedence over the blood family. Thus we have practices such as the "holy kiss" (normally one kisses only blood relatives and perhaps very close friends), the terminology of "brother" and "sister," and the transfer of the authority of the head of the family to Jesus (one does not obey the head of one's blood family when he conflicts with the directives of Jesus, although, following the practice of Jesus, one tries to be a peacemaker when such peacemaking does not conflict with the directives of Jesus). "Fictive" does not mean "not real" or "imaginary" but is rather a sociological term for "not blood." For the early Jesus movement one's fictive family was more real, not less real, than one's blood family.

ment rather than the terms of exaltation (e.g., "blessed") that were used in the period of the apostolic fathers. Thus, if our author is a later pseudepigrapher, he is really good at remembering such details about the earlier period of the Jesus movement.

Notice that Paul is referred to as "our" beloved brother. Our author can use the second person plural when he is including himself with his addressees ("our God and Savior Jesus Christ" [1:1] or "Jesus our Lord" [1:2]), when he refers to himself together with an undefined group around him ("a faith as precious as ours"; 1:1), and when he refers to himself together with the other members of the Twelve who witnessed the Transfiguration ("We did not follow cleverly invented stories when we told you about the power and coming of our Lord Jesus Christ, but we were eyewitnesses of his majesty"; 1:16).[10] But it is clear that he is not given to the use of the epistolary "we," for he shifts to "I" when he is speaking of his own personal commitment (1:12-15; 3:1-2).[11] Thus in our passage he is clearly including himself in a group that values Paul. But what group is it? Bauckham and Vögtle follow Schrage in arguing that "our" is the group of apostles, so Paul is a beloved fellow apostle to the apostles.[12] On the other hand, Mayor believes that the reference is to "Christians generally."[13]

In all probability we need to find a middle way. That is, if one feels that 2 Peter was written after there was a definite sense of an apostolic "college," then certainly "our" refers to this group. But in our comments above on 2 Pet 3:1 we have questioned this idea. On the other hand, each of the places where Paul uses this exact linguistic formulation he is referring to a valued colleague and co-worker, but not necessarily to someone whom he would call an apostle. Nor is he referring to the group of apos-

10. The reference group for the first "we" is debated. It could mean "we apostles" (including those missionaries who first brought the good news to 2 Peter's addressees) or "we followers of Jesus," that is, Peter and the apostolic group or Peter and the group around him (whether that group be his local community of the Jesus movement or whether it be Peter and his colleagues, as there is compelling evidence in both the NT and tradition to make us believe that Peter, like Paul, worked with a team of co-workers and apprentices around him). See the further discussion of "our" in our verse. Clearly the "we" associated with the claim to be eyewitnesses must refer to the members of the Twelve who saw the Transfiguration.

11. Paul also does not seem to use the epistolary "we," but rather uses "we" when he is including his colleagues or co-authors. We need to remember that more than one of his letters is a co-authored work, so more than one voice is speaking, although at this distance we cannot separate what Paul dictated and what came from Timothy or Silas.

12. Bauckham, *Jude, 2 Peter*; Vögtle, *Der Judasbrief, der zweite Petrusbrief*, 262; Schrage, *Der zweite Petrusbrief, der Judabrief*, 154; Schreiner, *1, 2 Peter, Jude*, 105.

13. Mayor, *Jude and II Peter*, 164.

tles in his "our" but to himself and those associated with him in his ministry (and in Colossians to Timothy, who was a co-author of the letter). Thus, while it is possible that Peter means "all followers of Jesus, you as well as us, consider Paul a beloved brother," the linguistic evidence points to his meaning "the group around me considers Paul a beloved brother." Anything more than this assumes a solution to the authorship question and then, often, uses this verse as evidence for making that assumption, ignoring the various parallels in the Pauline corpus and other NT literature.

Could Peter have referred to Paul as "our beloved brother"? On the basis of Gal 2:11-14, usually combined with some assumption about early Catholicism and its tendency to reconcile the unreconciled and especially Peter and Paul, it is often assumed that this could not be the case and that this phrase is patent evidence that we are dealing with a pseudepigrapher writing in the name of Peter. However, just as we noted above that the fact that the letter refers to Paul in terms that were current in the second half of the first century but not in the apostolic fathers is compatible with the assertion that but does not prove that the letter is really written by Peter (a discerning writer immersed in such writings could use the earlier style), so this term of collegial affection does not prove the opposite. One text that everyone accepts as genuine (Gal 2:11-14) tells us that Paul once sharply rebuked Peter in public. We are not told the outcome of this conflict, which some take to mean that Peter never backed down and the conflict went on, and others take to mean that Paul realizes his readers know they were reconciled. But even taking the more negative interpretation of that silence (and any argument from silence is weak) and ignoring the post-Galatians texts that show Paul and Peter in agreement (Acts 15:7ff. suffers from the fact that its relationship to Galatians 2 is disputed; 1 Cor 9:5; 15:5 are certainly not negative about Peter, but also do not say anything about his relationship to Paul), there is no reason to believe that the conflict between Peter and Paul was not reconciled (as the iconic tradition asserts). It is difficult to believe that an author like Paul who wrote so much about reconciliation and peace in the community would not have put significant effort into such a reconciliation.[14] Furthermore, on anyone's reckoning a minimum of ten or fifteen years have passed. No one who has a valued colleague with whom he or she once had a sharp disagreement (and this author has more than one person in

14. The Petrine tradition also includes the theme of peace (1 Pet 3:11; 2 Pet 3:14), but the authorship of both works is disputed. At a minimum they show that someone writing in the name of Peter would find communal harmony an appropriate theme to mention.

that category) would doubt the possibility that such reconciliation was possible.

What is clear is that Paul has written to these believers.[15] The problem is that this Pauline letter (or letters) has been identified with a number of those in the Pauline corpus.[16] Sometimes this is done on the basis of assumptions about the addressees of 2 Peter (e.g., Rome, or the same recipients as 1 Peter) and sometimes on the basis of content (i.e., which Pauline letter or letters contain the theme of 2 Pet 3:14-15 or that of the whole of 2 Peter 3). The fact is that 2 Peter gives no clear indication of where its addressees live, and the idea of living a holy life in the light of waiting for the Parousia of Christ is so common in the NT, including the Pauline letters, that, as we see has been done, a case can be made out for most of Paul's letters. That these believers have received a letter from Paul does narrow the field of addressees somewhat (even though we know that some letters of Paul were lost, there is no evidence that he wrote to any group outside his area of ministry, with the one exception of Romans, so it is probable, but not absolutely necessary, that the addressees live within Paul's area of ministry). But the attempt to identify the particular letter and thus the addressees is futile. Our author is not referring to a specific passage in a letter, but to the general agreement of Paul to what he has taught. We cannot get more specific than this, even though we would very much like to.

Our author does note that Paul wrote "with the wisdom that God gave him." (The Greek text has "the wisdom that was given to him," but the passive is probably a so-called "divine passive," referring in the passive to God as the giver, so the NIV interprets it rightly.) Paul (1 Cor 12:8; Eph 1:17; Col 1:19) and James (Jas 1:5), among others in the NT, refer to wisdom as a divine gift. James mentions that one asks God for wisdom and that God gives generously. Paul cites wisdom as a gift of the Spirit and in Eph 1:17 refers to a "spirit of wisdom and revelation." What our author is doing is attributing divine inspiration to Paul, parallel to that

15. Kelly, *The Epistles of Peter and of Jude*, 371-73, argues that the "you" is really all Christians and that this is simply an anticipation of "all his letters" of 2 Pet 3:16, that is, an indication of the collection of the Pauline corpus. However, as Bauckham, *Jude, 2 Peter*, argues, this defies the grammar of the two verses, for we first have "just as . . . wrote you" in 3:15 and then in 3:16 we have "as also in all his letters" (our translation for the NIV gives the sense, but obscures this point of grammar). Thus we have a comparison, one letter or letters addressed to the group compared to some wider group of Paul's letters. The author does not appear to mean that these two references to Pauline writing mean the same thing.

16. Mayor, *Jude and II Peter*, 164, prefers Romans, but notes that 1 Corinthians, Galatians, Ephesians, Colossians, 1 and 2 Thessalonians, and even Hebrews (or combinations of two or three of these letters) have been suggested by various commentators over the years.

which he attributes to the prophets in 1:20-21, but referring to a gift of the Spirit rather than to the Spirit itself, that is, to how the inspiration was appropriated by Paul rather than to the agent of inspiration.[17] Thus he is arguing that Paul, who had written to these addressees and who wrote under the inspiration of divine wisdom, confirms, at least in a general sense, the position that 2 Peter has just taken.

**16** But it was not just in the letter that Paul had written to the addressees of 2 Peter that he had written about the topics of concern to our author. He writes about "these matters" in "all his letters." On the one hand, this remark shows that it is likely misguided to try to determine which Pauline letter was written to these addressees (since Paul treats the same topics in all his letters). On the other hand, it shows that our author is aware of several Pauline letters. This knowledge again raises the dating issue. We know that Paul himself on one occasion had requested that churches share his letters: "After this letter has been read to you, see that it is also read in the church of the Laodiceans and that you in turn read the letter from Laodicea" (Col 4:16). But it is a big jump in time from Colossians to the first concrete evidence we have of people who know more than one letter. This evidence shows up in *1 Clement,* who not only knows Romans but can also write to the Corinthians, "Take up the epistle of the blessed Apostle Paul" (*1 Clem.* 47:1). It appears later in *2 Clement* and in Ignatius's *Ephesians.*[18] Thus we are on solid ground when we assume that a collection of the Pauline letters existed by the end of the first century.[19] It is also likely that some Pauline letters circulated independently of a collection (which is what one would expect as one church hears that another has a letter that might prove helpful in their situation),[20] and that there were collections of a few Pauline letters before there was a collection of all of his letters.[21] All

17. The parallel to 1:21 has been shown by Martino Conti, "La Sophia di 2 Petr. 3.15," *Rivista Biblica* 17 (1969) 121-38.

18. Ignatius, *Eph.* 12:2, refers to Paul, "who in all his Epistles makes mention of you in Christ Jesus." (Although one wonders how Ignatius thought the Ephesians were mentioned in every Pauline letter he knew.) On the evidence for 2 Clement's knowledge of a collection, see Karl P. Donfried, *The Setting of Second Clement in Early Christianity* (NovTSup 38; Leiden: E. J. Brill, 1974), 93-95.

19. Jack Finegan, "The Original Form of the Pauline Collection," *HTR* 49 (1956) 85-104. See also Walter Schmithals, "Zur Abfassung und ältesten Sammlung der paulinischen Hauptbriefe" ["On the Composition and Earliest Collection of the Major Epistles of Paul"], *ZNW* 51 (1960) 225-45.

20. Harry Gamble, "The Redaction of the Pauline Letters and the Formation of the Pauline Corpus," *JBL* 94 (1971) 403-18.

21. Mary Lucetta Mowry, "The Early Circulation of Paul's Letters," *JBL* 63 (1944) 73-86.

of this is quite logical since Paul was a valued teacher in his circle of communities and, as he left an area and especially as he died, his letters were his continuing voice. Thus churches would share letters and, as they obtained funds (a few hundred dollars to a couple thousand dollars in today's money), make copies. Copies would turn into collections, especially since it was possible to use one scroll for several of the shorter letters. Probably by the end of the first century the complete collection (i.e., all extant letters) was circulating to at least a limited degree (remember, these copies did not come cheap). The issue is which stage in this process 2 Peter is indicating.

The fact is that while Neyrey lists sixteen terms and four themes that 2 Peter shares with Paul, which come from Romans, 1 and 2 Corinthians, Philippians, and 1 Thessalonians,[22] the only really plausible parallels are Rom 2:4 and 2 Pet 3:9, 15, 1 Thess 5:2 and 2 Pet 3:10, and a possible reflection of Romans in 2 Pet 2:19. The rest of the parallels are all to terms and ideas that were relatively common in the early Jesus movement or in the surrounding Greco-Roman culture; thus independent use is as or more likely than influence from Paul. Thus it is incorrect to assume that 2 Peter knows the whole Pauline collection and thus must be dated close to or after the end of the first century. He appears to know only two or three Pauline letters, and perhaps he has heard of, but not seen, others as traveling believers reported what they used in their communities. These data could fit a wide range of dates in the second half of the first century, depending on where one assumes our author was living when he wrote 2 Peter.[23]

Clearly our author believes that Paul's writings in general agree with the position that he has laid out in the previous verses of 2 Peter 3, but also that he realizes that Paul's writings are difficult. From our perspective that is just what we would expect, since a letter is one half of a dialogue that takes place without either body language or immediate feedback. Thus what was clear to the original recipients might not be clear to a reader who knew the culture yet did not know the specific situation of the original recipients. Furthermore, the lack of immediate feedback means that Paul himself may not be aware of misunderstandings

22. Neyrey, *2 Peter, Jude*, 133-34.

23. Since Rome was the central node in the empire, one suspects that the letters of Paul were known relatively quickly in that city, and because pre-A.D. 70 Jerusalem was so important to the early Christian movement, perhaps to a lesser degree there as well (Galatians, both Corinthian letters, both Thessalonian letters, and Romans at least were written before Paul was imprisoned in Caesarea). In the minds of many scholars, Colossians, Philippians, Philemon, and perhaps Ephesians were also written before the end of Paul's third missionary journey.

that he is engendering in his readers,[24] let alone in those who do not know the situation of his original readers. Thus our author says that Paul's letters "contain some things that are hard to understand." The term for "hard to understand" *(dysnoētos)* is not found elsewhere in biblical Greek and is rare in nonbiblical Greek (only fourteen occurrences in the period from five centuries B.C. to three centuries A.D.), but its meaning is clear enough: it refers to exactly what the NIV says, that is, "something that is hard to understand."[25] Perhaps its most interesting use is in Hermas, *Sim.* 9:14:4, where Hermas asks for an interpretation of a vision he has received since the vision is "difficult for people to understand."

While our author recognizes that some of what Paul writes is difficult to understand (which is a great comfort to contemporary commentators), he does not inform us how difficult *he* finds Paul to understand. It is likely that he does have to work on understanding some of what Paul says (e.g., if he knows Romans, the broken grammatical construction in Rom 5:12 may have given him pause for thought), but his concern is not with people like himself who are well instructed in the faith but with "ignorant and unstable" people, whom he views as distorting Paul's teaching. The "ignorant" person (the term appears only here in the NT) is not the person who is stupid, but the person who is uninstructed. Philo uses the term eleven times, and Josephus, *Ant.* 12.191 (12.4.7) writes, "Joseph [son of Tobias, A.D. 200] had once a mind to know which of his sons had the best disposition to virtue; and when he sent them severally to those that had then the best reputation for instructing youth, the rest of his children, by reason of their sloth and unwillingness to take pains, returned to him foolish and unlearned."[26]

The term "unstable" has appeared earlier in our letter (2:14; cf. the verbal form of the contrasting idea in 1:12). Together the two words form the picture of a people who may be highly intelligent and well educated, but when it comes to knowing the narrative of Scripture and the major concepts of what we now know as the NT (in those days it would have been largely oral teaching) they are uninstructed and therefore unstable.

24. It is possible that 2 Thessalonians corrects a misunderstanding that Paul has when writing 1 Thessalonians, that is, that the Thessalonians wrote (or sent an oral message) back to Paul after receiving 1 Thessalonians, "Thanks for the information about the resurrection of the dead at the return of the Lord, but the issue floating around here is not that there will be no resurrection of the dead, but that the return of the Lord has already happened and we have missed it." If that were the case, we and the church through the ages are happy that the misunderstanding happened so that we have both pieces of instruction.

25. Johannes Behm, *"noeō, nous ktl.," TDNT* 4:693.

26. The term also occurs in several non-Jewish Greek writers, including the philosopher Epictetus, who lived in the first century.

Their knowledge is only superficial, so they are prey to the false teachers. They are like the student whom this writer once had who on an exam translated a passage in Romans from Greek as, "Therefore being justified by works without faith . . . ," apparently without realizing that it was impossible that Paul could have written that and therefore that his translation was faulty (as his professor would point out). This description shows the need for good catechesis in the church; that is, we should not simply expect that those newly committed to Jesus will simply pick up biblical knowledge, including the overall narrative and the main themes of Scripture, by sitting in church services, but we should set about to deliberately inculcate such knowledge in them so that, being rooted in the whole story, they will not easily be led astray.

For our author the issue is that such people "distort" Paul's letters "as they do the other Scriptures," and the result is "their own destruction." The term for "distort" has two meanings, the first of which is to "torture" or "torment" (a person, including oneself, with anxiety) and the second of which is to "twist, distort" "something so that a false meaning results."[27] It occurs only once in biblical Greek, in 2 Sam 22:27, LXX (2 Kgdms 22:27 in LXX terminology): the NIV translates that verse, "to the pure you show yourself pure, but to the crooked you show yourself shrewd." The LXX could be translated, "with the distorted you will be distorted" or "with the twisted you will be twisted." In 2 Samuel the twisting is passive, but in our passage it is active: these uninstructed and unstable people are twisting Paul.

Our author appears to be attributing guilt to these people. First, while being uninstructed can be simply an unfortunate situation (think about people who desire an education but cannot afford one), it can, as we saw in the quotation above from Josephus, be the result of refusing instruction. Second, distorting something is an active process. It is more than saying, "I do not understand this," or even than saying, "I do not like this," but rather implies an active abuse of a text, a twisting of its meaning to fit one's own purposes. Third, and most decisive, their distortions will result in their own destruction, which is what the false teachers receive in 2 Pet 2:1-2 and the ungodly sufferer in 2 Pet 3:7. Thus it looks as if the primary people in view here are not the victims of the false teachers of ch. 2 (2:14, 18) or those taken in by the "scoffers" of ch. 3, but rather the false teachers or "scoffers" themselves. Naturally their victims would be included to the extent that they picked up the way that these "teachers" abused Paul and the other Scriptures and distorted such writings themselves, but the focus seems to be on the leaders. They have refused the in-

27. "*Strebloō,*" BAG 771.

struction of our author and the rest of the tradition; they are misusing Paul and finding novel ways to interpret Scripture to be compatible with their views.

How were they misusing Paul and the other Scriptures? We can only speculate as to the answer to this question, but some possibilities suggest themselves. We know that later Gnostics would use Paul's doctrine of grace to justify their antinomian views.[28] There are certainly strains of "grace" teaching in the church today that do just that, that suggest that sin may not be a good idea, but since we are saved by grace our ongoing sin has no effect on our salvation. There is also the possibility that they distorted Paul's teaching on the resurrection (e.g., 1 Corinthians 15) so as to come up with a purely spiritual resurrection (one that happened at conversion or one that happened at death) and so do away with the need for a day of judgment. Again, parts of the church today interpret 1 Corinthians 15 that way. Finally, they may have distorted Paul and then rejected their distortion of Paul: "Paul teaches these weird ideas, and so it is clear that he did not know what he was talking about and we can safely dismiss what he has to say about the Parousia." All of these and more are possibilities, but the fact is that 2 Peter does not give us enough information about how these "unstable" people were using Paul for us to know.[29]

What we do know is that he does not try to defend Paul, but cites him as an accepted authority who, he believes, supports his position if interpreted appropriately. His addressees had received a letter from Paul, so they are as likely as not in the Pauline group of churches, a group that would value Paul as an authority. Given that there was no NT when 2 Peter was written and that our author might not even have had a written gospel that he knew he shared with his addressees, this citing of Paul was about as close as he could come to citing the authority of the NT in support of one's views today.[30]

28. Cf. Elaine H. Pagels, *The Gnostic Paul: Gnostic Exegesis of the Pauline Letters* (Philadelphia: Fortress, 1975), 66-67, who documents this for second-century Gnostics. Bauckham, *Jude, 2 Peter,* 332, suggests that such texts as Rom 4:15; 5:20; 8:1-2; 1 Cor 6:12; 2 Cor 3:17 may have been used in their arguments for "freedom." Paul himself had to counter such interpretations of his teaching: Rom 3:8; 6:15; Gal 5:13.

29. This leads Neyrey, *2 Peter, Jude,* 250, to suggest that our author is simply making "a claim of legitimacy in virtue of a tradition which is held always by all people everywhere. . . . Hence, the particularities of Paul's letters are ignored in favor of his acceptance as a representative of the tradition."

30. We discussed above that there is no reason to suppose that in light of the Peter–Paul conflict in Gal 2:11-14 there would be a lasting Peter–Paul antipathy (except in the eyes of contemporary scholars influenced by F. C. Baur and the Tübingen School — see the references in E. Earle Ellis, *Paul and His Recent Interpreters* [Grand Rapids: William B. Eerdmans, 1961]). Thus it should not surprise us that a Peter (whether one views him as

Interestingly he cites Paul along with "the other Scriptures." It is clear that this term refers to those works our author considers authoritative writings (the word "Scripture" means "writing"), for that is how the term "the Scriptures" is used in the NT (e.g., Rom 4:3; 9:17; 10:11; 1 Cor 15:3; Gal 3:8; 4:30; 1 Tim 5:18; Jas 2:8; cf. 2 Pet 1:20, which shows that even when the definite article is not used, usually such texts are meant). Naturally this included the Torah (Pentateuch), Prophets, and Writings that most Jews recognized (depending on when one dates 2 Peter, not all Jews recognized the Writings as authoritative), but also, given that 2 Peter, like most people in the early Jesus movement, cited the Scriptures in their Greek form, the extra books and additions to books found in what we call the Septuagint (LXX). Furthermore, since this is before any clear canon consciousness developed, it appears that the designation also includes some books that we would not include, such as the unknown work cited by James (Jas 4:5) or *1 Enoch,* the content of which is cited by 2 Peter and the exact words of which are cited by Jude. Thus in the absence of later discussions about the canon and the binding of Scripture into codices (what we now refer to when we speak of "books" — before this there were separate scrolls), the term was not as clearly bounded as it is today. Whatever the exact delimitations of our author's Scriptures, clearly he is including Paul among them. There is really no other way to interpret the term "other."[31]

Does this fact that Paul is included among the "Scriptures" mean that we must date 2 Peter late in the first century? It is true that it is in the apostolic fathers that we first see absolutely clear examples of writings from the first generation of the Jesus movement being cited alongside the Jewish Scriptures (*Barn.* 4:14; 2 *Clem.* 2:4; 14:2; Polycarp, *Phil.* 12:1). Possibly Bauckham is correct that 1 Tim 5:18 (which quotes the saying of Jesus we know from Matt 10:10 alongside an OT text) shows that already at that time the writings of the Jesus movement were being considered Scripture.[32] But even if 1 Tim 5:18 is a citation of the written Matthew (or a written source of Matthew), which some scholars will certainly dispute, it is a citation of the teaching of Jesus, the Lord and Master. This would not mean that Paul was being considered Scripture at the same time.

---

the real Peter or someone writing in his name — see the Introduction to this book, pp. 145-49) cites Paul positively.

31. Bauckham, *Jude, 2 Peter,* 333, cites Green, *Second Peter and Jude,* 147-49 (although Bauckham does not give page numbers) as supporting the idea that "other" distinguishes Paul from the OT writings. In reality Green is citing Bigg as holding that position, while he himself favors a position similar to the one we are outlining.

32. Bauckham, *Jude, 2 Peter,* 333. The even earlier 1 Cor 6:2 and 7:10 appear to refer to specific sayings of Jesus, but they do not refer to them as "Scripture" or cite them alongside OT texts.

Even the passages quoted by the apostolic fathers cite a gospel in two of the four cases, and one of the four (2 *Clem.* 14:2) simply refers to "the Scriptures and the apostles" without indicating whether non-Gospel apostolic writings were intended (although it would not be surprising if they were — at least one unknown writing is cited in 2 *Clem.* 14:3).

The truth is that we will likely never pin down when the psychological barrier between "the Scriptures" and the newly produced writings of the Jesus movement (including the writings of Paul) was crossed; it was probably crossed at different times in different communities and even in different individuals within the various communities. If a community had been founded by Paul, they certainly believed that they had heard "the word of the Lord" from him as he preached; he had been their source of truth and enlightenment, including their source of how to interpret the Jewish Scriptures. What would happen when such a community received a letter from Paul or a copy of a letter Paul had written to another community? Surely it would be valued from the start. Would they have had a chest somewhere in the group of house churches where they kept what Jewish Scriptures they owned and into which they now put this valued letter from Paul?[33] Would the letters from their founder not have been read alongside the Jewish Scriptures? We cannot document the "when," but under such circumstances it would not be at all surprising if such a community had not quickly mentioned Paul's writings (such as they had) and the Jewish writings (i.e., the Scriptures) in the same breath. We would be unwise to expect this to have happened before Paul permanently left the area, but his leaving or his subsequent death would have surely elevated the value of these writings since the living voice was not available. It is anyone's guess how soon that happened in any given community. And without knowing the history of the community or communities to which 2 Peter is addressed, his grouping of Paul's letters with "the Scriptures" is impossible to use as a tool for dating the book.

What is clear is that the specious arguments from these "scoffers"/false teachers are not helping them in their cause. They are not convincing our author that they are right. Instead, they are displaying that they have not learned the true tradition, that they are not reading the passages they cite in the light of the whole narrative. These teachers probably see their interpretation as justifying their position. Our author sees it as rationalization that will lead to their own destruction (i.e., eschatological

33. That is what Green, *Second Peter and Jude*, 147-48, reasonably argues. Of course, copies of the Jewish Scriptures were expensive, so it is unlikely that each house church had a full set, and it would not be surprising if many groups of house churches (i.e., city churches) could not collectively afford a full set.

judgment). He uses the emphatic "their own," which could mean that they were predicting dire consequences for the orthodox, among whom our author includes himself, but that they will themselves suffer dire consequences. It will not be Paul or the Scriptures that suffer; it will not be those who are well taught in the Scriptures and thus stable (assuming, as 2 Peter does, that being well taught implies a life conformed to what was taught); it will be they themselves, who think that they have justified their position over against that of the orthodox — they will suffer dire consequences when the Lord they have denied with their behavior returns in a coming that they do not believe will happen.

## IV. LETTER CLOSING (3:17-18)

Our author is almost finished. He has said what he needs to say. What remains is a final purpose statement — exhortation (purpose statements are often found at the end of Greek letters) and a closing benediction (perhaps a type of replacement for the health wish that is frequently part of the closing of a Greek letter) and doxology.

> [17]*Therefore, dear friends, since you already know this, be on your guard so that you may not be carried away by the error of lawless men and fall from your secure position.* [18]*But grow in the grace and knowledge of our Lord and Savior Jesus Christ. To him be glory both now and forever! Amen.*

**17** Again our author addresses his addressees, signaling that a new block of thought is beginning. In this case it is his final block of thought. The expression "dear friends" ("beloved") we have encountered before (3:1, 14), and have argued that it (one word in Greek) indicates a sense of endearment. Yet the NIV does us a disservice when it starts its translation of our verse with "Therefore, dear friends." This is because there is an emphatic "you" that starts the sentence in Greek. "*You,* therefore, dear friends" contrasts with the implied "them" of the "ignorant and unstable people" in the previous verse. Those people distorted the Scriptures and Paul and therefore did not know, but "*you*" "already know."[1] This fits with the theme of the letter, that Peter is reminding

1. Bigg, *St. Peter and St. Jude,* 301, argues regarding the participle in our verse that "*proginōskontes* ["since you already know," NIV] is equivalent to *ginōskontes* ["above all, you must understand," NIV]" of 1:20. In Acts 26:5 it means that the Jewish leaders previ-

them, not telling them something of which they are totally unaware (1:12-15; 3:1, 8, 15, the last two verses more by way of implication than as verses using a verb of reminder).[2] In essence he is saying, "You already know truth that the false teachers do not; you already knew this before I wrote, since I am just reminding you, and you still know it now." Whether this is a charitable assumption on his part (i.e., his addressees could have forgotten what they were taught or never really have learned it properly, but he is charitably assuming that they do know it) or not, we cannot tell. Our author's interest, however, is not in when or to what degree they knew this information beforehand, but that they know it now. That is what leads to the main point of the verse.

Our author's chief interest, then, is that they "be on [their] guard." This is the main verb of the sentence. While this verb can mean things like "keeping" the law (Mark 10:20 par. Matt 19:20 par. Luke 18:21; cf. Acts 7:53; 21:24; Rom 2:26; Gal 6:13), its meaning here is more closely related to that in such passages as Luke 12:15 ("Watch out! Be on your guard against all kinds of greed; a man's life does not consist in the abundance of his possessions."); 1 Tim 6:20 ("guard what has been entrusted to your care"); 2 Tim 4:15 ("You too should be on your guard against him, because he strongly opposed our message"); and 1 John 5:21 ("Dear children, keep yourselves from idols").[3]

What are these people to be on their guard about? The answer is, "so that you may not be carried away by the error of lawless men and fall from your secure position." "Error" for our author is the situation of those who are outside the community of the followers of Jesus (2 Pet 2:18; cf. Jude 11,

---

ously knew Paul for a long time, in Rom 8:29 and 11:2 it indicates people whom God already knew before the events under consideration, and in 1 Pet 1:20 it indicates that Christ was known before the foundation of the world (i.e., Christ was not a second plan after other plans of God had failed, but he was the plan from before creation). In each case the verb indicates, not a knowing first of all, but a knowing beforehand.

2. In saying this we are taking issue with Bauckham, *Jude, 2 Peter*, 337, who interprets this verse thus: "The fiction of Peter's prophecy is resumed from 2:1-3; 3:3-4. Peter is represented as having predicted the rise of the false teachers after his death, so that his readers, who, according to the fiction, are supposed to receive the letter before his death (1:13), will be forewarned even before they encounter the false teachers." Naturally, in Bauckham's view the whole work is a testament that the readers would understand was written in the name of Peter rather than by Peter, so the fiction is transparent and not a deception. However, given the reminder theme of the letter, our verse, at least, does not support this "fiction," but rather plays into that theme and fits naturally with 3:16 (where a present tense is used) rather than 3:16 being a slip into the present tense.

3. The verb also appears in the NT in the sense of guarding someone or something in prison, or guarding one's house: 2 Pet 2:5; Luke 2:8; 8:26; 11:21; Acts 22:20; 23:15; 28:16. It also occurs in a metaphorical sense in John 12:25; 17:12; 2 Thess 3:3; 2 Tim 1:12; Jude 24. In this latter sense, it is often God who is doing the guarding.

where it characterizes Balaam, and 2 Pet 2:15, where the verbal form of our word is used for Balaam), and "lawless people" for him were the people of Sodom (2 Pet 2:7); in both passages he is implying that error or lawlessness is also the situation of the false teachers, whose lack of morality he is unmasking in ch. 2. Being "carried away" is what happened to Barnabas in Gal 2:13, where, despite being a colleague of Paul, he lost his bearings and joined Peter and other Jews in separating himself from Gentiles in the celebration of the Lord's Supper (which was then a full meal).[4] The fact is that most people do not set about to err or to give themselves over to lawlessness. However, group pressure, the spirit of the age, plausible arguments, and the like can lead to one's being carried away by error, perhaps because one is ignorant of or ignoring the fact that the proponents of the error are in fact lawless. Before they notice, they are themselves involved in lawlessness, and then, perhaps, either caught in a web of rationalization or else feeling trapped because they feel too guilty to return.

Peter's answer to this danger is to "be on your guard so that you may not . . . fall from your secure position." We have already met instability in our letter: 3:16 points out that the uninstructed and unstable are those who distort the Scriptures, and 2:14 that unstable persons are vulnerable to the seduction of false teachers. But since the author of 2 Peter is, as we have seen, reminding his readers of what they already know, it is clear that they are in a stable (NIV, "secure") position.[5] This is the position that he has described in 1:3-4. Yet following 2 Pet 1:3-4 and its presentation of a secure and stable position, we have an encouragement to growth in virtue and the reminder that "if you do these things, you will never fall" (2 Pet 1:10, using a different verb, but with a closely related idea). Thus it should not surprise us that the book closes with a warning not to fall from a stable position. While "falling" can be literal in the NT (e.g., Acts 12:7) or literal with a metaphorical meaning (Jas 1:11; 1 Pet 1:24), the sense here is clearly metaphorical and rather close to Paul's in Gal 5:4 ("You have fallen away from grace"). That is, to fall from one's secure or stable position is to become apostate, to leave meaningful commitment to Jesus as Lord, as the false teachers have done.[6] If one is on

4. Rom 12:16 is the only other use of this term in the NT, and there it has a positive meaning.

5. The term occurs only here in the NT or the LXX, but for background on related terms, see Günther Harder, *"stērizō ktl.," TDNT* 7:653-57, although he does not handle our passage well, making too many assumptions about 2 Peter.

6. Our word means "to fall from," in our case "stability" and in Paul's case "grace." However, the simple word "to fall" is also frequently used in the NT for apostasy, as in Rom 11:11, 22; 1 Cor 10:12; Heb 4:11; Rev 2:5, or the judgment of whether or not one is true to one's pledge of loyalty to Jesus (versus being apostate), as in Rom 14:4; Jas 5:12.

one's guard, one will be aware of the danger and so not fall from the wonderful privileges and freedoms that he or she has received in Christ.

This, then, is the purpose of this book. It is a reminder in case the addressees have forgotten. It is a wake-up call, in case they are letting down their guard. It is a pointing out of the error of lawless men and women so that, seeing the error and its danger, the addressees will recoil from it and remain secure. Now that he has fulfilled his purpose and believes that his addressees are on their guard and will remain secure, our author can close his letter.

**18** The final letter closing is a general exhortation that serves as a benediction, to which is attached a doxology. We need to examine this more closely.

First, notice how similar this is to other NT letters, as seen in the chart on page 313.[7] While the other letters frequently include greetings and/or final instructions or information (Neyrey calls these postscripts),[8] which we have removed in the examples below, they often, like our letter, include a final general exhortation (1 Corinthians, 2 Corinthians, Galatians, 1 Timothy) and a blessing that includes grace (in fact, all except Romans, Hebrews, and 1 Peter mention grace). Furthermore, it is not unusual for letter closings to include a doxology, either before or after their greetings/postscript and their wishing grace on the addressees. We will highlight these doxologies in boldface in the table on page 314. As a final comparison, let us look compare 2 Peter with Jude in terms of their closing, underlining common elements:

| *Jude 24-25* | *2 Peter 3:17-18* |
|---|---|
| To him who is able to keep you from <u>falling</u> and to present you before his glorious presence without fault and with great joy — to the only God our <u>Savior</u> be <u>glory</u>, majesty, power and authority, through <u>Jesus Christ our Lord</u>, before all ages, <u>now and forevermore</u>! Amen. | Therefore, dear friends, since you already know this, be on your guard so that you may not be carried away by the error of lawless men and <u>fall</u> from your secure position. But grow in the grace and knowledge of <u>our Lord</u> and <u>Savior Jesus Christ</u>. To him be <u>glory</u> both <u>now and forever</u>! Amen. |

7. James and 1-3 John are not in the chart, for they have a different type of ending, James and 1 John ending with their purpose statement without a doxology or benediction, and 2-3 John ending with a statement about an expected visit and then a brief peace wish.

8. Neyrey, *2 Peter, Jude*, 246-47.

*1 Corinthians 16:22-24*

If anyone does not love the Lord — a curse be on him. Come, O Lord! The grace of the Lord Jesus be with you. My love to all of you in Christ Jesus. Amen.

*2 Corinthians 13:11, 14*

Finally, brothers, good-by. Aim for perfection, listen to my appeal, be of one mind, live in peace. And the God of love and peace will be with you.

May the grace of the Lord Jesus Christ, and the love of God, and the fellowship of the Holy Spirit be with you all.

*Galatians 6:16-18*

Peace and mercy to all who follow this rule, even to the Israel of God. Finally, let no one cause me trouble, for I bear on my body the marks of Jesus.

The grace of our Lord Jesus Christ be with your spirit, brothers. Amen.

*Ephesians 6:23-24*

Peace to the brothers, and love with faith from God the Father and the Lord Jesus Christ.

Grace to all who love our Lord Jesus Christ with an undying love.

*1 Thessalonians 5:23-24, 28*

May God himself, the God of peace, sanctify you through and through. May your whole spirit, soul and body be kept blameless at the coming of our Lord Jesus Christ. The one who calls you is faithful and he will do it.

The grace of our Lord Jesus Christ be with you.

*2 Thessalonians 3:16, 18*

Now may the Lord of peace himself give you peace at all times and in every way. The Lord be with all of you.

The grace of our Lord Jesus Christ be with you all.

*1 Timothy 6:20-21*

Timothy, guard what has been entrusted to your care. Turn away from godless chatter and the opposing ideas of what is falsely called knowledge, which some have professed and in so doing have wandered from the faith.

Grace be with you.

*Titus 3:15b*

Grace be with you all.

*Philemon 25*

The grace of the Lord Jesus Christ be with your spirit.

*Revelation 22:20-21*

He who testifies to these things says, "Yes, I am coming soon." Amen. Come, Lord Jesus.

The grace of the Lord Jesus be with God's people. Amen.

| *Romans 16:25-27* | *Philippians 4:20, 23* | *2 Timothy 4:18, 22* | *Hebrews 13:20-21, 25* | *1 Peter 5:10-11, 14* |
|---|---|---|---|---|
| **Now to him who is able to establish you by my gospel and the proclamation of Jesus Christ, according to the revelation of the mystery hidden for long ages past, but now revealed and made known through the prophetic writings by the command of the eternal God, so that all nations might believe and obey him — to the only wise God be glory forever through Jesus Christ! Amen.** | **To our God and Father be glory for ever and ever. Amen.**<br><br>The grace of the Lord Jesus Christ be with your spirit. Amen. | The Lord will rescue me from every evil attack and will bring me safely to his heavenly kingdom.<br><br>**To him be glory forever and ever. Amen.** The Lord be with your spirit.<br><br>Grace be with you. | May the God of peace, who through the blood of the eternal covenant brought back from the dead our Lord Jesus, that great Shepherd of the sheep, equip you with everything good for doing his will, and may he work in us what is pleasing to him, through Jesus Christ,<br><br>**to whom be glory forever and ever. Amen.**<br><br>Grace be with you all. | And the God of all grace, who called you to his eternal glory in Christ, after you have suffered a little while, will himself restore you and make you strong, firm and steadfast.<br><br>**To him be the power forever and ever. Amen.**<br><br>Greet one another with a kiss of love. Peace to all of you who are in Christ. |

Both refer to falling, although Jude calls on God to keep his readers from falling, while 2 Peter exhorts his addressees to guard themselves from falling. Jude clearly implies a secure or stable position, while our author states that his addressees have one. Both include a doxology using similar titles and names, although Jude attributes the Savior title to God and separates Jesus from God. Both call for glory to be given to God or Jesus, ending with a "now and forever" formula (slightly different in the two cases). Many of these elements are quite common in the NT, as we have seen in the other letter endings. But given that we know that 2 Peter has used Jude, we should not rule out 2 Peter's being inspired by Jude's closing in writing his own.

Looking at our final verse in more detail, we first notice that it forms something of an inclusion *(inclusio)* with 2 Pet 1:2 ("Grace and peace be yours in abundance through the knowledge of God and of Jesus our Lord"). That is, we have the same elements of grace and knowledge and Jesus (along with his title, "our Lord"), even if, as we shall see, some of the terms are slightly different in form. That the full title "our Lord and Savior Jesus Christ" is not found in 2 Pet 1:2 is not surprising, for it is found in 1:11 and, as "our God and Savior Jesus Christ," in 1:1. Furthermore, 1:5-11 is about growing in the grace and knowledge that one already has. Thus we see that 2 Pet 3:18 makes specific reference back to 1:2, but a general reference back to 1:1-11. Our author is clearly signaling that he is closing his work by putting a closing "bracket" to match his opening "bracket."

The specific wish (since there is a general tendency for letter closings to contain benedictions or health wishes, we are taking this to be as much a wish or benediction as a command) is that they continue to grow "in the grace and knowledge of our Lord and Savior Jesus Christ," which is similar to the wishes of 2 Cor 10:15; Eph 4:15; 1 Pet 2:2. Our author is wise and realizes that if they attempt to stand still, they will have a far greater tendency to fall than if they are moving forward. Commitment to Jesus works best as a centered set, which means that we define the members of the set in relationship to the center (in this case, Jesus Christ) and their direction in relationship to the center (in this case toward) rather than as a bounded set, which would mean that we define the members of the set in relationship to the boundary. Often Christians have used the latter definition, focusing on such issues as whether the person is outside the boundary and thus in heresy or apostasy or whether the person has crossed the boundary and so is saved (after which we have often breathed a sigh of relief and relaxed in a way that would seem rather strange to 2 Peter). Our author's wisdom says that safety is found in moving toward Jesus Christ. Direction is critical; speed is almost immaterial. If one is moving in the right direction, one is far more secure than if one is simply trying to "hold your ground."

But what is it that our author wants his addressees to grow in? That is a disputed point because the grammar of the phrase is not clear. Is it "in grace and in the knowledge of our Lord and Savior Jesus Christ" (only "knowledge" being "of our Lord") or "in the grace and knowledge of our Lord and Savior Jesus Christ"? Among the English translations, the NIV, NKJV, NLV, NRSV, RSV, ASV, ESV, TEV, NET Bible, and NASV all use the latter translation, while only the KJV and NAB use the former translation. Commentators are equally divided because there is no definite article ("the") in the Greek text, so without the article to indicate the grouping, one has to decide whether the "in" is functioning as a grouping agent, as it sometimes does, or not. The problem here is that normally "grace" is understood as "the grace Jesus gives" (Greek subjective genitive) and in our letter "knowledge" has been understood as a coming to know or a growing in the knowledge of Jesus (Greek objective genitive). Thus if grace and knowledge are viewed as a single unit, we seem to have Jesus functioning in two ways in a single phrase, as the subject (giver) of grace and the object of knowledge. Thus some commentators follow the translation of the KJV and NAB: we are talking about two different things, grace and the knowledge of our Lord Jesus Christ.[9] Others argue that despite the awkwardness, we are talking about two things grouped with Jesus, the grace he gives and our knowledge of him.[10] Still others avoid a decision.[11]

Vögtle, however, grasps the nettle a different way in that he argues that both grace and knowledge are gifts of Jesus (i.e., we have two subjective genitives).[12] That grace is the favor granted by God or Jesus, much as a potentate grants his favor to those whom he wills, is not disputed. At issue is the meaning of knowledge. It is true that here we do not have the Greek term that indicates the knowledge that is a coming to know Jesus (2 Pet 1:2; 2:20).[13] The term that we do have, however, can be used for knowing Jesus (2 Cor 2:14; 4:6; Phil 3:8; cf. Col 2:3) or salvation (Luke 1:77), but often it is used in the more general way of religious or other knowledge in general, and especially as a virtue that one can grow in (as in 2 Pet 1:5) or a gift from God (2 Cor 12:8; 13:2). More specifically, knowing Jesus can be just such a divine gift (2 Cor 4:6; cf. 2 Cor 2:14).

It seems to us, therefore, that what we have here are two gifts of Jesus: we continue growing (the present tense of the imperative indicates something that is ongoing, not something new) in the grace/favor that

9. Kelly, *The Epistles of Peter and of Jude*, 375; Mayor, *Jude and II Peter*, 170; Skaggs, *1, 2 Peter, Jude*, 143; Kraftchick, *Jude, 2 Peter*, 177; Schreiner, *1, 2 Peter, Jude*, 401; Spicq, *Les Épitres de Saint Pierre*, 264; Bauckham, *Jude, 2 Peter*, 337-38.

10. Hillyer, *1 and 2 Peter, Jude*, 225; Bigg, *The Epistles of St. Peter and St. Jude*, 303-04, explaining that there are two words for knowledge, *gnōsis* and *epignōsis*, the latter being knowledge of Jesus and the former being knowledge that Jesus gives, our verse having the former; Lucas and Green, *The Message of 2 Peter and Jude*, 156-57.

11. Schelkle, *Der Petrusbrief, der Judasbrief*, 239; Green, *Second Peter and Jude*, 150-151, although Green, unlike Schelkle, does discuss the options.

12. Vögtle, *Der Judasbrief, der zweite Petrusbrief*, 265.

13. Although, while this meaning for the term works out well within 2 Peter, it does not work for all uses outside of 2 Peter, for in some instances it appears to mean a growth in knowledge after one's initial commitment to Jesus (Eph 1:17; 4:13; Phil 1:9; Col 1:9; 3:10; cf. Rom 1:28; Phlm 6). This term is used most consistently in the NT of initial knowledge in the phrase "knowledge of the truth": 1 Tim 2:4; 2:25; 3:7; Titus 1:1; Heb 10:26. Are we inappropriately privileging this later literature if we say that it alone shows the meaning accepted by 2 Peter?

Jesus gives and in the knowledge that he gives, a knowledge that is surely a knowledge of him (since without growing in knowledge of God and of Jesus it is difficult to conceive of any growth in the Christian sphere that could be called true knowledge), but at the same time more than just knowledge of him, including knowledge of the Scriptures, knowledge that allows us to discern the falsehood of the false teachers and to recognize their seduction, knowledge that keeps us stable in every way. This is what our author wishes for his addressees and would surely wish for us, if he had known of us.

Having mentioned "our Lord and Savior Jesus Christ" for the final time (see the comments on 2 Pet 1:1, 2, and 11 for discussion of this phrase), our author adds a doxology, which, as we saw in the tables above, is not uncommon at the end of letters from the early Jesus movement. What is a bit unusual is that this one is to Jesus and not to God. However, while it is unusual, it is not unprecedented, for of the six doxologies we found in letter closings above (the number "six" includes Jude 24-25), four are to God the Father, and two are to Jesus (2 Tim 4:18; Heb 13:21). Furthermore, to this we should add the doxology at the beginning of the apocalyptic letter Rev 1:5-6 (i.e. Revelation is an apocalypse with a letter structure surrounding it). All of these are later works in terms of the NT collection, although it is disputed how late each of them was written.[14] What is clear is that in a work that begins by speaking of "our great God and Savior Jesus Christ" it is not surprising that we have a doxology to him (i.e., a form of worship) at the end.

This doxology ascribes to him "glory" (Greek *doxa* and therefore the term "doxology"), that is, ultimate honor, on an eternal basis. The "now" is what his followers are doing in the present, but the phrase "forever" is unusual in that usually the Greek expression "unto the ages" is used for "forever" but here in 2 Peter is "unto the day of the ages." Given that the Parousia has been a major topic of this letter, it is likely that Bauckham is correct to see this as meaning "the eschatological age as a day which will dawn at the Parousia."[15] That such a "day" can be a long period of time is clear from Sir 18:10 ("Like a drop of water from the sea and a grain of sand, so are a few years among the days of eternity"; NRSV), which is itself dependent on Ps 90:4 ("For a thousand years in your sight are like a day that has just gone by, or like a watch in the night"), understood to indicate the incomprehensibility of God's perspective of time. The "days of

14. For instance, was Revelation written in A.D. 69 or perhaps A.D. 96, and was Hebrews written before or after A.D. 70?

15. Bauckham, *Jude, 2 Peter,* 338. He cites in particular "the day" referred to in 2 Pet 1:19, but of course there are other synonyms for this day that appear throughout the letter.

eternity" are, then, without limit. It is this temporal limitlessness that our author wishes with respect to the honor of our Lord and Savior Jesus Christ. May he be honored now, as he is among us who are his followers and, unseen by human beings, in the halls of heaven where he and his Father wait patiently, enduring the evil of humanity, and may he be honored openly and fully on the day of his Parousia, a day that stretches limitlessly onward. Thus may he be honored eternally.

# *Index of Modern Authors*

# Index of Subjects

# Index of Scripture References

*References in parentheses show the LXX equivalent of the English references.*

## OLD TESTAMENT

# Index of Extrabiblical Literature

## DEAD SEA SCROLLS

## RABBINIC WRITINGS



## JEWISH WRITERS

## EARLY CHRISTIAN WRITINGS

## GREEK AND ROMAN LITERATURE